CHANGING CAPITALISMS?

Changing Capitalisms?

Internationalization, Institutional Change, and Systems of Economic Organization

Edited by

GLENN MORGAN,
RICHARD WHITLEY,
and
ELI MOEN

OXFORD

UNIVERSITY PRESS

OXFORD
UNIVERSITY PRESS

Great Clarendon Street, Oxford OX2 6DP

Oxford University Press is a department of the University of Oxford.
It furthers the University's objective of excellence in research, scholarship,
and education by publishing worldwide in

Oxford New York

Auckland Cape Town Dar es Salaam Hong Kong Karachi
Kuala Lumpur Madrid Melbourne Mexico City Nairobi
New Delhi Shanghai Taipei Toronto

With offices in

Argentina Austria Brazil Chile Czech Republic France Greece
Guatemala Hungary Italy Japan Poland Portugal Singapore
South Korea Switzerland Thailand Turkey Ukraine Vietnam

Oxford is a registered trade mark of Oxford University Press
in the UK and in certain other countries

Published in the United States
by Oxford University Press Inc., New York

British Library Cataloguing in Publication Data
Data available

Library of Congress Cataloging in Publication Data
Data available

Typeset by Newgen Imaging Systems (P) Ltd., Chennai, India
Printed in Great Britain
on acid-free paper by
Biddles Ltd, King's Lynn

ISBN 978–0–19–927563–2
ISBN 978–0–19–920528–8 (Pbk.)

Preface

The contributions to this book derive from a workshop held in Oslo in May 2003 sponsored by the University of Oslo and the Norwegian Research Council. Our thanks go to them for funding this event. The workshop was designed to reflect on the development of the programme of research broadly characterized under terms such as 'national business systems' and 'varieties of capitalism'. As well as the authors of the chapters, the following people contributed to the meeting and participated in the discussion: Robert Boyer, Steve Casper, Richard Hyman, Atle Midttun, Lars Mjøset, Bart Nooteboom, Diana Sharpe, and Risto Tainio. A number of people helped by commenting on second versions of various of the papers in preparation for publication; these included Gregory Jackson, Mark Lehrer, Ray Loveridge, Chris Smith, and Kathy Thelen. David Musson and Matthew Derbyshire at Oxford University Press have, as ever, been helpful in bringing the project from the drawing board to fruition.

Glenn Morgan
Warwick Business School
University of Warwick

Richard Whitley
Manchester Business School

Eli Moen
University of Oslo

May 2004

Contents

**Part II. Changing Firm Capabilities Within and
Across Institutional Frameworks**

Afterwords

List of contributors

COLIN CROUCH, Warwick Business School, University of Warwick

RICHARD DEEG, Temple University, Philadelphia

MARIE-LAURE DJELIC, ESSEC, Paris

MICHEL GOYER, Warwick Business School, University of Warwick

BOB HANCKÉ, London School of Economics

GARY HERRIGEL, University of Chicago

PEER HULL KRISTENSEN, International Centre for Business and Politics, Copenhagen Business School

CHRISTEL LANE, University of Cambridge

KARI LILJA, Helsinki School of Economics

ELI MOEN, Norwegian School of Management, Oslo

GLENN MORGAN, Warwick Business School, University of Warwick

SIGRID QUACK, Wissenschaftszentrum, Berlin

ARNDT SORGE, University of Groningen

RICHARD WHITLEY, Manchester Business School

VOLKER WITTKE, SOFI, Gottingen

1

Introduction: Changing Capitalisms? Internationalization, Institutional Change, and Systems of Economic Organization

GLENN MORGAN

The last decade has seen a remarkable resurgence of interest in the differences between market economies and their roots in contrasting institutional arrangements. Whether comparing business systems, social systems of production, forms of *regulation* or varieties of capitalism, many studies have emphasized the viability and persistence of distinctive systems of economic coordination and control in developed market economies (Berger and Dore 1996; Boyer and Drache 1996; Crouch and Streeck 1997; Hall and Soskice 2001; Hollingsworth and Boyer 1997; Quack et al. 2000; Whitley 1999; Whitley and Kristensen 1996, 1997). These systems vary between institutional contexts, especially those governing capital and labour markets, and have been shown to generate contrasting economic outcomes, particularly in terms of technological development.

Over much the same period, the revival of institutional economics and evolutionary approaches to understanding the firm have combined with work in strategic management to develop the resource or competence-based theory of the firm. Building on the ideas of Edith Penrose (Penrose 1959) and George Richardson (Richardson 1972), this approach focuses attention on how firms create distinctive capabilities through establishing routines that coordinate complementary activities and skills for particular strategic purposes. It sees economic outcomes as resulting from varied patterns of competition and cooperation between firms with differently developed path dependent knowledge and abilities. It is therefore as concerned with the internal generation of distinctive collective competences as with the operation of external selection environments (Chandler et al. 1998; Dosi and Teece 1998; Langlois and Robertson 1995; Mowery and Nelson 1999; Nelson and Winter 1982; Nooteboom 2000; Penrose 1959; Pitelis 2002; Richardson 1972).

For much of the 1990s these two strands of research remained distinct. Those focusing on the institutional frameworks of market economies were primarily concerned with identifying complementarities between institutional arrangements that explained coherence and continuity. Within specific institutional contexts, firms were seen as responding to competitive pressures in similar ways such that outcomes were substantially structured by institutional arrangements. On the other hand, those focusing on the dynamics of firm behaviour studied how firms develop new capacities and are able to learn new ways of doing things. The emphasis here was on experimentation, learning, and innovation linked to the idea of a diversity of performance outcomes at the firm level, in turn leading to continuously evolving patterns of sector organization.

More recently, it has become increasingly recognized that these approaches need to be modified and brought together. In particular, greater attention is now being paid to the analysis of different kinds of path dependence and forms of complementarity, as well as to the circumstances in which they become significant and change. Varieties of institutional integration, the surprising maintenance of 'deviant' or alternative traditions and processes within particular systems, and the existence of unpredictable yet consequential policy options that can lead to breaks in path dependency are increasingly being considered by students of business systems and varieties of capitalism. Such contradictions and divergences result in the need for a more open-ended analysis of how firms relate to institutions as a diversity of potential resources rather than as determinant constraining forces (see, for example, Amable 2003; Djelic and Quack 2003; Schmidt 2002; Yamamura and Streeck 2003).

Equally, the detailed connections between firm learning and institutional contexts have become more closely examined in studies of how the dynamics of firms' innovation strategies are closely related to their ability to weave new and unexpected outcomes from the opportunities provided by specific institutional contexts (see, for example, Amin and Cohendet 2004; Casper and Whitley 2004; Crouch et al. 2001; Gambardella and Malerba 1999; Hancké 2002). Other work on multinationals has also indicated that location in diverse institutional contexts gives firms and other actors opportunities, not always seized, to create unique sets of competences and engage in institutional arbitrage (Morgan et al. 2001). These firm-level actions may in turn contribute to change in institutional frameworks by altering the distribution of power and influence between different types of firms and other actors in a particular context.

This convergence between the dynamic capabilities and similar approaches to understanding firm variation and behaviour in different contexts with the analysis of institutional complementarities, contradictions, and change has great potential for our understanding of the dynamics of capitalist societies and economies in the twenty-first century. By suggesting how differently organized owners, managers, and employees construct and change different kinds of organizational capabilities and strategies in contrasting institutional environments, it provides the basis for identifying the processes through which distinctive patterns of economic organization, specialization, and performance become established and changed.

The integration of these approaches provides the context for this book. Each chapter combines to varying degrees an understanding of both the mutability of institutional arrangements and the dynamics of firm-level responses to institutional contexts. As such, the book goes significantly beyond a number of approaches in this field by rejecting the idea that firms are simply the passive recipients of a predetermined set of institutional resources constructed at the national level, and that firm behaviour simply reflects the constraints of its institutional context.

To take the cohesion of national institutional contexts first, many of the present contributions indicate that these have higher levels of diversity than has been previously supposed. The chapters explore a variety of explanations for this diversity and suggest three key points. The first is the need to explore in much greater theoretical and conceptual detail the nature of the 'systemic' linkages between institutions in a national context. The tendency to assume that these linkages are either equally 'tight' or equally 'complementary' is challenged in many of the chapters (e.g. Deeg, Crouch, and Whitley, Chapters 2, 7, and 8, respectively) and an attempt is made to understand further the range of variation in institutional linkages and complementarities.

The second is that whatever complementarities and linkages emerge need to be seen not as 'universal' characteristics of a particular context but as historically constituted and variable. Furthermore, this process of historical constitution is not an inevitable outcome of a particular set of circumstances but a result of skilful actions on the part of key groups within a society struggling over power and resources. In this sense, the contributions also represent a challenge to certain forms of path dependency argument, opening up possibilities of 'crooked paths' and changing institutional forms (Djelic and Quack, Sorge, Deeg, Lane, and Hancké and Goyer in Chapters 6, 5, 2, 4, and 3, respectively). There is clearly a need to 'take history seriously' and see any particular institutional formation not as an expression of an inner 'essence' to a national context but as an outcome of particular causal paths.

The third point concerns the nature of the 'national' as a structuring context for institutions and firms and in particular, its relationship to the international. It has been common to many institutionalist accounts to conceptualize the 'nation-state' as a self-enclosed system of inter-relationships that is 'at risk' of disruption by international processes. Characteristically, authors describe the 'threat of globalization' to this or that national system as though these are two distinct and separate entities. The chapters in this book challenge this view and argue that the two levels have been mutually constitutive since the emergence and development of nation-states and the modern world system in the sixteenth and seventeenth centuries. The tightness of fit within national systems is frequently related to how they are inserted or placed within the interstate political and economic system and the degrees of freedom this provides for certain actors from both inside and outside the system (see, for example, the discussions on Germany in the post-war period in Djelic and Quack (Chapter 6) and Sorge (Chapter 5); more generally Whitley (Chapter 8); Deeg (Chapter 2); Kristensen (Chapter 13); and Morgan (Chapter 14)). Thus, the significance of this outer context in the current period has to be seen not as, in itself, a 'new' process but as a new form of an old process.

In summary, the view of the national institutional context that arises from these contributions is that the degree of 'fit' and complementarity between institutions is variable. This variability is historically consti-tuted and not predetermined, it is interdependent with, and mutually constitutive of, the international context. This does not mean that models of 'divergent capitalisms' are not useful but rather that the way we use them must become much more sensitive to their nature as 'models'. They are not the reality itself but one of the main tools by which we identify the interesting questions in a particular context, a point emphasized by Kristensen (see Chapter 13) in his reference to the distinction between the 'logic of things' and 'the things of logic'. Our models are logical constructions about how 'things' (institutions) fit together; our research is about how things actually do or do not fit together in a messy empirical reality. By exploring the gap, we leave the logic of systems and enter the realm of action as played out in history with all its elements of contingency, indeterminacy, and unpredictability. Without the 'things of logic', we have no guides but if we mistake these for the 'logic of things', we end up cutting ourselves off from the interesting questions about institutions and change and reproducing timeless and ahistorical models.

The book develops this general argument in relation to the implications for firms. In this model of the institutional context, the owners and managers of firms are rarely limited in their choices of strategy and structure to a single model of 'rules of the game'. They can, to varying degrees, make other choices about which game they wish to be in, though opting out of dominant rules of the game creates new costs as well as new possibilities both for the firm that opts out and for those firms which decide to stay in the existing game (e.g. the discussions in Deeg, Lane, Hancké and Goyer, and Whitley, Chapters 2, 4, 3, and 8, respectively). The growing openness of the international economy, for example, fundamentally affects this process as it offers the possibility of new games with new pay-offs as well as new risks for firms if they internationalize (Morgan and Quack, Chapter 10; Moen and Lilja, Chapter 12). The result of institutional mutability and variety is that those directing firms are active participants in their own fate; they do not simply reproduce a dominant recipe, but on the contrary search for their own position in markets. This reflects our growing understanding of firms as highly dynamic actors.

The firm as an organization in competitive markets is an active learning agency continually combining and recombining elements in its external and internal environment in order to develop the distinctive capacities that will enable it to survive. Its selection environment is characterized by relatively rapid feedback effects that have short-term impacts on survival and growth.[1] This selection environment, however, is not Darwinian but on the contrary one in which firms can learn and seek to adapt themselves more appropriately to the environment. This learning, in turn, has two dimensions—internal and external. In internal terms, the firm as an authoritatively structured set of relationships can be changed in response to adverse market signals. In external terms, the firm can respond to adverse market conditions by restructuring its relationships with other economic actors and with

[1] There are, of course, many mediating social, institutional, and economic factors in specific markets that may moderate a 'harsh selection' context but even so this is a fundamentally different selection process than that which occurs at the institutional level itself (see Morgan, Chapter 14 for more detailed discussion of this point).

institutions. Thus, firms are inherently dynamic and changing both at the individual and the population level.

These arguments are developed in varying ways by the contributors to this book. In the first part of the book, the main focus of the analysis is on institutions and understanding issues of complementarity, contradiction, and change within national and international contexts. These discussions introduce the implications for firms as the authors construct their theoretical and empirical accounts of how institutions emerge and change. The second part of the book focuses more specifically on the firm level and considers how firms relate to institutional contexts. Here the dynamism of the firm and how it actively uses and reconstitutes institutional settings is the primary focus, though a key critical perspective in this discussion is the difficulties for the multinational firm in managing across different institutional contexts (a theme already well established in previous contributions from many of the authors in Morgan et al. 2001). Finally, an overview section offers perspectives on future developments for this type of research.

1.1. Part I: Institutional Complementarity, Contradiction, and Change in Business Systems

Part I comprises a series of chapters reflecting on how national institutional contexts cohere and change. Five of the chapters are particularly concerned to relate the theme of institutional change to Germany (Deeg, Lane, Sorge, Hancké and Goyer,[2] and Djelic and Quack in Chapters 2, 4, 5, 3, and 6, respectively) while the other two deal more generally with the theme of institutional complementarity (Crouch and Whitley in Chapters 7 and 8, respectively).

The centrality of Germany to these debates is not surprising as the 'German model' was often held up in the 1980s and early 1990s as a form of 'divergent capitalism' that delivered a distinctive set of economic and social outcomes from that which characterized US capitalism. Together with Japan, the survival and indeed the prospering of Germany in the 1980s when the United States and the United Kingdom were undergoing painful processes of industrial restructuring undermined previous arguments of convergence towards the Anglo-American model and led to an interest in multiple models of capitalism. What Hall and Soskice (2001) labelled

---

[2] These authors also illustrate their arguments by reference to changes in France.

the German 'coordinated market economy', was seen as working on the basis of 'patient capital', strongly coordinated inter-firm networks and the dual training system to produce diversified quality production. After unification the German economy moved into recession in the 1990s and it seemed that the model was under exogenous pressure to change—to become more financially and shareholder driven, less hidebound by agreements with suppliers and labour and more flexible in its work system. Thus, the German model has been a central focus in debates about how institutional complementarities emerge and give benefits to their participants. More recently it has become a test case in how such complementarities can be undermined by exogenous changes and what this means for the 'model'.

The authors of these contributions which discuss Germany can in turn be divided between those whose main interest is to describe and conceptualize the current changes (Deeg, Chapter 2; Lane, Chapter 5; Hancké and Goyer, Chapter 3) and those who wish to illuminate current debates by taking a longer term historical perspective on whether there was ever a German model in the first place (Sorge and Djelic and Quack in Chapters 5 and 6, respectively). In relation to the first set of contributions Deeg's Chapter 2 and that of Hancké and Goyer (Chapter 3) are concerned to warn against the idea that exogenous changes will destroy the German model. Deeg's argument rests on his broader view that complementarities are not one dimensional. They exist with different degrees of intensity depending on the institutions that are being considered as well as on the time at which the phenomenon is being considered. As complementarities loosen between particular institutions, Deeg argues, actors may look for ways of acting that sustain the parts of the system that survive. Thus the system may become bifurcated and elements of it more loosely connected but this may still allow it to survive and deliver, if in modified form, some of the main benefits which sustained it at an earlier time. Thus a stronger orientation to shareholder value at the level of corporate governance and financial markets is not necessarily incompatible with institutions of codetermination.

Hancké and Goyer make a similar argument though their focus is primarily on the actors in the system. For them, actors are permanently evaluating their position within institutional contexts and seeking new ways to use institutions. Furthermore, institutions do not tightly define the scripts that actors can follow. There may be deviant readings of existing institutional scripts as well as hangovers from previous eras marginalized and ignored but potentially available for resuscitation.

As actors face new problems or seek to define new opportunities, they draw selectively on this range of possibilities. Of course, the outcomes of these processes are structured by existing arrays of institutions and therefore the development of new scripts may be precarious, but there are circumstances in which new directions can emerge. Thus in their empirical discussion of changes in France and Germany, they emphasize the way in which firms, rather than being trapped in institutional constraints, use their freedom to construct a new institutional framework with elements of existing old and new policies and institutions that met their needs.

Lane is sceptical of these approaches. For her, the 'German model' was a tightly integrated set of institutions and social relationships; take away a key element of this model and it is impossible to expect that the rest of the system or the actors within it can either continue in the same old way or readjust incrementally to the loss. She argues that large German firms are becoming more dominated by shareholder value considerations as they internationalize and these are leading managers to place pressures on the codetermination system, cutting employment, increasing insecurity, and undermining labour solidarity. She rejects the view that what is emerging is a hybrid form, arguing that isomorphic pressures arising from shareholder value demands are leading to a convergence on the Anglo-American model of corporate governance. As one piece of the model is taken away, the rest will fall.

The more historical accounts by Sorge and Djelic and Quack revisit this question in different ways. Sorge's Chapter 5 take a long historical view to demonstrate his scepticism about the idea of the 'German model'. He shows that the 'German model' as constructed by analysts in the 1980s reflects a particular combination of forces that existed in Germany in the period from the late 1960s through to the 1980s. At different points in German history, the 'German model' could have been constructed very differently, for example, as an exemplary 'liberal market' system. He argues that the viability of attaching labels such as liberal and nonliberal to whole societies over lengthy periods is contestable. Sorge likens institutions to the furniture in a room; they lend themselves to certain purposes and keep us from doing other things but the furniture can be removed, renovated or moved about. The furniture in itself does not define the meaning given to it. This arises from the way in which actors interpret and use the furniture. Thus the 'German model' of the 1970s and 1980s used some of the 'institutional furniture' that had been constructed in

Germany over the last 100 years but it used it in different ways than previously because of the way in which actors interpreted their context at that particular time. Other furniture that was then discarded may be brought to the fore later or new furniture added. Again the message of Sorge is that institutions constrain but they do not determine; it is actors and the meanings which they construct for their contexts that make the difference.

Djelic and Quack's Chapter 6 illustrates this well through taking two specific examples of institutional change in Germany in the immediate post-war period. They consider how German competition law was reconstructed in a way that was more liberal and 'free market' than the cartel-like nature of German capitalism in some earlier periods of German history. They reveal how this was achieved through a combination of alliances between the strand of liberal economics that had survived in certain parts of German academia and political life, and the powers of US advisers in the immediate post-war period. In combination, these forces gave German competition law a very liberal tinge, throughout the period characterized as that of 'coordinated capitalism'. This meant that although German firms gained the benefits of coordination and cooperation through their institutional linkages to banks, to labour and along supplier networks, there was strong competition in product markets. Without this competition, the system would have lacked the key elements of dynamism which were essential to its success in overseas markets. Thus it was the combination of these principles which was crucial.

In terms of the following chapter by Crouch, the development of competition law in Germany reflected the emergence of a distinctive form of complementarity, that is, one where one set of institutional arrangements (in this case competition law) makes up for the potential problems created by another set of institutions (e.g. the highly 'insider' nature of corporate governance and inter-firm supply relationships which create cooperation between banks and firms). What was created was a balance between competition and cooperation that generated a distinctive set of advantages for German firms in comparison to their rivals from other institutional contexts. Djelic and Quack emphasize, though, that achieving this complementarity was not predetermined but an outcome of skilful actors using their powers in particular ways at appropriate times, similarly to Aoki's (2001) analysis of the development of the Japanese main bank system.

They reinforce this point by illustrating how in another area, that of the structure of banking, institutional reforms designed to decentralize the German banking system and stop the large banks from reforming and reasserting control over the economy failed to gain support within Germany itself and were easily overturned by the mid-1950s. Thus for them, historical outcomes cannot be predetermined and institutional formation is best thought of as a crooked path developing according to distinctive logics depending on the skills of actors and the possibilities of the context.

In his more theoretical discussion, Crouch suggests that institutional complementarity needs to be understood in terms of how institutions can create powerful and effective balances in social systems. Any particular institutional context may, in this argument, be characterized by divergent principles and institutions that exist in a creative tension and reflect a broader sociopolitical compromise between key actors. Sustaining these differences, however, requires barriers that prevent the dominant institutional logic from swallowing up the less powerful logic. Crouch argues quite explicitly that it is crucial that this is achieved as 'institutional heterogeneity' will facilitate innovation both by presenting actors with alternative strategies when existing paths seem blocked and by making it possible for them to make new combinations among elements of various paths. If actors do not have variety and diversity of institutions to draw on, they are not able to innovate with all the dangers that arise from this. The issue that Crouch poses therefore is: how to develop governance mechanisms that will ensure that diversity survives but does not become so strong that there is no institutional coherence or complementarity?

Whitley's Chapter 8 can in effect be seen as an attempt to answer this question by distinguishing between different types of 'national business systems' according to their coherence and homogeneity in contrasting institutional regimes. He argues that 'the more states organize and homogenize economic actors, the rules governing their interaction and the organization of interest representation, the more we would expect them to develop nationally distinctive business systems'. Essentially he suggests that arm's length states, acting as 'regulators' managing the terms and conditions on which firms interact, tend not to specify the kinds of economic actors and groups that can participate in markets. More promotional states, on the other hand, seek to direct economic activity in greater detail and to organize interest groups in particular ways in order to achieve developmental goals (the dominant developmental state), or to sustain social harmony (the business corporatist state) or finally to achieve social democratic goals of fairness (the inclusive corporatist state). These three types of state differ in the degree to which they encourage the involvement of other groups in the process of directing economic activity.

In the dominant developmental state, the goals for key strategic businesses are set and imposed by the state elite. In the business corporatist state, there is involvement of big business interest groups in the process but little recognition of the voice of employees or of smaller firms. In the inclusive corporatist state, the employees and small and medium-sized firms have a voice guaranteed to them through the institutions of the society and decisions are reached through some form of consensus. Rules are applied to all participants in the economy. Thus, Whitley argues that diversity of economic actors is greatest in institutional regimes that combine arm's length states with particular complementary institutions, and this in turn facilitates change.

In dominant developmental states, outside the key sectors with which the elite is concerned there will be a variety of practices. In business corporatist states with complementary institutions, Whitley suggests that there will be two sorts of variation. The first difference occurs between the big business sector and the rest of the economy; the former will tend to institutionalize internal labour markets and long-term employment which will be in part at the expense of the latter that will act as a flexible buffer allowing the large firms to grow or shrink their businesses according to market conditions without changing the levels and conditions of their core employees. The second sort of variation will be between the big firms themselves as they build distinctive patterns of skills and incorporation of employees without constraints from strong external labour markets, industry level trade unions, industry associations, or state bodies. In inclusive corporatist institutionalist regimes, variations are smallest as societal level rules about contracts, systems of codetermination and industrial relations, skills, and quality standards are imposed on all firms with few amendments. In Whitley's view, these internal variations have not yet been much affected by internationalizing developments as international regulations are mainly based on creating a market (the classic role of the state in the arms' length economies) and not on prescribing detailed procedures for how firms work, though this is clearly a debate within the European Union. He therefore describes the conditions in which different 'national business systems' become established but in a way that explicitly recognizes the governance of variety and diversity within them.

Overall, this section offers a considerable challenge to existing views of 'divergent capitalisms'. By opening up to more scrutiny the issue of how institutions are constructed and how complementarities emerge, the chapters reveal the importance of carefully distinguishing our 'models' of divergent capitalisms from the processes that real societies undergo as institutions and complementarities are constructed. This is a historically specific process, full of uncertainties and unpredictabilities in which skilful actors try to draw on the variety of resources within particular contexts to establish new and varied patterns of behaviour. In effect, our analysis has moved from an assumption of institutional homogeneity and reproduction to one of institutional heterogeneity and the structured governance of diversity and change.

1.2. Part II: Changing Firm Capabilities Within and Across Institutional Frameworks

If institutions are heterogeneous, what about firms? Firms face strong selection environments and as such they are engaged in a continuous search for ways to ensure their survival. Traditionally, institutionalists have tended not to pay much attention to firm variety. One strand of the institutionalist tradition, in fact, emphasizes that isomorphic pressures tend to force firms to take on similar structures and strategies as this guarantees wider societal legitimacy. Increasingly, however, the issue of distinctive firm capabilities is emerging as a matter for theoretical consideration and empirical research within the framework of national business systems analysis. Three factors have been crucial here.

First, there is the growing influence of the Penrosian view of the firm as a set of unique competences and capabilities that has to be constructed and managed in an effective way if it is to survive in highly competitive environments. Second, there is the issue of multinational firms that, according to the arguments of many recent authors (such as Bartlett and Ghoshal 1989; Dunning 2000), construct unique competences on the basis of combining the assets of different institutional locations into a new and unique mix. Thus, the very diversity of multinational firms makes isomorphism less likely. Third, there is the growing centrality of innovation to understandings of firm dynamics and market developments. The rewards that go to innovation tend to be so high that strategies based on isomorphism can rarely succeed in guaranteeing firm survival. Difference has to be cultivated if the rewards from innovation are to be achieved. The chapters in this part reflect the implications of these processes for institutional analysis.

Two of the chapters explicitly consider multinational firms and the difficulties that such firms have in developing distinctively cross-national capabilities and competences. Whitley, in his chapter on multinational firms (Chapter 9), argues that most studies of how institutional frameworks affect the development of different organizational capabilities have focused on nationally cohesive and distinctive settings. Rather less attention has been devoted to the kinds of idiosyncratic competitive competences that firms operating in diverse institutional contexts are able to generate. In particular, the extent to which, and ways in which, multinational companies (MNCs) develop distinctive kinds of organizational capabilities at the international level remain relatively unexplored from a comparative institutionalist perspective. The ability of such firms to integrate new knowledge and skills across national subsidiaries is often assumed rather than demonstrated, and there are significant difficulties in transferring situationally specific innovation capabilities between countries with contrasting institutional frameworks.

In particular, to what extent and how do different kinds of MNCs generate firm-specific organizational capabilities through international problem-solving activities and careers? His basic argument is that while many companies with major facilities in different countries may develop distinctive organizational capabilities at the national and regional levels, by no means all of them do so internationally. Their organizational capabilities as MNCs are little different from those of their domestic organization, together perhaps with those generated by some subsidiaries. The coordination of economic activities in different countries does not, then, necessarily produce distinctive cross-national collective capabilities, and so MNCs do not constitute a distinctive kind of company from the competence-based view of the firm. Rather, the extent to which international firms do form cross-national capabilities that are distinct from national and regional ones varies considerably.

Morgan and Quack's discussion of the internationalization of professional services companies illustrates some of these issues by showing that for these firms, the process of internationalization is highly complex. They suggest four possible routes to internationalization but argue that each of them creates organizational problems that cannot be easily solved. Thus while internationalization may seem like a good idea for these firms (as it potentially delivers benefits to clients), in organizational terms, it is not at all clear how different national bodies of knowledge, career expectations, partnership power structures can actually be brought together within a single international firm capable of developing distinctive transnational competences. This reflects the continuing commitment of most professionals to their home labour markets and home-based career and prestige hierarchies. The development of distinctive cross-national competences and capabilities within these firms is clearly limited.

The following two Chapters in this part, (11 and 12), focus more on firms within particular national contexts. Herrigel and Wittke examine the development of supplier relationships in the auto industry in the United States and Germany. In theory, these are two distinct institutional settings and therefore the ways in which firms manage their supplier relationships should reflect this institutional difference. However, Herrigel and Wittke argue that that actors in the United States and Germany are

to a surprising extent neither significantly constrained nor especially enabled by the institutional architecture of the political economy. Indeed, in many ways the institutional architectures in both the US and Germany, as coherent systems have been overtaken by events and stand awkwardly by as actors seek to construct new relations and forms of governance alongside them.

They argue that institutions may help actors solve governance problems but if not they are ignored or changed. The result is both greater heterogeneity in the possible forms of supplier relationships and greater overlap between US and German firms in terms of their commitment to one model—that of sustained contingent collaborations. How this model gets institutionalized clearly varies in the different settings but this is contingent not on institutional constraints but on how skilful actors use resources in their environment.

Moen and Lilja offer a very relevant example of this interaction of firms and institutions in their discussion of Finland and Nokia. From one reading of its history up to the early 1990s, Finland's institutional structure fitted together tightly in a way which suited its heavy dependence on the forest sector and the paper and pulp industry. Large investments with long payback periods in industries that were highly oligopolistic on the international scale were sustained by close and cooperative relationships between firms and banks, and within firms between managers, engineers and other skilled employees. However within a five-year period, Nokia became the biggest company in Finland and related high-tech industries became the dominant sector in the Finnish economy. What the authors reveal is a twofold process.

On the one hand, Nokia as a firm developed a distinctive set of innovative capacities that enabled it to grow rapidly and to internationalize key parts of its structure. On the other hand, Finnish society itself begins to change, partly through Nokia's direct intervention in the policy process and partly through its influence as a model of action. Most importantly, however, the authors argue that the horizontal forms of coordination that sustained the forest sector specialization of Finland in a previous era became the means by which a restructuring of institutions is commenced so that in particular the higher technical skills required of engineers in telecoms and associated areas become available to Nokia. In Sorge's terms, the owners of the furniture recognized that it had to be rearranged and renewed if it was going to be attractive and fit for a future in which Nokia (not the traditional pulp and paper firms) would be the dominant economic actor in Finland. The dynamic firm requires the 'dynamic' society, one that is coordinated and managed in a way that generates the resources that the company needs for the future. This is not so much a question of the elite imposing a solution on to society but rather one of using the institutions of coordination that already exist to develop new institutional solutions that facilitate firm dynamism.

1.3. Conclusions

The final two Chapters 13 and 14 take an overview of these debates. Kristensen, in his contribution, broadens the discussion by likening the key issues of institutional change in the current period to Elias' analysis of the 'civilizing process' (Elias 1994). In other work, Kristensen (with Zeitlin) has pointed out that multinationals have not yet established a constitutional order that establishes appropriate and agreed relationships between its various component parts (Kristensen and Zeitlin 2001, 2005). Instead, they are consumed by various degrees of visible and invisible conflict and competition between groups within them. Similarly in terms of their outward actions, they engage opportunistically with established institutional settings, thus weakening them and reducing their effectiveness. Both internally and externally, therefore, multinationals are in danger of destroying the institutional preconditions that made them possible in the first place. Kristensen argues that this makes it essential that countervailing forces are established to 'civilize' multinationals.

Inside the firm, this means the development of cross-national forms of legitimacy and responsibility based on formal and informal links between sites, their managers and employees. Externally it means the establishment of new voices of interest representation at the level of international and national institutions. Tilly (2001) has described the problem of current economic organization as 'back to the seventeenth century', an era of competing sovereignties, unstable institutions, and unclear rules of the game. As institutional settings become more diverse, establishing stable organizational forms that can be effective in these contexts becomes increasingly difficult. The two are inter-related; we need an adequate theory of societal change as much as we need an adequate theory of the firm in order to create, in Elias' terms, a new 'civilizing process' or more prosaically, build new institutional settlements in the current era.

In his final overview, Morgan emphasizes the importance of linking a dynamic view of firms with a dynamic view of institutions. He argues that firms are involved in tight market selection environments and they survive and grow by developing core capabilities through unique combinations of resources drawn from inside and outside the firm. Thus firms are unlikely to be passive recipients of institutional environments; on the contrary they are driven to be innovative and to look for new and unexpected resources in institutions. Institutions in turn are not functional outcomes of economic requirements. Institutions are political in nature, representing social compromises. They are not fixed but change as actors develop new resources from both the national and the international contexts. The metaphor of complementarities needs to be treated carefully. How tightly institutions interrelate is an empirical matter; it is in the realm of the 'logic of things' not the 'things of logic'. Once we take this seriously it is soon possible to identify divergences from central logics that have emerged over time. Empirical research can delve more deeply into these processes and show how contexts are continuously undergoing change and elaboration under the pressure of social, economic, and political actors.

In conclusion, the chapters in this book suggest that an essential goal is to move towards more empirically driven accounts of how institutions form and interact across various levels and spheres and how this relates to the dynamism of firms. They show that the dynamism of firms is constructed through the diversity of institutions rather than through their homogeneity. In considering this interaction more explicitly, the issue of 'changing capitalisms' can move more centrally onto our agenda, not as a way of dissolving the insights of previous authors within this tradition but rather as a means of sloughing off the many easy and simplistic criticisms that have been made of this tradition. The result should be a positive drive towards more empirically informed, historically grounded, and theoretically challenging studies of the interrelationships between firms and institutions in the constitution of changing capitalisms.

REFERENCES

Amable, B. (2003). *The Diversity of Modern Capitalism*, Oxford: Oxford University Press.

Amin, A. and Cohendet, P. (2004). *Architectures of Knowledge: Firms, Capabilities and Communities*, Oxford: Oxford University Press.

Aoki, M. (2001). *Toward a Comparative Institutional Analysis*, Cambridge, MA: The MIT Press.

Bartlett, C. A. and Ghoshal, S. (1989). *Managing Across Borders: The Transnational Solution*. London: Century Business.

Berger, S. and Dore, R. (1996). *National Diversity and Global Capitalism*. Ithaca, NY: Cornell University Press.

Boyer, R. and Drache, D. (1996). *States Against Markets: The Limits of Globalization*. London: Routledge.

Casper, S. and Whitley, R. (2004). 'Managing Competences in Entrepreneurial Technology Firms: A Comparative Institutional Analysis of Germany, Sweden and the UK'. *Research Policy* 33, 89–106.

Chandler, A. D., Hagstrom, P., and Solvell, O. (1998). *The Dynamic Firm*. Oxford: Oxford University Press.

Crouch, C. and Streeck, W. (1997). *Political Economy of Modern Capitalism*. London: Sage.

——, Le Gales, P., Trigilia, C., and Voelzkow, H. (2001). *Local Production Systems in Europe: Rise or Demise?* Oxford: Oxford University Press.

Djelic, M.-L. and Quack, S. (2003). *Globalization and Institutions: Redefining the Rules of the Economic Game*. Cheltenham, UK: Edward Elgar.

Dunning, J. (2000). 'The Eclectic Paradigm as an Envelope for Economic and Business Theories of MNC Activity'. *International Business Review* 9: 163–90.

Elias, N. (1994). The *Civilizing Process*. Oxford: Blackwell.

Gambardella, A. and Malerba, F. (1999). *The Organization of Economic Innovation in Europe*. Cambridge: Cambridge University Press.

Hall, P. and Soskice, D. (2001). *Varieties of Capitalism*. Oxford: Oxford University Press.

Hancké, B. (2002). *Large Firms and Institutional Change: Industrial Renewal and Economic Restructuring in France*. Oxford: Oxford University Press.

Hollingsworth, J. R. and Boyer, R. (1997). *Contemporary Capitalism: The Embeddedness of Institutions*. Cambridge: Cambridge University Press.

Kristensen, P. H. and Zeitlin, J. (2001). 'The Making of a Global Firm'. In: G. Morgan, R. Whitley, and P. H. Kristensen (eds.), *The Multinational Firm: Organizing Across Institutional and National Divides*, pp. 172–95.

———— (2005). *Local Players in Global Games: The Strategic Constitution of a Multinational Corporation*, Oxford: Oxford University Press.

Langlois, R. and Robertson, P. (1995). *Firms, Markets, and Economic Change*, London: Routledge.

Morgan, G., Whitley, R., and Kristensen, P. H. (eds) (2001). *The Multinational Firm: Organizing Across Institutional and National Divides*. Oxford: Oxford University Press.

Mowery, D. C. and Nelson, R. R. (1999). *Sources of Industrial Leadership*. Cambridge: Cambridge University Press.

Nelson, R. R. and Winter, S. G. (1982). *An Evolutionary Theory of Economic Change*. Cambridge, MA: Belknap Press of Harvard University.

Nooteboom, B. (2000). *Learning and Innovation in Organizations and Economies*. Oxford: Oxford University Press.

Penrose, E. (1959). *The Theory of the Growth of the Firm*. Oxford: Oxford University Press.

Pitelis, C. (ed.) (2002). *The Growth of the Firms: The Legacy of Edith Penrose*. Oxford: Oxford University Press.

Quack, S., Morgan, G., and Whitley, R. (2000). *National Capitalisms, Global Competition, and Economic Performance*. Amsterdam: John Benjamins Publishing.

Richardson, G. (1972). 'The Organisation of Industry'. *Economic Journal*, 82 883–96.

Schmidt, V. A. (2002). *The Futures of European Capitalism*. Oxford: Oxford University Press.

Tilly, C. (2001). 'Welcome to the Seventeenth Century'. In: P. DiMaggio (ed.), *The Twenty-First Century Firm: Changing Economic Organization in International Perspective*. Princeton: Princeton University Press, pp. 200–9.

Whitley, R. (1999). *Divergent Capitalisms*. Oxford: Oxford University Press.

—— and Kristensen, P. H. (eds.) (1996). *The Changing European Firm*. London: Routledge.

———— *Governance at Work*. Oxford: Oxford University Press.

Yamamura, K. and Streeck, W. (2003). *The End of Diversity? Prospects for German and Japanese Capitalism*. Ithaca: Cornell University Press.

PART I

INSTITUTIONAL COMPLEMENTARITY, CONTRADICTION, AND CHANGE IN BUSINESS SYSTEMS

2

Path Dependency, Institutional Complementarity, and Change in National Business Systems

RICHARD DEEG

2.1. Introduction

The concept of path dependency is widely invoked in the social sciences to explain institutional continuity and—to a lesser extent—institutional change. This is no less true of the various literatures which characterize and theorize about national business systems or models of capitalism. Yet, outside its formal application in economics to specific firms or technologies (e.g. Arthur 1994), the theory of path dependence is surprisingly underdeveloped. The exceptional efforts of North (1990) and others notwithstanding, the application of path dependent arguments to social and political institutions still lacks adequate theoretical specification and empirical examination. In this chapter I will attempt to advance theory building on institutional change broadly and institutional change in national business systems or regimes more narrowly.[1] I begin this effort by exploring the extent to which path dependency theory is useful in explaining institutional stability and change in national regimes. I am particularly interested in exploring change in the formal rules (typically codified in law or legal regulation) that govern national regimes. I believe this may be an underexplored category of institutional change as it involves large coordination challenges involving both market and political actors.

The author wishes to acknowledge the helpful comments of Gregory Jackson and this volume's editors.

[1] I will use the term 'national regimes' as a generic, catch-all term for the various analytical frameworks—'varieties of capitalism', 'national business systems', 'production regimes', 'social systems of production', 'regulation theory', etc.—which share broadly similar assumptions about the institutional underpinnings of national economies.

I will argue that path dependency theory can be useful in this endeavour, but there are both shortcomings in the theory itself and limits to its utility in explaining stability and change. Thus, I seek to move forward by identifying the manner and conditions under which path dependency is operative in national regimes.

The chapter has three major sections. The first provides a brief and limited review of institutional theory—path dependency theory in particular—and relates these to national regimes approaches. The second presents a critical discussion of these theories, suggests modifications, and raises issues needing further development. The final section attempts to elucidate the theoretical arguments by presenting a brief case study of change in the German financial and corporate governance subsystems.

2.2. **Path Dependency Theory and Institutional Change**

This section provides a necessarily truncated review of path dependency theory and related theories of institutional change. It contains three parts. The first is a brief exploration of sources of institutional stability or resilience, including path dependency (I will deliberately avoid an explicit discussion of theories of institutional choice or origins per se). The second explores sources of institutional change. The final part lays out specific mechanisms of institutional change that are useful in explaining changes in national regimes.

In this chapter I start from the theory of path dependence as articulated largely by Pierson (2000) and Mahoney (2000). Their theory is largely consistent with that developed in economics by Arthur, North, and others, but is adapted to political and sociological institutions. I consider the Pierson–Mahoney theory among the most promising for the analysis of national regimes, in part because it is a more narrowly conceived and therefore potentially rigorous theory of path dependence. In this theory, a path dependent process is one characterized by a self-reinforcing sequence of events. Following the branching metaphor, each event (or choice point) in the sequence sets the direction (and thus precludes others) of subsequent events. Events early in the sequence often matter more in determining the overall path trajectory because their effects may be exaggerated downstream. As events move down the path, change becomes more bounded, that is, previously viable options are increasingly remote (costlier to adopt). A path begins with a critical juncture, that is, a point in time in which at least two alternative paths are (more or less) equally probable but movement toward one is initially chosen or favoured. Mahoney (2000) has argued that this initial move should be contingent, that is, not explained by prior events or initial conditions.

The initial step in one direction is then reinforced through positive feedback or self-reinforcing mechanisms.[2] These mechanisms include *large set-up or initial costs*—once actors have made a substantial investment in a given path they have a strong incentive to sustain the path to recover their costs; *learning effects* may also strengthen the path, because as actors learn to utilize more effectively the institutions constituting this path, it enhances their value and utility; *coordination effects* take root when other actors follow the initial actors in their commitment to a given path and thus enhance the benefits accruing to all actors from this path; *adaptive expectations* are a fourth source of positive feedback when actors adopt or support a particular path because they expect others to do so.[3]

A final source of positive feedback deserves special attention, since it is regarded by many as often quite substantial and it—implicitly or explicitly—underlies virtually all theories of national regimes: this source is *institutional complementarity, interdependence, or coherence.*[4] For reasons to be made clear below, in this chapter I will use the term 'coherence' to refer to this concept. There are various definitions of coherence, but conceptually they are, in my view, quite similar. Whitley (Chapter 8, this volume), for example, understands coherence as the degree to which social institutions encourage similar kinds of economic actors to behave in similar ways and reinforce each other's effects on systems of coordination and control in the economy. Hall and Soskice (2001: 17), following Aoki, see coherence as when '. . . the presence (or efficiency) of one [institution] increases the returns (or efficiency of) the other'. What is common to these and other conceptions of coherence, in my view, is the core idea that the coexistence of two (or more) institutions together affects the strategic choices of actors and/or will enhance the ability of actors to achieve their objectives

---

[2] Mahoney has argued that path dependence may also follow a 'reactive' or non-reinforcing sequence. In this case early events give rise to backlash events that transform or reverse the early events. See also Morgan and Kubo (n.d.).

[3] In more recent work, Pierson (2004) has used the concept of 'asset specificity' to characterize set up costs and learning and coordination effects mechanisms.

[4] See also Pierson (2004); North (1990); also Whitley, Chapter 8, this volume; Hall and Soskice (2001). For Aoki (2001) institutional complementarity is not only a key factor explaining institutional stability but the essential factor that creates path dependency.

(which may include many objectives, not just maximizing economic gains).

Here, I propose that we distinguish three sources or types of coherence (the first two I draw from Crouch 2002).

1. In the first, institutions cohere through a *logic of similarity*—institutions with similar properties are found together as actors adopt similar approaches or institutional solutions to different spheres of action. This may be the result of the expansion of a 'logic of appropriateness'. For example, Vitols (2001*b*) argues that to the extent 'shareholder value' as a norm for corporate management is spreading in Germany, it is doing so to a great extent following this logic.

2. The second form is an opposed *logic of complementarity* in which one institution makes up for the *deficiencies* of the other (i.e. provides a 'missing ingredient'), thus raising the returns to actors from the first institution. For example, when strong familial social support networks offset the vicissitudes of a highly liberalized labour market. In such cases the existence of the former make the latter more socially and politically acceptable, thus allowing the society to gain the advantages of a liberal labour market.

3. The third form of coherence lies at the heart of most theories of national regimes. This form of coherence embodies the mutually reinforcing effects of compatible incentive structures in different sub-systems of an economy: we might call this a *logic of synergy*. Assume a given individual economic actor—such as a firm—operates in many subsystems of the economy; if the incentive structures across these subsystems reinforce particular strategies by that actor, they cohere by a logic of synergy. Estevez-Abe et al. (2001: 182), for example, write that the resilience of particular welfare production regimes is 'reinforced by institutions—collective wage-bargaining systems, business organizations, employee representation, and financial systems—that facilitate the credible commitment of actors to particular strategies, such as wage restraint and long-term employment, that are necessary to sustain cooperation in the provision of specific skills'. A logic of synergy may arise through deliberate strategic coordination by actors across institutional domains—Aoki (2001) calls this 'strategic complementarity'—or it may arise through a process akin to evolutionary (functional) selection or co-evolution (see also Streeck and Yamamura 2001). Thus, even where subsystems may not create mutually reinforcing incentive structures, subsystem similarity may develop because it precludes possible reductions in institutional efficiency through negative feedback or

externalities from other institutions operating on different principles (see also Whitley 1999: 41).

Distinguishing different sources or types of coherence is, in my view, an important step forward in developing theories of institutional change. For one, it is conceivable that different sources of coherence may be generally 'stronger' or 'weaker' in their effects. In other words, a 'strong' form of coherence exists when changes in one institution lead to changes in cohering or interdependent institutions. Intuitively it seems that a logic of complementarity would create the strongest coherence, because the functionality of a set of institutions for given actors would be eroded or compromised in the absence of the complementing institutions. Conversely, a logic of similarity might arguably be weaker because it may not rest on material interests. However, this is clearly an empirical question in need of further exploration.

In addition to those just discussed, there are other sources of institutional resilience or stability that are not necessarily self-reinforcing (though they may be), but nonetheless may work against change. Most important among these would be the application of *power* or authority by actors to preserve a given institutional path. Deep-seated *legitimacy* can also stabilize a path (Clemens and Cook 1999; Mahoney 2000). *Coordination or collective action problems* can also inhibit institutional change: Once actors have coordinated on one institution (equilibrium), they should have no incentive to unilaterally alter their behaviour, and even if they do, the cost of coordinating around another equilibrium may outweigh potential gains (Pierson, 2004; also Schwartz 2002). Change in politically constituted institutions may also be inhibited by the number and character of *veto points* which allow actors, even weaker ones, to block change. By politically constituted I mean those formal institutions that result by the direct actions and intentions of political actors operating within formal political institutions (in practical terms, this means laws, government regulations, and official policies). The theory of path dependence thus suggests that the longer an institution has been in place, the more resilient to change it will be and the more likely that any changes will be incremental. Given enough time and enough self-reinforcing mechanisms, a path will, according to Pierson, develop a 'deep equilibrium', that is, become highly resistant to change and likely to endure for a long period of time (see Pierson 2004: Chapter 5).

Given this theory of path dependency, then, how do institutions change? 'Strong' versions of path dependency (such as Pierson's)

imply that only an 'exogenous shock'—an event outside the path
that radically alters the incentives/constraints confronting actors on
the path—can lead to the end of the path. Short of this, change is
incremental or 'on-path'. Actors may gradually modify aspects of the
path, but the overall trajectory is unchanged. As I will argue below,
such strong versions of path dependent change are too limiting to
cover the full extent of real institutional change. Fortunately, other
scholars—who acknowledge path dependency in some form—have
provided us with compelling arguments for mechanisms of change
that may arise endogenously within the path that arguably lead to new
paths.

Thelen (2001, 2003), for instance, has argued that mechanisms of
change can operate at the same time as mechanisms of reproduction of a given path. Over time, however, the mechanisms of change
may outweigh those reproducing the path, leading to a major change
in the overall trajectory of the path. She highlights two mechanisms
in particular that may lead to such change. The first is 'institutional
layering' when actors use institutional material already available but
in new ways or combinations, or new institutions are added 'on top' of
existing ones.[5] The other mechanism is 'conversion' in which existing
institutions are turned to new purposes. Thelen (2003) also highlights
the role of 'marginal actors', especially in a political sense, who may
use such mechanisms to turn a path in a direction more favourable to
their interests.

This draws our attention to another source of change that I will also
highlight later, namely, that the interests of actors on the path may
change such that they seek to radically alter the path they are on. Such
shifts in interests may result from exogenous shocks but also from
endogenous changes in the path (Aoki 2001; Deeg 2001). For example,
unanticipated institutional effects or developments—which are highly
likely in complex systems—may lead actors to reassess their interests
vis-à-vis the institutions (see Pierson 2004). Such actors may then use
entrepreneurial skills, power, or access to other social networks or
institutional ideas in an effort to alter the institutions of the path (e.g.
Hacker 2002: 60; also Crouch 2002). Given a shift in interests, actors
may use various mechanisms of change such as layering, conversion,
or also diffusion, that is, draw on alternative notions of appropriate

---

[5] This is, in essence, an argument of bricolage—a concept already established in sociological
institutionalism. Crouch and Farrell (2002) make a similar argument in suggesting that actors may
borrow institutional innovations from other paths, especially those that are 'near' to the actors.

action or norms that alter other actors' behaviour, which may then culminate in institutional change. Stated somewhat differently, actors can appropriate and promulgate selected ideas that help them overcome the constraints of structure. Many theorists focusing on ideational sources of change, however, emphasize that ideas may also have independent causal force of their own, that is, are not mere tools in the hands of powerful actors (e.g. Lieberman 2002; see also Lehmbruch 2001).

2.2.1. *Path dependency in national regimes analyses*

Because of their common institutionalist roots, nearly all the approaches to national regimes draw on some or all of the above-mentioned sources of institutional resilience. In most of these schools there is also (at least implicitly) an assumption of path dependency, although the conception of path dependency employed varies considerably and not all of them adopt a path dependency model of the increasing returns type. Nonetheless, many are consistent with the assumption of path dependency in the form of increasing returns or positive feedback model. In the 'varieties of capitalism' approach, for instance, asset specificity—for example, joint investments, adaptive learning, and reciprocal relationships—plays an especially prominent role as a source of positive feedback (Hall and Soskice 2001).

What many such approaches share in common is an assumption that increasing returns or positive feedback effects are very strong in the form of institutional coherence (most typically presuming a logic of synergy). Again, using the varieties of capitalism approach as an example, this coherence is used to explain how coordinated market economies' (CMEs') production model based on skilled labour is sustained by the mutually constituted effects of a wide range of institutions governing collective bargaining, codetermination, vocational training, and industrial finance (Hall and Soskice 2001: 18–19). Together these institutions create, among other things, a context for long-term investment in relationships and skills. Thus the CME coheres as a national model or regime.[6]

The 'varieties of capitalism' literature is not alone in arguing (or assuming) for substantial coherence at the national level (which translates into a powerful source of path dependency). Indeed, it would make no sense to talk about national business systems, social

---

[6] Whitley (Chapter 8, this volume) goes further by arguing that CMEs exhibit stronger institutional coherence than LMEs.

systems of production or varieties of capitalism if there were not at belief in some form of significant coherence across subsystems of the economy (see, for example, Albert 1993; Whitley 1999). While these are usually summated at the national level as a unit of analysis, even where some literatures may use subnational units of analysis—such as an industrial sector (or region)—similar assumptions of institutional coherence are usually present (e.g. Lindberg et al. 1991: 32). In some cases this coherence may be seen to represent little more than institutional isomorphism (logic of similarity) and not, therefore, increasing returns or path dependence. But the literatures of interest to me here generally assume increasing returns and significant institutional coherence. Moreover, even those who may not assume coherence at the national level as a source of path dependency may still assume that individual institutions or institutional systems below this level exhibit increasing returns effects.

Several recent studies and theorists within these various schools have lately begun to question notions of tight coherence or coupling (e.g. Crouch 2002; Jackson 2003; Morgan and Kubo 2002). More generally, the implications of 'loose coupling' are underexplored in the institutionalist literature (Pierson 2004). Thus, in the second part of this chapter I jump on this bandwagon and attempt to adapt and modify increasing returns path dependency theory to help us better understand patterns of change which defy tight coupling assumptions, as well as the implications of such change for the future development of national regimes.

2.3. Theoretical Modifications and National Regimes

In this section I explore, first, a key weakness in path dependency theory and the resultant problem for its application to national regimes. The theoretical weakness is the problematic reliance on exogenous shock arguments to explain institutional change. Moving away from such reliance, I will argue, makes it much easier for us to explore theoretically—and explain empirical observations—institutional interdependencies or coherence as a source of path dependence.

The second theoretical issue I will broach is how we might explain changes in formal rules (institutions) governing economic behaviour when such rule changes require coordination between economic and political actors. I believe this line of inquiry is worthy of explicit attention because the major kinds of institutional changes in national regimes of interest involve changes in politically constituted institutions (rules). My discussion suggests not that we need new theoretical tools to explain such changes, but there are additional issues and considerations—as well as challenges—associated with such efforts.

2.3.1. *What is a path?*

For all the widespread use of the concept of an institutional path, there are surprisingly few efforts to define it specifically. It is too often simply assumed that we all know what it is and that we all share the same conception. But the very definition of a path is crucial to any theory of path dependency and change. Drawing on previous work (Deeg 2001: 14), I define an institutional path by its logic, that is, a distinct pattern of institutionally rooted constraints and incentives that create typical strategies, routine approaches to problems, and shared decision rules that produce predictable patterns of behaviour. Such a definition of a path moves us away from simply equating a path with the continuation of a formal institution or institutional system in itself.[7] This, in turn, generates several advantages.

First, it allows us to recognize key elements (reproductive mechanisms) of a path that may not be obviously part of the institution or system. I believe this also helps distinguish between 'on-path' and 'off-path' kinds of changes. Since virtually all institutions undergo some modification over time, we are continuously confronted with the challenge of how to characterize that change, that is, when are changes 'major' or path altering, and when are they merely movement along the existing path/trajectory?[8] Using a definition of a path as a 'logic' allows for the possibility that some institutions may be altered or changed, but if the patterns of actor behaviour, strategies, etc. remain largely unchanged (i.e. the logic), then we are seeing on-path change. This

---

[7] Many theorists (e.g. Pierson 2000; Mahoney 2000) define a path as a sequence of causally connected events. But this would seem to focus purely on the behavioural dimension of paths, that is, the actions and reactions of actors to preceding events. It does not address the structural dimension of the path, that is, the institutions that constrain the behaviour of actors (and make it predictable) by establishing a matrix of (dis-)incentives. A definition of a path should incorporate both dimensions.

[8] Knill and Lenschow (2001) pursue this question as well and provide, in my view, a similar argument to the one that I am advancing here. Following their schema, my approach here is somewhat de-emphasizing structure as the constitutive element of a path and emphasizing agent behaviour, though the two obviously cannot be completely separated and are part of a given path.

relates to the issue of institutional coherence (discussed more below), in that it allows for the possibility that institutional changes in one subsystem may not necessarily alter the path of a coherent one (this, in turn, may depend upon the type or source of coherence), as the logic of the latter may be sustained nonetheless through institutional innovation within that system (path) or the emergence of other institutions that might substitute for the ones altered in the first (e.g. by providing functional equivalence). Thus, while both subsystems may exhibit notable institutional change, only one may be off-path change. Finally, this definition also proves useful to identifying the beginning and end of a given path when path change occurs without some obvious exogenous shock (punctuated equilibrium) or contingent event.[9] That is, we can demarcate a path change when there is a major change in its logic.

But this definition still leaves open the question of what it is that is path dependent. It seems useful to me to distinguish at least three levels of analysis for understanding institutional change in political economies: (1) individual institutions and organizations—firms, government agencies, electoral systems, etc.; (2) institutional systems or complexes—a banking system, an industrial sector, a welfare system; (3) a national political economy or regime (what I call a meta-path). Making this distinction serves several purposes. First, it will facilitate exploration of endogenous and exogenous sources of change. For path dependent theories this distinction is crucial since—according to the strong version—only exogenous shocks can move institutional change off-path. Second, it will facilitate theorizing about the possibility (and reality) of path changes at or within one level but path stability at another.[10] It is also possible that path dependency may be more or less common at each of these levels.[11]

---

[9] Schwartz has argued that without being able to rely on the punctuated equilibrium (exogenous shock) metaphor to explain path change, path dependency arguments fall apart (2002: 3). I have argued elsewhere as well against a simple reliance upon exogenous shock arguments but have suggested that path dependency can still be salvaged (Deeg 2001).

[10] Knill and Lenschow (2001) also address this particular issue, arguing that the level of analysis one chooses to examine a given phenomenon is likely to determine whether one finds institutional continuity or discontinuity.

[11] Schwartz, for example, has argued that social and political organizations are generally subject to decreasing (not increasing, as path dependency assumes) returns, thus suggesting that the paths of individual organizations are sustained by other (non-path dependent) mechanisms (2002). I think this is probably true in many cases, though even when this may be the case, it may not preclude the possibility that increasing returns to the system as a whole (because of interdependence) may overwhelm decreasing returns to particular organizations within it.

2.3.2. *Across the exogenous–endogenous divide*

As has now been established, national regime approaches generally give primacy to the national level of analysis (the meta-path). In other words, nations are distinguished at the national level in their political economic institutional paths, for example, coordinated market versus liberal market economies (Hall and Soskice 2001; see also Amable 2003; Whitley 1999). Because of the presumed high level of institutional interdependence, individual organizations and institutional systems or complexes within that nation are subordinated to its national institutional logic, that is, the path or logic of the first two levels is heavily constrained by the third. Deviations remain anomalous and marginal. Major institutional change in one institutional subsystem within a nation is virtually precluded in this perspective, for it would then fail to cohere with the remaining systems. For such theories, then, tight institutional interdependence implies that endogenous is equated with domestic institutions, events, and actions, and exogenous with those emanating from outside national borders. While this is often empirically and theoretically correct, as we all know the national boundary is hardly such a neat dividing line (a theme treated extensively by Djelic and Quack, Chapter 6, this volume). For example, national actors (governments, firms, associations, etc.) participate directly or indirectly in the formulation of EU directives on finance. In such cases are EU interventions exogenous to the national system or (at least partially) endogenous?

Giving primacy to the national level also makes it difficult to analyse change of particular institutional systems within a given nation independent from other systems within the nation (from a path dependency perspective).[12] This is so because the coherence or presumed interdependence of the separate systems breaks down the exogenous–endogenous distinction upon which path dependent theories are predicated. According to path dependency theory, a switch to a new path only comes from an exogenous shock that renders the existing path unviable. But, if there is tight coherence across subsystems, what is exogenous and endogenous? For example, if the German banking system switches to a new path because of changes in domestic tax laws, is this an exogenous shock because these laws

---

[12] Even when an assumption of strong institutional interdependence at the national level is not being made, as long as there is any presumption of such interdependence (e.g. between two individual institutions) the problem of distinguishing exogenous from endogenous rears its ugly head.

are not part of the banking system strictly speaking (even though such laws prior to their changes significantly influenced banks' strategies)? Imagine a scenario in which these changes in tax laws were an unintended consequence of prior changes in the banking sector? Are they then an endogenous source of change? More than anything else, these questions point to the need for institutionalists to be much more self-aware and self-critical about the boundary issue, that is, distinguishing between exogenous and endogenous. As I will soon argue (and others have as well), in recent years we have witnessed a tremendous amount of institutional change within advanced capitalist economies and much of that change appears disjointed, asynchronous, and independently evolving across different spheres or systems of institutions within given national economies.

Using once again the national regimes framework, it would predict on-path or evolutionary change for organizations and institutional systems within a given nation. Only an exogenous (international) shock would force off-path change and then it would require widespread change across all key domestic institutional systems (which is exactly Lane's argument, (see Chapter 4, this volume), about Germany). But, as noted already, it appears possible for one institutional system within a nation to change off-path to a logic that is different from other systems and the logic of the national model (see also Crouch and Farrell 2002; Höpner 2001; Jackson 2003). Moreover, the change in a given institutional system may also occur as a result of factors endogenous to that system. Indeed, generally I would argue (as do Aoki 2001; and Djelic and Quack, Chapter 6, this volume) that off-path changes are likely to result from a combination of exogenous and endogenous factors.

How do we extricate ourselves from this problem? One possibility is to abandon path dependency arguments that require a clear exogenous–endogenous distinction or simply abandon path dependency arguments altogether.[13] Another possibility is to employ a more abstract definition of endogenous and exogenous, that is, to abandon more simple distinctions that equate endogenous with national and exogenous with international; or endogenous with everything that happens within a formally defined institution or institutional system and exogenous with everything outside it. A more abstract

---

[13] For an extensive critique and rejection of path dependency theory see Schwartz (2002); there have also been efforts to modify path dependency theory that help to overcome this problem at least to some degree (e.g. Crouch and Farrell 2002; Deeg 2001; Thelen 2000).

definition opens the possibility that endogenous sources of change may in fact be ones that, to many, appear to emanate outside the formal 'boundaries' of an institution or system (or national regime).

I propose we consider endogenous sources of change to include actions, events, or processes that result directly from the key mechanisms of path reproduction, that is, the changes in the mechanisms of reproduction (e.g. distribution of assets or power of actors, or actors' beliefs) which occur as a result of their own development and ultimately undermine or alter these mechanisms, thus upsetting the institutional equilibrium or path (see also Deeg 2001: 11). Using this definition allows one to argue, for example, that the close relationship (relational contracting) between large banks and non-financial firms was a key mechanism of reproduction in *both* the German financial and corporate governance subsystems (though each also has separate mechanisms). Thus changes in this relationship are endogenous to the financial system (as well as corporate governance) even though non-financial firms are formally outside the financial system.

More abstractly, endogenous institutional changes can arise through changes in actor goals and preferences. Shifts in preferences/goals are endogenous, for example, when they occur in response to unintended consequences of prior choices (events) or the long-term effects of institutions comprising the path within which these actors operate (which are distinct from their short-term effects). 'Generational turnover' or actor discontinuity within a given institutional path can also be a source of endogenous change (see also Pierson 2004: 154–73). Since successive generations of actors may not share the same goals and preferences and interpretive frameworks of their predecessors, they may seek to alter institutions. Such an argument presumes, of course, that actors, while constrained by their institutional context, are not determined by it. To be clear, actors are in many ways the product of their institutional environment, that is, their beliefs, preferences, and material resources are shaped (or in some cases, given) by the institutional context. This is another reason why institutions are typically change resistant. But without rehashing the age-old structure–agency debate here, it is important to clarify the point—actors are nonetheless able to innovate from within the path. Actors, for example, can learn from other institutional domains and use this to alter their own (see Crouch 2002).

There is also no reason to assume that increasing returns effects, in social and political institutions, are necessarily of a given strength or are indefinite. We should see path dependence as a variable concept. Moreover, arguing that off-path institutional change can arise from endogenous sources also means acknowledging that increasing returns effects can level off or turn into decreasing returns. While this makes theorizing more difficult—indeed, quite messy—and vulnerable to logical inconsistencies, it seems to fit better the evidence arising out of a growing body of case studies.

2.3.3. *Increasing returns and institutional coherence*

How might we account for the repeated observation that major institutional subsystems within national capitalisms are changing at varying rates and to varying degrees? Wide variation in change rates and degree of change across subsystems may be an indication of declining coherence or interdependence, or may simply reveal that the presumed coherence was, in fact, not present. Building on Morgan and Kubo (2002), I suggest five *patterns* of coherence or interdependence (not necessarily mutually exclusive) across the subsystems of a national regime which can be found in empirical studies of national regimes. These five are distinguished roughly by their position on a continuum from lesser to higher coherence, with higher coherence meaning increasing probability that altering one institution or subsystem will force changes in other institutions or subsystems. The *source* of coherence in any one of these categories could, in principle, be any one (or combination) of the three noted earlier (similarity, complementarity, or synergy).

1. *Loose Integration*. In this pattern there is loose integration and thus one subsystem may follow (or change to) a different logic from the others without affecting the rest.

2. *Increasing Differentiation*. In this pattern increased differentiation across subsystems leads to efforts to isolate or create a buffer between a subsystem that no longer fits the dominant logic of the broader system and the rest of the subsystems. Successful buffering will leave the remaining subsystems unchanged. This pattern represents a slightly higher level of coherence than loose integration because in this pattern a changing subsystem necessitates a response by others.

3. *Variable Complementarity*. The brief case study I present later (see also Goyer 2002) suggests a third possibility. Namely, that subsystems can cohere or complement each other in different ways under different conditions. In other words, subsystems do not 'fit' together like pieces of a jigsaw puzzle in which each part can only match up with

another in one specific way. In this pattern one subsystem may change substantially (move off-path) while complementary ones change to a much lesser degree (remain on-path). Yet, coherence or complementarity remains because the 'unchanged' system may draw on new features or effects of the changed subsystem that help it sustain its old path or logic. Or, conversely, the more radically changed subsystem may find new ways to remain compatible with, or draw certain synergies from, the relatively unchanged subsystems.

4. *Multiple, Coexisting Orders.* A fourth possible pattern of institutional coherence is one in which multiple 'orders' or regimes coexist within a given national regime (in this case, though, it might more accurately be labelled 'incoherence'). Each order would, in some sense, be a complete political economic system in its own right. Orders are constituted by a coherent set of institutions, organizations, and governing ideological or cultural principles (see also Lieberman 2002: 703). Orders may be 'layered' in the sense of coexisting with some overlap or points of intersection between them, and in the sense that one may be dominant. An order may also be latent within a national regime. For example, a previously stronger order may have diminished over time yet left important institutional and ideational legacies behind which might later be revived (see also Djelic and Quack, Chapter 6, this volume). This conception of orders suggests that they are likely to be characterized by increasing returns effects due to institutional coherence (but limited to institutions within the order), as well as other sources of positive feedback. Change in national regimes characterized by multiple orders may arise either endogenously—when friction between orders increases, for example—or exogenously, as when changed external circumstances favour the rise (or replacement) of one order over another. The volumes by Streeck and Yamamura (2001, 2003), for example, provide ample empirical evidence (and theoretical exploration) of how the tensions between liberal and nonliberal orders have played out over time in Germany and Japan.[14]

5. *Tight Integration.* The final pattern assumes tight integration across subsystems and thus change in one will lead to change in the others in order to restore a high level of coherence. The work of Hall and Soskice (2001), for instance, fits within this category.

The final issue I raise in this section (admittedly without providing much theoretical direction) is whether we can make a general

[14] To be clear, this is not the only possible typology of orders. It is conceivable, for example, for alternative nonliberal forms of order to coexist within the same national regime.

argument about which kinds of (sub)systems in national regimes may be more easily 'isolated' from others? In other words, are some kinds of subsystems less central to sustaining particular kinds of national regimes and thus more radically changed without altering the overall system? This strikes me as a promising, but as yet mostly unexplored, possibility. For example, one hypothesis might be that financial regimes can more readily undergo substantial (off-path) institutional change without forcing remaining subsystems within a national regime to move in step. In the varieties of capitalism school, for example, long-term finance provided by banks with close relationships to firms is viewed as an essential complement to the particular production strategies, training systems, and industrial relations systems that define CMEs (Estevez-Abe et al. 2001: 182). By this reasoning, the loss of relational banking should undermine the whole national regime, as Hall and Soskice (2001: 64) explicitly suggest would happen. But the brief case study of Germany I present below suggests the opposite may, in fact, be the case. More generally, the importance of the financial system for the corporate sector arguably varies 'naturally' over time. For example, during periods of high corporate self-financing firms are less dependent on the financial system and could probably manage well with a variety of financial systems. Major financial system change during such a period might then have limited effects on other subsystems. Thus the importance of a given subsystem to others may be conditioned by temporality.

The underlying question at hand, though, is whether another subsystem—such as the coordinated wage bargaining system—could be 'lost' or radically changed without undermining the logic of the national regime? While I cannot provide a direct answer to this question, my research suggests that financial systems may be more 'expendable' to CMEs. If this is the case, it tells us much about the role of institutional coherence in national regimes: it could be that national regimes are less coherent than often presumed, or that the financial system is not (or no longer) actually an important element of distinction among different regime types.

2.3.4. *Institutional change and the economics–politics nexus*

The discussion in this chapter is intended to illuminate in particular issues and approaches related to the explanation of off-path kinds of institutional change in national business systems. Such major change generally requires actors to change the higher-order *formal* institutions or 'rules of the game'. While 'rules of the game' may be informal, it is hard to imagine that any of the major kinds of institutional systems or regimes of interest to us do not also rest to a significant degree upon formal rules (institutions) that are politically constituted or codified— either in a statutory form or in formal political regulation. In other words, of concern here is not the 'normal' adjustment by economic actors within the economy (on-path change) to new market developments (i.e. change/path dependency at the first level of individual organizations and firms).[15] The kinds of off-path institutional changes of interest to me invariably involved extensive change through strategic (and non-strategic) coordination between market and political actors.

Explaining institutional change in formal, politically codified rules which govern economic actors presents some unique challenges. The first challenge is the rising level of actor complexity, as the creation and change of such institutions requires interaction and coordination by both market and political actors. Aside from the general difficulty of achieving coordination among increasing numbers of actors, there are reasons to believe that economic and political actors may be operating on a different logic.[16] While we may assume that economic actors are concerned primarily with production efficiency gains and profit, political actors may share these goals but are also likely to pursue other and more diverse goals simultaneously which may conflict with the former.

It is also conceivable that economic and political actors tend to operate on different timeframes. Thus, on the one hand, political parties (and even more so individual politicians) might conceivably have relatively short time horizons guiding their preferences regarding changes in institutional rules governing the economy. Market actors, on the other hand, may have somewhat longer time horizons if they expect their own tenure to last longer, or if they coordinate among themselves in the pursuit of common, long-term objectives, though, it is also conceivable that political actors may pursue long-term objectives. Either way, coordination among actors operating on different time horizons presents greater obstacles.

Another difference is that market actors seeking changes in higher-order institutions are presumably doing so in response to market pressures they face. In other words, competitive market pressures weigh

---

[15] There is some controversy as to whether formal or informal institutions are more resistant to change. Carey (2000) argues the former while North (1990) argues the latter. But this point is not important to me since undoubtedly both kinds of institutions are important and difficult to change.

[16] In this section I am drawing selectively and adapting from Pierson (forthcoming: 159–79).

heavily upon the preferences of economic actors. While political actors have their own competitive pressures, these do not arise directly out of economic market competition but competition in the political arena. Thus political actors may be far more reluctant to support institutional change because: (1) they may not suffer the same adverse consequences as market actors do from lack of change; (2) the consequences of institutional change for political actors may be more ambiguous than for market actors (thus while market actors may be 'weeded' out of the market by failure to respond to new competition, political actors may not); (3) political actors may continue to derive benefits (increasing returns) from the status quo even while market actors may not; or (4) political actors may not 'learn' the same lessons as market actors do from a given change in the terms of market competition, in turn leading to divergent preferences over institutional change. The converse, of course, might be true as well: political actors may be more willing to change institutions if, for example, the potential sunk costs for them are much lower than for market actors. To be clear, these are just some conceivable constellations of preferences, time horizons, and sources of competitive pressures acting upon market and political actors.

What all of this drives at is that changing higher-order institutional rules, and thus moving national regimes or even subsystems into off-path forms of change, is complicated by the economics–politics nexus (for a similar argument, see Lehmbruch 2001). The coordination difficulties arising from the economics–politics nexus will act as a source of institutional resilience, but not necessarily constitute a path dependent (increasing returns) situation. Coordination between market and political actors may, on the other hand, create path dependency if each set of actors is pursuing coherent (synergistic) strategies in their respective spheres (see also Aoki 2001). For example, if political actors adopt the pursuit of financial market deregulation as a strategy for success in political competition while financial institutions pursue this same deregulation as a part of their own market strategies, the two are mutually reinforcing (synergistic), and create positive feedback.

2.4. Analysing Change in German Finance and Corporate Governance

How do we characterize the extent of change in the German finance and corporate governance systems? What are the sources of resilience and of change? How is it that some institutions undergo radical change while others do not? Is this in fact possible, given the presumed interdependencies among the key institutions (subsystems) which comprise the national regime? In this part of the chapter I wish to explore these questions—to a greater or lesser degree—utilizing the above theoretical discussion. I will argue that the German financial and corporate governance systems—which, for analytical reasons, I treat as separate subsystems despite their close relatedness—have each changed to a new institutional path. But this new path is more complex than the old one: the new path entails a growing dualism within the financial and corporate governance systems. In other words, a 'carve out' is taking place in which a small number of firms (mostly very large ones) have created a new institutional path for themselves that incorporates substantial elements of a liberal market model (order). To be clear, this new path is a hybridized one in that many key elements of the old system remain. Nonetheless, I argue it is a new path for reasons explained below. This argument is consistent with the observation already made by several studies of Germany that indicate a rising internal heterogeneity or incoherence among the institutions that comprise its national political economy (e.g. Höpner 2001; Jackson 2003).

The path of the post-war German financial system was characterized by the logic of a bank-based system. This had several dimensions. First is that banks and non-financial firms developed long-term relationships (relational contracting) based on long-term financial commitments (whether loans or equity) in which trust became an important element. Banks pursued relationship banking. In the German case the logic also included a shared decision-making system based on corporatist (consensual) rule making within a tight policy community. Another dimension was the logic of group competition in which the savings and cooperative banks cooperated extensively with other banks of the same type in the effort to compete head-to-head with commercial banks in all market segments. Finally, we can argue that a key element of the 'old' system's logic was that of insider control in corporate governance. This governance system was closely connected to the corporate strategies of both individual banks and large non-financial firms. For instance, German banks' strategy for individual success (i.e. their business models) rested upon efforts to promote industrial development and competitiveness throughout the economy via network relations to firms. Conversely, the business models (corporate strategies) and corporate governance system rested on the assumption of 'patient' or dedicated capital.

The mechanisms of reproduction (sources of resilience) closely follow this logic. One key mechanism was the increasing returns accruing to the finance and corporate governance systems due to their coherence—a coherence following a pattern of tight coupling and based on synergies. Another was the coordination gains realized through the insider system of corporate governance, for example, protection from hostile takeover, information about other firms, and rewards for long-term success. A third key mechanism of reproduction was the stable distribution of power among the three banking groups. This power stability (and parity) undergirded consensual decision-making over the rules governing the financial system.

There are numerous reasons why the German financial system moved to a new path. First, the major strategies (and behaviour) of large banks changed from a focus on commercial banking based on long-term relations with large firms (relational financing) to investment banking (see Beyer 2002; Deeg 2001). Broadly speaking, in relational financing, banks make an implicit promise to assist firms in future situations of financial difficulty. In return, firms pay a slightly higher cost for funds (an 'insurance premium', so to speak) and provide banks access to inside information so that the former may monitor management (see also Aoki 2001). In investment banking, relationships may be long-term, but do not rest on an implicit promise by the bank to assist the firm if it gets into trouble. The relationship is more contractual in this case. In Germany, the move to investment banking means the (still ongoing) withdrawal of banks from their insider position in German corporate governance. Investment banking success is based on capital market activities and deal-based transactions with non-financial firms. This is why we see banks withdrawing from board seats and reducing and diversifying their holdings. As a corporate strategy, the logic of investment banking is opposed to that of the old commercial banking strategy; the latter, in effect, was a strategy of risk reduction by 'getting closer' to clients (through equity holdings, board seats, etc.), while the former is a strategy of risk reduction through 'gaining distance' from clients (diversification in assets, 'quick entry/exit', deal-based transactions: see also Beyer 2002).[17] Despite the decline of securities markets over the last few years, this general direction of evolution continues.

---

[17] Relational and investment banking often coexist within the same financial system, but one is usually dominant or exclusive within a given financial institution. Those which try to combine the two often find this possible but problematic.

Rule or decision-making over financial system rules has also become more conflictual. The logic (and practice) of group competition is eroding (though not gone) as the cooperative banks become more like a single banking concern while cooperation among savings banks suffers serious strains.[18] The German financial system is also on a new path because the key rules (laws and regulations) and norms that govern it have been extensively changed in order to foster the growth of securities markets and the reorientation of investors and banks toward basing their respective strategies on success in these markets (again, Deeg 2001). Finally, promoting securities markets in Germany was pursued primarily through change in the financial system itself, but with related (but not in themselves path altering) changes in tax, bankruptcy, accounting, and corporate laws.

Has the German corporate governance system moved to a new path? There is substantial recent research which could suggest that the corporate governance system has also moved on to a new path (e.g. Goyer 2002; Höpner 2001; Jackson 2003; for an opposing argument, see Bebchuk and Roe 1999). The logic (and managerial practices) of shareholder capitalism has pervaded a small but significant portion of corporate Germany. The institutions that created strong incentives (rents) for large, insider shareholders to maintain the system have been weakened. Aggregate indicators of share ownership generally show little change in the overall level of concentration since the 1980s (Höpner 2001). However, a disaggregated look shows a very different story. Ownership concentration has declined dramatically for a small but economically very significant group of firms (e.g. Deutsche Bank, Siemens), in part due to the rapid growth of shares held by institutional investors. The density of the equity and personal (via board seats) networks that linked many large firms and banks has also declined quite substantially and continues to do so (Beyer 2002; Höpner 2001).[19] The Eichel Tax Reform of 2002 is expected to accelerate the decline in equity links. Banks have dramatically reduced the number of board seats they occupy. Jackson (2003) has made an explicit argument that the German corporate governance system has moved on to a new (hybrid) path

---

[18] The loss of state guarantees for their assets, mandated by the European Union, will force savings banks toward greater commercial orientation and profit making. Mergers among banks is in many ways replacing cooperation among them. The greater pressure toward profitability may also affect the ability of savings (and cooperative) banks to maintain their traditional relations to firms (though it is still premature to suggest that this type of relationship is over).

[19] In just two years from 1996 to 1998, for instance, the number of capital ties among the 100 largest firms in Germany declined from 169 to 108 (Höpner 2002).

(Höpner 2001 concurs) in which a portion of corporate Germany has moved to an 'enlightened' form of shareholder capitalism (one that retains, inter alia, labour–management cooperation).

On the other hand, while the moves by many German firms to adopt a shareholder value approach to management are significant, change is highly differentiated. As in the banking system, firms appear to be bifurcating between the relatively few yet very large firms that, for various reasons, embrace shareholder value and all that it signifies, and the greater number of firms who have shunned or only made weak efforts to adopt the shareholder approach (Höpner 2001; Jürgens et al. 2000; Ziegler 2000). Thus while Lane (Chapter 4, this volume) foresees shareholder value as spreading throughout Germany because of tight institutional integration (and a logic of synergy), other studies suggest that the spread of shareholder value to other firms is limited and often follows a logic of similarity, that is, shareholder value is adopted as rhetoric that lends legitimacy to other goals being pursued by management (Jürgens et al. 2000; Vitols 2001*b*).

Moreover, even for those firms that have embraced the 'new', so much of the 'old' remains that their strategies for adapting to the new terms of international competition are quite different from those of US or French corporations (see Goyer 2002; Jackson 2003). For example, there is little evidence that any broader move to shareholder capitalism requires a reduction or elimination of worker participation institutions in Germany, and there appears to be little political interest in explicitly weakening these institutions (Ziegler 2000: 212). Many large German firms, even those that are emphasizing shareholder value, continue to believe that the interests of other stakeholders— employees, customers, and society in general—must still be balanced against shareholder interests.[20] Cioffi (2002: 26–7) has also argued forcefully that the KonTraG (*Gesetz zur Kontrolle und Transparenz im Unternehmensbereich*) of 1998—the first major reform of company law since the 1960s and one intended to augment financial market modernization efforts—did not alter the internal relations among corporate stakeholders. It upheld the key normative principles of codetermination and stakeholder capitalism, in part by leaving untouched the fiduciary responsibility of managers is the firm as a whole without given primacy to any particular constituency. Thus from a formal

---

[20] A survey done in 2000 of top managers found 72 per cent put the interests of shareholders, employees, and the public interest on an equal footing, while only 7 per cent espoused shareholder pre-eminence (Jackson 2003).

legal perspective the KonTraG did not place shareholders above other stakeholders.

Perhaps the best way to characterize change in German corporate governance is to distinguish between inter-firm and intra-firm dimensions. The intra-firm dimensions—the institutions structuring relations among the management, owners, employees—appear to be relatively stable. As noted above, Cioffi makes a compelling argument that the legal norm of shareholder supremacy could not be inserted into company law. Codetermination, at least formally, has even been extended under the Schröder government. Works councils and supervisory board codetermination have not hindered firm restructuring or even, as Mannesmann showed, a hostile takeover. In other words, the old neocorporatist system for internal governance is intact but adapting to a much-strengthened emphasis on corporate profitability.[21] In these changes Lane (Chapter 4, this volume) sees codetermination as turning into an empty shell—formal worker participation but with no power to affect outcomes. But this presumes that labour has lost all power to influence management, and this seems implausible to me, and as long as labour has some power, the ability to formally participate in codetermination cannot be trivialized.

Inter-firm relations (or perhaps extra-firm relations) have more obviously changed. The protective insider network is gone for many firms (especially the banks). Management is more transparent and, at least formally, more vulnerable to market sanctions or the sanctions of its own (minority) shareholders.

This leaves us, however, with a still unresolved and sticky issue: how much does an institutional system need to change before it constitutes a new path (logic)? If we look at the financial system or corporate governance system as a whole, the picture is muddy and we are forced to make an (highly contestable) assertion about whether 'the glass is half full or empty'. However, if we follow the argument about the emerging dualism or bifurcation in these systems, between firms (and banks) who are participating in the 'game' with new rules and those staying in the old 'game', it becomes easier to assert that one portion of these systems has in fact developed a new logic and thus a new path. In other words—and to overstate the point—there is no longer

---

[21] See Höpner (2001), for example. Though Rehder (2002) has suggested that intra-firm relations between management and employees have also undergone a path change; the constitutional exercise of worker rights within firms is being replaced with contractually negotiated rights.

a single financial or corporate governance system but two of each. Here, I am making a claim for the emergence of an alternative order (pattern 4 discussed above).

Moreover, the decline of insider corporate governance also suggests that the manner in which the financial and corporate governance systems are linked or coupled to each other has also changed (i.e. declining synergy). The mutual dependence between banks and firms is declining, suggesting that the future developmental paths of each system may in fact occur more independently of each other. This creates the possibility, for example, that the major financial institutions in Germany will continue to develop their investment bank focus regardless of future progress toward development of an 'equity culture' and securities markets, or the spread of shareholder value orientation, in Germany. For these institutions the domestic market, while still important, is not enough for their future growth and thus they will develop based on European and international success. Conversely, German corporate managers can still choose to maintain an insider and stakeholder oriented approach, so long as their ownership remains concentrated. And even those firms which embrace shareholder value are often doing so not because of pressures from capital markets per se, or a perceived need to develop German securities markets, but for their own reasons—to pursue certain product market strategies or simply enhance their own power and autonomy (see Höpner 2001; Jackson 2003). To bring it back to an earlier theoretical point, the financial and corporate governance systems arguably no longer share (or share fewer) key mechanisms of path reproduction: thus increasing returns due to synergies (coherence) between the two have declined.

To the extent that bifurcation within, and decoupling across, the two systems has occurred, it obviously raises doubts about the argument that the institutional (sub)systems of a national economy must evolve in a manner that sustains tight coupling. At the first level of analysis—individual organizations—we find many that have moved on to a new path while others have not. At the second level of analysis—institutional systems—we find a bifurcation entailing path change for some portion of the system but not the rest. At the level of meta-path, we have the question of whether the German political economy has shifted to a new path. Changes in the financial and corporate governance systems alone do not, in my view, amount to a change in the German meta-path. For this to happen we must also see a path change in other key systems, minimally including the organization of production and innovation and the organization of interests (especially the role of labour). It is not clear that we have seen such a change in these other pieces of the meta-path (though they too have clearly changed in various ways).

Goyer (2002), making a similar point, has shown that the German industrial relations system (and codetermination) appears compatible with the new emphasis on transparency and shareholder value just as it was with the old insider system of corporate governance. Yet this does not mean that institutional interdependencies are weak or nonexistent. Like Goyer, Höpner (2002) suggests that two institutional systems can complement each other in different ways under different conditions, creating the possibility that major changes in one system may only require minor changes in other, interdependent systems. Thus the growing emphasis on shareholder value (returns) is made coherent with codetermination when workers and owners 'team up' to use this as a means to pursue their common interest in controlling management. When pursuing shareholder value is understood to mean increasing corporate transparency (as has largely been the case in Germany (see Goyer 2002)), both investors and workers see this as a gain. Thus a codetermined corporate governance system can be made complementary (variable complementarity, under my earlier scheme) with a securities market-oriented financial system (see also Aguilera and Jackson 2003).

One might counter with the argument that the path-altering institutional changes that have been documented in Germany have created incoherence and thus an unstable situation (see Lane, Chapter 4, this volume). We might thus expect Germany to move in either of two directions—further along the continuum toward a liberal market economy (which would include path-altering changes in other institutional systems), or a re-establishment of the old path through either a reversal of some crucial changes or their evisceration through additional reforms. This would be consistent with the varieties of capitalism argument that in between the coordinated market and the liberal market model is an inhospitable no-man's land (Hall and Soskice 2001). But this may not be the case. One possibility is that the new path is stable because it creates a 'model within a model', that is, a liberal market order within a coordinated market order. The 'sub-model' may be stable in that it has internal coherence because institutions in various institutional systems have been sufficiently altered to make them work in a synergistic fashion. Yet, the overall national regime may remain on the same path because the rules (institutions) are sufficiently flexible to allow actors to choose between the two models or orders.[22]

Returning to my earlier theoretical points about the boundary question, there is still the question of whether path change in finance and corporate governance was driven by endogenous or exogenous forces, or both? Given space limitations, I will not attempt a complete argument here. Elsewhere I developed a fuller argument that change in the German financial system began endogenously with a decline in financial dependence of large firms on banks (Deeg 2001). This was later supplemented by exogenous pressures for change. The pattern of pressures for change in corporate governance appears to follow that of the financial system fairly closely. A primary source of change in corporate governance was the decline in the traditional bank–large firm relationship. For reasons suggested earlier, I view this as an endogenous source of change albeit one that appears to be at first glance an exogenous one, namely, banks—to large degree—were the major promoters of change in German corporate governance because they needed these changes to realize their ambition of developing German securities markets (see also Cioffi 2002). Yet, the banks were pushing for corporate governance reform in the 1990s because of the decline of the traditional relationship with large firms that began in the late 1970s and the growth of foreign competition starting in the 1980s. Thus bank pressure for change was, by my earlier definition, an endogenous source of change.[23] The success of the banks in fostering securities trading and foreign investment in Germany, in turn, opened the door to exogenous pressures for change, for example, demands by foreign institutional investors for greater transparency.

This brings me to the final point of the section and that is the politics of change (the economics–politics nexus). Change in the finance and corporate governance system was driven to a great extent by a coalition of economic and political actors (the 'Frankfurt Coalition')—which included, among others, the major commercial banks, the government of Hesse, and actors within the federal bureaucracy, especially the Finance Ministry (for more see Lütz 2002). Over the last decade political party actors became increasingly proactive in this reform process with the most far-reaching reforms promoted—ironically—by the Social

---

[22] There is certainly precedent for this, as the work of Piore and Sabel (1984), Herrigel (1996) and others show that substantial deviation in the organization of production on a regional/sectoral level has existed throughout the industrial era in Germany and other nations.

[23] Similarly, the banks (and other financial market promoters) have sought changes in tax laws and the pension system to stimulate demand for equities (see Cioffi 2002; Deeg 1999, 2001).

Democratic Party as part of a long-term political strategy (see Höpner 2002). As one would expect, change required the coordination and exercise of political power by pro-reform groups. More than that, not surprisingly, change involved a new (or perhaps revival of an old) 'discourse' centred around the need to legitimate and establish an ideational framework for the emergence of a new institutional order along the lines indicated earlier, that is, the liberal market 'sub-model' or regime within a still broadly coordinated market regime. Following Lehmbruch (2001), we could term this a 'discourse coalition' to indicate the coordination of action among these actors based on a shared belief system. It also reflects mutually reinforcing (synergistic) strategies by economic and political actors in their respective spheres of competition. My own view is to see the use of discourse as a political tool by actors with material interests in change, but there is also no reason to exclude a priori the possibility that certain ideas—such as 'shareholder value'—have had independent causal force on change in Germany (see also Lieberman 2002).

There is also the possibility that the emergence of a liberal market order within the finance and corporate governance systems is, in fact, partially a *re*-emergence. Vitols (2001*a,b*) has argued that liberal ideas and institutions were quite strong in the German financial system during the industrialization era and only in the 1930s did a more nonliberal set of institutions ('order') become dominant. This raises the possibility (admittedly needing investigation), that the current pattern of change is driven in part by actors drawing upon ideas, institutional legacies and the like that were, in some way, already at hand within Germany. What all this points to, again, is the lesson that off-path institutional change at the level of (subsystems) requires extensive coordination and mobilization by reformist market and political actors. Though one should note that the requisite level of political involvement could arguably vary significantly across different subsystems, depending upon the extent to which the subsystem rests upon politically codified institutions.

2.5. Conclusion

In the conclusion I wish to focus attention on four broad issues raised by the theoretical discussion and empirical case presented in this chapter relevant to further research. The first addresses the question of whether looser coupling across subsystems of national regimes means that such systems and regimes are less path dependent (and/or resist-ant to change). The answer, of course, requires empirical investigation, but I think theory suggests that no such general claim can be made at this point. A subsystem itself might have a high level of 'internally' generated path dependency. Or, its path dependency might depend a lot on coherence with other subsystems and if these erode, then the subsystem itself is vulnerable to change. For example, the system of codetermination in Germany (broadly understood) seems to have a high level of path dependency on its own, as it seems to remain rel-atively robust in the face of far-reaching change in related subsystems. Perhaps this is because it is based to a much greater extent on polit-ically codified institutions, that is, a legal framework. Conversely, the insider character of the corporate governance system involving equity links and personal interlocks was based more on a congruence of firm strategies and less on specific 'parchment' institutions (though it had these too and they needed to be changed). With change in the corporate strategies of just a small number of key firms (e.g. Deutsche Bank and Allianz), this system seems to be greatly changing (Beyer 2002 lays out a similar argument). At the national regime level, then, looser coupling may not necessarily mean weaker path dependency since constituent subsystems may derive their own stability (path dependence) from other sources. Radical (off-path) change in one subsystem may, in fact, be less destabilizing to such a system. In other words—and contrary to present orthodoxy—a more loosely coupled national regime may turn out to be *more* resilient to change than a tightly coupled one.

This leads to the closely related second issue, and that is whether we can generate and test hypotheses about the patterns of change in national regimes based on the different *sources* and *patterns* of subsystem cohesion. I have suggested some possibilities in this chapter, but much more could obviously be done. In the same vein, we need to better identify and distinguish path dependency as a source of resilience from other, non-path dependent sources.

The third issue—one raised earlier, but without a satisfying discussion—is whether some subsystems categorically are more eas-ily 'decoupled' without affecting other subsystems? Earlier, I offered the financial system as just such a candidate. Why might this be so? In the case of CMEs the financial system is seen as crucial to promoting certain product market strategies based on high levels of investment in specific assets and long-term horizons. Thus long-term finance is a 'necessary' complement. But perhaps product market strategies and managerial horizons depend far more on other complementary institutions. In the German case, strong codetermination and collective bargaining (along with entrenched political interests) may be sufficient to maintain such strategies. Or, perhaps such a national regime has institutional 'redundancies'—taking away one cohering institution still leaves enough to carry on the job.

The final issue is one not addressed in the chapter but one I find especially important and challenging (and therefore worth noting here): how do we measure increasing returns to an institutional system or a 'meta-path'? How do we measure increasing returns to political institutions? To the kinds of formal institutions that are politically codified yet govern market actors? For example, coherence among the myriad laws and regulations governing financial actors are arguably a source of increasing returns, but how do we measure these returns to individual market actors? Even more perplexing, how can we measure non-monetary returns for political actors such increased power, legitimacy, or political support. Here we lack the price mechanisms (and thus cost/revenue efficiency calculus) to quantify returns. To make path dependency a truly useful and powerful analytical tool for understanding change in social and political institutions, we will need to solve this ultimate challenge.

REFERENCES

Aguilera, Ruth V. and Jackson, Gregory (2003). 'The Cross-National Diversity of Corporate Governance: Dimensions and Determinants'. *Academy of Management Review* 28: 447–66.

Albert, Michel (1993). *Capitalism versus Capitalism: How America's Obsession with Individual Achievement and Short-Term Profit Has Led it to the Brink of Collapse*. New York: Four Walls Eight Windows.

Amable, Bruno (2003). *The Diversity of Modern Capitalism*. Oxford: Oxford University Press.

Aoki, Masahiko (2001). *Toward a Comparative Institutional Analysis*. Cambridge, MA: MIT Press.

Arthur, W. Brian (1994). *Increasing Returns and Path Dependence in the Economy*. Ann Arbor: University of Michigan Press.

Bebchuk, Lucian Arye and Roe, Mark J. (1999). 'A Theory of Path Dependence in Corporate Ownership and Governance'. *Stanford Law Review* 52: 127–70.

Beyer, Jürgen (2002). 'Deutschland AG a.D.: Deutsche Bank, Allianz und das Verflechtungszentrum grosser deutscher Unternehmen'. Max Planck Institute for the Study of Societies, Working paper 04/4, March.

Carey, John M. (2000). 'Parchment, Equilibria, and Institutions'. *Comparative Political Studies* 33: 735–61.

Clemens, Elisabeth S. and Cook, James M. (1999). 'Politics and Institutionalism: Explaining Durability and Change'. *Annual Review of Sociology* 25: 441–66.

Cioffi, John W. (2002). 'Restructuring "Germany, Inc.": The Politics of Company and Takeover Law Reform in Germany and the European Union'. Institute of European Studies, University of California, Berkeley, Working paper PEIF-1.

Crouch, Colin (2002). 'The Problem of Innovation in Typologies of Capitalism'. Unpublished manuscript.

—— and Farrell, Henry (2002). 'Breaking the Path of Institutional Development? Alternatives to the New Determinism'. Max Planck Institute for the Study of Societies, Discussion paper 02/5.

Deeg, Richard (1999). *Finance Capitalism Unveiled: Banks and the German Political Economy*. Ann Arbor: University of Michigan Press.

—— (2001). 'Institutional Change and the Uses and Limits of Path Dependency: The Case of German Finance'. Max Planck Institute for the Study of Societies, Discussion paper 01/6.

Estevez-Abe, Margarita, Torben Iversen, and Soskice, David (2001). 'Social Protection and the Formation of Skills: A Reinterpretation of the Welfare State'. In: Peter A. Hall and David Soskice (eds.), *Varieties of Capitalism: The Foundations of Comparative Advantage*. Oxford: Oxford University Press.

Goyer, Michel (2002). 'Refocusing and Corporate Governance in France and Germany: The Centrality of Workplace Institutions'. Presented at the Annual Meeting of the American Political Science Association, Boston, MA, 28 August–1 September.

Hacker, Jacob S. (2002). *The Divided Welfare State: The Battle Over Public and Private Social Benefits in the United States*. Cambridge: Cambridge University Press.

Hall, Peter A. and Soskice, David (eds.) (2001). *Varieties of Capitalism: The Foundations of Comparative Advantage*. Oxford: Oxford University Press.

Herrigel, Gary (1996). *Industrial Constructions: The Sources of German Industrial Power*. Cambridge: Cambridge University Press.

Höpner, Martin (2001). 'Corporate Governance in Transition: Ten Empirical Findings on Shareholder Value and Industrial Relations in Germany'. Max Planck Institute for the Study of Societies, Discussion paper 01/5.

—— (2002). 'European Corporate Governance Reform and the German Party Paradox'. Unpublished manuscript.

Jackson, Gregory (2003). 'Corporate Governance in Germany and Japan: Liberalization Pressures and Responses during the 1990s'. In: Streeck, Wolfgang and Yamamura, Kozo (eds.), *The End of Diversity: Prospects for German and Japanese Capitalism*. Ithaca: Cornell University Press.

Jürgens, Ulrich, Rupp, Joachim, Vitols, Katrin, and Jäschke-Werthmann, Bärbel (2000). 'Corporate Governance and Shareholder Value in Deutschland'. Discussion Paper of the Social Science Research Centre, Berlin, FS II 00-202.

Knill, Christoph and Lenschow, Andrea (2001). ' "Seek and Ye Shall Find!" Linking Different Perspectives on Institutional Change'. *Comparative Political Studies* 34: 187–215.

Lehmbruch, Gerhard (2001). 'The Institutional Embedding of Market Economies: The German "Model" and Its Impact on Japan'. In: Wolfgang Streeck and Kozo Yamamura (eds.), *The Origins of Nonliberal Capitalism: Germany and Japan in Comparison*. Ithaca: Cornell University Press.

Lieberman, Robert C. (2002). 'Ideas, Institutions, and Political Order: Explaining Political Change'. *American Political Science Review* 96: 697–712.

Lindberg, Leon N., Campbell, John L., and Hollingsworth, J. Rogers (1991). 'Economic Governance and the Analysis of Structural Change in the American Economy'. In: John L. Campbell, J. Rogers Hollingsworth, and Leon N. Lindberg (eds.), *Governance of the American Economy*. Cambridge: Cambridge University Press.

Lütz, Susanne (2002). *Der Staat und die Globalisierung von Finanzmärkten: Regulative Politik in Deutschland, Grossbritannien, und den USA*. Frankfurt: Campus.

Mahoney, James (2000). 'Path Dependence in Historical Sociology'. *Theory and Society* 29: 507–48.

Morgan, Glen and Kubo, Izumi (2002). 'Beyond Path Dependency? Constructing New Models for Institutional Change: The Case of Capital Markets in Japan'. Unpublished manuscript.

North, Douglas (1990). *Institutions, Institutional Change and Economic Performance*. Cambridge: Cambridge University Press.

Pierson, Paul (2000). 'Increasing Returns, Path Dependence, and the Study of Politics'. *American Political Science Review* 94: 251–67.

—— (2004). *Politics in Time: History, Institutions and Social Analysis*. Princeton: Princeton University Press.

Piore, Michael and Sabel, Charles (1984). *The Second Industrial Divide*. New York: Basic Books.

Rehder, Britta (2002). 'Pfadwechsel ohne Systembruch: Der Beitrag betrieblicher Bündnisse für Beschäftigungssicherung und Wettbewerbsfähigkeit zum Wandel der Arbeitsbeziehung in Deutschland'. Ph.D. dissertation, Humboldt University.

Schwartz, Herman (2002). 'Down the Wrong Path: Path Dependence, Markets, and Increasing Returns'. Unpublished manuscript.

Streeck, Wolfgang and Yamamura, Kozo (eds.) (2001). *The Origins of Nonliberal Capitalism: Germany and Japan in Comparison*. Ithaca: Cornell University Press.

Streeck, Wolfgang and Yamamura, Kozo (eds.) (2003). *The End of Diversity: Prospects for German and Japanese Capitalism*. Ithaca: Cornell University Press.

Thelen, Kathleen (2000). 'Timing and Temporality in the Analysis of Institutional Evolution and Change'. *Studies in American Political Development* 14 (Spring): 101–08.

Thelen, Kathleen (2003). 'How Institutions Evolve: Insights from Comparative-Historical Analysis'. In: Mahoney, James and Rueschemeyer, Dietrich (eds.), *Comparative-Historical Analysis in the Social Sciences*. Cambridge: Cambridge University Press.

Vitols, Sigurt (2001*a*). 'The Origins of Bank-Based and Market-Based Financial Systems: Germany, Japan and the United States'. In: Streeck, Wolfgang, and Yamamura, Kozo (eds.), *The Origins of Nonliberal Capitalism: Germany and Japan in Comparison*. Ithaca: Cornell University Press.

——(2001*b*). 'Varieties of Corporate Governance: Comparing Germany and the UK'. In: Peter A. Hall and David Soskice (eds.), *Varieties of Capitalism: The Foundations of Comparative Advantage*. Oxford: Oxford University Press.

Whitley, Richard (1999). *Divergent Capitalisms: The Social Structuring and Change of Business Systems*. Oxford: Oxford University Press.

Ziegler, Nicholas (2000). 'Corporate Governance and the Politics of Property Rights in Germany'. *Politics and Society* 28: 195–221.

3

Degrees of Freedom: Rethinking the Institutional Analysis of Economic Change

BOB HANCKÉ AND MICHEL GOYER

No self-respecting economist, political scientist, or sociologist today ignores the importance of institutions. In standard economics, institutional analysis has found a central place: endogenous growth theory, transaction costs economics, as well as the new economics of organization imply an active incorporation of institutions into theory; and since the seminal article by March and Olsen (1984), even hard core behavioural political science has been forced to come to terms with the structuring effect of institutions, while game-theoretic approaches in political science underscore the role of institutions in shaping outcome sets.

This chapter builds on and acknowledges these contributions of institutionalism, but is critical of some of its implications for the analysis of economic change. We agree with the (often unspoken) claim that institutional frameworks preclude certain trajectories of change: particular adjustment paths are highly unlikely, and probably impossible, because of how they rely on the presence of other elements in an institutional framework. What we take issue with is a tendency in this literature to reify institutional frameworks, which runs the risk of leading to an institutionally determined teleology. Institutional frameworks, we will argue, have the capacity to offer alternative adjustment paths that cannot simply be 'read off': how actors operate in particular institutional frameworks, and how they 'learn' to operate within it, matters for their effects. Similar institutions can therefore lead to

We would like to thank Richard Bronk, Steven Casper, Scott Cooper, Peer Hull Kristensen, Glenn Morgan, David Soskice, Richard Whitley, and the participants in the Oslo workshop for helpful discussions and comments.

different outcomes, and institutional frameworks can offer actors new adjustment paths beyond the immediately visible ones.

Our critique addresses both actual and potential problems that we see with the literature. While many authors are sensitive to the points we raise, too often the implications of these points seem to be ignored. Our aim with this chapter is to take stock of this implicit debate within institutionalism and use it as a means to improve institutional theory.

The chapter starts by reviewing the standard arguments on institutions and economic change, and then present our alternative view. Section 3.2 presents empirical material on economic adjustment from France and Germany. This suggests that the creative use of elements of the institutional frameworks by critical actors, and the re-articulation of existing elements, allowed them to adopt paths that were probably impossible to predict with the use of the conventional views on economic adjustment in these countries. Section 3.3 concludes.

3.1. The Contributions and Limits of Institutional Theory

From two decades of research within the 'new institutionalism' in political economy, economic sociology, and comparative business studies a broad consensus is emerging on the relation between institutions, economic action, and economic change. According to this view, institutional frameworks powerfully shape the reaction space of actors in a two-step process. The first step is related to the role of institutions in defining the scope and nature of new problems. Since institutional frameworks operate as filters for environmental stimuli, actors perceive similar challenges very differently in differently organized societies (Hall and Soskice 2001; Locke and Thelen 1995). The second step deals with the set of possible solutions that actors may perceive for the problems they identified. Since institutions are logically prior to interests in this view, the formation of preferences by economic actors is an endogenous result of the existing institutional structure (Berger 1981; Hall 1986; Steinmo et al. 1992), and in this process, institutions are not neutral (Zysman 1994: 244). In sum, actors pursue their strategies in accordance with the definition of both the problems and their interests as they have been shaped by the institutional structure.

A classic example of this line of argument is Streeck's study (1989) on how German and US car producers both faced a crisis in the early 1980s, but responded very differently. The German manufacturers, eager to capitalize on the 'Made in Germany' label, went up-market, while the US producers primarily saw their crisis as a cost crisis, and thus started searching for cost reductions. The German strategy directly resulted from the constraints imposed by (among other things) the system of labour relations with strong unions at their core, which precluded a cost-based strategy, and the ability of these very institutions to constructively offer alternative paths; the effect was a move up the quality scale into less price-sensitive market segments. In contrast, labour law has allowed US producers to de-unionize large parts of their production system, and impose a series of cost savings which often took the form of massive workforce reductions in order to compete with Japanese producers on price.

Two related but analytically distinct implications for the analysis of economic action are associated with this view: one is that different institutional frameworks lead to divergence across market economies; the second is that they contribute significantly to maintaining differences across, and continuities within, nations. Both of these outcomes are related to the notion of path dependency, which itself emphasizes three issues: the importance of starting points, the role of (institutional) inefficiencies, and the importance of critical junctures (Deeg, Chapter 2, this volume; Herrigel and Wittke, Chapter 11, this volume). Early events, often of a formative nature, thus have a great influence on the sequence and character of future events (Pierson 2000: 252). The importance of being first is a direct function of the presence of increasing returns to scale, the importance of switching costs, and the way early events set limits on the range of possible future developments (Arthur 1994; Crouch and Farrell 2002; Pierson 2000). The institutional structure of a system of corporate governance, for example, depends on the initial structure in which domestic firms were first embedded (Bebchuk and Roe 1999).

Divergence across nations is a result of institutionally determined differences in power relations among actors, privileging some while demobilizing others (Hall 1986: 19; Pierson 2000; Steinmo et al. 1992). Institutional frameworks affect the power of actors in several different ways: their ability to overcome collective action dilemmas, their access to the decision-making process, and the resources at hand. By structuring both preferences and power, the institutional framework faced by domestic companies and other actors constitute a 'matrix of incentives and constraints that militates toward some kinds of firm behaviour and away from others' (Hall 1997: 181).

Finally, the process of institutional formation is critical and infrequent. There are critical junctures characterized by institutional change

that send countries, firms, and other actors along different developmental paths that are then extremely difficult to reverse (Hall and
Taylor 1996: 942; Thelen 1999: 387). The metaphor of the branches
on a tree is insightful. Once you start going down on a particular
branch, other branches down the tree are precluded. Any evaluation of this debate has to start by acknowledging how much this
view of institutions and institutional change has helped us in understanding economic adjustment. In most general terms, it has made us
aware of the role of history in defining the range of possible adjustment paths (see, for example, Hall 1986; Hall and Soskice 2001;
Pierson 1994). It has also allowed us to capture better why some
experiments in institutional reform fail (Levy 1999; Wood 1997), why
economic adjustment, including workplace restructuring, took different forms in different countries (Streeck 1989, 1996; Turner 1991),
and why competitive pressures in international markets have not
led to a single sustainable model of capitalism (Hall and Soskice
2001). In all these cases, existing institutional frameworks limited the
range of options for economic actors, structured their incentives to
favour the initial path, and this was reflected in the differences in the
outcomes.

Yet this position may overstate the power of institutional
frameworks—and therefore of the nature of the constraints that actors
may perceive. One part of this objection is empirical. Multiple adjustment paths and patterns of business organization often coexist within
the same institutional framework: even among the small group of
OECD countries, there are differences between companies, sectors,
and regions within each of the countries. Within German capitalism, for example, there are many instances of weakly regulated
labour markets, where the hard codetermination laws that govern
the economy in the ideal–typical version found in textbooks do not
hold sway, and where primary and secondary working conditions
are set unilaterally (within a minimum legal framework) instead of
negotiated between strong actors (Hassel 1999; Herrigel and Wittke,
Chapter 11, this volume). Conversely, some companies in the United
States have, against the odds, been able to successfully rely on cooperative labour relations, shop-floor workers' participation in self-steered
teams, and strategic comanagement (Rubinstein and Kochan 2001).
And the German political economy increasingly accommodates very
different models of regional economic development, ranging from
the symmetric model associated with the south-west of the country
(Herrigel 1996), to a considerably more hierarchical model of relations

between large firms and their suppliers as in the east of the country (Casper 1997).

Are these internal variations just noise, as highly ideal–typical treatments of (frequently national) institutional frameworks assume, or is there a logic to and perhaps a hierarchy among these multiple patterns (Crouch and Farrell 2002)? Rather than treating this as just random variation and thus defined away, the first question should be how these different patterns coexist. Since institutional adaptation often involves the resuscitation of existing but ignored elements of the dominant framework (as in institutional 'bricolage' or in the generalization of what was initially a niche strategy to the rest of the economy—the case of 'diversified quality production' in Germany, as Piore and Sabel (1984) have argued), understanding how these different elements are mutually articulated becomes a necessity for understanding change.

Our final objection to some of the applications of institutional theories deals with the question of what to make of paths that were ultimately not chosen. First of all, there is a basic methodological issue: how do we know they were not chosen? If choice entails an active option for one of at least two alternatives, we have to be able to demonstrate that these alternatives were actually there, if only in the sense that they were debated as a possibility. Failure to do so has vast methodological implications, since it implies that we are unable to distinguish between a lack of (awareness of) alternatives—the operational opposite of 'choice'—and choosing a particular option. But even if we assume the existence of alternative paths, the question that needs to be answered is why these were not chosen when the chance was offered. Is this 'choice' (or rather 'non-choice') explained by the mechanisms at the heart of the path dependency argument (positive feedback and switching costs), or by other, perhaps very different mechanisms such as sudden exogenously determined reversals in the economic or political fortunes of some of the actors? Correlation is not causation, as we never cease to tell our students; yet, when it comes to the institutional analysis of economic adjustment, we all too often accept lower standards of proof.[1]

[1] Wood (1997) offers a good example of how this should be done. After demonstrating that the first Kohl government had a very ambitious agenda in economic policy, which included tax cuts, a restructuring of key labour market institutions (works councils and training system), privatizations, and deregulation, his analysis shows how and why German employers were very reluctant to go along with this programme. Their interest was to avoid a complete overhaul of the system, especially in labour relations, because it might endanger their product market strategies, which had been highly successful until then. Thus, a coalition emerged, which included the workers' wing of the ruling party, employers, and unions, against the (for German standards

The reaction against these deterministic views of institutions has appeared in two forms of constructivism. The first is the 'soft' constructivist position that institutions do not solely regulate economic action, but are elements of a quasi-constitutional order that 'produces' as much as regulates actors and their outcomes; rather than seeing both as independent, this view stresses their mutual construction. The best examples of this position are found in the literature on comparative capitalism, which often started from the deterministic views and then reintroduced actors in a more dynamic conception. Both Hall and Soskice (2001) and Whitley (1999), for example, demonstrate how the capabilities and resources that economic actors have at their disposal are a function of the institutional frameworks they find themselves in.

The second form of constructivism establishes a more radical break with the prevailing form of institutionalism. It emphasizes strategic action, and takes that to its logical conclusion: there are, in principle, no limits to the types of solutions that economic actors can bring to bear on problems they identify; indeed, since even the identification and conceptualization of a problem is socially constructed, institutions cannot be assumed to have any fixed quality whatsoever—neither for identifying problems, nor for finding solutions (Sabel and Zeitlin 1997). If institutional frameworks matter, it is because they offer elements to construct novel strategies—but these elements are always subject to a protracted process of redefinition and reconstruction, often up to the point that they may have little to do with what they were initially.

The problem with these constructivist views is that the soft view is not sufficiently distinct from the deterministic position, whereas the radical one has moved too far in the opposite direction. Regarding actors as constituted by institutions also imputes an institutionally determined rationality to the situation: actors still pursue interests, but these interests are a direct function of the institutional framework they find themselves in. This implicit teleology evokes echoes of Wrong's critique of sociology's 'over-socialized conceptions' of actors (Wrong 1961): actors, either individually or collectively, do think, evaluate, develop strategies, and act upon these considerations. Treating each of these steps in the process as determined by the rules and norms that govern individuals, groups, and organizations, misses the point that

---

radical) reform proposals, and the reforms died a silent death. Thelen (2000) takes the analysis further and demonstrates that parallel strategic considerations were at the basis of German employers' reluctance to adopt similar (but even more modest) reforms in the mid-1990s.

actors can do unexpected things that do not necessarily follow directly from the institutional framework. Since actors are able to learn from the previous generation (of actors and of actions), they can quickly find themselves a step ahead of the institutional framework as they knew it. Institutional frameworks may constrain, in other words, but they may also offer new possibilities as a result of these constraints, because they allow for forms of learning that may extend beyond the possibilities recognized in the initial framework.

But the openness of institutional frameworks is, despite what radical constructivists seem to assert, not without limits. As Culpepper (2003) demonstrated, for example, without an adequate social and institutional infrastructure, it is impossible to construct high-skill training systems *de novo*. Attempts in the 1970s by successive Labour and Tory governments in the United Kingdom to forge a system of wage bargaining that helped check rampant inflation, failed largely because of the absence of underpinning institutions (Regini 1984). And as many countries in Eastern Europe are finding out today, building the institutions of capitalism involves more than simply importing them from abroad, especially if none of the necessary supporting institutions is present. As we will see in the case studies in the next section of this chapter, institutions do set limits on the direction of potential adjustment paths, even in extreme crisis situations. The initially healthy reaction by the radical constructivists to the single-scenario determinism of the dominant institutionalist theories may therefore have been an overreaction. Any notion of systemic institutional coherence (Aoki 2001; Hall and Soskice 2001) implies that particular paths are excluded or impossible: institutions do offer 'negative scenarios'.

The position we defend here builds directly on these criticisms and has two components. The first is related to the underlying model of change. We think that the punctuated equilibrium metaphor which has invaded the analysis of change in political economy (and, to a lesser extent, economic sociology) over the last few decades (Krasner 1984) has led to a profound misunderstanding of processes of social, economic, and institutional change—a point noted early on, incidentally, in a famous essay by one of the 'fathers' of punctuated equilibrium theory in biology (Gould 1980). Human society does not evolve according to a slow-speed Darwinian model in which multiple generations are required to select small beneficial changes, and in which long periods of stasis are interrupted by sudden sharp crises and rapid changes. Instead it evolves according to a model that is closer to what Lamarck had in mind, in which traits acquired in one generation

are transmitted to the next: human beings—and the social arte-
facts they construct, such as interest groups, companies, and other
organizations—learn, both across and within generations.[2]

This argument has two immediate implications. First, change, rather
than the stasis invoked by the punctuated equilibrium models, characterizes human societies, and organizations, as actors are permanently
evaluating their position and the returns on that position. In addition,
and in large part as a result, change can be extremely fast in principle, probably limited only by the speed with which actors recognize
that a particular set-up does not serve their interests broadly defined.
Institutional frameworks are therefore caught in an almost permanent
process of redefinition, which allows actors operating within them to
explore interpretations that can be very different from the ones that
were initially intended.

Second, while institutional frameworks may be considerably more
malleable and open than the conventional views assume, systemic
constraints of internal coherence impose limits on this openness. This
appears to us as one of the most important lessons from the institutionalist analysis of comparative economic organization over the last two
decades. We leave open for the time being whether these systemic constraints are best conceived of in terms of a tightly coupled system with
a single-point equilibrium (Aoki 2001; Hall and Soskice 2001) or of a
looser, Weberian-inspired 'elective affinity' model (Lane 1995; Whitley
1999). What matters in our view is the emerging consensus in political economy and economic sociology that institutional cherry-picking
rarely works as planned, precisely because (to push that metaphor) the
cherries are hanging on a tree that they need in order to grow.

In the next section we develop our argument through summary
accounts of how large firms in France and Germany adjusted to different pressures for change. In this process, as we will show, the
institutional framework that they found themselves in acted as a constraint by precluding particular options. At the same time, however,
many of these firms managed to exploit endogenous but often hidden
degrees of freedom that the institutional framework offered. In the
first account, on industrial renewal in France since the early 1980s, we

---

[2] Note that we are not suggesting, as the literature on policy learning does, that this is an
apolitical process. Learning can be of a purely didactic type, but almost certainly involves deeply
political processes: the construction of a problem, the inventory and development of resources
(including power) at the disposal of protagonists, and the actual negotiations are an integral
part of what we call 'learning' in the Lamarckian sense. Jacoby (2000) develops some of these
arguments when discussing institutional transfer.

will show not only that French policy-makers were unable to emulate the German model which was the main signpost for their attempts to rejuvenate French industry, but also that the 'orphaned' institutions that emerged as a result of these attempts, became the object of a process of active reinterpretation by large firms—the leaders, by default, in French industrial adjustment during that period.

The second summary discusses the introduction of shareholder value in Germany. Despite the very similar pressures to those that occurred in other countries, most notably in the Anglo-Saxon economies in the 1980s, and which could have forced the corporate governance system in Germany down a similar path of rapidly expanding equity markets and outsider models of corporate governance, large firms in Germany adopted a model which carefully balanced workers' and shareholders' interests.

3.2. Surprising Reorganizations of Large Firms in France and Germany

Methodologically, both of these accounts can be read as critical cases for the view that institutional frameworks constrain actors in their search for solutions to new problems. The study of large firm adjustment in France has to be considered against the background of the conventional images of the French business system, often dating back to Crozier's seminal studies in the 1960s, which still inform much of today's economic sociology and political–economic analysis of the French economy. According to that view, French business is caught in a vicious circle of low trust and therefore hierarchical workplaces, high state involvement to overcome the problems that result from this workplace set-up, and therefore an endemic incapacity of economic actors—firms, associations, and trade unions—to change without central state intervention. Imagine now that such a centralized state-centred framework is facing an increasingly competitive international economy and that protectionism no longer is a viable political option because of European integration. The outcome is, or ought to be, a profound crisis without an endogenous solution, precisely because the central state seems to be the last actor to be able to provide that. Yet large firms in France not only managed to adjust quite successfully; they did so without relying on the state for guidance by exploiting the (perhaps limited but real) existing degrees of freedom they discovered in their institutional environment.

The second case study is constructed in a parallel way. Germany's institutional framework is considered to be highly restrictive in ways that often remind us of the 'stalemate society' that France was supposed to be. As a result, when large firms became exposed to pressures from international capital markets, large publicly quoted firms in Germany were facing several problems: the need to become more transparent, construct compatible incentive structures throughout the company, and more attention to the demands of institutional investors. At the same time, however, the system of codetermination, which gives workers and their representatives hard and soft participation rights in the companies, imposed hard constraints on how management could implement reforms that addressed their needs. Yet, the German codetermination system turned into an asset for corporate governance reform, and the reforms themselves strengthened the codetermination system because they imposed additional transparency on the companies. The apparently overwhelming constraint in this case study is the presence of several institutional constraints on the ability of managers to conduct the business strategy of the firm.

Note, first of all, that the institutional frameworks for economic action in these two cases have always been considered to be very different in comparative analyses (Levy 1999: 23–56; Maurice et al. 1986; Ziegler 1997; Zysman 1977, 1983). Then consider the outcomes: in both cases, the initial limits on the system imposed by the institutional frameworks restricted the nature of the options that large firms were able to engage. In both cases, adjustment followed a path that reflected the preexisting institutional framework. At the same time, however, the limits imposed by the institutional framework tell us little about the path actually adopted by the large firms in their adjustment, since in both cases the large firms reconfigured important elements in their environment so that they became compatible with the types of strategic solutions they were searching for. Institutional frameworks may have constrained the firms in their adjustment path, but they did not condemn them to a particular form of adjustment.

3.2.1. *The surprising modernization of French industry*

By the early 1980s, the French economic development model, which had served the country well up until then (see Boyer 1997; Levy 1999 for succinct accounts of the post-war French model), had ground to a halt. Economic growth slumped, inflation soared, productivity fell sharply, and corporate profitability followed suit. While it might be tempting to attribute this crisis to growing international competition which created competitiveness problems for the large firms, a closer look reveals that the difficulties of the French model were the result of an internal crisis of the French production regime, and exacerbated by the macroeconomic policies of the government between 1976 and 1983. Large firms faced a dramatic productivity and profitability crisis, and the macroeconomic stabilization policies pursued by the Left government after the U-turn in 1983 had two direct consequences for them. It made the 'traditional' French solution, which consisted of the state subsidizing the companies out of the crisis, impossible because of budget constraints and European competition policy. Additionally, the tight monetary policies, which led to high interest rates in support of the franc, aggravated the financial problems of the highly indebted large firms.

Between 1981 and 1984, French governments developed initiatives in three fields that were designed to support a forced reorganization of French industry while allowing the broad macroeconomic policy to pay off in the areas of labour relations, regional development, and finance. Policy-makers were actively looking for inspiration in Germany, and attempted to import what they considered as mature institutions that critically contributed to German economic success onto French soil. The Auroux laws, the largest package of labour reforms in French history, were meant to create an industrial relations system that would simultaneously defuse the perennial workplace conflict and modernize the decision-making structures inside French companies. The Defferre reform package involved a series of measures that decentralized decision-making in many areas, one of which was economic development, towards the regions. The underlying aim was, with the strength of local economies in Germany in mind, to build the conditions for similar dynamic local industrial tissues in different regions in France. Finally, the financial system was reorganized to make banks more responsive to the needs of industry. Again, the German house-bank system, which involved close ties between banks and companies, served as an example.

This German-inspired road turned out to be impossible to adopt, and as a result the well-intended reforms ultimately failed to produce the results they envisioned. The Auroux reforms ended up weakening instead of strengthening the unions, and the workplace reforms that did come about were not only very modest judged by their initial goals, but became building blocks in a management strategy to increase labour productivity. The decentralization of economic policy-making created a host of regional institutions for economic development, but with very little effect on how local industrial structures were organized. Finally, by rapidly introducing competition for both deposits and credits, the financial reform not only weakened the (previously highly protected) French banking sector, it also failed to live up to its goal of bringing the worlds of finance and industry closer to one another. As Levy (1999) convincingly argues in a review of these different policy initiatives, the reforms faced two types of problems: the first was that the actors that were supposed to be empowered by the new initiatives were too weak to carry them through on their own; the second was, ironically, that without the state, the actors that were supposed to be empowered—the trade unions, the banks, and regional economic actors—were unable to use the decentralization policies. Since none of the supporting institutions was in place, the policies fell on very dry soil, and ultimately failed.

However, while the policies may have failed because they targeted the wrong actors, large firms, through a process of trial and error, ended up deploying them as tools for their own restructuring—thereby radically altering the meaning and impact of the policies and institutions in the process. In many cases, management in the large firms had—or at least might have had—a reasonably clear idea about where to go, but was incapable of envisioning ways to get there because the French institutional framework constrained most of its steps: in 1984–5, at the apex of the crisis, the state was the outright owner of a large part of the economy, indirectly controlled the bulk of industrial credit as a result of the nationalized banking sector, indirectly set wage rates for the economy through the minimum wage, and induced strategies of economic development through indicative planning.

Large firms in France therefore had to reorganize their ties with the state, first and foremost the ownership patterns that linked them directly to the state—a process for which they relied on the new instruments that were born out of the financial deregulation-cum-privatization policies of the 1980s. In the nationalized companies-management used the privatization policies to construct a corporate governance system that acted as a protective shield against both a potentially intrusive state and potentially highly nervous short-term capital markets. In the state-owned public services, the same was achieved through permanent renegotiation of the relationship between management and the state: stemming the losses of these companies required a profound internal reorganization which emphasized profitability, and these (internal and external) goals were written into the planning contracts between state and management, leading to increased operational autonomy of the latter. And in the private companies, management autonomy either never posed a problem, because the ownership and control structures provided management with the autonomy for restructuring it needed; or structures that secured autonomy had to be created.[3]

After this redefinition of the relative position of management *vis-à-vis* company owners, the second step was very similar in the different large companies: they set goals for their internal reorganization, and attempted to adjust their workforce and supplier system by introducing new organizational models that were slowly becoming standard organizational models in many other countries as well. Here, however, the old problems of the French model resurfaced under a new guise. Neither workers nor suppliers had the capacity to follow the companies in that new strategy. Many workers were low-skilled, which endangered a productivity drive, the labour relations system was conflictual rather than cooperative, and suppliers were technologically underdeveloped, organizationally weak, and underfinanced. The large firms squared the circle by relying heavily on a wide collection of state policies that dealt with a reorganization of the labour market to restructure their workforce. At the same time, they used the new institutions for local economic development to reorganize their supplier base: they enlisted municipal and regional development agencies, technology centres, training institutes, and employment offices to support their suppliers in the forced upgrade.

Thus, while the 'German' option of decentralized production that relied on workers' skills, cooperative labour relations, deep competencies of suppliers, and an active involvement of banks in corporate governance turned out to be unfeasible because the underlying centralized and adversarial institutional framework was unable to accommodate such a shift, French industry adjusted by finding its own route. The large firms adjusted, not as a result of trajectories imposed by the state, but by actively constructing a new institutional environment that fitted with what they perceived as their new needs, using these new tools to further their internal adjustment, and explore new markets. In order to accomplish this, they borrowed elements from failed government

---

[3] In some cases, this could take a long time and be subject to significant internal tensions which for a long time blocked any attempt at organizational restructuring and heavily burdened the future adjustment of the company, as in Moulinex (see Hancké 2002: Chapter 6).

policies in the areas of corporate governance (to secure independence from the state and capital markets), and from decentralizing policies in labour relations and economic planning (to support their productivity drives). The French institutional framework of the 1980s may have precluded the preferred up-market option, but it also offered creative large firms instruments for their adjustment.

3.2.2. *Corporate governance reform and codetermination in Germany*

The German system of corporate governance has been described as the paradigm case of coordinated market economies in advanced capitalism. The central institutions governing the German system, themselves tightly linked in a wider framework, included a concentrated ownership structure with friendly domestic banks and firms at its core, a reliance on bank loans and retained earnings as a source of finance, accounting and disclosure standards that favour the accumulation of hidden reserves, and therefore do not accurately reflect market value, and a system of industrial relations characterized by the participation of employees at the firm level through codetermination rights at the plant and board levels (Hall and Soskice 2001; Thelen 1991; Zysman 1983).

The cosy world of German corporate governance was rocked by developments in the 1990s, both at the domestic and international level, that significantly contributed to the rise of shareholder value as a key reference point for companies (compare Deeg, Chapter 2; Lane, Chapter 4, this volume). One critical driver was probably financial liberalization, which had two important consequences. On the one hand, it pushed up interest rates as banks were forced to compete for deposits with new competitors; on the other, the use of derivatives and other exotic financial instruments exploded. The high cost of capital and the availability of alternatives encouraged large German companies to tap into international financial markets (Deeg 1999). In addition to financial liberalization, an increasing percentage of takeovers in the United States and in other advanced industrialized countries have been financed by equity swaps (Rappaport and Sirower 1999: 147–51), which implies that firms with a higher market capitalization possess a substantial advantage in the global M&A marketplace (Coffee 1999: 649). At the same time, the ownership structure of German companies evolved from one centered upon domestic banks and non-financial enterprises to one in which financially committed institutional investors became more important, which has increased substantial pressures for greater financial returns, and therefore put pressure on its system of corporate governance—and of the position of employees within it (Höpner 2001: 6).

The institutional framework that prevailed in Germany in the 1980s and 1990s, and the rights and position of works councils in the firm in particular, foreclosed the option of rapid and deep restructuring of large firms. While legal participation rights of works councils are strong in social matters, weaker over personal issues, and modest in economic and financial matters (Müller-Jentsch 1995), they have been able to use their veto power strategically in some areas through linking outcomes there to other issues where they have weaker rights. The works council at the Volkswagen's Braunschweig plant, for example, used its codetermination rights on working times and wage grades to demand an expansion of the skills and training funds for affected workers in the 1980s (Thelen 1991: 213). In addition, the position of organized labour and the works councils in the training system has enabled them to impose significant constraints on hiring new personnel when a company scaled back its activities to a few core competencies: since new training programmes have to be approved by an expert body in which organized labour holds half the seats, they have de facto veto power over these programmes.

While the existing institutional framework of German corporate governance significantly limited the availability of options, and of a trajectory based on deregulation in particular, it also offered a series of possible adjustment paths. One possible outcome—often lamented in the German and international business press—was immobilism as a result of the mutual veto positions of all the actors; a creative reconfiguration of the institutions of the other. However, the German system of corporate governance has been characterized by considerable change. Some large companies have adopted elements of shareholder value priorities in their strategy (Goyer 2003; Höpner 2001). Of all the changes in the German system of corporate governance over the last decade, the adoption of financial transparency was perhaps the most important one (see Goyer 2003: 191–8). In 1996, only nine firms of Germany's largest 120 were using an international accounting standard. By 2001 that figure had risen to 96, and this figure included all the members of the DAX 30 stock market index. In contrast, other measures usually associated with shareholder value, such as a focus on core business activities, have not become a new model for German firms.

The adoption of financial transparency as a strategy of shareholder value demonstrates the flexibility of the German institutional framework. At their core, international accounting standards make it close to impossible to accumulate hidden reserves, and as a result reflect the market value of the firm better than the conventional German standards. Moreover, quarterly reports force firms to provide plenty of additional information on a continual basis while making cross-subsidies between units more visible. These effects protect the interests of outside shareholders in the firm. But financial transparency also has the effect of increasing the information available to employees, especially in a 'thick information' setting like the German one—thus increasing their ability to monitor management. It should therefore not come as a surprise that employees have generally supported the introduction of greater financial transparency (Höpner 2001: 27).

This suggests that the institutions of corporate governance can complement each other in different ways under different conditions. The firm-level codetermination scheme found in Germany is perfectly compatible with financial transparency under a shareholder value-oriented system—as it was under the previous bank-based financial system in which German accounting standards protected firms against short-term financial demands. Since the adoption of greater financial transparency was a negotiated process with employee representatives (Höpner 2001: 27–8), workers can act as informed and credible participants in the process of firm adjustment, thereby reducing managerial incentives to act in a unilateral manner. The active participation of employees in firm restructuring has allowed the institutions of codetermination to both resist the deregulatory consequences associated with the advent of flexibility and of shareholder value strategies, and to turn them into instruments that reinforce existing employee representation models.

Moreover, the negotiated adoption of some shareholder value strategies in Germany took place in an overall context in which employees have been able to shape the patterns of adjustment to changes on world markets. In particular, the use of firm-level agreements has been a new element of the interaction between works councils and management in Germany. Works councils have also used their position to negotiate comprehensive restructuring packages designed to allow for the introduction of shareholder value measures without relying on wage cuts, dismissals, and external labour flexibility (Streeck 2001: 26). Over half of the 100 largest German companies have negotiated 'location agreement' and 'employment pacts', trading wages for job security, in the latter half of the 1990s. And slightly fewer than 20 of these have also included specific investment plans for the next 2–4 years in exchange for more flexible work shifts and a reduction in company bonuses and wages. The aim of these plant agreements was to improve the competitiveness of firms in a context of global competition, and they therefore make portfolio restructuring through dismissals of workers in peripheral units a less attractive option.

What lesson does the transformation of German corporate governance entail for the study of institutions? The German political economy—and its system of corporate governance in particular—has often been analysed as a mixture of constraints and incentives (Streeck 1991). The ability of management to implement strategies of adjustment in a unilateral manner is constrained by several factors, most notably the legal rights of works councils and trade unions. On the other hand, and in contrast to the arrangements found elsewhere, the institutional arrangements of German companies provide management with opportunities to include employees in the development and conduct of the business strategy of the firm (Thelen 1991).

While we agree with this view, we would emphasize that some of the enabling features of the German model are not related to the institutions per se, but result from experimenting and learning by actors. The various constraining elements of the German institutional framework—barriers on dismissals, legal rights of works councils, training requirements, and others—could be introduced by legislation in other countries. By contrast, only some of the enabling arrangements of the German system—such as associational governance of training or the inability of firms to poach skilled workers—could be copied via legislation.

For example, in many large firms, works councils have used their legal rights to become de facto co-managers of the firm, and thereby have often been key actors in the introduction of competitiveness-enhancing rationalization schemes (Herrigel and Wittke, Chapter 11, this volume; Müller-Jentsch 1995). The willingness of works councils to become positively involved in the business strategy of the firm reflects the choices and strategies of actors in light of two key developments. The first is the decentralization of wage bargaining in Germany—and the rise in importance of several new firm-level

issues—has increased the importance of works councils at the expense
of national unions. However, the decentralization of wage bargaining is not unique to Germany, and its consequences on the behaviour
of works councils differ across nations as the French and Swedish
cases demonstrate (Howell 1992; Thelen 1993). In these two countries, the weakness of firm-level works councils entailed that the
decentralization of wage bargaining meant that either trade unions
faced a major identity crisis that required fundamental institutional
changes (Sweden) or that firm-level flexibility came to be associated
with straightforward deregulation of the labour market (France). The
decentralization of wage bargaining and the rise of importance of firm-
level issues, however, cannot by themselves account for the strategy
and actions of works councils in Germany.

The second development is the negotiated introduction of shareholder value strategies in Germany—but which is not unique to the
field of corporate governance. Economic adjustment over the last
fifteen years has often been framed by negotiations between employees and management at the national level. One can point to the
tripartite committee on the Alliance for Jobs and the process of social
concertation as embodied in social pacts as prime examples of the
negotiated adjustment of the German political economy (Regini 2000).
Package deals linking issues across several policy fields—employment
and social policies, wage bargaining, welfare reform—have been the
main outcome of these negotiations.[4]

The negotiated character of changes in German corporate governance and other policy areas accounts for the willingness of works
councils to become active participants in the strategy of the firm,
since it has provided employees with the ability to act as informed
and credible participants in the process of firm adjustment, thereby
reducing managerial incentives to act in a unilateral manner. The
active participation of employees in firm restructuring has led to a
situation without the potentially deregulatory consequences associated with the advent of flexibility and of shareholder value strategies.
Codetermination therefore seems to have evolved from a set of institutions designed to reconcile class conflict into a framework in which
the competitiveness requirements are internalized in part by the ability of works councils to act as a strategic partner for management
(Höpner 2001).

---

[4] See also the above discussion on the introduction of firm-level agreements on location and
employment in Germany.

3.3. **Conclusion**

This chapter has argued that the dominant view of institutions in contemporary political economy increasingly seems to miss important dynamic elements of economic change. Most importantly the view of change associated with this approach—path dependency—is unable to make proper sense of two disturbing elements. The first is how to analyse the coexistence of different organizational patterns within one national economy. In essence, the dominant views define those away as statistical noise. The second was how to make sense of possible adjustment paths that were 'not chosen'—were they the result of the feedback mechanisms at the basis of the path dependency view? Both problems follow from an inadequate conceptualization of the interaction between institutional frameworks and actors that underlies the dominant view.

The two summaries of corporate adjustment in France and Germany over the last two decades demonstrated the need for a view that treated institutions not simply as constraints under which actors optimize adjustment paths. Rather than simply imposing constraints, as we demonstrated, institutional frameworks also provide elements that actors can creatively use to build responses to new challenges. In the case of large firm adjustment in France, the initial road, inspired by the institutions that were associated with German economic success, was impossible because many of the underlying arrangements found in Germany were simply not present in France. But, instead of being trapped in this situation, firms then began to actively construct a new institutional framework, with elements of existing old and new policies and institutions that met their needs. Similarly, instead of being caught in the maelstrom of shareholder value, which supposedly pits managers and owners against workers, the codetermination system in Germany became a crucial institutional vehicle for managing external pressures.

This suggests that institutions embody multiple potential scripts. Historical institutionalism seems to (and, in all fairness, often does) give convincing ex post explanations for why one of these scripts prevailed. However, it is frequently unclear if two conditions held: were there real alternatives that were actively debated, and did the ultimate choice follow from the rational calculus of actors? Explaining why some options were not chosen is therefore equally important as why some were chosen; the burden of proof is—especially in the case of historical continuity—as much on 'why not?' as on 'why'.

This is not a call for establishing counterfactual histories, or for disappearing down a methodological black hole in trying to answer the usually overdetermined question of why something did not happen (Emigh 1997). What we suggest is that explaining institutional continuity—perhaps especially continuity—resulting from path dependency requires more careful research designs, often of a comparative nature, to demonstrate how choices were made, and that these choices reflected the rational calculus mechanisms at the basis of path dependency arguments.

But the path dependency arguments have made a few important methodological and theoretical contributions, to which we should remain attentive. The chances for success of institutional change or reform are not distributed symmetrically. It is, for example, much easier to actively deregulate a labour market (as Thatcher and Reagan demonstrated in the 1980s), than to build a new, non-market based, institutional framework (as the French discovered—see Culpepper 2002). Similarly, some piecemeal reforms of elements in institutional frameworks might be simply impossible because they are inconsistent with other elements in the framework. Even in its weakest version, institutional complementarities impose a degree of institutional congruence that cannot simply be ignored.[5]

As a result, some adjustment paths may be impossible—the French political economy, for example, may have had many options open, but the German road that policy-makers aspired to was definitely not one of them (Culpepper 2001; Hancké 2002; Levy 1999). However, identifying what is impossible says little about what is possible. This is where the limits of the historical–institutionalist approach, as exemplified in the path dependency argument, become apparent.

REFERENCES

Amable, Bruno (2000). 'Institutional Complementarity and Diversity of Social Systems of Innovation and Production'. *Review of International Political Economy* 7(4): 645–87.

Aoki, Masahiko (2001). *Toward a Comparative Institutional Analysis*. Cambridge, MA: MIT Press.

---

[5] Amable (2000) suggests to think in terms of 'hierarchies' of institutions: some institutions within a framework set parameters for the development and operation of other institutions.

Arthur, Brian (1994). *Increasing Returns and Path Dependence in the Economy*. Ann Arbor: University of Michigan Press.

Bebchuk, Lucian and Roe, Mark (1999). 'A Theory of Path Dependence in Corporate Ownership and Governance'. *Stanford Law Review* 52: 127–70.

Berger, Suzanne (1981). 'Introduction'. In: S. Berger (ed.), *Organizing Interests in Western Europe*. Cambridge: Cambridge University Press.

Boyer, Robert (1997). 'French Statism at the Crossroads'. In: C. Crouch and W. Streeck (eds.), *Political Economy of Modern Capitalism*. London: Francis Pinter.

Casper, Steve (1997). 'Automobile Supplier Network Organisation in East Germany: A Challenge to the German Model of Industrial Organisation'. *Industry and Innovation* 4(1): 97–113.

Coffee, John (1999). 'The Future as History: The Prospects for Global Convergence in Corporate Governance and Its Implications'. *Northwestern University Law Review* 93: 641–707.

Crouch, Colin, and Farrell, Henri (2002). 'Breaking the Path of Institutional Development: Alternatives to the New Determinism in Political Economy'. Cologne: Max Planck Institue working paper.

Crozier, Michel (1964). Le phénomène bureaucratique. Paris: Le Seuil.

Culpepper, Pepper D. (2001). 'Employers' Associations, Public Policy, and The Politics of Decentralized Cooperation'. In: P. A. Hall and D. Soskice (eds.), *Varieties of Capitalism: The Foundation of Comparative Institutional Advantage*. Oxford: Oxford University Press.

—————— (2003). *Creating Cooperation: How States Develop Human Capital in Europe*. Ithaca: NY: Cornell University Press.

Deeg, Richard (1999). *Finance Capitalism Unveiled: Banks and the German Political Economy*. Ann Arbor: University of Michigan Press.

Djelic, Marie-Laure (1998). *Exporting the American Model: The Postwar Transformation of European Business*. Oxford, New York: Oxford University Press.

Emigh, Rebecca Jean (1997). 'The Power of Negative Thinking: The Use of Negative Case Methodology in the Development of Sociological Theory'. *Theory and Society* 26: 649–84.

Finegold, David and Soskice, David W. (1988). 'The Failure of Training in Britain: Analysis and Prescription'. *Oxford Review of Economic Policy* 4(3): 21–53.

Gilson, Ronald and Roe, Mark (1999). 'Lifetime Employment: Labor Peace and the Evolution of Japanese Corporate Governance'. *Columbia Law Review* 99: 508–40.

Gould, Stephen Jay (1980). *The Panda's Thumb*. London; New York: Penguin.

Goyer, Michel (2003). 'Corporate Governance, Employees, and the Focus on Core Competencies in France and Germany'. In: Curtis Milhaupt (ed.),

Global Markets, Domestic Institutions: Corporate Law and Governance in a New Era of Cross-Border Deals. New York: Columbia University Press.

Hall, Peter A. (1986). *Governing the Economy. The Politics of State Intervention in Britain and France.* Oxford: Oxford University Press.

—— (1997). 'Politics and Markets in the Industrialized Nations: Interests, Institutions and Ideas in Comparative Political Economy'. In: Mark Irving, Lichbach, and Alan Zuckerman (eds.), *Comparative Politics, Rationality, Culture and Structure.* New York: Cambridge University Press.

—— and Soskice, David (2001). 'Varieties of Capitalism: The Institutional Foundations of Comparative Advantage'. In: P. A. Hall and D. Soskice (eds.), *Varieties of Capitalism: The Institutional Foundations of Competitiveness.* Oxford: Oxford University Press.

—— and Taylor, Rosemary C. R. (1996). 'Political Science and the Three New Institutionalisms'. *Political Studies* 44: 952–73.

Hancké, Bob (2002). *Large Firms and Institutional Change: Industrial Renewal and Economic Restructuring in France.* Oxford: Oxford University Press.

Hassel, Anke (1999). 'The Erosion of the German System of Industrial Relations'. *British Journal of Industrial Relations* 37(3): 483–506.

Herrigel, Gary (1996). *Industrial Constructions. The Sources of German Industrial Power.* Cambridge, NY: Cambridge University Press.

Höpner, Martin (2001). 'Corporate Governance in Transition: Ten Empirical Findings on Shareholder Value and Industrial Relations in Germany'. Discussion paper 01/5, Max Planck Institute, Cologne.

Howell, Chris (1992). *Regulating Labour. The State and Industrial Relations in France.* Princeton: Princeton University Press.

Jacoby, Wade (2000). *Imitation and Politics: Redesigning Modern Germany.* Ithaca, NY: Cornell University Press.

Krasner, Stephen D. (1984). 'Approaches to the State. Alternative Conceptions and Historical Dynamics'. *Comparative Politics* 16(2): 223–46.

Lane, Christel (1995). *Industry and Society in Europe: Stability and Change in Britain, Germany, and France.* Aldershot: Edward Elgar.

Leibowitz, Stan and Stephen Margolis (1995). 'Path Dependence, Lock-In, and History'. *Journal of Law, Economics, and Organization* 11: 205–26.

Levy, Jonah (1999). *Tocqueville's Revenge. Dilemmas of Institutional Reform in Post-Dirigiste France.* Cambridge, MA: Harvard University Press.

Locke, Richard M. and Thelen, Kathleen (1995). 'Apples and Oranges Revisited: Contextualized Comparison and the Study of Comparative Labor Politics'. *Politics and Society* 23(3): 337–68.

March, J. G. and Olsen, J. P. (1984). 'The New Institutionalism: Organizational Factors in Political Life'. *American Political Science Review* 78(3): 734–49.

Markovits, Andrei S. (1986). *The Politics of the West German Unions.* Ithaca, NY: Cornell University Press.

Maurice, Marc, François Sellier, and Sylvestre, Jean-Jacques (1986). *The Social Foundations of Industrial Power*. Cambridge, MA: MIT Press.

Müller-Jentsch, Walter (1995). 'Germany: From Collective Voice to Co-Management'. Joel Rogers and Wolfgang Streeck (eds.), *Works Councils: Consultation, Representation and Cooperation in Industrial Relations*. Chicago: University of Chicago Press.

North, Douglas C. (1990). *Institutions, Institutional Change and Economic Performance*. Cambridge: Cambridge University Press.

O'Sullivan, Mary (2000). *Contests for Corporate Control: Corporate Governance and Economic Performance in the United States*. New York: Oxford University Press.

OECD (1991). 'Trends in Trade Union Membership'. *OECD Employment Outlook 1991*. Paris: OECD.

Pierson, Paul (1994). *Dismantling the Welfare State?* Cambridge: Cambridge University Press.

—— (2000). 'Increasing Returns, Path Dependence and the Study of Politics'. *American Political Science Review* 94(2): 251–68.

Piore, Michael J. and Sabel, Charles F. (1984). *The Second Industrial Divide: Possibilities for Prosperity*. New York: Basic Books.

Rappaport, Alfred and Sirower, Mark (1999). 'Stock or Cash? The Trade-Offs for Buyers and Sellers in Mergers and Acquisitions'. *Harvard Business Review* 77(6): 147–58.

Regini, Marino (1984). 'The Conditions for Political Exchange: How Concertation Emerged and Collapsed in Italy and Great Britain'. In: John H. Goldthorpe (ed.), *Order and Conflict in Contemporary Capitalism. Studies in the Political Economy of Western European Nations*. New York: Oxford University Press, pp. 124–42.

—— (2000). 'Between Deregulation and Social Pacts: The Responses of European Economies to Globalization'. *Politics & Society* 28: 5–33.

Rubinstein, Saul A. and Kochan, Thomas A. (eds.) (2001). *Learning from Saturn: Possibilities for Corporate Governance and Employee Relations*. Ithaca, NY: ILR Press.

Sabel, Charles F. (1982). *Work and Politics*. Cambridge: Cambridge University Press.

—— (1995). *Intelligible Differences: On Deliberate Strategy and the Exploration of Possibility in Economic Life*. Working Paper, Columbia Law School.

—— and Zeitlin, Jonathan (1997). 'Stories, Strategies, Structures: Rethinking Historical Alternatives to Mass Production'. In: C. F. Sabel and J. Zeitlin (eds.), *World of Possibilities: Flexibility and Mass Production in Western Industrialization*. Cambridge: Cambridge University Press.

Shleifer, Andrei and Summers, Lawrence (1988). 'Breach of Trust in Hostile Takeovers'. In: Alan Auerbach (ed.), *Corporate Takeovers: Causes and Consequences*. Chicago: University of Chicago Press.

Steinmo, Sven, Thelen, Kathleen, and Longstreth, Frank (eds.) (1992). *Structuring Politics: Historical Institutionalism in Comparative Analysis*. Cambridge: Cambridge University Press.

Streeck, Wolfgang (1984). 'Neo-Corporatist Industrial Relations and the Economic Crisis in West Germany. In Order and Conflict in Contemporary Capitalism'. In: J. H. Goldthorpe (ed.), *Studies in the Political Economy of Western European Nations*. New York: Oxford University Press.

—— (1989). 'Successful Adjustment to Turbulent Markets'. In: P. Katzenstein (ed.), *Toward the Third Republic. Industry and Politics in West Germany*. Ithaca, NY: Cornell University Press.

—— (1991). 'On the Institutional Conditions of Diversified Quality Production'. In: E. Matzner and W. Streeck (eds.), *Beyond Keynesianism. The Socio-Economics of Full Employment*. Brookfield, VT: Elgar.

—— (1996). 'Lean Production in the German Automobile Industry? A Test Case for Convergence Theory'. In: S. Berger and R. Dore (eds.), *National Diversity and Global Capitalism*. Ithaca, NY: Cornell University Press.

—— (2001). 'The Transformation of Corporate Organization in Europe: An Overview'. Paper presented to the first conference of the Saint-Gobain Foundation.

Swidler, Ann (1986). 'Culture in Action: Symbols and Strategies'. *American Sociological Review* 51(2): 273–86.

Thelen, Kathleen (1991). *Unions of Parts: Labor Politics in Postwar Germany*. Ithaca, NY: Cornell University Press.

—— (1993). 'West European Labor in Transition: Sweden and Germany Compared'. *World Politics* 46: 23–49.

—— (1999). 'Historical Institutionalism in Comparative Politics'. *Annual Review of Political Science* 2: 369–404.

—— (2000). 'Why German Employers Cannot Bring Themselves to Dismantle the German Model'. In: T. Iversen, J. Pontusson, and D. Soskice (eds.), *Unions, Employers and Central Banks. Macroeconomic Coordination and Institutional Change in Social Market Economies*. Cambridge: Cambridge University Press.

Turner, Lowell (1991). *Democracy at Work. Changing World Markets and the Future of Labor Unions*. Ithaca, NY: Cornell University Press.

Whitley, Richard (1999). *Divergent Capitalisms: The Social Structuring and Change of Business Systems*. Oxford: Oxford University Press.

Williamson, Oliver E. (1988). *The Economic Institutions of Capitalism: Firms, Markets, Relational Contracting*. New York: Free Press.

Wood, Stewart (1997). 'Weakening Codetermination? Works Councils Reform in West Germany in 1980s'. Berlin: WZB Discussion paper 97-302.

Wrong, Dennis (1961). 'The Oversocialized Conception of Man in Modern Society'. *American Sociological Review* 26: 183–93.

Ziegler, J. Nicholas (1997). *Governing Ideas. Strategies for Innovation in France and Germany*. Ithaca, NY: Cornell University Press.

Zysman, John (1977). *Political Strategies for Industrial Order. State, Market and Industry in France*. Berkeley, CA: University of California Press.

—— (1983). *Governments, Markets and Growth*. Ithaca, NY: Cornell University Press.

—— (1994). 'How Institutions Create Historically Rooted Trajectories of Growth'. *Industrial and Corporate Change* 3(2): 243–83.

4

Institutional Transformation and System Change: Changes in the Corporate Governance of German Corporations

CHRISTEL LANE

4.1. Introduction

After the collapse of state socialism, the focus of debate in the social sciences came to rest on differences within the capitalist world between different models of capitalist organization. Just ten years on, the debate has shifted further, and now there are being voiced both triumphant claims and fears that one model of capitalism—that of competitive or liberal market capitalism—is reshaping the institutions of other models. The fundamental and long-established differences between what has come to be known as organized or coordinated market economies and competitive or liberal market economies are said to be in the process of erosion.

This new debate has focused on changes in capital markets, corporate financing and their implications for corporate governance—institutions widely held to be cornerstones of models of capitalism. Financial systems influence the allocation and use of capital (in the forms of shares) and shape modes of corporate governance. Forms of corporate governance, in turn, structure most other relationships within firms and even in society as a whole, as they are inherently connected with a redistribution of power and material welfare. Hence, there is strong concern, particularly but not only on the part of labour, with the consequences of any processes of change from the model of 'coordinated' to that of a 'liberal market' economy for the redistribution of surplus and control to various stakeholders in the firm.

Transformation of corporate governance has been most pronounced in coordinated market economies, and the impetus for, and advocacy of, change have come chiefly from the United States (O'Sullivan 2000). As Germany has been long portrayed as the paradigm case of coordinated capitalism (Deeg 2001; Hall and Soskice 2001), with many built-in institutional obstacles to erosion, debate around the German case is of particular interest. If the hitherto very cohesive German system can be shown to be in the process of fundamental change, then other continental European business systems also may be vulnerable.

The widely observed processes of institutional change have initiated a fresh debate on institutional transformation and how it might best be conceptualized. Four positions may be distinguished in this debate: (1) an argument for system transformation and convergence; (2) claims for system reproduction, albeit with partial adjustment of the old model; (3) a diagnosis positing the emergence of a hybrid model of capitalism; and (4) an argument positing a more flexible establishment of complementarity between institutional arrangements in different subsystems. Deeg (Chapter 2, this volume) calls this 'variable complementarity', defined as 'subsystems [which] cohere or complement each other in different ways under different conditions' (ibid.: 13–14). Variable complementarity can come about either through a process of functional conversion of an existing subsystem, as actors utilize changes in power relations to (re)assert their interests (Thelen 2000, 2003), or through the adaptation of expectations on the part of new institutional actors, to gain congruence with the existing system logic.

This chapter seeks to clarify the extent and exact nature of current transformations in the German system of corporate governance and political economy, as well as identify sources of change. It offers both an extended theoretical analysis and an empirical substantiation of institutional change. To this purpose, it will provide first, a discussion of institutional transformation and, second, an outline and evaluation of changes in the German system of corporate governance. Although the empirical investigation thus centres solely on the German case, the theoretical treatment of institutional transformation is intended to have a significance beyond the single case.

I shall make the contentious claim that a process of convergence is, indeed, occurring. Convergence has been variously defined, and in this work it means one-sided adaptation of the 'coordinated market economy' model to that of the 'liberal market economy' (LME). It is being recognized that existing German institutions will mediate the impact of the 'liberal market economy' model. Hence, convergence will not result in the creation of a German variety of capitalism which becomes identical to Anglo-American capitalism in all its features. Nevertheless, the transformation of the underlying system logic will lead to fundamental and far-reaching changes in all institutional subsystems.

My argument eschews a functionalist assumption that convergence is occurring because LMEs have shown superior economic or social performance and that imitation by the less efficient is compelling. Instead I will show that convergence will have far-reaching and maybe unintended consequences which might undermine the viability of the successful German production paradigm of diversified quality production. As such, the outcome will be highly negative for one important actor integral to that paradigm—labour. Last, I am not assuming that convergence is inevitable. I shall suggest that the process is reversible, if there is sufficient political will.

The Anglo-American system of corporate governance, in turn, is not static and is undergoing some significant changes. (See Pendleton and Gospel (2003) and O'Sullivan (2000) on changes in the British and US systems, respectively.) However, these transformations are viewed by this author as adjustments of the existing model, rather than systemic changes. Changes have been introduced in a voluntaristic manner to enhance system legitimacy, and no underlying dynamic or driver of change has been identified by either set of authors.

Change in patterns of corporate governance is a highly complex process, going far beyond changes in regulation of the capital market and the adoption of new company codes of good practice. In contrast to the chapter by Deeg (Chapter 2, this volume), which mainly focuses on developments in the financial system and corporate governance, this chapter undertakes a more comprehensive analysis also of consequences, including strategic and structural changes within firms, as well as changes in the institutions of labour. Such a tracing of the interdependencies between financial system, corporate governance and firm-internal transformation makes it difficult to accept Deeg's claims that 'financial systems may be more "expendable" to CMEs' and that 'the financial system is not (or no longer) actually an important element of distinction among different regime types' (Deeg, Chapter 2, this volume: 15). To the contrary, I see the financial system, in Amable's (2003: 67 ff.) terms, as being at the top of the institutional hierarchy in that it incorporates upper-level constitutional rules which determine the design and mode of change of institutional subsystems, consisting of lower-level rules.

Evidence for an in-depth assessment will be drawn from my own study of German companies in one important industry—chemicals/pharmaceuticals and from a range of secondary sources on firms in other industries.

The chapter is structured as follows. Section 4.2 outlines the theoretical framework adopted. It presents a more extended conceptualization of the nature of institutional reproduction and change, with a special focus on the notions of institutional logic, coherence/complementarity, hybridization, and functional conversion. Section 4.3 presents and analyses the empirical evidence on institutional change and persistence. In Section 4.3.1, I introduce a brief historical sketch of the German model of corporate governance up to the mid-1990s, to enable an assessment of change. This will be followed in Section 4.3.2 by an analysis of the changes in formal and informal institutional arrangements at the levels of both the financial system and of the firm. It evaluates the consequences of change for various corporate stakeholders, as well as their opportunities to influence the direction of change or mediate its impact. In Section 4.3.3, the focus is on persistence of institutional arrangements and any enduring divergence of the German model from the Anglo-American one. Section 4.3.4 considers the balance of persistence and change. It critically examines existing evaluations/explanations of such coexistence. In section 4.3.5, it is concluded that the concept of convergence more aptly characterizes emergent tendencies of change and that we may expect acceleration of the transformation process in the coming decades. The Conclusion debates the import of the analysis made in Section 4.3 for the debate on convergence versus divergence, in the context of the theoretical understanding of institutional change detailed in Section 4.2. I conclude by raising the question of whether the process is reversible and what actors might have the motivation and the power to initiate a reversal or containment of financial liberalization.

4.2. A Theoretical Analysis of Institutional Persistence and Change

Theoretical analyses of varieties of capitalism conducted during the last decade or so have differed in the degree to which they have systematically considered institutional change. Works published mainly during the 1990s, such as Berger and Dore (1997), Hollingsworth and Boyer (1997), Kitschelt et al. (1999), Lane (1995), Whitley (1992, 1999), have assumed system persistence. More recent works discuss change but do not necessarily problematise and/or explain it. Thus, Vivien Schmidt's (2002) analysis of the Futures of European Capitalisms, despite much empirical coverage of change, offers little theoretical analysis of transformation which is mainly viewed as within-system change. Hall and Soskice (2001), although very aware of institutional change in the empirical chapters, in their theoretical positions nevertheless have remained beholden to a focus on institutional reproduction. In this, they and other authors discussed above have been influenced both by the notion of what constitutes system transformation and by an emphasis on system coherence or interlocking complementarity of institutional ensembles.

From Hall and Soskice's (2001: 16) 'rational actor' perspective, institutional complementarity is said to exist when the presence or absence of one institution affects the efficiency of the other. This is seen to inhibit fundamental socio-economic change and instead promotes institutional reproduction. For sociological institutionalists, in contrast, institutional complementarity is derived from the assumption that there is an institutional logic expressed in concrete practices and organizational arrangements which influences what social roles, relationships, and strategies are conceivable, efficacious and legitimate (Biggart and Guillen 1999: 725). Institutional logics are viewed as sense-making constructs and focus on taken-for-granted organizational arrangements. Both these approaches, as well as the work of Whitley (1999), envisage a system logic and internal coherence (rather than variable complementarity). Hence they have suggested that underlying logics are changed only with great difficulty, implying that only extreme external shocks are able to effect system transformation. Although change is not ruled out entirely, 'within system' incremental change has been theoretically privileged.

More recently, in the face of empirically observable, wide-ranging change in core institutional arrangements, analysts have begun to question four interconnected assumptions of the above approaches: (1) that system change necessarily has to be of the radical big-bang nature (most contributors to this volume); (2) that it can be brought about only by external shocks (Deeg 2001, Chapter 2, this volume; Djelic and Quack, Chapter 6, this volume; Mahoney 2001; Thelen 2000, 2003); (3) whether discrete institutions may change independently from the rest (Becker 2001; Deeg, Chapter 2, this volume; Lane 2000; Morgan and Kubo 2005; Thelen 2000, 2003; Vitols 2001; some contributors to Yamamura and Streeck 2003); and

(4) whether complementarity may not be more variable and flexible than previously assumed (Beyer and Hassel 2002; Höpner 2001; Höpner and Jackson 2001; Jackson 2003; Streeck 2001; most contributors to this volume). (Some of these authors take multiple positions.) A related but slightly different perspective has been developed by Amable (2003). He posits institutional complementarity and diffusion of change from one institutional subsystem to another. But strangely, conformity to a single system logic is not considered a necessity (ibid.: 6), and one is left wondering what produces the system coherence he otherwise assumes.

The above analysts therefore dwell on more evolutionary and cumulative change. They place great importance also on the influence of internal actors in bringing about change. Most important, they do not assume an unchanging system coherence. Instead, some posit hybridization of systems and may identify buffers which prevent change in one part of the system, affecting other parts (Morgan and Kubo 2002). Finally, complementarity now is viewed in a more fluid and negotiable manner which envisages the evolution of a new alignment of interests (e.g. Beyer and Hassel 2002; Deeg, Chapter 2, this volume; Sorge, Chapter 5, this volume) and which permits the choice of multiple scenarios for action or paths (Hancké and Goyer, Chapter 3, this volume). Last, despite this new intense preoccupation with institutional change (cf. Schmidt 2002; Yamamura and Streeck 2003), analysts only diagnose within-system change, and radical transformation in the form of convergence, although admitted for an institutional subsystem, is ruled out for the system as a whole.

These critics have elaborated a much more sophisticated and valid notion of institutional change and have significantly advanced our understanding of institutional reproduction and transformation. But their analyses nevertheless do not fully satisfy on theoretical grounds, nor are theoretical claims backed up by sufficient/convincing empirical support. Some argue for new alignments of interests, without sufficient theoretical justification and/or empirical support for this position (e.g. Beyer and Hassel 2002; Jackson 2003), or they mistake continuity of formal institutional structures for preservation of the old system logic (Höpner and Jackson 2001). Last, they argue for multiple paths within one institutional subsystem, without distinguishing between variety within a prevailing logic and variety beyond such a logic (e.g. Hancké and Goyer, Chapter 3, this volume).

I concur with the above analysts that transformation can result from cumulative change and that a consideration of internal actors' interests and negotiating power is vital when trying to understand the process of change. In other respects, however, this chapter takes a more radical stance.

Although I accept that institutional ensembles may change independently from each other, I contend, in contrast to Deeg (Chapter 2, this volume), that this does not necessarily indicate loose coupling, but merely a time delay in change feeding through from one subsystem to another. Dissenting also from Amable (2003), I argue that the resulting opposed logics and lack of coherence can prevail only for a transition period. Instead, I follow Biggart and Guillen (1999), Whitley (1999), and Hall and Soskice (2001) in their claim that there is an inherent strain for system coherence or complementarity. This is based on an underlying institutional logic, which cannot be disrupted in the longer run if the system is to retain stability. This logic not only structures incentives, but also aids sense making. It defines interpretative schemes, expectations and goals, making some scenarios for action legitimate and others illegitimate.

Institutions are not viewed as totally constraining actors—indeed, the latter have been viewed as bringing about institutional transformation. It is being assumed, though, that once a system logic has been accepted by multiple key actors it imposes certain limits for action, which cannot be ignored in the longer run without incurring sanctions. Otherwise institutions would be unable to provide scenarios for action which make sense for and/or are considered legitimate by actors, located in different institutional subsystems. Hence I conclude that loose coupling between key institutional components has its limits and that hybridization—defined by Deeg (Chapter 2, this volume) as the coexistence of multiple orders or regimes within one overarching national regime—can only be unstable and temporary. Actors cannot make strategic decisions based on, for example, a market logic in one arena and resort to a more communal logic in another arena of decision-making—a point also supported by Streeck and Yamamura (2003: 35). If, as Deeg (Chapter 2, this volume) and Amable (2003) suggest, different logics can only prevail if buffers are erected between subsystems, it needs to be indicated how this can be achieved in a national economy where both sectors and firms have a high degree of interdependence.

Two further theoretical questions have to be answered. First, how does one know whether institutional innovation is within-system or bounded change, or whether it has led to the adoption of a new path and a more fundamental system change. System change has occurred when a new logic has replaced the old one, that is, when it is accepted by most influential actors in the political economy. It is being assumed that the system of corporate governance, which defines relations of control both between and within firms, as well as pinpointing their main stakeholders, is crucial to the definition of the institutional logic linking all parts of the system.

Second, how does system change differ from hybridization? Hybridization usually implies that complementarity no longer exists and that different parts of the system are dominated by different logics. Transformation in one major subsystem is considered compatible with stability in another subsystem (e.g. Deeg, Chapter 2, this volume; Jackson 2003). Thus, to illustrate, the logic of the LME may be accepted by actors in the capital market and in large listed firms, but not by unlisted large companies or by small and medium-sized firms and their banks (Deeg 2001). Or, alternatively, the new logic may dictate strategy in product markets but not in firm-internal systems of codetermination (Höpner and Jackson 2001).

To sum up the argument so far, it has been suggested that (actual or imminent) transformation of core institutional arrangements of the German political economy has been more striking than reproduction and that it is necessary to arrive at a theoretical understanding of this momentous process. It has been argued that hybridization generally is an unstable temporary phenomenon. If a cumulative change in a central institution has fundamentally changed the logic which governs relations within that system, and if it is supported by both external pressures and by powerful actors within the system, hybridization is not likely to endure. The power and/or legitimacy of internal champions of change will lead to a spillover into other parts of the system, even into those more remote from the stock market. Complementarity eventually will be restored. I therefore shall argue in this chapter that we must expect the adoption of a new path. As adoption of an entirely new path rarely occurs, convergence to the currently hegemonic Anglo-American model is the more likely outcome. We can expect this to be a drawn-out process, characterized by negotiation and conflictual confrontation.

These theoretical claims will be substantiated in the empirical part of this chapter, focusing on contemporary changes in the system of corporate governance (Sections 4.3.2–4.3.4). First, though, a short description of the German system of corporate governance during the post-war period and up to the middle 1990s will be provided. This will identify the institutional logic and coherence of that system, as well as provide a base line against which more recent transformation may be assessed.

4.3. Empirical Evidence and Analysis

4.3.1. *Historical sketch of the German financial system and form of corporate governance*

Throughout the post-war period, until the mid-1990s, the German financial system and mode of corporate governance showed a high degree of stability, distinguishing it, for example, from the French system (Morin 2000). It has often been described as being diametrically opposed to the system of outsider control, prevalent in Britain (Lane 1995, 2000) and in the United States (O'Sullivan 2000).

Among sources of capital for German firms, retained earnings has been the most significant, leaving firms highly autonomous (Deutsche Bundesbank 1997: 37, quoted by Becker 2001: 31). Bank debt has been low, and listing on the stock market was common only among a small proportion of the largest firms. Due to a number of reasons, the stock market remained underdeveloped and insignificant both for domestic and foreign investors. Hence stock market capitalization has been low in comparison with Britain, the United States, and even Japan. Thus, during the period of 1982–91, stock market capitalization stood at only 20 per cent of GDP, compared with 75 per cent in the United Kingdom (Mayer 2000: 1). Ownership in German firms has been relatively concentrated, and family ownership is still significant even in some very large firms. Cross ownership of non-financial firms has been very pronounced, and interlocking directorships have been highly developed (Windolf 2000). For all these reasons, hostile takeover was almost unknown. Banks have been important insiders in German firms, occupying a high proportion of seats on supervisory boards, although their ownership stakes during recent decades have not been high. Their importance as insider controllers has been based primarily on their ability to cast proxy votes on behalf of the many smaller investors whose shares they administer.

Important rights of control have been vested in the supervisory board. It is independent from the management board, and seats on it are held in varying proportions by representatives of owners and employees. Relatively effective employee codetermination has been a distinctive feature of the German system of corporate governance.

Such a system of corporate governance has implications for a wider range of stakeholders. Top managers in this system are said to be more accountable to both large owners, banks, employees, and even the local community. Decision-making is more consensus-oriented and may even be described as more collective.

There has, however, been a relatively low constraint to deliver very high returns to shareholders, and instead stability of the firm, market growth, together with adequate profits, have been management goals. Financial control of organizational subunits has been relatively lax, financial transparency of companies low, and small investors have had no means to safeguard adequate returns on their investment.

Managers usually have made their career in a given industry and advanced to top positions within the internal labour market. These circumstances have enabled managers to pursue strategies, oriented towards longer term returns. Employees possess legally guaranteed rights of control, both through representation on works councils and on the supervisory board. Unions are not formally represented in firms but strongly rely on works councils for information and recruitment of new members. Labour representatives have exercised their rights to safeguard their skills, their employment security and an equitable distribution of surplus between various stakeholders. Thus, both managerial and employees' orientations have been congruent with and formed the basis of the German production paradigm of diversified quality production (Streeck 1992).

Both works councils and board representation have been utilized in a manner which combines cooperation with management on some issues with a more oppositional stance on others. Despite some variation between firms and industries in the balance between partnership and conflict (Kaedtler and Sperling 2003), the German system as a whole has been aptly described as one of *Konfliktpartnerschaft* (conflictual partnership) (Müller-Jentsch 1993). During the 1990s, both the level of union membership and of the number of works councils have declined, as a consequence of both increased competition in global markets and of reunification.

The underlying logic, informing all parts of the German political economy, has been shaped by a network type of control. This has aimed for stability and growth, rather than for short-term high returns on investment. This network has included employees as important stakeholders in the firm, entitled to a fair share of surplus and to co-decision-making in areas directly affecting their current and future well-being. A logic of cooperation both within networks and in individual companies, rather than one of market competition, has prevailed.

4.3.2. *Recent institutional changes in the German financial system and system of corporate governance*

4.3.2.1. *Sources and promoters of change*

This network system of corporate governance has begun to change during the second half of the 1990s, and it is suggested that both exogenous and endogenous sources of change, as well as actors, need to be considered. The external impetus for change has come from three main sources, and there is considerable interdependence between them. Many analyses of changes in the German model of capitalism have focused mainly on the transformation of the financial system and of capital markets (e.g. Deeg, Chapter 2, this volume; Heinze 2001). Only a consideration of all three sources and a recognition of their mutually reinforcing impact, however, is able to capture the full force for change.

The first source of transformation has been liberalization of international capital markets and the greater readiness of hitherto 'national' capital to seek out the most profitable opportunities for investing capital wherever this may be in the world. This has entailed the modernization of capital markets in continental Europe—particularly in France and Germany—and the spread of the Anglo-American model of organizing them. Such modernization has introduced new market actors—investment funds—and has established enhanced legitimacy for and wide acceptance of their primary goal—improved shareholder value. This, in turn, has put pressures on listed firms to restructure their operations in line with fund managers' expectations, particularly to reduce product diversity and concentrate on what is considered core business. Failure to de-diversify is sanctioned by the so-called conglomerate discount on the share prices of such firms. Greater pressure for enhanced profits and dividends has forced managers to turn previously integrated organizational sub-units into independent profit centres, eliminating cross-subsidization. Capital market actors thus have introduced the logic of the market into firms and have been able to influence their strategic decision-making.

Intensified competition in product markets, and a much increased importance of innovation and of shorter innovation cycles to prevail in such competition, has been the second source of change. It has made it more important to attain sufficient size and market power to prevail against international competitors, and this has exerted pressure for capital concentration, through merger and acquisition. This, in turn, sometimes has precipitated listing on stock markets.

A third source of change in corporate governance have been new cultural or ideological orientations, shaped by three processes of cultural diffusion. Here, the reference is to the concept of shareholder value and associated motivations, cognitions, and scenarios for action. These have been widely propagated by consultancy firms which are often of Anglo-American origin. They have been absorbed by German managers through participation in new programmes of management education, particularly the MBA, and, last, during extended spells of direct exposure to Anglo-American business environments as expatriate managers of German subsidiaries, particularly in the United States.

All these external pressures, it will be shown below, have not simply been imposed on unwilling financial and non-financial firms. Core and powerful economic actors have begun to identify their own interests with those of capital market actors and to actively promote internal change. Many political actors have suffered a crisis of confidence about the German innovation system and about the fit of German institutional arrangement with a much less regulated international economy (Streeck and Yamamura 2003: 3). They therefore have given legislative support to financial liberalization and no longer step in to alleviate its consequences.

However, opinions on what model of capitalism is appropriate and desirable for Germany have differed both within parties and between them. Thus, the current and previous social democratic/Green coalition governments have been sending out conflicting messages. The new Takeover Law, in force since 1 January 2002, permits the target management to put into place anti-takeover defences, provided these have either received support from 75 per cent of shareholders or have been authorized in advance by the supervisory board (Deakin et al. 2002). Also opposition to the introduction of a new liberal EU directive on takeovers has been opposed by German members of the European parliament, leading to its narrow defeat. Last, the ongoing debates about labour market reform show large pockets of resistance to market liberalization within the Social Democratic Party. There is no indication as to how these conflicting stances towards organizing labour and capital markets are to be reconciled.

4.3.2.2. *Changes in capital markets*

Wide-ranging changes in German capital markets have been effected by both important market actors and by government changes in legislation. A long list of changes from the mid-1990s onwards (for an exhaustive list, see Höpner 2001 and Jackson 2003) by 1998 had led to the modernization of the German stock market on the US/UK model. Particularly significant steps have been: the creation of a unified market in Frankfurt, to become the privatized *Deutsche Boerse*; the creation, in 1994, of a federal authority for market supervision; the establishment of legal rules and conventions, creating greater transparency in firm structures and actions; safeguarding of the rights of minority owners; the removal of some hurdles to hostile takeover; and the creation of the initially successful *Neuer Markt* for smaller, technology-intensive firms. The latter caused a wider diffusion and acceptance of the market principle both among smaller firms and small German investors.

Other government legislation fuelled the expansion and influence of the stock market on firms. Among these were the legal authorization of share-buy-backs and of stock options as part of managers' reward package, in order to realign incentives; the introduction of a semi-voluntary company code to encourage greater transparency and accountability of firms to investors. The most far-reaching piece of legislation, however, passed in 2000 and implemented in 2002, is the exemption from tax payments of sales of blocks of shares, previously tied up in cross-holdings. It is expected that this tax reform, encouraging investors' withdrawal from long-term shareholdings in underperforming companies, will unravel the German system of cross shareholding. It thus is likely to dissolve the large block holdings and destroy the network character of corporate control. This, in turn, will constrain companies to become more reliant on stock markets. The resulting greater dispersion of holdings then will provide investment opportunities for outsiders, thus making firms more vulnerable to takeovers. In sum, these developments would knock out the basis of the current German system of insider control. This will put into question the long-termism that patient capital has permitted, as well as undermine the cooperative character of inter- and intra-firm relations.

Banks took an active part in bringing about these changes (Höpner 2001) and, in turn, changed their roles, both in capital markets and within firms. Banks had begun to recognize that their business in large firms had been diminishing (Becker 2001; Deeg 2001) and, simultaneously, that more money could be made in investment banking and active asset management. Many banks already had begun to put greater emphasis on short and middle-term increases in share values of the companies in their ownership portfolio (Becker 2001: 316). Banks' partial disengagement from insider control is evident in their reduced representation on company supervisory boards (Luetz 2000) and, more dramatically, from the surrender of a significant portion of board chairmanships. Thus, between 1992 and 1999, banks' share of chairmanships fell from 44 to 23 per cent in the largest forty companies (Höpner 2001). They additionally now have slightly less control over proxy votes (Deeg 2001; Jackson 2003). The giant insurance company Allianz, although not withdrawing from boards to the same degree, has changed its strategy towards more active asset management, in the same way as Deutsche Bank (Heinze 2001; Höpner 2003b: 22) and Munich Re, another insurer (O'Sullivan 2003). Together, these developments indicate banks' reduced willingness and capacity for insider monitoring. As Deutsche Bank and Allianz between them are the most significant owners of large listed companies, their change of strategy cannot but be highly consequential for cross shareholding networks.

4.3.2.3. *Changes within firms*

The number of companies listed on the German main stock market has increased very slightly as has listing on foreign markets (O'Sullivan 2003: 16). Additionally, the number of IPOs, on the *Neuer Markt*, increased dramatically since 1998 (ibid.), indicating a change in psychology among managers of younger firms. The proportion of shares owned by foreign institutional investors increased from 4 per cent in 1990 to 13 per cent in 1998 (Deeg 2001: 27, footnote 39; O'Sullivan 2003). Also the degree of dispersion of share ownership has risen slightly. Those companies already quoted undertook a number of changes, significantly affecting corporate governance, organizational structures and strategies and the relations with other stakeholders. However, only a minority of firms—around 10 per cent—significantly changed their ownership structure and became exposed to takeover (Heinze 2001). A market for corporate control, it is widely agreed, has not yet developed. But the market nevertheless is shaping many managers' expectations and interests, as external monitoring of listed companies has become prevalent. Even companies not exposed to shareholder pressures have adopted elements of the notion of 'shareholder value' to legitimate restructuring and a greater performance orientation.

Hence the influence of the stock market on managerial attitudes, goals, and strategies of companies has been pervasive, affecting both listed and unlisted internationally oriented companies. Although there is little evidence that investment funds are exerting strong direct external control over managers, the indirect influence of the stock market, via the movement of share prices, has been considerable. The listed companies have responded to external market monitoring in different ways. Some investor stipulations have been widely followed, whereas others have been accepted by only selected companies. These responses are evident not only in a fairly common adoption, among larger companies, of greater cultivation of investor relations, of international accounting standards and in the issuing of quarterly reports (Beyer and Hassel 2002). They are additionally expressed in more fundamental changes of strategy and structure, relating to enterprise goals, such as mode of growth, selection of product portfolio, incentive structures, and system of payment (Becker 2001; Höpner 2001). Examples from one industry will illustrate this, but there exist sufficient research findings on firms in other industries (mainly produced by teams working at the Max Planck Institute in Cologne) to support a conclusion that this a more general trend.

As firm size is becoming more crucial to survival in global markets, more firms have had to dilute owner control and become listed to raise the additional capital needed for expansion (e.g. Merck KgaA, Altana, and Fresenius) or to swap shares in mergers. Concern with the movement of company share price then motivates managers to introduce various strategy changes, welcomed and rewarded by capital market actors. Some or all of the following changes in strategy and structure have been implemented by companies in the chemical/pharmaceutical industry: introduction of sometimes ambitious targets for growth in turnover and profits (most large companies in the industry); changes in organizational structure to enable better control of performance by both top managements and capital market actors, as well as to facilitate spinning out and/or listing of organizational subunits (Hoechst, Bayer, and Fresenius); introduction of share options or equivalent schemes to align managerial incentives with those of investors (all major companies in the industry); introduction of reward systems for employees, tied to the company's or business unit's performance (all large companies in the industry); some reduction of product diversity to enhance transparency and a greater shift to the more profitable pharmaceuticals segment (executed most consequentially by Hoechst/Aventis and more hesitantly by most of the other companies) (Company

Annual Reports 2001/02; Becker 2001). All these measures go beyond merely signalling to investors and instead have involved concrete and consequential organizational and attitudinal transformations.

Unlisted firms and those still substantially under family control have responded to a lesser degree. But they nevertheless have been compelled to make partial adjustments as they operate in the same competitive environment as the companies, exposed to stock market control. Thus Boehringer Ingelheim, still family-owned, nevertheless has introduced changes in organizational structure which force managers to take more responsibility for their units' performance and has introduced 'shareholder value' indicators for purposes of internal control. Additionally, Boehringer, as well as Merck KgaA (over 70 per cent family-owned) have introduced a functional equivalent to a share option scheme, in order to attract and retain high calibre top managers (Becker 2001: 299, 310). In sum, important aspects of managerial strategies have been decisively shaped by changes in corporate governance, even if there is still resistance on some aspects and different firms have adapted at different speeds and to different degrees.

Managers are not merely responding to new sets of incentives, but many of the younger managers, on the basis of US training or experience, have developed different world views and use different sense-making constructs from those current in the traditional German business system. Many are less committed to the traditional German company culture and have adopted some of the attitudes and values of their Anglo-American counterparts (Faust et al. 2000). Large corporations now seek to appoint more entrepreneurially oriented generalist managers, and 'intrapreneurship' is more prevalent in many managers' world view than the old bureaucratic model (ibid.: 272 ff.). Career patterns of higher managers are becoming more similar to those of Anglo-American managers, as evidenced in the dramatic decline in the average time in post during the 1990s (Höpner 2001)—a feature more conducive to adopting a strong stance on raising short-term profitability. Financial and business specialists now are more likely to be selected for promotion to management boards (Becker 2001; Höpner 2001), necessarily causing partial displacement of the traditionally strongly entrenched production-oriented engineers. More generally, the new generation of German top managers recognizes the importance of financial indicators and targets as bases for strategic decision-making. Such practices are regarded as modern management approaches, the adoption of which enhances managerial reputation (Becker 2001: 274).

All these changes in strategy, structure, and reward systems have impacted on employees and on organized labour in companies and at industry level. Negative repercussions for employee stakeholders have been various. The famed German employment security has been eroded in some large 'shareholder value' companies, such as the former Hoechst, Siemens, and Daimler-Chrysler, where the sale or closure of subunits has resulted in massive job reduction. (See also Faust et al. 2000, on the greatly increased feeling of insecurity among managerial employees.) 'Shareholder value' firms now spend a higher share of net value generated on dividends and a lower proportion on labour (Beyer and Hassel 2002: 15, reporting on a survey of the fifty-nine largest German companies). They have not reduced spending on labour but, by cutting the level of employment, have intensified labour for remaining employees (ibid.). In 'shareholder value' companies, a greater proportion of employees' pay is now variable (Kurdelbusch 2001), creating insecurity, as well as under-mining labour solidarity. The solidarity created by representation on company-wide works councils has been weakened by linking pay more strongly to performance of individual company subunits. In the words of Rehder (2002), quoted by Deeg (Chapter 2, this volume), 'the constitutional exercise of worker rights within firms is being replaced with contractually negotiated rights'. A much increased focus by employees on the profitability and survival of their employing company also has made employee representatives less willing to cooperate with unions to achieve wider industry goals (Höpner 2001: 27).

The evidence presented above makes it difficult to accept the claim, made by Jürgens et al. (2000) and endorsed by Deeg (Chapter 2, this volume), that 'the greater number of firms ... have shunned or only made weak efforts to adopt the share holder approach'. While one may argue about the exact number of firms directly affected, isomorphic pressures to adapt have been strong in many sectors and firms.

4.3.3. *Persistence of the German model*

The story told so far has provided a one-sided picture. Many features of the old system of corporate governance persist, and convergence to and divergence from the Anglo-American model exist side by side in a complex mixture. An assessment of the degree of persistence has to bear in mind, however, that German companies have only achieved financial internationalization since the late 1990s.

The most glaring example of persistence of the old financial system is that German firms have not been rushing to become listed on the main stock market which, in comparative perspective, remains strongly undercapitalized. Hence only the large flagship companies, and not all of those, are subject to direct stock market pressure, and family owner-ship of even very large companies persists. Individual shareholding, although greatly increased, remains low by international standards and thus retards the development of a shareholder psychology.

Among listed companies, ownership concentration, often sustained by cross-ownership of shares, remains significant. Average size of voting blocks of nearly 50 per cent may be opposed to blocks of less than 10 per cent in UK companies (Mayer 2000: 2). This continues to obstruct the development of an outsider system of control and of a market for corporate control. The influence of foreign investment funds—the most insistent claimants for shareholder value—has been significant in only a small proportion of cases—about 10 per cent of large listed companies.

There has been no change in company law, and the system of code-termination still is intact, although both works councils and unions have been weakened during the 1990s. Reduced cooperation between works councils and unions and a migration of negotiation to the company level, which preceded changes in corporate governance, has obvious negative implications for the whole system of collect-ive bargaining. Employee stakeholders still retain some degree of influence, if not control, within the enterprise. The two-tier board, designed for insider control, remains in place although it is difficult to assess the actual amount of control labour can still exert. The part-nership component of the German model of 'conflictual partnership', by and large, is still upheld but its conflictual element has been weakened.

In sum, persistence of features of the 'insider' or 'network' system thus is still impressive, but the points clearly have been set for trans-formation. Processes of capital disentanglement had already started before the Eichel Law was passed in 2000 (Höpner 2003b: 22 ff.), and labour has become a weakened stakeholder. In the absence of a strong coalition, opposing liberalization, the developments in capital markets and firms outlined in Section 4.2 may be expected to undermine most of the hitherto persistent features in the coming decades.

4.3.4. *Balance of change and persistence: hybridization?*

The discussion under Section 4.3.2 has shown that the German system of corporate governance has experienced far-reaching change in its underlying logic, indicating significant convergence with the Anglo-American system. But, at the same time, it shows stubborn resistance to change on some central features of corporate governance. Although most analysts nevertheless agree that the German financial system and form of corporate governance have shown a high degree of adaptation to the Anglo-American model, they nevertheless stop short of positing convergence for German capitalism as a whole. Instead, some authors are suggesting that convergence has not gone beyond a few large companies. Others assert that complementary institutional subsystems persist in only marginally changed form, or that mutual adaptation between the interests of labour and shareholders is likely to occur. Hence these scholars either conceptualize current transformations as a process of hybridization (Becker 2001; Deeg 2001; Höpner and Jackson 2002; Vitols 2001), as functional conversion of existing institutional complexes (Hancké and Goyer, Chapter 3, this volume; Höpner and Jackson 2001), or as the elaboration of a new 'within-system' complementarity (Beyer and Hassel 2002; Sorge, Chapter 5, this volume). Functional conversion, according to Thelen (2000: 105), occurs when exogenous shocks empower new actors who harness existing organizational forms in the service of new ends. Establishment of a new complementarity, in contrast, envisages that new external actors adapt their goals towards existing structures and interests.

One diagnosis of hybridization is based on the belief that the great internal heterogeneity of the German economy creates highly diverse contingencies for firms and hence, despite some common pressures, precludes convergent development (Becker 2001; Deeg 2001; Jackson 2003; Vitols 2001). The focus is particularly on diversity within or between sectors, firms of differing size and type, as well as divergent degree of exposure to global pressures.

How persuasive are the various hybridization claims? The argument about diversity between firms, in my view, underestimates the pressure for isomorphic adaptation (DiMaggio and Powell 1991) which emanates from the example of the large flagship companies, the business press and consultancy firms and overestimates the capacity, in practical terms, of one set of firms to insulate themselves against the 'performance' culture adopted by another set.

Such isomorphic adaptation, contrary to Becker (2001) and Vitols (2001), can be shown to have taken place in the chemical/pharmaceutical industry. A close analysis of recent developments of the then three chemical/pharmaceutical giants—Hoechst, Bayer, and BASF—shows that Hoechst was merely the first, in 1996/97, to choose a strategy of liberalization, evident in de-diversification and radical organizational and legal restructuring. Bayer and BASF, although originally much more wedded to the retention of a diverse product portfolio and a traditional integrated organizational structure, since then have begun to embark on a similar path. In 2002, Bayer began to restructure itself into a holding company, with legally independent subsidiaries—a pattern highly reminiscent of the Hoechst model. The push to proceed in this way clearly came from the capital market. According to the company's web site, this new structure gives greater transparency for internal resource allocation, for the capital market and for stockholders (Bayer web site, 13 August 2002). Since then, Bayer has divested itself of its chemical activities, to concentrate on the more profitable pharmaceuticals and crop sciences segments. Organizational restructuring also may be a preparation for the planned acquisition of or merger with another pharmaceutical company, to further increase the focus on this business area, favoured by the capital market. BASF, too, has sought to gain more focus, albeit in a different direction from Hoechst. In 2000, it shed its business in pharmaceuticals to concentrate on chemicals. (Its subsidiary Knoll, which had the largest part of the pharmaceutical operations, was sold to Abbott Laboratories.) Thus, the three companies have not adopted identical strategies, but all have changed, albeit at different speeds, in the direction, rewarded by the stock market.

Nor is diversity as pronounced when we move to other industries or to firms in lower size classes. Although the pharmaceutical industry is among the most highly internationalized ones there now exists hardly any industry sheltered from competitive pressures in international markets for capital and goods and services. The studies by Beyer and Hassel (2001), Höpner (2001), Zugehoer (2001), and Höpner (2003b: 21) well illustrate that the shareholder value orientation is prevalent also in other industries. Even industries with a low level of internationalization are exposed to pressures from inward investors and companies within them, if listed, are not immune from takeover.

Furthermore, competitive pressures affect both large and medium-sized firms, albeit to different degrees. In Germany, interaction between large companies and SMEs is particularly pronounced, and a buffer insulating one firm segment from the other is difficult to imagine. Firms in both size classes have to seek funds to increase their size or to increase investment in R&D, in order to stay ahead in the international competitive race. Nor are smaller firms totally exempt from pressures as large firms have to pass on cost pressures to their smaller suppliers. The existence, until recently, of the *Neuer Markt*, too, has familiarized smaller firms with market practices and values. Smaller firms also are no longer necessarily shielded by their banks. Commercial banks themselves now are subject to pressures from 'shareholder value'. Pressures on non-commercial savings banks to become more profit-oriented in the longer run will force them, too, to pass these on to their SME clients. This will come to a head after the imminent demise, due to a planned EU directive, of most of the privileges currently still enjoyed by savings banks (Lane and Quack 2001).

Managers, as suggested by Becker (2001), do indeed differ in the extent to which they acknowledge and accept the new pressures for greater transparency and shareholder value. But their perceptions, interests, and motivations are increasingly being shaped by the ideology of shareholder value, and generational change also is evident. Some managers have embraced the new ideology with alacrity as, for example, the chief executives of Hoechst (until 1999) and Daimler-Chrysler, others have done so more partially (the CEOs of Bayer and Siemens) or more reluctantly (the previous CEO of Merck) when the adverse consequences of non-compliance for stock price became obvious.

A second set of arguments often associated with hybridization, based on the recognition of the importance to the current production paradigm of industrial participation, emphasises functional conversion. The view of Höpner and Jackson (2001) that 'shareholder value and codetermination do get along fine' exemplifies this stance. They suggest that many works councils now see their main function as supporting management goals of enhancing efficiency and competitiveness (ibid.). Institutionalized practices of codetermination, they say, have changed from being an institutional structure for negotiating issues of a 'class' type, to one mainly supporting the company goal of enhanced efficiency. German labour, however, is not newly empowered, as Thelen's (2000) concept stipulates, but, to the contrary, adapts from a position of weakness. Hence the claim by Höpner and Jackson (2001) that the institution of codetermination is persisting, despite the changed logic of the system of corporate governance, does not convince. Adherence to the 'shareholder value' principle by management means putting investors first, and many of the activities undertaken to satisfy investors go counter to employees' interests, as already detailed in Section 4.3.2. What persists in many cases is only an institutional shell, emptied of the old ideological content which allowed bodies of codetermination to execute checks on and provide a counterweight to the power of capital. In the words of Streeck and Yamamura (2003: 43), 'an institutional analysis that fails to recognize such transformation as a major change, a change that affects the institution of codetermination in a fundamental way, misses the essence of what it observes'. The assumption of a stance of co-management would be better described by the term 'loss of function', than by that of 'functional conversion'.

Furthermore, the system of co-determination and the stakeholder company is now no longer sacrosanct and has been attacked by several different influential constituencies (Callaghan 2003: 8–9). The Commission, which drafted the new corporate governance code, is planning to introduce a new investor-friendly measure. This would permit companies, with more than half their employees overseas, to opt out of being bound by codetermination (*Financial Times*, 8 November 2002: 9). The Head of the influential national industry association, the BDI, is known to be another vocal critic. On 18 June 2003, VIP, an association of institutional shareholders, joined the fray. 58.3 per cent of shareholders in Lufthansa adopted a motion, criticizing the vice-chairman of the company's supervisory board, the leader of the trade union Verdi, for supporting a recent, highly damaging strike in the company. A conflict of interests by union members of the supervisory board, highlighted by their motion, additionally has been identified by J. Schwalbach, a professor of business economics and the chairman of a forthcoming conference on the future of codetermination (*Financial Times*, 20 June 2003: 8). In sum, criticism of codetermination from a variety of quarters makes it appear likely that a fundamental institutional reform now is on the cards. In the light of this, it seems doubtful whether labour, through works councils and board codetermination procedures, can still exert decisive influence on events in other subsystems. It does no longer seem tenable to claim, as does Deeg (Chapter 2, this volume: 48), that 'the system of co-determination in Germany seems . . . to remain relatively robust in the face of far-reaching change in related sub-systems'.

A stronger argument in favour of a new complementarity between corporate governance and the institutions of labour has been advanced by Beyer and Hassel (2002) and Jackson (2003). Implicitly adopting the view of Biggart and Guillen (1999) that a certain system logic 'breeds' certain capabilities, conducive to cultivation of particular market niches, they rightly point to the indispensability to the German production paradigm of high levels of human capital development and consensual decision-making. They bank less on the strength and ability of labour to preserve the old paradigm, than place trust in managers and investors not to undermine it. In support of their claim, they point to empirical evidence that, to date, wage levels have not fallen and commitment to a high-skill economy has not noticeably weakened. However, they neglect to note that payment for this expensive system of training now is under strain.

Beyer and Hassel (2002) further claim that investors have not shown themselves opposed to the expensive training system and may recognize that this system enables German firms to deliver higher value. They suggest that institutional investors might be willing to forego short-term profit maximization in favour of longer term gains. Beyer and Hassel (2002), as well as Jackson (2003), thus are citing the arguments of 'enlightened shareholder value' and refer to the professed willingness of some fund managers to support the 'high road' of achieving simultaneous gain both for shareholders and other stake-holders. But unfortunately, at the time of writing, these professed enlightened goals hardly have been put to the test.

Furthermore, although many managers and policy makers will no doubt wish to preserve the venerable paradigm of 'diversified quality production', powerful constraints for profit maximization will make this a much more problematic endeavour than is recognized by Beyer and Hassel (2002) and Jackson (2003). Their argument attributes more subtle behaviour to investors than is possible in an arm's length market environment with short time horizons, where resources usually flow to producers who are likely to guarantee the highest returns in the shorter run. Their assumption that patience by stock holders will necessarily be rewarded by higher future yields from German producers is dubious. There is no evidence that the German production system of diversified quality production can deliver such comparatively high returns on investment as can be gained in the new economy.

The points made above seriously question whether the various theses on hybridization, functional conversion, and the development of a new complementarity between the systems of corporate governance and of industrial relations will continue to be useful for the analysis of developmental trends in the German variety of capitalism. The third scenario cannot be ruled out, but the theoretical basis for any new complementarity has not been specified, and empirical evidence for the emergence of a critical mass of enlightened shareholders is lacking. The next section therefore will again pose the case for more radical institutional transformation. To do so, I will identify the underlying pressures which will eventually destabilize the hybrid system and/or bring into conflict incompatible interests and goals and advance the process of convergence. I shall also pinpoint the developments already under way which indicate such a progressive trend.

4.3.5. *Pressures for system convergence*

As acknowledged by Deeg (2001) and O'Sullivan (2003), the changes in the capital market now are so well established that they have become irreversible. They have created a new logic for corporate governance which will prove compelling in the longer run. (This conclusion is also supported by Streeck and Yamamura 2003: 42.) This is all the more likely because these changes have been accepted and promoted by powerful internal actors—German commercial banks and insurance companies, as well as top managers of large companies. The gains from the switch to outsider control have amply compensated the large commercial banks for the progressive attenuation of insider control, and their interests now are firmly aligned with a stock market oriented economy (Becker 2001).

An equally import precipitant of the process of convergence has come from political reform and legal change. O'Sullivan (2003) and Streeck and Yamamura (2003) plausibly attribute changes in capital markets to policy-makers' realization that German firms have been lagging in the 'new economy', due to the structure of the German capital market, particularly the resulting shortage of venture capital. Among the many remedial measures adopted, the introduction of the so-called Eichel tax reform, which encourages the unravelling of the system of cross-shareholding by non-financial companies, is likely to prove the most consequential. Two considerations make it likely that network dissolution will occur. First, such dissolution was already well under way when the Law was enacted, and further disentanglement has occurred since then (Höpner 2003b: 23; O'Sullivan 2003). Thus, between 1996 and 1998 alone, the holdings of non-financial companies had declined from 37.6 to 30.5 per cent, and these shares seem to have been bought up by foreign investors (Deutsche Bundesbank, Gesamtwirtschaftliche Finanzierungsrechnung, quoted by O'Sullivan 2003: 16). Second, it appears highly likely that the vast opportunities for gain, entailed by withdrawing underperforming ownership stakes for utilization in more lucrative investments, will be seized by both financial and non-financial firms. Indeed, both Deutsche Bank and Allianz already have signalled their intention to follow this course of action (Heinze 2001). Such a development would further transform the system of corporate governance, leading to de-concentration of capital holdings, much increased stock market listing, new openings for foreign investment funds and hence to a market for corporate control. The image of 'stalactite change', that is, of a 'minuscule drop of water falling from the vault of a cave', chosen by Djelic and Quack (2003, Chapter 6, this volume) to portray the nature of institutional change, cannot said to apply to this instance of change. To the contrary, it is a dramatic change, likely to deal the death knell to the old entrenched German system of cross-shareholding and the system of insider control it has been upholding.

Pressures for convergence have come not only from capital market actors, but they also have been more or less enthusiastically embraced by a significant group of company managers. These managers' interests are better served by a transformation of the German model of corporate governance, or, alternatively, they have been socialized into a new business culture, either by managing outside Germany or by studying in US universities. The weakening of the institutions of labour, too, is part of a progressive trend. It is due to structural transformations in the German economy, such as a move towards sectors (services) and firms (small and medium-sized and 'new economy' ones) where organization of labour is much more difficult and unions and works councils tend to be less well represented, as well as to the weakness of the German economy's employment generation. Although German labour is not yet as weak as its British or US counterpart it seems that an effective campaign against marketization is beyond its organizing capability.

Last, pressures for convergence have existed for only a relatively short period of time, starting in the mid- to late-1990s. If they have been able to unleash such fundamental change in so many areas in this short time span we must expect that many hitherto persistent features of the German variety of capitalism will be swept away during the coming decade.

4.4. **Conclusions**

The preceding theoretical analysis and empirical description of changes in the German model of corporate governance since the mid-1990s have considered both the nature and the outcomes of change. They have attempted to make evident the complexity of the change process and have shown that diffusion of change from one institutional constellation to others has occurred with a time delay. This has led to a hitherto lower degree of change in the industrial relations/labour relations system than in the financial system and mode of corporate governance. This delay may be due to labour resistance, or it may simply constitute a delayed reaction.

I have explored whether the outcome or direction of change in German capitalism can best be conceptualised as persistence of the model of coordinated market capitalism, adapted through functional conversion and the achievement of a new complementarity, as hybridization, incorporating elements of both the 'coordinated' and 'liberal market' economy models, or as imminent convergence to the model of 'liberal market' capitalism.

The virtual consensus of most analysts of the transformations in the German political economy has been that, despite much persistence of traditional 'coordinated market' features, change in the core area of corporate governance has been far-reaching. Change has proceeded too far and is supported by too many powerful 'within system' actors to be reversible. There is, however, little agreement on how radical change in one subsystem has affected the system as a whole. In contrast to other analyses both in this volume and elsewhere, this chapter has concluded that the typification of this process of change as either hybridization, functional conversion and/or the establishment of a new complementarity is unhelpful. The new logic of corporate governance already is diffusing into other sections of the economy— beyond the DAX 30 firms—and to other institutional subsystems. It has affected basic aspects of company strategic focus, organizational structure and reward systems. These, in turn, have impacted on the utilization and development of human resources, as well as shaping labour relations and the tenor of cooperation in works councils. This process of diffusion is bound to become more prevalent in coming decades. In this way, it eventually will lead to convergence with the Anglo-American model.

The trend towards convergence is not simply attributed to external constraints. Furthermore, the concern with a system logic has not precluded a strong focus on actors, capable of changing this logic. The process of convergence is shown to be receiving support from powerful actors within the German political economy, particularly from large banks and insurance companies and from many of the large internationally oriented German companies, but also from government ministers.

I have not argued that the German variety of capitalism already has converged towards the Anglo-American type. I have merely identified a developmental tendency and predict an intensification of this tendency in the coming decade. Such convergence will not entail the copying of all details of the model of liberal market capitalism, but, above all else, it will involve the embrace of the underlying logic of 'shareholder value'. The latter then might be implemented in a manner more congruent with German institution-alized practices. Such implementation will, however, fall short of hybridization.

Occurrence of convergence to liberal market capitalism is not merely of theoretical interest. It will have far-reaching practical consequences, detrimental to the continued viability of the model of diversified quality production, to employees and to organized labour, as well as increasing the level of social inequality in German society. It is, therefore, important to ask whether there are any powerful or influ-ential supporters within Germany of the status quo who might be able to erect buffers between the capital market and institutions of labour and industrial relations. The question thus becomes whether the proven importance of viewing labour as a stakeholder would result in the adoption of a model which can satisfy the demands of both international investors and labour.

In contrast to Höpner (2001), Beyer and Hassel (2002) and Sorge (Chapter 5, this volume), I am sceptical that the old model of a coordinated market economy is likely to be restored. My pess-imism about evolving a new complementarity is based on three arguments. First, it has not been shown what the basis for such a new complementarity would be. What resources can labour mobilize to preserve or re-establish stability in the subsystem of industrial relations? If a cooperative inter-firm network and the long-termism it has encouraged have been greatly weakened by the transforma-tion of corporate governance, what resources can managers call on to maintain the costly training system and the cooperative style in labour relations? None of the above authors has provided answers to these questions.

Last, functional conversion of the institutions of codetermination is not likely to save them as industrial relations entities, facilitating the exertion of meaningful countervailing powers. Although the structures may persist, their rationale will be changed fundamentally. The fact that they are legally secured cannot, as Deeg (Chapter 2, this volume) claims, prevent this development. They will no longer be an avenue through which labour may exert a significant amount of insider control—the feature which has long endowed the German variety of capitalism with its distinctive character.

But the future is never as closed as my pessimistic prognosis makes it appear, and events may occur to halt or reverse the convergence process. Given the lingering strength of social institutional embeddedness of the German model, together with the absence of a clear policy direction which endorses the 'liberal market' model, there may yet emerge a coalition of industrial managers, employees, and politicians working for a new as yet inchoate compromise solution. Particularly among politicians in both main parties (the Social-Democratic Party, SPD and the Christian Democratic Union, CDU) there is not yet any consensus on (Höpner 2003a), nor a coherent strategy for a future direction of the economy and for the institutional supports this requires. Also the blocking by German MEPs of a liberal takeover directive has shown that support in Germany for 'free market' policies is by no means universal or guaranteed. This, in theory, leaves open the possibility of a restoration of the old model through the building of a coalition at the macro-level against free-market policies and the erection of protective barriers between institutional complexes. (This possibility is also envisaged by Amable 2003: 24.) At the present time, however, the emergence of such a coalition is not evident, and the close integration of the German economy into both the European Union and the international economy would make such a project difficult to sustain.

Alternatively, the occurrence of powerful external shocks might stall or reverse the convergence process, and this might lead to a consolidation of the antiliberal economic and political faction. A chance for a halting or reversal of the convergence process lies in a strong and persistent de-legitimation of the Anglo-American system of corporate governance, or in a process of its convergence to the model of 'coordinated market economies'. 'Stock market' capitalism, since the collapse of the high-tech boom and of share prices more generally, is no longer as popular as it was during the early 1990s. Additionally, the 'Enron' syndrome has dented the faith in the US system of corporate governance, although the enactment of the 2002 Sarbanes-Oxley Act already has begun to restore investor confidence.

What are the chances for such developments occurring? Although some softening at the edges of the UK model in particular has been noted (Pendleton and Gospel 2003), a convincing case for convergence towards the model of a 'coordinated market economy' is still outstanding. Despite widespread disillusionment with the 'shareholder value' maxim, it would be premature to diagnose the demise of the liberal market economy. The renewed emergence of a wave of cross-border acquisitions and mergers suggests continuing reliance on and importance of the stock market. Thus, in conclusion, one cannot rule out a reversal of the process of system convergence in Germany, but at the current time there is no solid evidence that such a process is under way.

REFERENCES

Amable, B. (2003). *The Diversity of Modern Capitalism*. Oxford: Oxford University Press.

Becker, S. (2001). *Einfluss und Grenzen des Shareholder Value. Strategie- und Strukturwandel deutscher Grossunternehmen der chemischen und pharmazeutischen Industrie*. Frankfurt a. Main: Peter Lang.

Berger, S. and Dore, R. (eds.) (1997). *National Diversity and Global Capitalism*. Oxford: Oxford University Press.

Beyer, J. and Hassel, A. (2002). 'The Market for Corporate Control and Financial Internationalization of German Firms'. *Economy and Society*, 31(3): 309–32.

Biggart, N. W. and Guillen, M. F. (1999). 'Developing Difference: Social Organization and the Rise of the Auto Industries of South Korea, Taiwan, Spain, Argentina'. *American Sociological Review* 64(5): 722–47.

Callaghan, H. (2003). 'Battle of the Systems or Multi-level Game? Domestic Sources of Anglo-German Quarrels over EU Takeover Law and Worker Consultation'. Paper presented at the 15th Annual Conference of the Association for the Advancement of Socio-Economics. Aix-en-Provence, 27–29 June 2003.

Deakin, S., Hobbs, R., Nash, D., and Slinger, G. (2002). 'Implicit Contracts, Takeovers, and Corporate Governance in the Shadow of the City Code'. Working paper 254, ESRC Centre for Business Research, University of Cambridge, December.

Deeg, R. (2001). 'Institutional Change and the Uses and Limits of Path Dependency: The Case of German Finance'. 01/06. Unpublished paper, posted on web site www.mpi-fg-Koeln.mpg.de.

DiMaggio, P. and Powell, W. (1991). 'Introduction'. In: W. Powell and P. DiMaggio (eds.), *The New Institutionalism in Organizational Analysis.* Chicago: University of Chicago Press, pp. 1–38.

Djelic, M.-L. and Quack, S. (2003). 'Theoretical Building Blocks for a Research Agenda Linking Globalization and Institutions'. In: M.-L. Djelic and S. Quack (eds.), *Globalization and Institutions. Redefining the Rules of the Economic Game.* Cheltenham: Edward Elgar, pp. 15–36.

Faust, M., Jauch, P., and Notz, P. (2000). *Befreit und entwurzelt: Fuehrungskraefte auf dem Weg zum 'internen Unternehmer'.* Muenchen and Mehring: Rainer Hampp Verlag.

Hall, P. and Soskice, D. (2001). *Varieties of Capitalism.* Oxford: Oxford University Press.

Heinze, T. (2001). Transformation des Deutschen Unternehmenskontroll-Systems? *Koelner Zeitschrift f. Soziologie und Sozialpsychologie* 53(4): 641–74.

Höpner, M. (2001). 'Corporate Governance in Transition: Ten Empirical Findings on Shareholder Value and Industrial Relations'. Discussion paper 01/5, Max-Planck-Institut f. Gesellschaftsforschung, Cologne.

—— (2003*a*). 'European Corporate Governance Reform and the German Party Paradox'. Discussion paper 2003/04, Max Planck Institut f. Gesellschaftsforschung/Cologne.

—— (2003*b*). 'The Politics of the German Company Network'. Paper presented at the 15th Conference of the Society for the Advancement of Socio-Economics, Aix-en-Provence, 27–29 June 2003.

—— and Jackson, G. (2001). 'An Emergent Market for Corporate Control? The Mannesmann Takeover and German Corporate Governance'. MPIfG Discussion paper 01/4, Cologne: Max Planck Institut f. Gesellschaftsforschung.

—— and —— (2002). Das deutsche System der Corporate Governance zwischen Persistenz und Konvergenz. Replik auf den Beitrag von Thomas Heinze in Heft 4/2001 der *Koelner Zeitschrift f. Soziologie und Sozialpsychologie* 54(2): 362–8.

Hollingsworth, J. R. and Boyer, R. (eds.) (1997). *Contemporary Capitalism. The Embeddedness of Institutions.* Cambridge: Cambridge University Press.

Jackson, G. (2003). 'Corporate Governance in Germany and Japan: Liberalization Pressures and Responses During the 1990s'. In: K. Yamamura and W. Streeck (eds.), *The End of Diversity.* Ithaca and London: Cornell University Press, pp. 261–305.

Jürgens, U. et al. (2000). 'Shareholder Value in an Adverse Environment: The German Case'. *Economy and Society* 29(1): 54–79.

Kaedtler, J. and Sperling, H.-J. (2003). 'Globalization and Financialization as Triggers for Enterprise Reorganisation and the Impact on Industrial Relations'. *SOFI-Mitteilungen* 31 (July): 53–66.

Kitschelt, H., Lange, P., Marks, G., and Stephens, J. (eds.) (1999). *Continuity and Change in Contemporary Capitalism.* Cambridge: Cambridge University Press.

Kurdelbusch, A. (2001). 'The Upswing of Variable Pay in Germany—Evidence and Explanations'. Unpublished paper. Max-Planck-Institut f. Gesellschaftsforschung. Cologne.

Lane, C. (1995). *Industry and Society in Europe. Stability and Change in Britain, Germany and France*. Aldershot: Edward Elgar.

—— (2000). 'Globalization and the German Model of Capitalism—Erosion or Survival? *The British Journal of Sociology* 51(2): 207–34.

—— and Quack, S. (2001). 'How Banks Construct and Manage Risk. A Sociological Study of Small Firm Lending in Britain and Germany'. Working paper 217, Centre for Business Research, University of Cambridge.

Luetz, S. (2000). 'From Managed to Market Capitalism? German Finance in Transition'. *German Politics* 9: 149–71.

Mahoney, J. (2001). 'Path Dependence in Historical Sociology'. *Theory and Society* 29: 507–48.

Mayer, C. (2000). 'Corporate Governance in the UK'. *Hume Papers on Public Policy* 8(1): 1–9.

Morgan, G. and Kubo, I. (2005). 'Beyond Path Dependency? Constructing New Models for Institutional Change: The Case of Capital Markets in Japan'. *Socio-Economic Review* 3(1): 55–82.

Morin, F. (2000). 'A transformation in the French Model of Shareholding and Management'. *Economy and Society* 29(1): 36–53.

Müller-Jentsch, W. (ed.) (1993). *Konfliktpartnerschaft. Akteure und Institutionen der industriellen Beziehungen*. Muenchen und Mehring: Rainer Hampp Verlag.

O'Sullivan, M. A. (2000). *Contests for Corporate Control. Corporate Governance and Economic Performance in the United States and Germany*. Oxford: Oxford University Press.

O'Sullivan, M. (2003). 'The Political Economy of Comparative Corporate Governance'. Unpublished manuscript.

Pendleton, A. and Gospel, H. (2003). 'Markets and Relationships: Finance, Government and Labour in the United Kingdom'. Paper presented to the 15th Annual Conference of the Society for the Advancement of Socio-Economics. Aix-en-Provence, 27–29 June.

Schmidt, V. (2002). *The Futures of European Capitalism*. Oxford: Oxford University Press.

Streeck, W. (1992). *Social Institutions and Economic Performance*. London: Sage.

—— (2001). 'The Transformation of Corporate Organization in Europe: An Overview'. MPIfG Working paper 01/8, December 2001. Cologne: Max Planck Institut f. Gesellschaftsforschung.

—— and Yamamura, K. (2003). 'Introduction: Convergence or Diversity? Stability and Change in German and Japanese Capitalism'.

In: K. Yamamura and W. Streeck (eds.), *The End of Diversity?* Ithaca/London: Cornell University Press, pp. 1–50.

Thelen, K. (2000). 'Timing and Temporality in the Analysis of Institutional Evolution and Change'. *Studies in American Political Development* 14(1): 101–8.

—— (2003). 'How Institutions Evolve'. In: J. Mahoney and D. Rueschemeyer (eds.), *Comparative Historical Analysis in the Social Sciences*. Cambridge: Cambridge University Press, pp. 208–40.

Vitols, S. (2001). 'Viele Wege nach Rom? BASF, Bayer und Hoechst'. Unpublished Paper. Wissenschaftszentrum Berlin/Germany.

Whitley, R. (ed.) (1992). *European Business Systems. Firms and Markets in National Context*. London: Sage.

—— (1999). *Divergent Capitalisms. The Social Structuring and Change of Business Systems*. Oxford: Oxford University Press.

Windolf, P. (2000). *Corporate Networks in Europe and the United States*. Oxford: Oxford University Press.

Yamamura, K. and Streeck, W. (eds.) (2003). *The End of Diversity? Prospects for German and Japanese Capitalism*. Ithaca and London: Cornell University Press.

Zugehoer, R. (2001). 'Capital Market, Codetermination and Corporate Restructuring. A Comparative Study of Siemens and Veba'. Paper presented at the 13th Annual Meeting of the Society for the Advancement of Socio-Economics, Amsterdam, 28 June to 1 July.

5

Systemic Perspectives on Business Practices and Institutions. A Plea Beyond Comparative Statics

5.1. Introduction and Overview

Business system authors have mainly claimed to provide explanations within a comparative statics framework; the approach thus explains interdependencies between types on different system dimensions. This is useful for a first rough-and-ready explanation of diversity as it can be summarized for the present, and following general characteristics of a trajectory as it is reinterpreted from a recent vantage point. Its capacity for explaining change and evolution to more fine-grained varieties of business systems, in a systemic way, is however limited. This chapter argues that this can be improved, but requires going beyond comparative statics, to develop a dynamic perspective.

A first step is to analyse and distinguish different types of system differentiation: action systems and institutional systems. Business system change can be analysed as occurring through four essential mechanisms:

(1) tight coupling between action systems;
(2) loose coupling and evolutionary decoupling between characteristics within and across institutional subsystems;
(3) enactment of temporary equilibria between institutional subsystems, and between these and environments;

While writing this, I was a visitor at the Max Planck Institute for the Study of Societies, Cologne. The support of the Institute is very gratefully acknowledged.

(4) interacting systemic–internal and environmental impulses upsetting temporary equilibria and propelling towards search for new equilibria (overall institutional arrangements).

Together, these four mechanisms can be called 'non-identical reproduction'. This conceptualization of business systems dynamics comes out of societal analysis, an approach that has helped to provide empirical and theoretical foundations to NBS theory since its inception. It is illustrated and proved in the example of Germany. Any other country might have been selected for demonstration, but for Germany, a larger number of methodologically robust comparisons with other societies have been made available. This makes a treatment possible that can be substantiated by a comparison.

This analysis is developed step-wise. First, a consideration of system theory reveals different theory types that inform on differences in NBS. The implications of this theoretical pluralism inside NBS are developed. Different variants of NBS are then discussed.

5.2. Shades of Systems and Systemic Relations

NBS thinking has its point of departure in two key notions: there are economic and social institutions that govern business behaviour and what happens in business organizations, notably firms. Then, 'systems' denotes a systemic coherence within a society and economy, between different domains, spheres, arenas, or sets of characteristics. Institutions in different domains of a business system or national society are thus thought to be interdependent. They hold each other in place. On the other hand, we have to acknowledge change, including the change of institutions themselves. NBS authors are always subject to the dilemma that the power of the approach resides in the interdependency of institutions across societal domains but change undeniably unsettles the picture of institutions, including the nature of their interrelationships. This leads to the question: are institutions not really unrelated, contrary to NBS thinking? Can we therefore dispense with NBS and concentrate conceptualization on the mechanics of business system change?

First, the world of institutional notions and institutional theory is much more complex than appreciated in such a question. Second, the world of systems and their relations is much more complex. I offer a concept of institutional sets and systemic construction which is derived from societal analysis (Maurice et al. 1982), as an approach which is intentionally eclectic, that is, it combines theoretical strands which are often kept apart (Maurice and Sorge 2000).

A key point about any societal order is that it can be divided follow-ing two different criteria: the division of meanings and the division of labour. The flaw in NBS thinking was not to differentiate between the two. It is an old flaw inherited from structural functionalism, exem-plified and pioneered by Parsons (1964). Parsons had distinguished functional subsystems of society as systems of meaning: they were specified by an abstract function they fulfilled. Parsons then conceived the evolution of society as progressing towards a differentiation of society, such that functional differentiation, by abstract purposes or meanings, became identical with the differentiation of institutional entities, within the division of labour. NBS literature has thus con-flated functional and institutional differentiation or, at least, not been attentive to their difference.

The division of labour is a familiar concept; it relates to a systems differentiation between institutional subsystems, and these are aggreg-ates of social entities, individual social entities such as organizations, or departmental or functionally specific parts of the latter. The educa-tional system is, for example, one institutional subsystem of society. This system socializes people into roles by generating knowledge, skills, and normative orientations. However, the educational system is far from having a monopoly over all or most of the socializing func-tions allocated to it. Socialization also happens at play, in the street and elsewhere, in the family and also very much in work groups, enterprises, and indeed most places in which people do something together. Socialization into roles implies a different systemic differ-entiation and a different concept of systems than an institutional differentiation does. An act of socialization is part of the subsystem of socialization, as a functional subsystem which bounds all beha-viour meaningfully related to socialization. One first proposition is that institutional systems are perennially distinct from functional systems bounded by meaning, and no evolution will change that. But it is also perennially interesting to wonder how functional systems relate to institutionally bounded entities.

Institutions are too often addressed as characteristically inert, fol-lowing the one-sided entry of DiMaggio and Powell (1983) and neglecting the more recent and productive work of Oliver (1992, 1996). Institutional actors are always confronted with requirements and consequences that go against inertia. They have to bear regard to these if or when their action is to be meaningful (effective, legitimate, satisfying, rewarding, morally good—whatever). The pursuit of meaning thus opens up institutions and it counteracts inertia. There is a side to institutional entities and institutional behaviour which implies social construction, dialectics, and change. This side is captured by social action theory which has focused on the differentiation of action systems.

Systemic differentiation by meanings and associated action spaces can be coarse grained or very fine grained. In sociology, notably in French and German sociology (see Luhmann 1972) but also in the business and management approach established by de Leeuw (2000), such subsystems are called action systems or spaces. They are defined by abstract meanings of generic types, such as socialization, career progression, industrial relations, politics, economic exchange, or more refined meanings. There is no limit to the refinement of spaces bounded by meaning or function. Action spaces or subsystems have the perennial habit of cross-cutting the institutional division of labour in society: play and banter give rise to the identification of an action space, with its own meaning, and this subsystem also includes work organizations. Any behavioural act is potentially implicated in a multitude of action systems or spaces at the same time. The more refined our typology of action systems is, the greater the number of action spaces implicated by a behavioural act. Consequently, it is crucial to keep apart the 'specific' meaning of any behavioural act, which tends to be a heap of interrelated meanings, and the 'generic' meaning governing a cross-individual and wider action space.

NBS has been concerned with institutionally differentiated systems, following a more positivist approach, and it has tended to assume that institutional subsystems can also be identified as having specific meanings. For instance, economic organizations are very much filled with the meaning of utilitarian purposes and achieving tangible material results. But as we can see, this is a limited picture, for institutional entities such as economic organizations are also filled with other meanings, such as socialization, establishing biographical trajectories, or relaxing social intercourse. Other action systems therefore strongly figure inside them. This has been pointed out by symbolic interactionism and interpretivism (such as put forward by Berger and Luckmann 1971). It insists that the division of meaning by action spaces, which draws meaningful boundaries around distinct action orientations in society, always cross-cuts the institutional division of labour. Against Parsons, it tells us that we must always distinguish between action systems and institutional domains and entities. Rather than having unique meanings, institutional subsystems and entities always have lots of them, which makes for an inherent ambiguity. Furthermore, societies and also national business systems are not simply integrated because their institutional domains and entities have different functions and are therefore complementary. That is only 'systems integration' as Lockwood (1964) called it. 'Social integration' (following Lockwood's terms again) is constituted by action spaces bounded by society or the business system; such action spaces are tightly coupled, which reflects the idea that any behavioural act is governed by a multitude of different and interrelated meanings.

Positivism and interactionism or interpretivism are not meaningless clichés but widely accepted approaches of equal right. While positivism deals with social facts 'for what they are', interactionism, interpretivism, and other derivatives such as constructivism deal with them as 'what people make of them' (Burrell 2002: 32 ff.). As Burrell himself pointed out integration of paradigms may indeed be called for and productive, as long as pluralism is maintained. This is also the basis for my argument. It tries to point out that action spaces and institutional entities may overlap but are not the same; and we learn a lot about societies or business systems by researching how action spaces defined by specific meanings on the one hand and institutional entities on the other stand against each other, how and where they overlap and where they diverge.

Action systems have action of the same type as elements, and these are of the same type if they have the same meaning across all those individuals that perform this action. Of course, they are difficult to pinpoint empirically. But analytically, every time that we see people pursuing the same meaning, we see them as part of an action system. Whenever you do a transaction for an economic motive, you are part of the economic action system. Whenever or wherever you comfort someone or have an informal and friendly cup of tea, you are part of an action system which has no good standard designation, so you may call it 'personal re-assurance and comfort system'. And of course, if we distinguish upon closer inspection even more differentiated and specific meanings, then of course we differentiate the species further into sub-sorts. The main thing is that action systems are identified as crystallized around an identical meaning.

Institutional entities are collective 'bodies' (agencies, enterprises, churches, army divisions, Elvis Presley commemoration associations, trade unions, secret societies, mafia gangs, freemasons' lodges, parties, fast-food chains, football clubs, etc.), which are bound together by membership, governance (despotic or anarchical), goals, and action programmes. Many institutional entities are organizations in one form or another, but they may also be extended families, clans, or any other more archaic body with recognizable membership, a common purpose and a certain amount of social closure or exclusion. Action systems are bounded by meaning but do not have institutional boundaries, while institutional entities are bounded by membership but share in lots of action spaces.

Parsons had argued that societies become more and more functionally specific and differentiate subsystems accordingly. Thus, he thought that the division of labour in society went hand in hand with the division of meaning, such that differentiated institutional entities, in their respective subsystems, were becoming more and more concerned with a unique meaning or function. This is the conflation of institutional and action systemic differentiation which needs to be discarded according to interactionist approaches.

Action theorists put forward that sets of meaning evolve and become refined over time, cross-cutting the division of labour between institutional entities. Thus, for example, it would be silly to assume that schools and universities can ever absorb all the action with educational or socializing meaning in society. Instead, socialization into roles and notably education will remain and be developed, and not only in a residual role, within other institutional entities: rowing clubs, street gangs, but also enterprises and other organizations with a purpose totally different from education. Interaction theorists and interpretivists also alert us to the fact that institutions and meanings do not become linked to one another in stable one-to-one relationships. Institutions acquire peculiar and shifting positions within a welter of action spaces. Business systems may thus consist of combinations of institutional elements endowed with very different meanings. When specific meanings of institutions change, or when institutional ensembles such as those represented under different business system types change quality or composition, this calls business systems theory into question. It is notably Chapter 4 by Lane in this volume which points in this direction. However, NBS theory is not called into question if we see its systemic relationships and tight coupling vested in and between action spaces rather than institutional ensembles. Institutions and characteristics of institutional entities may be much more fleeting and shifting than NBS theory suggests. This may happen without going against the systemicness of NBS, if this systemicness is seen to reside in and between action spaces. Such phenomena will be addressed, in what follows, under the rubric of the decomposition and recombination of institutions, a keynote which is also struck by Djelic and Quack (Chapter 6, this volume). It relates to the idea that 'path dependencies' stylized in the varieties of capitalism literature should be better conceived as dependencies upon a crooked path, that is, dependencies which can be reformulated and rearranged at specific turning-points.

Action spaces are, in a way, 'furnished' by institutions. Institutional furniture is basically somewhat inert. But it does change over time. Even when it does change, by anything ranging from scrapping and re-equiument to redecoration or rearrangement, actors do not break with the style of the institutional furniture completely, at least not all the time or on every occasion. Even actors busily re-interpreting and changing institutions need, as a back-drop to the change they perform, a compensatory measure of stability or continuity. This inevitable relative inertia of institutional furniture or furniture style in the midst of change may be stronger in a particular action space. This is the more functionalist and positivist side of the present analysis. However, stable or inert institutional furniture in one action space, through the tight coupling of action spaces, brings about mutual adaptation between novel furniture and older furniture, in and across action spaces, leading to an eclectic combination of new and old institutional furniture. Its overall style thus keeps a distinct measure of continuity, both although, and because, it is regularly being challenged by new additions that replace specific and older furniture.

We can thus see that the extent of the division of labour is interesting for systems integration following Lockwood, but uninteresting with regard to social integration. Social integration is related to the 'quality' of the division of labour, expressed by whether it overlaps with, or cross-cuts, the division of meaning. A division of meaning in action systems cross-cutting the division of labour is socially integrative, whereas identity of the division of labour with the division of meaning in action systems is socially disruptive. This insight is also useful in the sociology of work and technology, where it can be used to explain how enterprises organize work processes and structures, not as a function of technology per se but task environmental settings (Sorge 1985). We need to be concerned about the 'quality' rather than the 'extent' of the division of labour, as had already become clear in the earlier distinction suggested by Durkheim, about the need to distinguish 'anomic' and socially integrative division of labour. The quality of the division of labour is expressed by its relation to the division of meaning. A division of labour thus becomes anomic when its components have very singular meanings, and this may be called alienating because it removes other meanings from the scene of an organizational entity.

Institutions structure and fill action spaces with rather inert furniture, as useful things which lend themselves to certain purposes, whereas they keep us from doing other things in that space. Inversely, the institutional furniture in any action space derives its meaning from a generic meaning which is attached to that action space. But the specific meaning of an institution is always under the conjoint impact of different action systems, tightly coupled as they are. Action spaces thus need institutional furniture in order to translate general meanings into concrete activities and tools, and institutions are meaningful in the terms of the action spaces into which they are inserted. Furthermore, the institutional furniture of action spaces can be removed, renovated, or moved about. This is institutional change.

The addition of action systems to NBS theory focused on institutional systems has the following advantages. It problematizes the meanings inherent to institutions, and the meaningful interrelationships between different institutions in one society. It directs attention at the meaningful construction and reconstruction of business systems, compared over time or between different societies. Action systems and the division of meaning they imply have to be considered more sharply and they have to be mapped with regard to institutional systems and their change. Action systems make for systemic coherence across societal or business system domains, and they do that even when institutional change is strong. They can do that because institutions and institutional ensembles such as in business system types are eclectic combinations which are valid for a time, as a temporary quasi-equilibrium. Even when such equilibria change fundamentally, the ensuing business system is never completely removed from a previous one but continuous with it. Interactionist thought thus gives conventional (positivist) NBS theory greater range and power; it can therefore be likened to the boosters attached to a rocket.

5.3. Standard and Extended Concepts of Business Systems, Variation, and Change

Business systems are subject to variation and change, over time and between societies and economies. The power of NBS theory resides in its capability to explain such variation and change. It can basically do this in two different ways. The first way, which is strongly presented in the writings of Whitley (2002, notably in the reasoning around the table on p. 179), is to argue that institutional variety across societies and over time shows a correspondence between the various dimensions of business systems. This works in the following way: NBS has two main conceptual arms, first, a concept of salient main dimensions in which systems vary and, second, a typology of business systems.

Such characteristics are general institutional descriptors. They are not enshrined dogmatically; if anyone came and drew a more complex and differentiated map of characteristics, Whitley would surely be very pleased and consider this a perfectly legitimate extension of his work. Indeed, the drift of Whitley's writings is to go for increasing complexity of the tables with which he summarizes the theoretical essentials of his arguments. The advantage of his concept is a systems typology much more refined than in the literature on varieties of capitalism which is overly fascinated with the contrast between Anglo-American and 'Rhineland' capitalism. NBS typologies put forward fairly consistent relations between characteristics across dimensions. Such essentials give NBS its tantalizing appeal, suggesting that there are typical and stable interrelationships across the whole range of characteristics. Specific types are then characterized by, not only accidental but stable interrelationships. Through such interrelationships, characteristics combine and congeal into types.

Here again, Whitley would certainly not mind if someone came and differentiated this typology further. For the one and only criterion for defining a particular business system is that stable and characteristic interrelationships between their dimensions can be ascertained, in such a way that what happens with regard to one characteristic is fairly closely coupled to what happens on other dimensions. Thus, no matter how complex Whitley or other NBS developers may one day engineer the typology to be, its attractiveness will always reside in the interrelationships posited, between salient characteristics within particular types. These interrelationships are central for an explanation and prediction of change. For what the NBS approach does is to state that the evolution of systems happens by a coevolution of characteristics. Very interesting propositions can be generated in this way. They are cast within a type of analysis which, following usage in economics, is called comparative statics. This is what Whitley has claimed to be the principal purpose of the approach.

For instance, in a collaborative business system such as there is in Germany, the theoretical statement applies that its propensity to finance investment out of credit rather than through retained earnings or share issue—and have low equity-to-debt ratios—is quite explicably interdependent with a stakeholder view of corporate control including codetermination, with generation of trust in the workforce by vocational training and job enrichment, and with more extensive cooperation between enterprises even when they compete in the same markets. Similarly, conceptually suggestive and corroborated examples for other business systems could be mentioned. They allow us to explain why institutional traits are stable: they are interdependent and in that way tend towards a lock-in or coevolution, and that allows us to predict change. So, for example, if through any external influence the equity-to-debt ratio of German enterprises were to increase, this would in all likelihood also imply that alliance coordination between enterprises and the generation and maintenance of trust in the workforce would be scaled down.

The distinctive logic of this reasoning is based on a systems analysis which emphasizes tight coupling. That, as argued above, is not a good systems-theoretical bargain although it generates propositions which at first sight are rather robust. For the attractive thing about NBS—tight coupling which leads to stable interrelationships—is the hallmark of action systems, and these are institutionally unspecific although they are furnished with institutions. Institutional systems should however be seen as loosely coupled, such that institutional change may entail recombination of characteristics. For example, it would have to be expected that increasing the equity-to-debt ratio might even be compatible with stronger trust in the work force. This could be so because it is perfectly conceivable that German enterprises, if threatened by the vicissitudes of the stock market, might feel particularly dependent on what they perceive as a central resource for coping with such vicissitudes: a well-trained and trustworthy workforce. In this way, it can be seen that tight coupling—between the organizing, socializing, and financing action systems—prevailed, whereas with regard to institutional subsystems, decoupling, and recombination of characteristics come in.

Once we thus extend the range of systems analysis facilitated by NBS, we can facilitate a more differentiated systems analysis, allowing for both loose and tight coupling, in the appropriate places: tightly coupled action systems provide for the coherence of business systems and indeed whole societies; loosely coupled and therefore changeable institutions can be combined into new patterns which are often surprising. NBS thus gains in range by the addition of a 'booster' to the rocket. The booster is interpretivism and interactionism, denoting the consideration of action systems. The main engine of the rocket is, and can remain to be, of positivist and functionalist construction. For a certain amount of institutional inertia, that is, specific meanings attached to institutional features, is inevitable.

Another complexity to be introduced concerns the range of factors affected by change in the first instance. Change may come into the business systems via one restricted factor. There may be something exogenously new which affects one factor directly, be it the equity-to-debt ratio, or intensification of vocational training, or incentives for or against alliance coordination. Its effect within the system can then be analysed using either purely positivist or boostered (positivist plus interactionist–interpretivist) theory. On the other hand, change can be visualized as extending to a variety of factors: it may be that changes with regard to both, capital versus credit financing and work systems organization and training systems, occur simultaneously and without clear relations between them. In this case, change is visualized as much more eclectic. Change may consist of a concoction of diverse and conflicting political influences, management hypes, and any other of the colourful flowers that blossom next to each other in the fertile ground of society, as an entity which is inherently and ceaselessly erratic, laden with emotional, affective, fashionable, and unreflectedly traditional motives. If we combine the positivism versus boostered positivism dimension with the initial range of change dimension we obtain Figure 5.1. It briefly sketches what the type of analysis resulting in each field implies for NBS.

Let us first discuss what happens in quadrants A and B. This very much remains within the comparative statics perspective emphasized

	Institutionally differentiated systems—positivism	Institutionally differentiated systems and action systems—positivism plus interpretivism
Change affects in the first instance: specific factors	A: Comparative statics: change affects other factors, on the basis of relations between them	B: Comparative statics plus change of meaning: theory is confirmed, but meaning of characteristics may change
Change affects whole sets of relations	C: Disconfirmation: theory is disconfirmed	D: Dialectics: partitioning of institutional spaces, and partitioned recombination of distinct or opposed characteristics

Figure 5.1. *Systems concepts, impact of change, and their theoretical implications*

by Whitley, and it may come with or without an interpretivist and interactionist booster. In the section that follows thereafter, I discuss quadrants C and notably D, which are more distinct because they imply disconfirmation of NBS or its development from comparative statics into dynamics. The dynamic analysis is linked to a dialectical approach. The reader will appreciate that there is no interpretivist and interactionist booster without a strong dose of dialectics. The intention is not to throw out NBS one-sidedly or downplay its positivist core engine. An analysis under the terms of quadrant A, which I would see as the mainstay of NBS so far, may be perfectly acceptable for certain purposes. It will be even better under the assumptions of quadrant B. But since a dynamic perspective allows us to do more than comparative statics does, a move from quadrant A to D is particularly enticing. It greatly amplifies the range of NBS thinking.

5.4. Dynamic Change in Business Systems: From Disconfirmation to Recombinant Dynamics

Dynamic change means that it leads to novel equilibria. Such equilibria would fundamentally upset the affinities put forward in NBS types, such as in the list of Whitley's six business system types mentioned above. This would mean that a business system at moment n would exhibit, say, a linkage of trust-based cooperation in the workforce with alliance coordination between enterprises and with credit-based financing, and at moment $t + 10$, or in a slightly different national case, has a deep capital base in finance. Change can be pictured here as attaching to a greater number of factors, which takes us to the second row in Figure 5.1, and which thereby makes for different kinds of affinities between system characteristics. Can we find such examples?

They might be those where change is stretched out over a lengthier span of time, or when it stretches over a critical juncture at which basic affinities become disjointed and rearranged. Take the case of Germany at three different moments: before the middle of the nineteenth century, from the end of the nineteenth century until about 1945, and after 1955. At any of the three moments Germany had reached different institutional equilibria, and it would have been dubious to characterize it as a 'socially coordinated market economy' at these points; the differences between the points in time are too great to be captured by one and the same type. A sequence of different institutional equlibria, consisting of different combinations of institutions which cannot be captured by one type, has a grave consequence if we do not use an interpretivist and interactionist booster. It makes us finish up in quadrant C. In this case, erratic recombinations of institutions over time render NBS useless. Why could there be any purpose in national business systems if there is no concrete institutional stability? Faced with this galling prospect, let us examine how the more appealing position in quadrant D (NBS with a booster added on) can cope with socio-economic and political change over time.

In Prussia, clearly the most dominant German state after 1813 and notably 1866 until 1945, the first half of the nineteenth century was marked by the Stein–Hardenberg reforms which had a profound impact on economic institutions. They instituted freedom of trade and contractual liberty, doing away with guild privileges (Zunftzwang) and monopolies, and introducing differentiated but general taxation. These reforms were probably even more economically liberal than France's, which had kept some monopolies. From an antiquated state as far as liberal economic institutions were concerned, Prussia thus moved up to a front position alongside that of England. Needless to say, liberalization was not as forthcoming on the side of political participation and parliamentary rule.

When economic institutions of Germany are discussed and compared, scholars have come to type German capitalism as 'nonliberal' (see contributions in Streeck and Yamamura 2001). But the origin of German capitalism in the Prussian reforms, certainly as far as contractual freedom and abolition of guilds are concerned, is as liberally English and French as can be. There also later came a pervasive programme to privatize mines which, in Continental states, had been traditional prerogatives of rulers, property 'below the soil' mostly belonging to them and not being eligible for private transactions or acquisition. Prussian economic liberalization was indeed embedded in a 'fairly' absolutist state, although provincial estates had been established throughout the kingdom. But the political side of liberalism is not the issue, in the discussion of economic institutions; the latter were thoroughly liberalized. It is not correct, at least not for this formative period, to state that 'liberal alternatives were historically suppressed and nonliberal patterns were institutionalized' (see the chapter by Geoffrey Jackson in Streeck and Yamamura 2001: 123). Institutionalization started off on a track which was decidedly economically liberal, and Lehmbruch has made this quite clear, in line with socio-historical research (see his chapter in Streeck and Yamamura 2001: 48–9).

It could be radically liberal because it came as a revolution from above, rather than emerging gradually through 'disincorporation' (local abolition of guild privileges) in English towns, upon their own discretion, and in a country which outside towns hardly had any effective constraint to incorporate economic activities. It took an admirer of Adam Smith, Prime Minister Hardenberg, to enact economic liberalism systematically. It was therefore nonliberal only in its political contextuality, which is however not part of the definition. Contracting in England was de facto bound to common law or informal but effective conventions, and these may at the time have been as effective as more formal or statutory rules on the continent of Europe. The whole history of industrial relations in England proves this point (Pollard 1978: 150 ff.). It may have been liberal in terms of statute law, but this did not signify absence of effective constraints and resurgence of regulation or other constraints. We do not have any methodologically sound historical comparison which allows us to state whether de facto liberalization was more or less intensive over a longer time, when we compare, for example, Prussia and England at the beginning of the nineteenth century. Statute and common law in England have of course mostly been more individualistic, facilitating individual contracting rather than collective contracting. But collective regulation and contracting may also enhance individual contracting, that is, their relation is dialectical. Describing whole institutional sets as liberal or nonliberal may thus be problematic.

The viability of attaching labels, of liberal and nonliberal forms of capitalism, to whole societies and for lengthy periods, is contestable. In the characteristic fascination of social science with institutional end-states as desirable and coherent outcomes of diverse evolutions, an alternation between, or combination of, corporatism and liberalism has come to be considered 'schizophrenic', to use a term chosen fit to apply by Rokkan et al. (1970: 97). History is always schizophrenic in the sense of not being governed following one and the same mindset, and so are major movements and their fundamental ideas in practice.

Economic institutions did not remain dominated by liberal policies in Prussia, and the second half of the nineteenth century saw the rise of corporatism, not as a smooth continuation of medieval traditions but a reaction to economic crises. This reassertion of corporatist interests followed on from the currents that had also led to the earlier minor renaissance of guilds and crafts in Prussia, in 1845. In a significant dialectical twist, reassertion of corporatist interests thus has followed strong waves of liberalization, in both Prussia and the whole of Germany. This continues the peculiar Prussian dialectic of liberalism being imposed from above, to which artisanal and small industry strata reacted by grass roots drives back to corporatism, particularly when the economy took a turn for the worse.

But the reaction was not locked into a crafts and small firms context. For it was not abandoned by the capitalists and financiers of the new Empire, which they might have done as initially devout liberals or paternalists, focused on the well-being of 'their' enterprise rather than the wider economy. Of course, the populations of firms prevalent in the Germany of the boom period (Gründerjahre) after 1872 had become vastly different from 1848, which would have made cumulative liberalism all the more plausible: there was substantial investment into public infrastructure, and more concentrated mechanical, electrical, and chemical industries had either started a process of firm growth and concentration, or were preparing it. The boom phase after unification in 1872 was not long-lived and led on to a relative decline in the seventies. But again, it is far from a foregone conclusion that enterprises should try to escape a downturn on the basis of collective solidarity, rather than liberal enterprise individualism.

From then on, corporatism emerged on mainly two fronts, and it is also related to the emergence of collective bargaining between unions and employers' associations. One front was the revival of guild corporatism in the artisanal sector of the economy, where it had been strong before the onset of liberalism, and the other was cartellization, mainly in the more concentrated industries or for bulk or large-scale production types. Kocka (1978: 563) observed:

The disruptions to growth, and the fall in prices from 1873 to the mid-1890s led to a rapid increase in the number of concerns cooperating in cartels, beginning in the 1880s. . . . The agreements reached in these contracts were at first usually aimed purely at a common price policy; the cartel gained stability when it also regulated the quantities of production for each firm and conditions of distribution.

Next to American firms but probably earlier, German enterprises thus became cartel-building record-holders. It might also have developed there, but legislation moved against it more rapidly, whereas in Germany, it took another half a century for this to happen. From the literature, it is clear that cartels were in the first instance a defensive mechanism to assure survival in a time of recession.

But it is not self-evident, by the fact of recession alone, that firms should engage in cartelization as spontaneously and promptly as they did in Germany. Other equally plausible scenarios would be further increasing concentration and bankruptcy, even an 'end game' in which only the presumably 'fittest' survive. Competition law would not have precluded this at the time. There must have been an institutional and cultural memory, and/or a conception of enterprise in which a 'community of fate', as Weber would have called it, of an albeit restricted population of producers having to confront whatever challenges markets might hold in the present or an uncertain future, came to the fore again.

If a cartel was only defensive, it would quickly disband in an upswing. But nothing of the sort happened in Germany. '... cartels continued to develop in the upswing conditions prevailing after the mid-1890s; they even increased thereafter. They served to limit competition, stabilize prices and profits, and they tended towards a monopoly control of the market' (Kocka 1978: 563. See also Wengenroth in Vogt 2002: 356–7). While corporatism by cartelization has a ring to it, of exploiting the customer and consumer, its re-inventers also had in mind what Clark (1940) later called 'workable competition', that is, one which assured returns sufficient to invest into new products and channels of distribution. Now, if we term economic liberalism a market order that avoids collusion between actual or latent competitors, then the authors in Streeck and Yamamura (2001) are surely right in calling it nonliberal.

Now, cartels also became endowed with a more modern idea, the facilitation of investment on the basis of sufficient and stable returns and margins, and the necessity of innovation and expansion. The time when cartels became more dynamic in this way, was also one in which capitalism and markets became truly international. But as a reaction to internationalization, the Second Reich also started to pursue a policy of imposing customs duties on imported goods; customs were certainly mainly defensive of the statics of the domestic market order (Wengenroth in Vogt 2002: 358).

Cartelization was a policy used to achieve, not only domestic distribution of demand but also dynamic effectiveness in an international market. Some cartels were already international. But even if German firms applied cartelization only domestically, where presumably the possibility to transact and enforce such agreements was greater, if they pursued this policy in order to generate funds for expansion and product development abroad, then the cartel did not have a purely static role.

Nonliberal cartelization and corporatism were however the corollary of competing in international and free markets. From the end of the nineteenth century until well into the 1950s, it was typical for German firms to differentiate 'export' and 'standard' products or models. Export models or products had greater quality and were more expensive, and they targeted a more demanding or munificent slice of the market. This expressed the importance given to exporting as a generalized quality mark, and to mobilization of resources for 'differentiated quality' production, as a point of attraction in branding and production that the firm held out to customers (Streeck 1992: Chapter 1; see also Sorge and Streeck 1988).

The other front of resurgent corporatism was public organization and governance in the artisanal sector. In Germany, this sector has always been conceived as large, including the more 'noble' trades such as goldsmiths, watchmakers, and other makers of more luxurious goods, but also plumbers, bricklayers, sawyers, cartwrights, carpenters, decorator painters, shoemakers, and further suppliers of more mundane products and services. Artisanal trades were also quick to gain ground in technologically new areas, such as electrical and electro-mechanical applications. Furthermore, training in artisanal apprenticeship was by far the most important human resource generation pool for the emerging industrial firms.

> The most significant contribution of the artisan sector lay in the supply of skills to industry ... There was, then, no dual economy in the quality of labour ... The craftsman's contribution has tended to be disparaged because of the presumed anachronistic influence of guilds on economic growth .... But guild regulations interfered more with personal convenience than with economic development. (Lee 1978: 455–6)

In 1886, about 43 per cent of all journeymen trained in artisanal trades changed jobs to be employed in manufacturing (Stein 1975: 51). It is therefore not surprising that artisans had a solid lobby, for not only did they defend vested interests but were also a convenient producer of a large reserve army of skilled manpower that industry could tap into. After the Trades and Industry Statute of the North German Confederation, which had been continued into the new Reich, the government in 1897 thus brought in legislation that provided for obligatory incorporation of artisanal trades, obligatory apprenticeship and examination, as well as further training and examination for master craftsmen (großer Befähigungsnachweis) (Lee 1978: 456; also Stein 1975: 75).

What we witness here is an institutional division such that a more incorporated artisanate was governed by different institutions than industry and non-artisanal services. But the logic of this partitioning is that human resource generation and utilization meant a steady and remarkable flow from the artisanate to industry. In this, there has never been any fundamental change until the present day. And in this respect, the internal diversity of an institutional order is not simply random variance but systematically structured in a way that makes 'things fall into place': it is the institutional partitioning which has helped to define working careers, not to obstruct them. Rather than the retrograde and inflexible residue of a world gone by, which it was made out to be in some literature, the artisanate has remained a socialization and talent pool from which careers typically pointed in the direction of more modern industry, not as a convenient escape but as a continued evolution. Lee wrote (1978: 456):

The vociferous disputes about the privileges of artisan organization can too easily distract attention...from the fact that on balance, the achievement of the guilds—in fostering commercial honesty, in adapting rapidly to the unprecedented demands for skill in the course of industrialization, and above all in encouraging high educational levels—entitles them to be considered positive rather than negative influences on the supply of skilled labour.

By the turn of the century, an institutional order had thus been established which can be termed nonliberal, on the fronts of cartelization, industry level collective bargaining and neocorporatist organization for artisanal occupations, linked with an early and rapidly advancing build-up of obligatory social insurance. But this nonliberalism responded to experience with pervasive liberalism earlier on. It drew lessons from it, rather than having suppressed alternatives to liberalization. And societies draw lessons typically in this way, recombining things from the 'garbage can' of history such as to respond to new stimuli. This eventually led to a new synthesis of capitalism, corporatism, and mercantilism, such that capitalism not only competed with (older) corporatism that had been pushed back, but coevolved with a modernized corporatism. So did liberalism (large contractual freedom in industry and commerce) coevolve with segmental corporatism in the artisanate, and with 'cartel corporatism' in concentrated industries. Furthermore, the whole evolution not only has domestic aspects but strong international overtones or motives, and from a more defensive posture it went over to one of penetrating international markets. If someone had been asked to define a 'German model' in 1900, the answer would have been: economic coordination by cartels linked with collective bargaining, segmental corporatism complementing more liberal contracting, plus governmentally ordained compulsory social security.

This sort of 'German model' (1900 version) to a large extent continued, except that in the Weimar Republic in 1922, a dualist system of vocational education and training (linking apprenticeship with more pervasive day release to Berufsschulen, technical colleges) was instituted to cover not only handicrafts but industry, commerce, and other services. In this system, local chambers (of industry and commerce, handicrafts, etc.) set training schedules following national guidelines and took care of examination and certification. What had been an artisanal model of education and training thus spread to the rest of the economy, and to this extent the institutional partitioning was reduced. But artisanal education and training continued to form a major pool of industrial recruitment and careers, which was helped by some effort of parallel definition of artisanal and industrial trades (in building, mechanical and electrical engineering above all). The pattern of interlinked cartelization, collective bargaining, tripartite social security, and corporatism was thus strengthened.

These were the major alternatives that presented themselves for socio-economic institutions in the Federal Republic, the third historical moment to be considered. First, there was a choice between more liberal and nonliberal recipes. The purely domestic and more recent tradition, as outlined above, was leaning much more towards a nonliberal 'German model' in a mix of the 1890, 1922, or even 1934 versions, with cartels, macroeconomic planning, collective agreements, and nationalized 'key industries', notably coal and steel, with different emphasis depending on political persuasions. The feeling was very much that a destitute economy in need of reconstruction and confronted with neighbours more likely to strengthen borders than soften them, needed precisely this. Both those that drew their conclusions from misuse of capitalist power and those that sought to establish new legitimacy for it, thus initially had greater sympathies for planning and coordinated regulation. The employers and entrepreneurs went for cartels and corporatist regulation, the unions, Social Democrats but also parts of the Christian Democrats for nationalization and national economic and social planning.

All this was described by Djelic (2001), based upon a thorough inspection of documents. This was the scene that awaited what Djelic termed 'exporting the American model', that is, a much more liberal slant to economic institutions than recent nonliberal domestic models allowed for. The 'American model', favoured by military administration in the American Zone of Occupation (Bavaria, Hessen, Southern Baden-Württemberg, and the American sector of Berlin) was emphatic about dissolving cartels and large monopolists such as the IG Farben in chemicals, pharmaceuticals, coal, steel, and also banking, on free entrepreneurship, checks against 'restriction of competition', keeping economic planning and price controls to a minimum, and doing away with much of the corporatist apparatus that had been built up. It was the conjoined influence of American military government and Ludwig Erhard as one potent force among others in the CDU that tipped the balance in favour of 'importing the American model'.

Without American support and active involvement throughout the 1950s . . . Ludwig Erhard and his team would certainly not have been able to push for a restrictive cartel act. By providing material and intellectual support to a small group of West Germans ready to fight cartels, by helping to ground their institutional power, the Americans had in the end a significant impact on the West German anticartel debate. (Djelic 2001: 170)

By that token, the building of socio-economic institutions came to constitute a systematic break with the recent past. It can be compared with Napoleonic influence and the Prussian reforms at the beginning of the nineteenth century. And, as Djelic's analysis shows, nowhere in occupied, or rebuilding, Europe was this foreign influence as great as in Germany. Interestingly enough, what was later stylized as a 'German model' in 1978, was formatively subject to an influence radically opposed to recent German institutions, like no other except for the Napoleonic period and the Prussian reforms. At the time when the French nationalized all banks and enterprises that had collaborated with wartime Germany, and built up national planning, Germany was becoming more profoundly Americanized than any other country in Europe. How could a supposedly 'German model' originate in such a period? If one had asked observers, at the end of the 1950s, if they had noticed a 'German model' being put together, they would have taken this to be a cabaret joke.

Once again, it is essential to look at the partitioning of institutional spaces and the recombination of distinct institutional principles under new auspices. First, it is true that not only in the economic order but also in enterprise management, the post-war period in Germany was one of the most extensive americanizations that has occurred anywhere. Suddenly, Germany again became a model school boy of liberalism. Until Margaret Thatcher came to power, Britain excelled by a higher amount of state-owned enterprises and public responsibility in the economy, including a lengthier history of post-war economic

rationing and planning. Germany abolished cartels and denational-
ized enterprises, split up industrial groups already before the Federal
Republic was founded in 1949, and instituted the most elaborate
watchdog over the practice of competition and avoidance of monopolistic behaviour in Europe in 1957 (Bundeskartellamt). But this
liberalization focused on the order of markets, specifically commodity
rather than labour markets, and the behaviour of firms within them.
Characteristically, and following the approach of the ordo-liberal
school, it thus both enhanced and restricted contractual freedom, and
it restricted it to the extent that contracts might limit competition by
the formation of de facto monopolies.

Another part of institutional space affected by Americanization is
business and management behaviour. In his work on managers and
management in West Germany, Lawrence observed in company visits
a general reaction: managers were pleased to have learned lessons from
the United States, which can be described as a pragmatic but purpose-
ful, unconventional, sober, analytical approach. Status distinctions in
the enterprise became delegitimated, social conventions more critically
examined and adapted to help solve problems, unreflected practice
changed in line with a perceived functional rationale. Social relations and business practice were becoming less personalized and more
matter-of-fact (Lawrence 1980). But Lawrence had rightly wondered
whether this fascination with American practices was not related to
the urge to do two things at the same time: one is sincerely to leave
behind constraining vestiges of a Nazi Führerprinzip which had been
strengthened in companies, as well as older conventional methods.
The other is to legitimate in a new way some populist and more egalitarian codes that had evolved, rather continuously, under the auspices
of nonliberal populism and culminated under the Nazis. It will not
have been easy for social actors to distinguish such reflections, for
egalitarian populism was laden with both connotations, of American
and Nazi types of modernization. One of the major post-war normative conceptualizations of 'sound business and management practice',
which at the time absorbed the writings of prominent American gurus
such a Peter Drucker, was the Harzburger Modell which at the time
was certainly not presented as a 'German model' but as a universalistic
doctrine. This 'model' was developed under the leadership of a former
SS officer from war economy management (Reinhard Höhn).

On the side of business and management tools, much of European
post-war reconstruction was of course inspired by the Marshall Plan
(European Recovery Program), and this in turn implied, not only

direct relief and loans, but also a large scale drive to upgrade productivity in Europe. In all the countries participating, consultancies were set up to act as mediators between American methods of productivity increase and local firms in Europe. There was thus a systemic drive to align European firms on more American methods of management and production, in the expectation that this would lead to an economic growth feeding on both latent or suppressed consumption needs and more efficient production. Djelic's (2001: 146) analysis for France reads as if productivity development was indeed more of an 'imported' tool-box. For Germany, she shows that the RKW (Rationalisierungskuratorium der Wirtschaft) became active since 1950, as an official promoter of productivity thinking in the economy and an agency helping the Marshall Plan effort (2001: 180). However, the RKW was then far from new; it already existed before the War, under the same acronym but a slightly different title: Reichskuratorium für Wirtschaftlichkeit. For both Weimar industrialists and the Nazis had also thought of productivity development. Next to the RKW, there were a host of other national institutions (for work study and industrial engineering: REFA, for technical education in colleges and within-industry: DATSCH and DINTA). Before US multinationals invested more strongly in Europe, there was clearly no other place in Europe which could touch Germany for emulation of macroregulation and productivity-enhancing Fordism.

A part of a Nazi corporate architecture in the past, the rebaptized RKW now figured as a massive country-wide consultancy jointly supervised by employers and trade unions. It is difficult to tell whether productivity measures promoted by the RKW before and after the War differed greatly. The Marshall Plan permitted direct learning from more mechanized and sophisticated mass production operations that at that time were few and far between in Europe. The question still remains to what extent advanced American methods could be transferred to Europe without substantial adaptation and change. This is not to suggest that the RKW continued doing the same thing as before. But in all likelihood, it was a gradual change from Nazi productivity policies to Marshall Plan ones, and Germans will have found it easy and convenient to extol their enthusiasm for things American. This required little actual behavioural reorientation, and it was rewarded with approval by the new powers, because it was visibly consequential for successful practice.

Yet, twenty years after the promotion of American capitalism and management in a way which was singular in Europe, Germany became stylized as having economic and social institutions which were quite different from liberal capitalism. The elements and logic of recent corporatist capitalism in Germany have been eminently summarized by Streeck ((1997), as well as other contributions of this author cited therein). In addition, one needs to mention a network of cross-holdings of shares, between large industrial groups, to stabilize ownership interests in view of the possibility that outside interests might via the stock market attempt to buy an enterprise against the intentions of its management or core stakeholders (Windolf 1994). Bank participation in the share capital of those companies that it services with loans (Hausbank) is also part of this pattern, as is the practice of financing investment out of bank loans as far as possible, without incurring the risk of under-capitalization.

Altogether, the type of institutional order which sums up such characteristics is the 'socially coordinated market economy' following Whitley (1992, 2002). But it is doubtful whether it became socially coordinated in goods markets. What we find for Germany after 1945 is to some extent an intermediate order, between radical liberalization and neocorporatism, bringing in and integrating unions and employee representatives even more than in the past, and shedding the dictatorial vestiges of Nazism and the nonliberal heritage of the second Reich and the Weimar Republic. But a typification across the board is less helpful for a good explanation of what the business system means, or how its division of meaning is meaningful and perceived to be such, by actors. Partitioning of institutional space is again central. For the codetermined neocorporatism which extends over the generation and allocation of all types of productive resources has come to constitute a nonliberal complement to a new and very liberal order of goods markets. Actors set the institutional scene in such a way as to generate human and capital resources in a nonliberal way, in order to confront heightened competition in goods markets. The logic which binds such opposed and complementary forces together, into a meaningful ensemble, is set within a longer term tradition characterized by seesaw movements of liberalization and corporatist quasi-government, with visibly wide swings. This has led to a partitioned articulation of opposed principles. And this is a central mechanism of societal differentiation which is lacking in NBS to date.

This differentiation does not simply imply a splitting-up into institutional spheres, occupations, strata, etc. It is distinctive for a creative division of meaning such that different meanings are allocated parts of partitioned institutional space, but are nevertheless complementary and thus contributive to an overarching meaning. When actors intuitively or explicitly acknowledge this coherence and take it for granted, they enact societal community and identity.

There are two possible conclusions one can draw from this sort of analysis. One is that on closer inspection, there are no stable associations between types on different business system dimensions, and this is the conclusion one inevitably gets to in quadrant C of Figure 5.1. For there is no clear association between them in the long run, and if the long run does not count in NBS, then one might as well abandon it. But with the interpretivist-interactionist booster in quadrant D, NBS is launched in a powerful way. In this case, it does not depend unilaterally on stable long term association between types. The business system instead features noteworthy decoupling and recombination of institutions without losing its long term identity based on tightly coupled action systems in the slightest. In a long-term perspective, NBS must therefore abandon the tight coupling of institutions, substitute the tight coupling of action systems to maintain systemic coherence and in this way analyse the sequential engineering of different institutional combinations and temporary equilibria. Quadrant D thus facilitates the evolutionary explanation of business systems.

5.5. A Summary

This chapter has attempted to show that NBS is not usefully imagined as a theoretically monolithic approach. Taking systems analysis seriously, we can derive theoretical variants of NBS which have their strengths and weaknesses for different purposes. The currently dominant variants of NBS have their strengths in cross-sectional international comparisons. But to analyse evolutionary change, a variant is needed which seeks the integrity of business systems, not in the stability of finely grained typologies, but in the dialectical recombination of distinct types as the central mechanism for generating specific and temporally valid business systems. Further theoretical implications of such an approach are developed by Hull Kristensen (Chapter 13, this volume). To provide such an account, this chapter has taken a longitudinal approach, in order to show how meanings and institutions are differently combined over time. To permit a longitudinal treatment, there has been a focus on Germany. It might equally have been put on any other country. Despite the country focus, the underlying material has been assembled from cross-societal comparisons, or it has rested on a comparative assessment which is implicit. An integral treatment combining longitudinal and cross-sectional analysis is of course ideal, and I have tried to approximate the ideal somewhat, by providing observations that can withstand the test of intersocietal comparison although they focus on statements with regard to one country.

REFERENCES

Berger, Peter L. and Luckmann, Thomas (1971). *The Social Construction of Reality. A Treatise in the Sociology of Knowledge*. Harmondsworth: Penguin.

Burrell, Gibson (2002). 'Organization Paradigms'. In: A. Sorge (ed.), *Organization*. London: Thomson Learning, pp. 25–42.

Clark, John M. (1940). 'Toward a concept of workable competition'. *American Economic Review* 30: 241–56.

DiMaggio, Paul J. and Powell, Walter W. (1983). 'The Iron Cage Revisited: Institutional Isomorphism and Collective Rationality in Organizational Fields'. *American Sociological Review* 48: 147–60.

Djelic, Marie-Laure (2001). *Exporting the American Model. The Post-War Transformation of European Business*. Oxford: Oxford University Press.

Dore, R. (1973). *British Factory–Japanese Factory: The Origins of National Diversity in Industrial Relations*. London: Allen and Unwin.

Höpner, Martin (2003). *Wer beherrscht die Unternehmen? Shareholder value und Mitbestimmung*. Frankfurt a.M.: Campus.

Kocka, Jürgen (1978). 'Entrepreneurs and Managers in German Industrialization'. In: see Mathias and Postan (eds.), pp. 492–589.

Lawrence, Peter (1980). *Managers and Management in West Germany*. London: Croom Helm.

Lee, J. J. (1978). 'Labour in German Industrialization'. In: Mathias and Postan (eds.), pp. 442–91.

Leeuw, A. C. J. de (2000). *Bedrijfskundig Management. Primair Proces, Strategie en Organisatie*. Assen: Van Gorcum.

Lockwood, David (1964). 'Social Integration and Systems Integration'. In: G. K. Zollschan and W. Hirsch (eds.), *Explorations in Social Change*. London: Routledge & Kegan Paul, pp. 244–57.

Luhmann, Niklas (1972). *Soziologische Aufklärung. Aufsätze zur Theorie sozialer Systeme*, Vol. 1, 3rd edn. Opladen: Westdeutscher Verlag.

Mathias, Peter and Postan, M. M. (eds.) (1978). *The Cambridge Economic History of Europe. VII. The Industrial Economies: Capital, Labour and Enterprise. Part 1*. Cambridge: Cambridge University Press.

Maurice, Marc and Sorge, Arndt (eds.) (2000). *Embedding Organizations. Societal Analysis of Actors, Organizations and Socio-Economic Context*. Amsterdam: John Benjamins.

——, Sorge, Arndt, and Warner, Malcolm (1980). 'Societal Differences in Organizing Manufacturing Units. A Comparison of France, West Germany and Great Britain'. *Organization Studies* 1: 59–86.

——, Sellier, François, and Silvestre, Jean-Jacques (1982). *Politique d'éducation et organisation industrielle en France et en Allemagne. Essai d'analyse sociétale.* Paris: Presses Universitaires de France.

Münch, Richard (1980). 'Talcott Parsons und die Theorie sozialen Handelns II: Die Kontinuität der Entwicklung'. *Soziale Welt* 31: 3–47.

Oliver, Christine (1992). 'The Antecedents of Deinstitutionalization'. *Organization Studies* 13: 563–88.

——(1996). 'The Institutional Embeddedness of Economic Activity'. In: J. A. C. Baum and J. E. Duttton (eds.), *Advances in Strategic Management,* Vol. 13. New York: JAI Press, pp. 163–86.

Parsons, Talcott (1964). *The Social System.* New York/London: Free Press/Collier-Macmillan.

Pollard, Sidney (1978). 'Labour in Great Britain'. In: see Mathias and Postan (eds.), pp. 97–179.

Rokkan, Stein, Campbell, A., Torsvik, P., and Valen, H. (1970). *Citizens, Elections, Parties. Approaches to the Comparative Study of the Process of Development.* Oslo: Universitetsforlaget.

Sorge, Arndt (1985). *Informationstechnik und Arbeit im sozialen Prozess. Arbeitsorganisation, Qualifikation und Produktivkraftentwicklung.* Frankfurt a.M.: Campus.

——and Warner, Malcolm (1986). *Comparative Factory Organisation. An Anglo-German Comparison of Management and Manpower in Manufacturing.* Aldershot: Gower.

——and Streeck, Wolfgang (1988). 'Industrial Relations and Technical Change: The Case for an Extended Perspective'. In: R. Hyman and W. Streeck (eds.), *New Technology and Industrial Relations.* Oxford: Blackwell, pp. 19–47.

Stein, Claus-Dieter (1975). *Die Rolle von Staat und Unternehmern bei der Berufsbildung von Industriearbeitern in der Weimarer Republik.* Berlin: Free University, Dept. of History: Master thesis (Staatsexa-mensarbeit).

Streeck, Wolfgang (1992). *Social Institutions and Economic Performance. Studies of Industrial Relations in Advanced Capitalist Economies.* London, Newbury Park, New Delhi: Sage.

——(1997). 'German Capitalism: Does it Exist? Can it Survive?' In: C. Crouch and W. Streeck (eds.), *Policial Economy of Modern Capitalism. Mapping Convergence and Diversity.* London: Sage, pp. 33–54.

Streeck, Wolfgang and Yamamura, Kozo (eds.) (2001). *The Origins of Nonliberal Capitalism. Germany and Japan in Comparison.* Ithaca, NY and London: Cornell University Press.

Vogt, Martin (ed.) (2002). *Deutsche Geschichte. Von den Anfängen bis zur Gegenwart*. Frankfurt a.M.: Fischer Taschenbuchverlag.

Whitley, Richard (2002). 'Business Systems'. In: A. Sorge (ed.), *Organization*. London: Thomson Learning, pp. 179–96.

Whitley, Richard (ed.) (1992). *European Business Systems*. London: Sage.

Windolf, Paul (1994). 'Die neuen Eigentümer. Eine Analyse des Marktes für Unternehmenskontrolle'. *Zeitschrift für Soziologie* 23: 79–93.

6

Rethinking Path Dependency: The Crooked Path of Institutional Change in Post-War Germany

MARIE-LAURE DJELIC AND SIGRID QUACK*

6.1. Introduction

At the end of the Second World War, American occupying forces denounced the German tradition of cartelization and its contribution to the building up of Nazi power. While Germany was far from being the only European country with a tradition of cartelization, it was probably the country where the systematic organization of markets had gone furthest by the mid-1940s. Fifty years later, cartels have been all but formally outlawed from the German economy through, in particular, the double effect of a national anti-cartel act and of European competition law. At first sight, this suggests that, over a period of fifty years or so, the German regime governing competition has been radically reoriented. It has moved away from a deep mistrust of market competition (defined here as opposed to any form of collusion between competitors) and a marked preference for systematic inter-firm cooperation towards an overall endorsement of the liberal competition principle and a negative perception of cartelization.

A path dependency argument could see the mark here of one of those rare but critical junctures, where an institutional system or subsystem enters a radically new path, usually as a result of pressures external to the system itself. However, an analysis of the transformation of the German competition regime shows the limits of conventional path dependency approaches in trying to account for such an episode of institutional change. The end of Nazi Germany and

* In alphabetical order. We thank the editors of this volume for highly helpful comments and suggestions on this chapter.

the Occupation period were indeed critical junctures—but with respect to the competition regime, they did not 'set into motion institutional patterns or event chains (with) deterministic properties' (Mahoney 2000: 507). Rather they marked the starting point of an ad hoc clearing process that would generate a crooked path. We follow that path, step by step, to propose an alternative theoretical frame to approach institutional change—what we call here path generation.

We look at the fate of the German competition regime by comparing what happened in product markets, on the one hand, and in the banking sector, on the other. The comparison of those two cases is interesting because, in spite of quite similar starting conditions, outcomes were different. This type of comparison has the potential—as we try to show in the last part of the chapter—to generate theoretical insights on institutional change in general. In both cases, the initial impulse for regime change was exogenous—the initiative coming from the Allied occupation government. This initial impulse was, in both cases, an attempt to increase competition where cooperation had been the dominant principle governing inter-firm relations. Struggles and confrontation evolved over a period of nearly ten years. Muddling through, give and take, negotiations, small steps forward followed by moments of backlash characterized the paths in both cases. In the end, in the case of product markets, the crooked path ultimately led to a significant transformation of formal institutions—away from cartelization and towards oligopolistic competition. With respect to the banking sector, however, drastic formal changes, originally introduced by the Allied occupation government, did not prove stable and disappeared.

This chapter has three main parts. First, we tell the story of the transformation of the competition regime in German product markets. We turn next to describe what happened in the German banking sector. A comparison of developments in those two cases illustrates and reveals the limits of conventional path dependency accounts. Finally, in the discussion section, we draw from this comparison a number of theoretical insights about institutional development and change.

6.2. Transforming the Competition Regime in German Product Markets

We first consider the reordering of product markets in Germany after the Second World War as an illustration of a process of path generation. This case is interesting because it reveals a tension between change and persistence, between a break with the historically dominant legacy of cartelization and the persistence of coordinated market behaviour, albeit in different forms—through mergers, for example, or through bank shareholding in firms. It also reveals the importance of foreign influences.

6.2.1. *The legacy of the past: organized capitalism in inter-war Germany*

When Hilferding wrote in 1923 about 'organized capitalism' in Germany, he referred to a complex system of institutional mechanisms allowing German companies to control and stabilize their markets to a significant extent. The most important of such mechanisms were cartels, combines and the bank–industry nexus (see also Sorge, Chapter 5, this volume)—all of which had their origins in the last decades of the nineteenth century but had come into existence for different reasons.

A severe but relatively short slump following the industrial boom of the 1870s provided the impetus for the emergence of the first cartels as 'voluntary agreements between independent enterprises of a similar type to secure a monopoly of the market' (Liefmann 1938: 7). The cartelization movement, however, lasted well beyond this period, increasing in scale and scope in buoyant times as much as in more difficult ones (Djelic 1998: 54–5). The scope and stability of these cartels naturally differed considerably between sectors. Basic industries and raw materials were regulated by a few strongly organized and stable cartels. In the finished goods industries, on the other hand, cartels tended to involve larger numbers of firms and they usually proved more fragile. The collapse of a particular cartel agreement in those industries was usually followed by a period of cut-throat competition that itself triggered the crystallization of new cartel agreements.

From the end of the nineteenth century onwards, the development of horizontal cartels on a large scale was complemented by the emergence of ownership-based links between firms known as *Konzerne*. Liefman (1938: 225) defines the *Konzerne* as 'a merger of firms that remain juridically independent of one another into a single unit for the purposes of productive technique, administration, trading or (especially) finance'. A key difference between cartels and *Konzerne* was that whereas cartels were on the whole horizontal associations aiming to limit and control competition between firms operating in similar product markets, *Konzerne* had often a vertical dimension or would even bring together firms from unrelated industries to which financial and banking partners could be added. According to Kocka and Siegrist (1979: 91–4) the first *Konzerne* were created in order to overcome bottle-necks in the supply chain and to counterbalance deficits in the technical and financial infrastructure of Germany at that time. The economic disruptions following the First World War were fertile ground for the multiplication of such combines. By 1927, the top one hundred corporations in Germany were practically all *Konzerne* (Siegrist 1980: 87–8 as mentioned in Herrigel 1996: 95).

The bank–company nexus similarly increased in importance from the last quarter of the nineteenth century and changed its nature and form significantly. Up to the end of the nineteenth century, large private banks acted predominantly as commercial banks (Quack 2004) and sought to limit their lending risk by encouraging companies to obtain long-term finance on capital markets. Banks would hold a portion of the securities they underwrote but these holdings were generally seen as temporary, waiting for buyers that could offer a reasonable price. At that time, banks would only rarely transform frozen credit into shareholdings (Edwards and Olgivie 1996; Vitols 2001: 8).

Links between banks and companies became much tighter with the economic crises of 1923–4 and 1929–33. German banks increasingly turned to transforming frozen credits into long-term industrial shareholdings as a way to save and stabilize companies that had run into trouble (Höpner and Krempel 2003). At the end of the Weimar Republic, German banks had gained a central position as mainsprings of national industrial policy. This position reflected the multiplicity of their roles as 'supervisory board members, creditors, share owners, organizers of consortiums, and executors of the voting rights of dispersed share owners' (Höpner and Krempel 2003: 8). The combination of these roles made German banks important intermediaries in the market for corporate control. But German banks were not only owners and providers of capital. For many German firms, they were also a source of stability and a buffer against competition and its consequences. This stability was reinforced by the long-standing tradition within the German banking sector of regulating competition through gentlemen's agreements. Initiated by professional associations, a number of these agreements or cartels were in time to be made compulsory by the state.

By the end of the 1930s, cartels and combines had proliferated and the links between banks and industrial companies had become extremely dense. Faced with recurrent economic crisis,

German politicians, lawyers, and economists had come increasingly to regard competition as potentially disruptive to the social order. They welcomed 'organized capitalism' as progress. While criticisms of cartels and their impact during the hyperinflation of 1923 led to a decree against abuses of cartels, this did not change the generally positive attitude in Germany to cartelization as a form of market coordination. Towards the end of the Weimar Republic, cartels increasingly became state regulated. Particularly during the Great Depression, the German government started to use compulsory cartels as a means of stabilizing industries facing crises—the banking sector being there an interesting illustration. Faced with the banking crisis of 1931, the Weimar government authorized the banking associations to set up a compulsory cartel on debit and credit interest rates.

During the Nazi period, a law on the formation of compulsory cartels was promulgated on 15 July 1933, becoming the basis for governmental intervention and state-led economic planning until the Second World War. Under the rigid centralized control put in place during the war, cartels were often not in the position to pursue and achieve their objectives. Voigt (1962: 187) states that at the end of the war the total number of cartels had declined to 650 'a large number of which were nothing more than mere shells'. Many of these shells, however, would become quickly revitalized, particularly in those industries that had been previously strongly cartelized. Attitudes towards the legitimacy of cartels as a means of economic coordination would prove deeply entrenched in a whole generation of business leaders that was soon to resume responsibility after the end of the war.

6.2.2. *The long post-war struggle for a German competition law*

A widely shared conviction that cartels and large combines had played an important role in the rise of the Nazi regime in Germany led the military governments at the Potsdam Conference to agree that German industry should be decartelized and deconcentrated after the war. Allied anti-cartel laws issued in 1947 prohibited cartels, combines, syndicates, or trusts (Damm 1958). On the American side, they grew out of the long-standing American antitrust tradition and reflected significant concerns about the role played by international cartels in undermining and even harming US security and defence before and during the Second World War (Berghahn 1986: 85; Djelic 1998: 82–3).

The British and French military governments followed the US policy of forbidding cartels as a means of destroying German war capacity. Their attitude towards cartel agreements—that were also common practice in Britain or France—was nevertheless much more lenient.

In 1949, the occupation statute was signed and Germany was allowed to return progressively to sovereignty. The American government insisted, however, that certain fields, among them decartelization and financial decentralization, would remain under the full control and scrutiny of the newly created Allied High Commission that took over at the end of the period of military government (Horstmann 1991: 192). In the treaty allowing Germany to return progressively to sovereignty, the American government demanded that German agencies prepare and submit their own competition law. This law, however, would replace the 1947 Allied legislation only after being fully validated and accepted by Allied authorities. The United States, and to a certain degree the United Kingdom, were thus in a position to exert significant influence on West German legislation, through political and economic coercion, including after the foundation of the Federal Republic of Germany in September 1949. This remained the case at least until the end of the occupation regime in 1954 (Djelic 1998: 81).

American policy makers were aware that radical transformations of the sort they were fostering would survive only if Germans actively appropriated them. From the beginning, the American military administration in Germany had tried to identify those Germans that would be sympathetic to their goals and thinking on and around competition. They found Eberhard Günther, who had been in charge of monitoring cartel agreements within the Ministry of Economics during the Weimar Republic. They also came to work with a number of 'ordo-liberal' economists, like Franz Böhm or Alfred Müller-Armack. The 'Freiburg school', with which those men were associated, had formulated in the 1930s an economic programme that was then highly heterodox in the German context. Ordo-liberals believed that competition, if nurtured and protected by a tight legal framework, was a basic precondition of political democracy. Early on, Americans had also identified Ludwig Erhard, at the time a relatively unknown professor of economics who had been in close contact with the Freiburg school for a number of years, as a potential local relay. In 1948, the Americans appointed Erhard chairman of the newly constituted German Economic Council (*Deutscher Wirtschaftsrat*).

As Economic Minister of the Federal Republic of Germany from 1949 onwards, he became a central figure in mediating between the demands of the American military government in Germany on one side and German resistance and opposition on the other. Erhard himself favoured a law that would combine strict opposition to cartels with a much more lenient approach to concentrations of economic power (Djelic 1998: 109–10). This, in fact, placed him close to the American antitrust tradition and to the position at the time of American occupation authorities.[1] His vision of a social market economy (*soziale Marktwirtschaft*) relied on a combination of large-scale firms and efficient competition that together would drive the German economy towards US-type consumer capitalism (Berghahn 1985: 185; Erhard 1958: 169–71).

During the early period of the drafting process, between 1949 and 1953, Erhard could count on the support of the Christian Democratic Party. He could also rely on representatives of the Liberal Party and, of course, he could turn if needed to the Allied High Commission. Within German industry, the retail trade sector and parts of the small and medium-sized business community—those represented in particular in the Association of Entrepreneurs (*Arbeitsgemeinschaft selbständiger Unternehmer*, AsU)—were in principle supportive of a ban on cartels. These actors hoped that such a ban could protect them against pressures from big business (Berghahn 1986). Nevertheless, even within those groups, the legitimacy of cartels was still deeply entrenched and it was acknowledged that there were necessary, or at least acceptable, exemptions (Hüttenberger 1976: 294; Robert 1976: 175).

Overall, though, support in Germany for Erhard's position was small and marginal. The majority of German business leaders were fiercely opposed to a ban on cartels (Hüttenberger 1976: 294; Robert 1976: 375–81). In spite of the 1947 Allied laws, there was informal coordination of market behaviour after the war that was quite reminiscent of inter-war cartelization. This was particularly so in those industries where pre-war cartels had been strong—raw materials, production, and investment goods industries. Opposition against any kind of cartel legislation was most likely to be found in these sectors (Voigt 1962: 188). But the opinion that cartels were necessary and

---

[1] This was the reason why a first German draft, written by a team of ordo-liberal experts and presented in 1949 to Erhard, was quickly filed away. This so-called 'Josten draft' was not only criticized by German business leaders who were against a strict prohibition of cartels. It was also in fact rejected by Erhard and the Americans on the grounds that it called for strong political and legal intervention in order to prevent concentrations of economic power (Robert 1976: 112–3).

legitimate ways to coordinate market strategies of firms was popular and widespread, well beyond those industries. Before the war, small and medium-sized firms in many industries, including mechanical engineering and consumer goods, had found protection behind cartel agreements. Price, term-fixing, and specialization agreements allowed weaker players to survive, protecting them in fact from the efficiency and productivity of larger firms. After the war, some of those smaller firms feared that a general prohibition of cartels would mean the end of such protection and trigger a process of concentration that would make it difficult for them to survive (Herrigel 1996: 172).

As soon as industry associations became re-established in the late 1940s and early 1950s they began to lobby fiercely. In particular, the Federal Association of German Industries (*Bundesverband Deutscher Industrien*, BDI) under the leadership of Fritz Berg became a vocal opponent of Erhard's project. The BDI argued that time was not yet ripe for a German economy fully based on the competition principle and that a prohibition of cartels would hamper economic reconstruction. Instead, the BDI favoured a legislation modelled on the double principle of abuse control and self-government by industry, as known from the Weimar Republic (Braunthal 1965; Damm 1958; Djelic 1998). On a more pragmatic level, the BDI and its sectoral member associations lobbied throughout the drafting process for exemptions and exceptions. Industry associations exerted constant pressure through direct contacts with specific ministries (i.e. finance or transport). They also lobbied elected representatives of the Parliament (*Bundestag*) and members of the upper house (*Bundesrat*). They pushed the idea that export, crises, rationalization, or specialization cartels were necessary and suggested that certain sectors should be fully exempted (Robert 1976: 181–5).[2] After long debates, the Economic Ministry finally submitted draft legislation to Parliament in 1952. The massive opposition stemming from business communities, however, and their active lobbying, meant that discussions of the bill were still pending at the time of the elections in October 1953.

Following the elections, a new attempt was made to reach an agreement. Ludwig Erhard created an ad hoc commission that brought together officials from the Ministry of Economic Affairs and a few

---

[2] In the pursuit of their aims, members of this camp did not hesitate to use rather crude methods of lobbying. For example, they threatened to reduce their campaign contributions for the 1953 elections and launched a virulent media campaign against Erhard, whom they accused of acting on American orders (Erhard 1963: Chapter 16).

members of the BDI. At the same time he attempted to tighten the links with those groups of industry (particularly the AsU and parts of the consumer goods industry) that did not benefit so much from cartels and were therefore more willing to accept a prohibition. Representatives of these groups became increasingly vocal from 1954 onwards, challenging the dominant position of the BDI and its leader Fritz Berg (Berghahn 1986; Braunthal 1965). In 1954, for example, a group of business leaders representing companies such as the Margarine-Verkaufs-Union, Württembergische Metallwarenfabrik, Krupp, Klöckner, or Mannesmann, sent an open letter to the Economic Minister where they argued that a prohibition of cartels was not necessarily negative for the German economy and that the BDI was far from representing the opinion of all its members (Robert 1976: 251–2).

The ad hoc commission finally agreed on a revised version in 1955. Erhard had insisted on the prohibition principle—the revised bill included a prohibition of cartels largely similar to the provisions of the Sherman Act—but had accepted a number of exceptions to the prohibition clause. Most of those exceptions had been proposed by industry representatives already during the first legislation period. The bill was presented to the Bundestag in 1955. Hostilities between the opposing camps were immediately reopened. Pressure now came not only from industry, but also from other ministries and politicians, in particular from some members of the Christian Democratic Party (Robert 1976: 371). With the end of the occupation regime in 1954, the threat of direct imposition of a law by the Americans was not so credible anymore. This allowed the opponents of a clear prohibition principle to exert more influence in the drafting process than before. Furthermore, in the course of the early 1950s, mergers between large companies brought the retail sector as well as small and medium-sized companies increasingly into opposition to a strict prohibition of cartels because they felt such legislation would be directed exclusively against them. In consequence, Erhard lost the support of a strong group that in the early 1950s had been an important ally (Hüttenberger 1976: 107). Hence, he had to accept a few more changes before the Law against Restraints on Competition (*Gesetz gegen Wettbewerbsbeschränkungen*, GWB) was finally passed in 1957.[3]

---

[3] The German Law against Restraints on Competition (*Gesetz gegen Wettbewerbsbeschränkungen*) is cited in the following in the version of 27 July 1957, as reprinted in Lehnich (1958: 89–127).

6.2.3. GWB: Magna Carta for change or a text hiding continuity?

At the end of the seven year-long fight for a German antitrust act, the result appeared at first sight significant. The Law against Restraints on Competition (abbreviated in German to GWB (*Gesetz gegen Wettbewerbsbeschränkungen*)) represented, at least formally, a clear departure for the German product markets from the legacy of economic coordination through cartelization. Cartel agreements with restrictive effects on competition were declared null and void (§ 1) and a newly created Federal Cartel Office (*Bundeskartellamt*) was in charge of monitoring obedience and pursuing offences and behaviours illegal under the GWB frame (§ 48).

The law, however, included a number of exceptions. These were essentially of two types. First, certain types of agreements were excluded from the general ban (§§ 2 – 7 GWB). Among these were term-fixing, rebate, and specialization agreements that had merely to be notified to the Federal Cartel Office. This type of exceptions reflected a compromise with the small and medium-sized business community. Structural crisis cartels and export cartels were also exempted from the general ban. The latter not only had to be notified, though, they also had to be approved by the Federal Cartel Office. Furthermore, the law gave the Economics Ministry full authority to allow cartels in exceptional circumstances, when the national interest or public welfare called for limits to competition (§ 8, section 1 GWB). Second, industries in which full market competition was not considered as appropriate or possible, were excluded entirely from the area in which the law was operative. This included the public sector (§ 98 GWB), transport and communication (§ 99), agriculture and forestry (§ 100), the banking and insurance sector (§ 102) and utilities (§ 103) (Voigt 1962: 191).

Although GWB created a space for exceptions, the general prohibition of price and quota cartels, as well as the establishment of a federal agency in charge of monitoring and, if necessary, sanctioning violations of the law, did affect the business behaviour of German companies—even though with considerable delay in many cases. It prevented, in particular, the re-emergence of thousands of cartels that had structured the economy during the inter-war period (Nawrocki 1973: 105). The overall number of cartel agreements, as registered with the Federal Cartel Office, remained low during the following decades.[4]

---

[4] During the period 1958–60 the Federal Cartel Office received 189 applications for cartel agreements (Voigt 1962: 195). In 1972, 212 cartel agreements were registered with the Federal

According to contemporary observers—even those who were rather critical of the exemptions associated with the law—during the first years of its existence the German legislation led to more fairness in competition and freedom in decision-making in many industries. The investment and expansion strategies of most companies were no longer driven by the 'cartel rhythm' that had been so characteristic of inter-war Germany (Voigt 1962: 204).

At the same time, the German law could not prevent companies from searching for ways to bypass it. This was made easy in fact by the formulation of § 1 that left informal cartel agreements and collusive behaviour outside the reach of the Federal Cartel Office. Neither was the law prepared to deal adequately with issues of misuse or abuse of economic power. Those issues arose in the late 1950s, together with increasing economic concentration (Nawrocki 1973; Voigt 1962).[5] During the 1960s, the Federal Cartel Office used information and persuasion to try and influence business attitudes. This was met with considerable reservation. In the early 1970s, cartel-friendly attitudes were still not exceptional within the German business community. This led the Federal Cartel Office in the 1970s to fine heavily a number of companies that had been shown to have violated the GWB (Nawrocki 1973: 103).

The impact of the GWB on company strategy and behaviour was therefore often not direct or immediate. Rather, it followed upon a long process of confrontation and contestation between different actors with opposing interests. Throughout this process, it was not always clear, who would have the upper hand. At critical points, the champions of cartel prohibition and in particular the Federal Cartel Office, were bolstered and helped by the development, in parallel, of a European competition regime. In some cases, the Federal Cartel Office even sought the active support of European competition institutions (Quack and Djelic 2005). The overall outcome of this more long-term process of normative and cognitive transformation was that cartel-like behaviour gradually and increasingly became regarded as inadequate and illegitimate by politicians, lawyers, and business leaders in Germany.

The slow move away from a legacy of cartelization in German product markets can be construed as a systematic break with the past. Whereas in the inter-war period product markets in Germany

Cartel Office in Germany the majority of which were export, term-fixing and specialization cartels (Nawrocki 1973: 119).

[5] The 1973 reform of the GWB dealt with those weaknesses. It extended the prohibition of cartels to collusive behaviour, improved the control of misuse of economic power and introduced a systematic control of mergers (Nawrocki 1973 : 111–2).

were predominantly governed by cartelization, the post-war period saw a significant move to a liberal market order in this area. Collusion between actual or potential competitors became not only prohibited by law but also increasingly regarded by a growing number of economic and societal actors as an inappropriate strategy to achieve a leading position in national and international markets. Among business leaders this reorientation was not only facilitated by a younger generation of managers taking over responsibility in the 1960s and 1970s (Berghahn 1986) but also by the strong impact of American management methods on German enterprise management (Djelic 1998).

Change, though, did not preclude continuities and the persistence of inter-firm coordination through other means in post-war Germany. One partial bridge with the past can be found in the growth of large German combines in the 1960s and 1970s, at this point often in the form of legally merged entities. Another element of partial continuity, at least up until the 1990s, was the stabilization, or even expansion, of the German company network linking German firms with financial institutions (Beyer 1998; Streeck and Höpner 2003; Windolf and Beyer 1995; Windolf and Schief 1999).

It would be misleading, however, to regard the evolution of the post-war company network in Germany as a modern substitute for the industrial cartels of the inter-war period (see also Shonfield 1977 [1965]: 254). Whereas cartels were directed at limiting the exposure of member firms to product market competition, the German company network can be seen as directed towards improving the competitiveness of its individual member firms in liberal (and increasingly internationalizing) product markets. It did so in a double sense: on the one hand, by providing flows of information on investment, technological development and market strategies it created opportunities for indirect coordination between firms of the same or related industries in Germany (Windolf and Beyer 1995: 24)—even though only rarely between direct competitors (Schönwitz and Weber 1982: 102). On the other hand, large blocs of cross-shareholding protected its member firms—at least well into the 1990s—from hostile takeovers and short-term capital market pressures (Höpner and Krempel 2003).

Hence, in our view, it is not sufficient to point to the continuities in structural, financial and personal inter-firm linkages. Instead a qualitative analysis of which actors attempted to regulate which kinds of competition with what kinds of results during distinct periods would be necessary. Höpner and Krempel (2003) show that the motivations and logics behind apparent continuities in inter-firm linkages have changed considerably over the last century. Their results indicate that links between companies, like other institutions, can be used as tools for different objectives and can mean different things in different periods. In particular, the conditions of emergence of those links may have little to do with their contemporary functionalities. The idea here is that behind stable labels and formal *façade*, institutional arrangements may be drifting progressively, changing quite significantly through time both in meaning and impact (Streeck and Thelen 2005: 36).

Altogether, a progressive but clear break in the dominant order of product markets—away from cartelization and towards liberalization and competition—has combined in the post-war period in German product markets with continued and reinvented forms of social coordination (this was the case also in labour markets, see Sorge, Chapter 5, this volume). Ironically, this unique combination can be seen as highly structuring of what was identified in the 1970s as a specific German model of production. In this respect, the Law against Restraints on Competition fostered an early move of German firms towards modernized forms of inter-firm coordination in liberalized product markets, which in other European countries did not take place before the 1990s (Lilja and Moen 2003: 158).

6.3. The Post-War Reorganization of the Competition Regime in the Banking Sector

Comparing the story of the German competition regime in product markets with what happened in the banking sector during the same period reveals both similarities and differences. In both cases, the initial impulse was exogenous—the initiative for change came from the Allied occupation government. In both cases, it is difficult to identify a moment or an event that could represent the type of critical juncture so important in path dependency arguments. Struggles and confrontations evolved over a period of nearly ten years and what appeared at one point in time as being a step in the direction of change could lead only a short time afterwards to severe backlash—and vice versa. In spite of similarities, however, outcomes in the longer run emerge as quite distinct.

In the case of product markets, the crooked path ultimately led to a significant transformation of formal institutions, that itself triggered and was reinforced by a progressive reorientation of economic actors away from cartelization and towards oligopolistic specialization. In the banking sector, on the other hand, quite drastic formal changes, originally introduced by the Allied occupation government, did not prove stable and were progressively displaced. The strength and coherence of German opposition combined with an evolving geopolitical context and a highly constrained and constraining local financial system to deflect and tame changes. Core actors of the German banking sector managed to defend and maintain cartelization in the financial sector well after the 1958 law prohibited cartelization in most industries and product markets.

6.3.1. *The allied banking project for Germany—a bone of contention*

The role and behaviour of German banks during the Nazi period was a sensitive issue after the Second World War—on a par with cartels and industrial concentration. The American government and its military administration in Germany wanted to severely punish German banks. They were also highly critical of the structure of the German banking system. Growing unrest, rumours about a currency reform and questions about the viability of the credit system made a reform of the banking system an urgent issue. When Joseph Dodge, an American banker, was put in charge of financial and banking policy within the American military government (OMGUS) in September 1945, it was high up on his agenda. Dodge favoured a far-reaching restructuring and decentralization of the German banking sector. OMGUS's programme for a 'democratic and demilitarized banking system' aimed at the introduction of more competition in the German banking sector through dissolution of the large private banks, the separation of investment from credit banking and a limitation of interlocking directorates between banks and industrial combines. Dodge viewed these measures as 'an integral part of our program to ensure that the German financial hierarchy will never play any part in disturbing the peace of the world' (cited in Horstmann 1991: 64). A novel banking structure should be established that was, here again, to be modelled upon the American experience (Holtfrerich 1995: 461).

The Dodge plan met considerable opposition in the Allied Control Council—the supreme allied authority body. The British military government was highly sceptical of a decentralization of the German banking system. It would not agree to any such measure as long as there was no mechanism set up allowing for a redistribution of financial flows between the different military zones. The Soviet military government opposed the American plans on the grounds that the currency reform should come before a reform of the banking system. In October 1946, the chairman of the Allied Control Council acknowledged that no agreement would be reached. Military governors were left to proceed as they wished in their respective zones of occupation (Holtfrerich 1995: 469; Horstmann 1991: 93).

Within the American zone, OMGUS sought German supporters of the Dodge plan. With very few exceptions, reactions among members of the Länder governments were quite negative.[6] Ludwig Erhard, then Economics Minister in the Land of Bavaria, rejected the Dodge plan uncompromisingly. The arguments advanced by German politicians were generally in line with the contents of a memorandum that had been prepared by representatives of the large German private banks. This memorandum had reached the Southern Länder governments already in October 1946—a sign that large German banks had early on begun to lobby German politicians with a view to prevent changes in the German banking system (Holtfrerich 1995: 472). The claim was that the German unified and universal banking system corresponded to the structure of the overall economy and therefore could not be dissolved into parts without endangering the stability and liquidity of that economy as a whole. Furthermore, a functioning system of banking credit was seen as crucial precondition for the reconstruction of the German economy (Horstmann 1991: 99).

Still, the threat that OMGUS would impose a law was real. Hence, governments of the Länder in the American zone prepared draft legislation for a decentralization of the banking system. In January 1947, central banks were set up in each Land within the American zone. Representatives of the private banks, however, objected to any cooperation with the Americans. In reaction, OMGUS issued an order in March 1946 launching decentralization for the private banks and making it clear that any informal contact across Land borders between branches of the same bank was illegal and would be punished (Horstmann 1991: 105). The governments of the Länder tried to

[6] The Land of Baden-Würrtemberg was the only one signalling cautious support of the Dodge plan. The Finance Minister, Dr Fritz Cahn-Garnier, himself a victim of persecution under the Nazi regime, and Otto Pfleiderer, head of department in the finance ministry, believed that decentralization of the banking system was an important dimension of political federalism. Pfleiderer also argued that a banking reform was a necessary 'complement to the policy of decartelization' (cited in Horstmann 1991: 107).

convince private banks to collaborate with OMGUS. Those attempts, however, were unsuccessful. In May 1947, the American military government came up with one more piece of legislation. Law no. 57 appointed state commissioners in charge of decentralization for each of the large private banks.

From 1947 onwards, Western occupying powers started talking about the possibility of having a bi- or trizonal central bank. The British military government was particularly convinced that this would be a mechanism facilitating the redistribution of financial flows across occupation zones. As a concrete result of these discussions, the Bank of German Counties (*Bank Deutscher Länder*) and the Allied banking commission started operating in Frankfurt in February 1948. As a counterpart, the British (and French) military governments agreed to a decentralization of private banks at the Land level in their zones also. Thus, by April 1948, it seemed as if key features of the Dodge plan were becoming reality in the three Western zones. The Reichsbank had been replaced by a federal system of central banks at the Land level. Out of the three large private German banks, thirty formally independent banks had been created. Both central and private banks could only operate within the borders of a Land. Apparently, the decentralization of the German banking sector had been achieved. The legal liquidation of the old private banks, however, proved difficult to implement because it required the cooperation of all four Allied governments. Opposition against a speedy liquidation did not only come from the Russian military government. There was resistance as well on the British side, and, of course within the German banking community.

6.3.2. *Reconcentration of the German banking sector*

In fact, there was hardly anybody within that community supporting the American decentralization plan. Top managers in large private banks had been suspended and often arrested by the Allied governments immediately after the war. Regional managers took over responsibility in the new local and decentralized banks and, in the American zone, state commissioners appointed by OMGUS had complete power. When they came back from captivity and de-nazification camps, however, the old German banking elites re-asserted their leadership. Soon, links and cooperation between banks across Land borders were re-established on an informal (and illegal) basis. At Deutsche Bank, for example, members of the pre-1945 board of directors started to meet again informally from 1947, sending out instructions on important issues to all decentralized units. One of those board members, Hermann J. Abs, had been in close contact since 1946 with the British military government. He became subsequently a key figure in the mobilization of private banks against a decentralization of the German banking sector (Holtfrerich 1995: 481–2).

At Dresdner Bank, the 'old circle' met regularly from mid-1948 onwards and secret messengers were circulating with information and money between the different Länder and military zones (Horstmann 1991: 178–9). Management through informal channels was made possible by the loyalty of regional managers to their previous 'mother bank'. Similarly, a number of the state commissioners appointed by the American military government had previously been active in the banking sector and sympathized openly or silently with a recentralization of private banks. Politicians as well as public opinion at the time were fully in agreement with the banking community. The decentralization of the banking sector was unpopular almost everywhere. Unlike in the competition field, where the ordo-liberals played a significant role, the Americans were unable to find supporters for their banking policy.

In 1950, the year when the Federal Republic of Germany was founded, Hermann J. Abs and Wilhelm Vocke, the president of the directorate of the *Bank Deutscher Länder*, presented their own propositions for the future of the German banking sector. A massive press campaign supported this German plan that opposed the American program and had the backing of German politicians, independent of party affiliation. A first victory for this German opposition came soon. The British military government sent a special memorandum to the financial committee of the Allied High Commission. This memorandum integrated in modified form the proposal of Hermann J. Abs for a revival of the large private German banks (Horstmann 1991: 211).

This led to heated controversies between the three Western powers that proved impossible to reconcile. As a result, Allied financial consultants formally called upon the German Minister of Finance, in March 1950, to develop a plan for the restructuring of the banking sector. In contrast to the equally unresolved reordering of the iron and steel industry, or of I. G. Farben, the initiative for future planning in the banking sector was handed over to the German side. This opportunity was quickly taken up by German bankers and politicians. In March 1952, a German law came into force that allowed a recombination of banking activities into three independent banks covering larger areas of the newly formed Federal Republic of Germany.[7] During parliamentary debates, members of the social-democratic and liberal parties argued for a full reconcentration of the banking sector. This was considered, however, politically unrealistic by the German government (Horstmann 1991: 281).

Of course, debates in Parliament did not go unnoticed amongst Allied representatives in Germany. When the draft legislation was submitted for approval in March 1952, the Allied High Commission formally demanded a reassurance that the three-banks model would not be immediately questioned itself. The government of the Federal Republic of Germany issued a secrete declaration of obligation (*Verpflichtungserklärung*). On 27 March 1952, in a letter to the Allied High Commission, Konrad Adenauer declared that the three-banks model would remain stable for the three years following enactment of the law. Geographical extension, in particular, of the domain of each bank was ruled out. Furthermore, the Finance Minister issued a declaration promising a reform of the right of banks to represent minority shareholders for whom they hold the shares (Horstmann 1991: 283).

Representatives from the private banks, however, were only waiting for the next opportunity to recombine further and to turn their three large banks into a single bank unified at the Federal level. When the Federal Republic of Germany regained full sovereignty in May 1955, this was immediately followed by calls from the private banks to remove the banking law. The drafting process for a new legislation started early in 1956, influenced by the suggestions of the German private banks. The law was passed rapidly without debates and with unanimous voting by the German parliament on 12 December 1956. It allowed for a recombination along the lines of the former banking groups starting in January 1957—the first possible date according to Adenauer's secrete declaration (Horstmann 1991: 294).

When compared to the original American plans for a reorganization of the German banking sector, the outcomes of the actual reform process appeared quite limited at the end of the 1950s. Instead, one finds significant evidence of continuity with respect to the structure and functioning of the German banking system across and beyond the Nazi period and the Second World War. The early American proposition to separate credit and investment banking had altogether disappeared

---

[7] *Gesetz über den Niederlassungsbereich von Kreditinstitutionen, Großbankengesetz.*

from the agenda. The same thing could be said of the plan to reduce
and limit industrial shareholdings by German banks. Since the 1952
law, it was apparently accepted that the managers of large banks were
the ones to be in charge of a reordering of the banking sector. This
meant, in fact, that those who were making the decisions and planning 'reform' were the very men who had been ruling the industry
before and during the Second World War. The 1956 legislation, finally,
meant the full re-establishment of universal large private banking in
Germany — nearly at the same time as the long-lasting struggle for a
competition law came to an end with a significant impact there on
formal rules of the game.

One important factor that could explain in part the failure of the
ambitious American plan was the absence of liquid and large-scale
stock markets. Banks were the only external providers of capital in
post-war Germany. In that context, attempts to split banks into small
units with little financial power and to detach them from their traditional ownership and personal links to industry were bound to be
unpopular and to generate resistance. All the more so that, after 1948,
the reconstruction of the German economy called for a joint mobilization of economic and financial resources. And this joint mobilization
was in fact being encouraged by the United States for geopolitical
reasons.

6.3.3. *Cooperation and competition in the German banking sector*

Overall, continuity defines the German banking sector in the period
after the Second World War. Since the financial crisis of the 1930s, the
German banking sector had been governed by cartel agreements that
included recommendations on interest rates. Soon after the Second
World War, banks and banking associations pleaded for a continuation
of these sector-specific restrictions on competition. Their main argument was that free competition in the banking sector would quickly
undermine the stability and security of the overall financial system.
The authorities in charge of bank supervision in the different Länder
generally accepted this argument and declared cartel agreements in
that sector valid in principle (Hausleutner 1970: 47–8, 86–7).

The planned Law against Restraints on Competition loomed as a
serious challenge to the existing coordination of interest rates and
more generally to restrictions on competition within the German banking sector. Unsurprisingly, banks and banking associations became

involved in the debate around the GWB from the start. They lobbied to have the financial sector exempted from the law. With the support of financial supervisory authorities, and of several Länder governments, they managed to obtain the insertion of a sectoral exception into the law against restraints on competition (GWB, see p. 146) (Hüttenberger 1976: 306; Robert 1976: 185, 341; Schmidt 1995: 22).[8] As a consequence, banks and banking associations could officially continue their practice of negotiated and coordinated interest rates. In 1967, the Federal government declared the existing interest rate decree as invalid in order to generate more competition in the banking sector—with little effect. Several banking associations argued that individual banks needed help and orientation (*Orientierungshilfe*) during the transition period that would lead to more competition. Hence, they went on proposing and registering recommendations on credit interest rates with the Federal Cartel Office (Hausleutner 1970: 111–2).

The exemption of the banking (and insurance) sector from the Law against Restraints on Competition (GWB) would be removed only in 1990. Three developments preceded and prepared the 1990 reform of §102 GWB. From the mid-1970s, the Federal Cartel Office (FCO) had systematically gone after collusive behaviour. Increasingly, it was taking a much more critical position on the issue of interest rates recommendations in the banking sector (Schmidt 1995: 77). Then, during the 1980s, the FCO received support from the EC's Directorate General IV, which launched an increasing number of investigations into cases of anti-competitive behaviour in the European financial sector. The European Court of Justice also helped by confirming that the European competition law was applicable without sectoral exemption in all those cases.

The European layer of competition law began to penetrate more and more national administrative and legal decision-making and finally constrained the relevant German actors to adapt national legislation to European standards (Quack and Djelic 2005; Schmidt 1995: 26). Furthermore, since the mid-1980s large private banks in Germany were going through strategic reorientation from national to international (often European) markets and from universal to investment banking (Morgan and Quack 1999; Vitols 2001). Liberalization of financial markets as well as increasing international competition between

---

[8] A special law concerned with the regulation of the banking sector (*Kreditwesengesetz (KWG)*), was enacted in July 1961. It indicated the conditions under which banks would be allowed to operate but did not touch upon questions of competition in this sector (Hausleutner 1970: 137 ff.).

banks undermined the collective capabilities of large private banks with respect to sectoral self-organization and market coordination (Höpner and Krempel 2003; Lütz 2002; Deeg and Lane, Chapters 2 and 4, respectively, this volume).

6.4. How Institutions Change: Rethinking the Idea of Path

The two stories we have described and contrasted in this chapter give a sense of how processes of institutional change can be complex, dense, and somewhat messy in real life. We have looked in this chapter at an important institutional subsystem—the competition regime—and at its fate in two parts of the German economy—product markets and the banking sector. A comparison of evolutions in those two cases provides us with an illustration of the conditions and limits for institutional change. We now pull together the main theoretical claims we can make on the basis of the empirical material provided in this chapter.

6.4.1. *A pincer movement*

In the stories we told above, a critical factor influencing the shift in competition regime in German product markets was the significant pressure brought to bear by the United States, and the alternative model this country provided. Additionally, though, for this shift to stabilize, it was crucial that it was supported by a local group who became committed to the American ideas in order to gain leverage for their own, preexisting, German intellectual tradition. The ordo-liberals had been marginal in Germany—both intellectually and institutionally—until the end of the Second World War. But they were German seeds upon which the American antitrust pressure could be grafted. The support of American occupation authorities brought a number of ordo-liberals into key institutional positions from which they could influence the political and, later on, the business communities. Over time they were also able to engage in public discussions over the pros and cons of an economic constitution for the newly founded Federal Republic of Germany, linking the choice of a new competition regime with general political issues of democracy and social justice. Hence, the reordering of product markets in post-war Germany started from the collaboration between dominant foreign and peripheral domestic actors. Once local actors had obtained access to important positions of power and were able to champion their project to broad parts of society, dynamics internal to Germany gained momentum and proved quite significant for the long-term stabilization of change.

We argue that change is more likely when institutional systems or subsystems are being attacked from both inside and outside, and foreign as well as domestic actors are able to mobilize various resources in favour of a common project (for more examples of that see Djelic 1998; Djelic and Quack 2003). The case of the banking sector in Germany is in part a counterfactual illustration of our claim. The Dodge plan did not have the expected impact, nor were its consequences long lasting, partly because it lacked the support of significant domestic actors. The small number of groups willing to link the decentralization of banks to broader debates on economic democracy and Federalism (such as a few political representatives in Baden-Württemberg) were not able to mobilize any significant support.

The case of the banking sector, however, points also to structural limitations creating significant constraints for actors with the desire to mobilize in the direction of the envisioned project. The under-development of stock markets in Germany meant that both American occupation authorities, as well as the very few domestic proponents of a decentralization of the banking sector, had difficulties in pointing to a viable alternative to universal banks—particularly in a situation in which financing was urgently needed for the economic reconstruction and financial markets were still predominantly national. Such structural limitations gave on the other hand the old banking elites significant leverage and the capacity to mobilize in their own interest.

6.4.2. *Layered dimensions of institutionalization*

The contrast of these processes of change in German product markets and banking sector highlights the multiple ways in which institutionalization occurs. When we think of institutions as collective, stabilizing or stabilized, rules of the game, we need to consider at least three dimensions. First, we have to consider the formal institutions or rules of the game, whether they be structurally embedded or codified in 'hard' or 'soft' law regimes. Second, our empirical material also tells us, that we should pay attention to individual and collective behaviours and interactions that set themselves in a relation of coevolution with formal institutions. Finally, we have to take into consideration contextual rationalities (Djelic and Durand 2004), the background logics or principles in which institutional systems or rules of the game are inscribed. There can be more, or less, fit between those three levels or dimensions. A tight fit and articulation between all three dimensions reveals a strong and stable institutional regime—at least at the moment of observation. On the other hand, decoupling or loose fit reveal, we suggest, pressures for and greater potentiality of institutional change and recomposition.

Challenges to and attacks upon institutional regimes can happen at all three levels in succession or concomitantly. The story of the reordering of product markets in Germany shows that quite clearly. One could argue that the process started with a formal rewriting of the law when the occupying powers issued a decree in 1947 prohibiting cartels, combines, syndicates, or trusts. At the same time, and for ten years after that, we document a process of loose coevolution. The local German champions of the antitrust movement were busy elaborating their own version of the formal law—but the impact of that process on the behaviour of economic actors was at best indirect and in any case delayed. Behaviours were, in the meantime, changing within certain groups and the overall balance of power within the German economy was shifting in favour of those groups that had either internalized market regulation (through hierarchies) or developed patterns of regulation alternative to cartels. Those changes in logics of action were only partly related to changes in formal rules of the game. Furthermore, the direction of causalities was not so clear and changes in behaviours and market interactions influenced the process of transformation of formal institutions, at least as much as the latter had an impact on logics of action.

In the end, though, where we start from probably matters less than the fact that, in time, changes aggregate and combine on all three dimensions. Consequential and long-lasting institutional system change calls for a transformation of formal rules, behaviours and underlying principles. This is bound, however, to be step by step and to require time. It is likely to involve and reflect a multiplicity of cumulative pressures exerting themselves from many angles on a particular institutional regime.

6.4.3. *Nestedness and reinforcing pressures*

The importance of nested and reinforcing pressures at other levels of collective action is a further conclusion to be drawn from this comparison. In parallel to the reordering of markets in Germany, an antitrust regime was being developed at the European level. Antitrust provisions emerged as an important feature of both the European Coal and

Steel Community (ECSC) as it was being structured, starting in 1951, and the European Economic Community (EEC), which was born with the Treaty of Rome in 1957 (Djelic 2002; Quack and Djelic 2005). The two processes—one of institutional change at the national level in Germany and one of institution building at the European level—had originally emerged and were initiated independently from each other. Those two processes, however, soon collided, colluded, fed, and reinforced each other.

This concomitant and partly interconnected development of anti-trust at the European level has, over the long run, been a stabilizing factor for the shift in competition regime in German product markets. A comparison with the post-war story of competition regime shift in Japan would tend to confirm that (Haley 2001). Although the Japanese story shared many features with the German one (Streeck and Yamamura 2003), the resulting institutional transformation in Japan was neither as significant nor as stable in the long run as it has been in Germany. One of the explanations, we propose, is that the shift in competition regime in German product markets was stabilized and reinforced through time by the development and emergence of another 'layer', as it were, of antitrust, at the transnational or European level. Such reinforcing pressure was entirely absent on the other hand in the Japanese story.

The story of the banking sector in Germany provides us with further evidence of the role and significance of reinforcing and nested pressures. The attempt at introducing more competitive logics within the German banking sector proved relatively short-lived and unsuccessful during the 1950s. We argued above that the relative lack of success of the change project in the German banking sector could be explained in part by the absence of local champions. The pincers had only one arm. At the same time, when we extend the banking story to look at more recent developments (the 1980s and 1990s), it becomes clear that the German banking sector has been experiencing major transformations (see also Lane, Chapter 4, this volume) after decades of stability and relative resistance to change. An important difference for this sector between then and now has been the emergence of reinforcing and nested pressures at the European and global level. European regulation has matured and progressively trickled down towards the German banking sector while the internationalization of financial markets has provided alternatives to industrial finance through domestic banks for many large corporate actors in Germany, and the political elite has become progressively reconciled to this.

6.4.4. *From path dependence to path generation*

This chapter suggests that the shift in competition regime in Germany since the end of the Second World War has emerged from a succession of critical junctures, and from a multi-step process of coevolution and hybridization of new rules of the game and preexisting practices. The path has been a crooked rather than a straight one and we argue that it could only be charted and ascertained a posteriori. Many of the stages and step-by-step evolutions could not have been fully anticipated or expected. We do not document a pattern of punctuated equilibrium—a single radical and abrupt jump from one competition regime to another. Nor do we give evidence, though, of evolutionary and inconsequential within path transformation. When we look at the period as a whole, the shift in competition regime was progressive and step by step and nevertheless highly consequential.

We propose that the idea of 'path generation' fits quite nicely with the process of institutional change we have described here and, more generally, suggest that the life and evolution of institutions may have more to do with processes of 'path generation' than with patterns of 'path dependence'.[9] There are a number of key differences between the two concepts. The idea of 'path dependence' implies a focus on the past. The past constrains or even determines the present or the future. In contrast, the idea of 'path generation' suggests at least as much a projection towards an open-ended future.

Another major difference concerns the degree of openness implied by both terms. In the less deterministic variants of the path dependence argument, the process is open-ended for a short while only, during the periods that coincide with critical junctures. But then the process is closed off, precisely through what happens during those moments. In our idea of 'path generation', on the other hand, the process is open-ended throughout. The multiplicity of critical junctures together with their partly unexpected consequences means that both the path itself and its consequences can be fully recognized and mapped only post hoc.

A third important difference between the concepts of path dependence and path generation has to do with the articulation between structures and agency. Path dependence arguments tend to be associated with passive models of action where behavioural patterns and

---

[9] See Garud and Karnoe (2001:6) for a parallel discussion of path creation and path dependencies in the field of entrepreneurship and technological innovation.

logics of action are merely constrained by and have to adapt to structural and institutional frames. Our idea of path generation reveals, on the other hand, a preoccupation with a process of coevolution and mutual interplay—where institutional frames constrain behaviours and agency, the latter in turn shaping, adapting and transforming the institutional and structural rules of the game in which they are embedded.

In contrast to the weak model of path dependence (Sewell 1996), the concept of path generation allows us to specify the conditions under which redirection of an existing path becomes likely. In our case study we have identified two such enabling conditions: a pincer movement of external and internal pressures for change and the ability of foreign and local actors to mobilize positional, relational, and discursive resources in favour of a planned change. Unlike in the strong variant of path dependence, on the other hand, a redirection of the path comes not from a single critical juncture but rather it emerges and is being constructed through a historical sequence of multiple junctures that cannot be fully anticipated. The path is a crooked one and it reflects long periods of struggle between countervailing pressures. This crooked path shows the historical interplay between pressures for continuity and stimuli for change—the reinforcing mechanisms identified by Mahoney (2000) and Pierson (2000) being challenged then by external and internal triggers for change.

The perspective on institutional change that emerges has been theorized elsewhere (Djelic and Quack 2003). We argue that the succession and combination, over a long period of time, of a series of incremental steps and junctures can lead in the end to consequential and significant change. Each single one of these incremental steps may appear in itself quite marginal and it may be absorbed and mitigated in part by the preexisting institutional frame.[10] However, the succession, aggregation, and combination of multiple and multilayered steps ultimately and with a longer term view of the process adds to the significance and heightens the impact of each single transformation. We use the image of 'stalactite change' (Djelic and Quack 2003: 309) and we see it as more useful to describe the way in which most national institutional systems change than the image of the 'Big Bang' often associated with punctuated equilibria models.

---

[10] See also Thelen (2003: 210) for a discussion of the 'cumulative effects of ongoing and often subtle changes' and Streeck and Thelen (2005) for another thorough analysis of 'incremental change with transformative results'.

REFERENCES

Berghahn, V. (1985). *Unternehmer und Politik in der Bundesrepublik*. Neue Historische Bibliothek. Frankfurt: Edition Suhrkamp.

—— (1986). *The Americanization of West German Industry*. Cambridge, UK: Cambridge University Press.

Beyer, J. (1998). *Managerherrschaft in Deutschland? 'Corporate Governance' unter Verflechtungsbedingungen*. Opladen/Wiesbaden: Westdeutscher Verlag.

Braunthal, G. (1965). *The Federation of German Industry in Politics*. Ithaca, NY: Cornell University Press.

Damm, W. (1958). 'National and International Factors Influencing Cartel Legislation in Germany'. Ph.D. dissertation. Chicago: University of Chicago.

Djelic, M. L. (1998). *Exporting the American Model*. Oxford: Oxford University Press.

—— (2002). 'Does Europe Mean Americanization? The Case of Competition'. *Competition and Change* 6(3): 223–50.

—— and Durand, R. (2004). 'Strong in the Morning, Dead in the Evening: Toward a Theory of Firm Selection for Strategic Management'. Working paper available upon request.

—— and Quack, S. (2003). *Globalization and Institutions: Redefining the Rules of the Economic Game*. Cheltenham: Edward Elgar.

Edwards, J. and Ogilvie, S. (1996). 'Universal Banks and German Industrialization'. *Economic History Review* 49: 1–29.

Erhard, L. (1958). *Prosperity Through Competition*. New York: Frederick Praeger.

—— (1963). *The Economics of Success*. Princeton: Van Nostrand.

Garud, R. and Karnoe, P. (eds.) (2001). *Path Dependence and Creation*. Mahwah and London: Lawrence Erlbaum Associates.

Haley, J. O. (2001). *Antitrust in Germany and Japan: The First Fifty Years: 1947–1998*. Seattle: University of Washington Press.

Hausleutner, J. P. (1970). 'Die Kartellrechtliche Bereichsausnahme für das Kreditgewerbe und die Fachaufsicht nach dem Kreditwesengesetz'. Köln.

Hilferding, R. (1923). *Das Finanzkapital*. Vienna: Verlag der Wiener Volksbuchhandlung.

Herrigel, G. (1996). *Industrial Constructions. The Sources of German Industrial Power*. Cambridge: Cambridge University Press.

Holtfrerich, C. L. (1995). 'Die Deutsche Bank vom Zweiten Weltkrieg über die Besatzungsherrschaft zur Rekonstruktion. 1945–1957'. In: L. Gall, G. Feldman, H. James, C. L. Holtfrerich, and H. E. Büschgen (eds.), *Die Deutsche Bank 1870–1995*. München: Verlag C. H. Beck, pp. 409–578.

Höpner, M. and Krempel, L. (2003). 'The Politics of the German Company Network'. MPIfG Working paper 03/9. Max Planck Institut für Gesellschaftsforschung Köln.

Horstmann, T. (1991). *'Die Alliierten und die deutschen Großbanken. Bankenpolitik nach dem Zweiten Weltkrieg in Westdeutschland.* Bonn: Bouvier Verlag.

Hüttenberger, P. (1976). 'Wirtschaftsordnung und Interessenpolitik in der Kartellgesetzgebung der Bundesrepublik. 1949–1957'. *Vierteljahreshefte für Zeitgeschichte* 24(3): 287–307.

Kocka, J. and Siegrist, H. (1979). 'Die hundert größten deutschen Industrieunternehmen im späten 19. und frühen 20. Jahrhundert. Expansion, Diversifikation und Integration im internationalen Vergleich'. In: N. Horn and J. Kocka (eds.), *Recht und Entwicklung der Großunternehmen im 19. und frühen 20. Jahrhundert: Wirtschafts-, sozial- und rechtshistorische Untersuchungen zur Industrialisierung in Deutschland, Frankreich, England und den USA.* Göttingen: Vandenhoeck & Ruprecht, pp. 55–122.

Lehmbruch, G. (2002). 'Der unitarische Bundesstaat in Deutschland: Pfadabhängigkeit und Wandel'. In: A Benz and G. Lehmbruch (eds.) *Föderalismus.* Wiesbaden: Westdeutscher Verlag, pp. 53–110.

Lehnich, O. (1958). *Gesetz gegen Wettbewerbsbeschränkungen (Kartellgesetz).* Köln, Berlin: Carl Heymanns Verlag KG.

Liefmann, R. (1938). *Cartels, Concerns and Trusts.* New York: Dutton.

Lilja, K. and Moen, E. (2003). 'Coordinating transnational competition: changing patterns in the European pulp and paper industry'. In: M.-L. Djelic and S. Quack (eds.), *Globalization and Institutions.* Cheltenham: Edward Elgar, pp. 137–60.

Lütz, S. (2002). *Der Staat und die Globalisierung von Finanzmärkten: Regulative Politik in Deutschland, Großbritannien und den USA.* Frankfurt a. M.: Campus.

Mahoney, J. (2000). 'Path Dependence in Historical Sociology'. *Theory and Society* 29: 507–48.

Morgan, G. and Quack, S. (1999). 'Confidence and Confidentiality: The Social Construction of Performance Standards in Banking'. In: S. Quack, G. Morgan, and R. Whitley (eds.), *National Capitalisms, Global Competition, and Economic Performance.* Amsterdam and Philadelphia: John Benjamins Publishing Company, pp. 131–57.

Nawrocki, J. (1973). *Komplott der ehrbaren Konzerne. Marktmanipulation, Wettbewerbsverzerrung, Preisdiktate.* Hamburg: Hoffmann und Campe.

OMGUS—Office of Military Government for Germany, US (1947). 'Explaining Decartelization to the Germans, 10 September', Vol. 18: #11/11-3/7.

Pierson, P. (2000). 'Increasing Returns, Path Dependence, and the Study of Politics'. *American Political Science Review* 94: 251–68.

Quack, S. (2004). 'Cross-Societal Diffusion During German Industrialisation. The Role of the "International" in the Emergence of "German" Capitalism'. Unpublished manuscript available upon request.

—— and Djelic, M. L. (2005). 'Adaptation, Recombination and Reinforcement: The Story of Antitrust and Competition Law in Germany and Europe'. In: W. Streeck and K. Thelen (eds.), *Beyond Continuity—Institutional Change in Advanced Political Economies*. Oxford: Oxford University Press.

Robert, R. (1976). 'Konzentrationspolitik in der Bundesrepublik—Das Beispiel der Entstehung des Gesetzes gegen Wettbewerbsbeschränkungen'. *Volkswirtschaftliche Schriften Nr. 250*. Berlin: Duncker & Humblot.

Schmidt, H. A. (1995). *Die Europäisierung des Kartellrechts im Bereich der Kredit- und Versicherungswirtschaft*. Baden-Baden: Nomos Verlagsgesellschaft.

Schönwitz, D. and Weber, H.-J. (1982). *Unternehmenskonzentration, personelle Verflechtungen und Wettbewerb: Eine untersuchung auf der Grundlage der hundert größten Konzerne der Bundesrepublik Deutschland*. Baden—Baden: Nomos Verlag.

Sewell, W. H. (1996). 'Three Temporalities: Toward an Eventful Sociology'. In: T. J. McDonald (ed.), *The Historic Turn in the Human Sciences*. Ann Arbor: University of Michigan Press, pp. 245–80.

Shonfield, A. (1977 [1965]). *Modern Capitalism. The Changing Balance of Public and Private Power*. Oxford, New York: Oxford University Press.

Siegrist, H. (1980). 'Deutsche Großunternehmung vom späten 19. Jahrhundert bis zur Weimarer Republik'. *Geschichte und Gesellschaft* 6: 87–8.

Streeck, W. and Höpner, M. (2003). 'Einleitung: Alle Macht dem Markt?'. In: W. Streeck Wolfgang and M. Höpner (eds.), *Alle Macht dem Markt? Fallstudien zur Abwicklung der Deutschland AG*. Frankfurt: Schriften des Max-Planck-Instituts für Gesellschaftsforschung Köln, Bd. 47, 1–49.

—— and Thelen, K. (2005). *Beyond Continuity—Institutional Change in Advanced Political Economies*. Oxford: Oxford University Press.

—— and Yamamura, K. (2003). 'Introduction: Convergence or Diversity? Stability and Change in German and Japanese Capitalism'. In: K. Yamamura and W. Streeck (eds.), *The End of Diversity. Prospects for German and Japanese Capitalism*. Ithaca, London: Cornell University Press, pp. 1–50.

Thelen, K. (2003). 'How Institutions Evolve. Insights from Comparative Historical Analysis'. In: J. Mahoney and D. Rueschemeyer (eds.), *Comparative Historical Analysis in the Social Sciences*. Cambridge, MA, pp. 208–40.

Vitols, S. (2001). 'The Origins of Bank-Based and Market-Based Financial Systems: Germany, Japan, and the United States'. Discussion paper FS I 01–302, Berlin: Wissenschaftszentrum Berlin für Sozialforschung (WZB).

Voigt, F. (1962). 'German Experience with Cartels and Their Control During Pre-War and Post-War Periods'. In: J. P. Miller (ed.), *Competition Cartels and their Regulation*. Amsterdam: North-Holland Publishing Company, pp. 169–213.

Windolf, P. and Beyer, J. (1995). 'Unternehmensverflechtung im internationalen Vergleich'. *Kölner Zeitschrift für Soziologie und Sozialpsychologie* 47(1): 1–36.

Windolf, P. and Schief, S. (1999). 'Unternehmensverflechtung in Ostdeutschland'. *Kölner Zeitschrift für Soziologie und Sozialpsychologie* 51(2): 260–82.

7

Complementarity and Fit in the Study of Comparative Capitalisms

COLIN CROUCH

An important component of almost all neo-institutionalist analysis of national systems of economic organization—or any other identified level at which a system can be observed—is the construction of *ensembles* that link institutions in one area within a given social formation to those in another. However, as some other contributors to this volume demonstrate (in particular Deeg's Chapter 2 and Morgan's concluding Chapter 14), the matter is not straightforward. This is so for a reason very familiar to sociologists: human actors will often regard the institutional context within which they find themselves as provisional and as capable of amendment by them. We may follow Morgan's final chapter in using the term 'institutional entrepreneurship' to describe this approach of actors to their contexts. It may be found in many situations, but we might expect it to be particularly common among firms, institutional entrepreneurship being a component of entrepreneurship in general. The fact that institutions are potentially malleable does not mean that their existence can be discounted. The fact that a river can be bridged does not mean that it does not exist; but it does mean that we should not regard it as an ultimate barrier to communication between communities living on its opposite banks.

We therefore need a theoretical approach that accepts the basic tenets of neo-institutionalist analysis, but which can also accommodate the responsiveness of institutions to actors. Institutions do constrain action; and institutions do tend to hang together as *ensembles*, particularly when they are sustained by the laws and formal institutions gathered around nation states. Even in a globalizing world, there is enough reality in these structures to justify retaining them as the basic building blocks of an account of the basic contexts of action. But, as Morgan for example shows, human institutions often do not have the rigid, ultimately constraining attribute of mechanical or many biological systems. For example, once an engineer has demonstrated to us that without an engine a car simply cannot deploy motive power (or a biologist that without a heart a mammal cannot live), we have no alternative but to accept the prognosis that follows the analysis. However, when a social scientist demonstrates that without a certain form of financial system certain investment projects will be impossible, it is always open to the institutional entrepreneur to say: 'Perhaps not; but let us see what we can do to fix up something else'. He has to accept the difficulty that the social scientist has identified, and has been well warned, but he is able to try to act creatively and defy the lessons of past experience.

In the following I shall explore this potential malleability of human institutional *ensembles* by taking advantage of an ambiguity embedded in the concept of complementarity. I take an approach to this institution similar to that adopted by Deeg in his Chapter 2. The idea of complementarity as something resting in the form taken by institutions themselves is commonly used to explicate the links that are considered to bind such *ensembles*, but the term is often deployed disconcertingly to refer to both similarity and contrast in this respect. These two logics of action are indeed both at work in all complex systems; it is possible that a complex system can endure only if it has certain features that hold together in a congruent manner, but also others that contrast with that manner. The problem concerns the temptation to confused reasoning caused by using the same concept, complementarity, to refer to both opposite phenomena.

The logic of the former principle is that the competence and learning capacity of important social actors depends partly on their being able to apply routine, formulaic solutions across a range of topics and problems. Institutional evolution probably favours situations where actors can do this over those where they must constantly reinvent the wheel and approach problems with little transferable experience. On the other hand, the logic of contrast is that constant repetition of similar formulae will leave actors unprepared for novelty and the need to change. Evolution will therefore favour systems that have a capacity to respond to challenges to their routines. Working out how these opposed principles fit together is a major challenge for neo-institutional analysis. It is a task that is not helped if complementarity, or any other concept, is used to weave both together through techniques of narrative, thick description and stylized facts that fail to confront the challenge. The following is an attempt to start on this task; it does not claim to be the final answer.

The first need is to secure a firm understanding of what we understand by principles of similarity and contrast, and how their opposed logics might operate within complex systems. For reasons that will be explained, I shall in fact use 'complementarity' to mean 'contrast' and related ideas, and shall therefore contrast it with similarity and never use it as a synonym for this.

7.1. Distinguishing Similarity and Complementarity

7.1.1. *Similarity*

Similarity among institutions within a society can be used as the rationale for their being found together when it can be shown that isomorphism emerges from the way in which 'a given set of national, regional, or sectoral institutions tends to create equilibrium forms of firm behaviour, combined with a broader set of factors that include the presence of specific public policies, social coalitions and socio-economic conditions' (Hall 1999). Hall and Gingerich (2004) take this further to argue that systems mixing institutions of different fundamental types (specifically, mixing coordinated and liberal market economy characteristics) will underperform pure types. This is a clear claim for the logic of similarity against that of complementarity, which prevents the authors indulging in ad hoc mixing of the two. The research methods used by Hall and Gingerich cannot discover the presence of complementarities in the sense of contrasts, because they start with broad generalizations about characteristics of systems, which methodologically exclude the possibility of exceptions within them that might constitute complementarities.

A further interesting implication of 'U-curve' theories of the Hall and Gingerich kind is that, though they are usually based on cross-sectional research (i.e. comparing a number of cases at one time), they seem to embody very strong and negative predictions for possibilities of change (see also Calmfors and Driffill 1988). They have two clear forms of advice to offer strategic actors located near one or other pole of the U-curve and wanting to improve their performance: either produce a purer example of the form to which they lie closer, or transform their situation into that at the opposite pole, accepting that for a considerable period this will bring worsening performance. This follows because, while they are gradually losing the characteristics of their existing system and acquiring the opposite one, they will at first have an increasingly mixed system, which the U-curve hypothesis predicts will necessarily bring a deteriorating performance in the short run. This powerful claim is valuable in accounting for many real cases of change: the United Kingdom during the 1980s and 1990s; possibly some countries in Eastern Europe at the present time.

One cannot criticize these implications of the U-curve; they provide valuable hypotheses for testing. One can, however, question whether cross-sectional studies enable us to talk about what happens during *change over time*. This doubt is caused by the realization that reflexive, creative actors, able to perceive what is happening to their institutions and possessing (limited) ability to try to interact with the lessons of their experience and innovate, are in a different position from the set of separate, contemporary actors involved in cross-sectional research.

The idea of *Wahlverwandschaft* or elective affinity is often used to describe the process whereby institutions across many different parts of a society find some kind of fit together, mainly through cognitive processes and social learning (Ebbinghaus and Manow 2001*a*; Powell and DiMaggio 1991: 63–82; Shalev 2001). As Hall and Soskice put it (2001*a*: 17–21), particular institutions tend to develop similar capacities in neighbouring spheres, such as corporate governance, vocational training, and collective bargaining. Kitschelt et al. (1999*a*) similarly assert that there is an elective affinity which links types of production regime, patterns of socio-economic inequality and protection through welfare states, and the constitution of corporate political actors in parties and interest groups. In the same vein, Goodin et al. (1999) argue that different types of welfare state are integral to different forms of economy, though they only consider the tax transfer aspects of welfare regimes. Whitley (1997) sees patterns of similarity linking the training system and the role of employers and workers' organizations in running it, the academic stratification of the labour market, the strengths and policies of the state concerning the integration of the pre-industrial training system, the extent to which owners are locked into the fate of the firms into which they invest, their trust in the formal institutions governing property rights and other economic issues, and systemic trust in general, which is in turn linked to types of financial markets, and the nature and form of legitimation of authority relations.

Streeck (2001) proposes that German and Japanese capitalism are distinguished from the Anglo-American variety by their distinctive and isomorphic financial systems, corporate governance, worker citizenship, approaches to employment, welfare states, industrial relations, training, and wage distribution. There is similarly widespread agreement among economic historians that the common law system of Anglophone countries was more favourable to the growth of the free-market economy than the civil codes of most of continental Europe. The common law approach does not permit a central authority to frame an a priori comprehensive code, but it evolves gradually in synchrony with, and in the same manner as, developments in the market economy itself.

7.1.2. *Complementarity*

Complementarity should be used to identify the opposite kind of institutional link: in the everyday sense of the word two things are 'complementary' when one *makes up for the deficiencies* of the other. For example, computer scientists speak of complementary binary numerical series—a model of which considerable use will be made below. One can call this 'perfect' complementarity. There are many institutional examples. For example, several studies of the United Kingdom during the 1980s and 1990s argue that the relative independence of parliament from the centralized governments during much of that period enabled the establishment and maintenance of a free-market economy (Gamble 1988; Wood 2001: 254–6). Centralized strength is the opposite of the characteristics of the free market itself, and is linked to it by the logic of perfect complementarity. Indeed, Wood has elsewhere (King and Wood 1999) explicitly contrasted the political economy of neoliberalism in the United Kingdom with that of the United States during the 1980s on these grounds. He is arguing that, by itself, the market cannot produce the kind of external, monopolistic, non-competitive power source required if the rules that the market itself requires are to be devised, enforced and revised. Drago (1998) has demonstrated at length how the quality of aloofness from organized interests often seen as characteristic of British government applied even more strongly to the Chilean dictatorship of Auguste Pinochet, a regime which could introduce a free-market level playing field because, having liquidated all opponents, it did not have to pay any attention to special lobbies on behalf of particular producer groups.

A further example would be non-transferable company pension schemes in US corporations, which offset the tendency towards high labour mobility of many other US labour market institutions. Another would be the highly portable skill qualifications of the German vocational training system, which offset the tendency towards low labour mobility of many other German labour market institutions. Another again would be the role of big institutional investors in the US economy, whose individual impact on a firm or whole sector can be so large that they cannot behave as in a pure market, but need to act strategically, often engaging in dialogue with firms' managements. They thereby offset the bias towards spot markets of some other US financial institutions, and make possible a supply of patient capital. In another example still, Carruthers, Babb, and Halliday (2001) have shown how central bank rules have become stricter while bankruptcy laws have become softer, the former being consistent with strict neoliberalism but the other not. The authors conclude:

... [bankruptcy law] is the institution which constitutes the legal preconditions for market pressure! Indeed, bankruptcy laws are being altered so as to ameliorate the market pressures that distressed corporations face. This does not invalidate the idea of institutional efficiency, but it casts doubt on the idea that market pressures drive institutions in the direction of ever-greater efficiency. (ibid. 119–20)

Similarly, a family pattern complementary to a free-market economy might be one that provides resources of emotional support and maintenance of the worker to offset the rigours and insecurities of the labour market (e.g. Parsons and Bales 1955).

There is another, looser, but very useful sense of complementarity of which there are many more examples. This is the economist's sense, which I shall call 'partial' complementarity. This is defined clearly as two goods, a fall in the price of one of which will lead to a rise in the demand for the other (for its adaptation to institutional analysis, see Amable 2000). This contrasts clearly with similarity: where goods are similar, to the extent that they might substitute for each other, the fall in the price of one leads to a *fall* in the demand for the other. Complementary goods differ from each other, and although they do not necessarily contrast in binomial fashion as with perfect complementarity, they are not just 'different'. They are linked in the specific way defined, and the character of that link has to be discovered.

Aoki (1994) defines them as institutions, the enhancement of one of which will assist provision of the other. For example, the studies by Streeck and Yamamura (2001) and Yamamura and Streeck (2003) of German and Japanese historical development shows how the bundle of characteristics of those economies came together because actors worked creatively to make them do so. Over a long period they then adjusted them to make them fit better. Later observers then erroneously think that they had been strategically planned. If we bear in mind the role of human creativity in forging these complementarities, we shall be aware that entrepreneurial actors may intervene at points of change and produce surprising new combinations that unsettle the *ceteris paribus*.

But, once released from the strict economist's sense and used more analogously—as in Aoki's definition—partial complementarity can easily lapse into similarity. It is important to avoid this in order to maintain the tension of these two principles.

7.1.3. *Distinguishing the concepts*

The logic of similarity and that of complementarity both clearly exist, and particular empirical *ensembles* combine elements of both. The logic of strict complementarity is that certain efficiencies are achieved when balancing or contrasting characteristics are found alongside each other: the advantages of the mongrel over the pedigree animal. The latter has heavily reinforced characteristics, which means that vulnerabilities are exaggerated, while the mongrel avoids such reinforcement and may therefore appear more 'balanced'. At the same time, of course, the pedigree animal, because it does have exaggerated characteristics, does some things particularly well. Animals used for specialized performance tasks like racing are always pedigree. Both types of animal offer advantages, but they are different types of advantage. The same may be true of *ensembles* of institutions. Those based on complementarities may be adept at certain activities; those based on similarities at others. This leads us to interesting research questions about when which type is appropriate; but it also creates a temptation for the analyst to use whichever of the two logics makes the more convincing story. Since the two principles are (in the strictest sense!) complementary, one or the other can always be employed, giving an impression of an explanatory achievement when all that has been done is a labelling exercise.

For example, Fioretos (2001: 234), dealing with a rare period (the early 1990s) when the German government could rely on its parliamentary majority far more confidently than the British, manages to give the usual argument about the British polity (stated above) a startling new twist. He maintains that *precisely because* of its parliamentary stability, the German government was more worried about its relations with nonparliamentary interest organizations; British government, worried about parliament, had no attention to spare for such interests. Fioretos is not wrong, as he accurately describes what he observed, but it is disconcerting when authors are able to interpret the same datum in directly opposed ways.

Theory-builders tend to move between opposite logics (similarity and complementarity) depending on which is more convincing because they construct their models by working from a small number of empirical cases which they regard as paradigmatic, and embed its characteristics—which contain a complex mass of similarities, complementarities, and mere accidents—into the theoretical type. There is then the danger that they present an overall account which looks plausible but which is not vulnerable to counterfactual test.

This risk is avoided if one always follows Max Weber, who argued that an ideal type should be developed as a 'one-sided accentuation' of logically implied characteristics, representing, that is, the imposition of a single rationale, *from which of course it is fully expected that empirical cases will diverge*. This does not permit mixing the logics of similarity and complementarity; the ideal type always presents the logic of similarity, never that of complementarity. It also requires a separation between the logic of structures for action, such as is involved in the construction of an ideal type, and the logic of actors' interests, which may be far less 'pure'.

A good example of alertness to this distinction appears in the work of Campbell and Pedersen (2001*a*: 257) on neoliberalism. Like King and Wood (1999), cited above, they note the internal heterogeneity of practical examples of neoliberal policies, and that instances of proclaimed neoliberal policies do not necessarily follow a thoroughgoing logic, but '. . . the development of neoliberal institutions in one area was compensated for by institutions based on different principles in other areas . . .; the adoption of neoliberalism was heavily mediated by other institutional principles'.

In other words, complementarity was mixed with similarity. Instead of adapting their idea of the logic of neoliberalism to be able to include the heterogeneous items, they explicitly note the 'impurity', and are therefore able to identify complementarity. And they see this as clearly vulnerable to empirical variation: they show how Danish neoliberalism differed considerably from the US form.

Theory can be permitted to combine contrasting rationales in this way if it posits either a central group of actors who can be considered to have skilfully fashioned major elements of the society after their interests (as in Campbell and Pedersen), or a compromise between identified major actors engaged in power struggle as discussed by Bruno Amable 2003. For example, the *régulationiste* literature (Boyer and Saillard 1995) was able to propose a homogenization of coherent Fordist principles across a wide range of institutions, because it was ultimately related to Marxist theory, which in turn sustains a thesis that all the institutions of a social formation will reflect the interests of a dominant class. (There is of course considerable diversity and ambiguity in Marxist theory whether an actor-centred or a function-alist account should be given of how this domination comes to be expressed.) Esping-Andersen's (1990) model of welfare-state forma-tion is an example of a logic of stylized compromises between opposed social and political forces, as the designation of the types in terms of political models implies. It is also possible to depict the establish-ment of particular kinds of governance as an outcome of sociopolitical struggle. Steinmo et al. (1992), Thelen (1999), Kristensen (1997*a,b*), Streeck and Yamamura (2001) and other historical institutionalists have similarly looked at the role of conflict and contention in the establishment of particular national sets of institutions.

If we do not adopt a functionalist approach, we shall want to post-pone the search for such links to the empirical application of a theory rather than its initial formulation (Streeck 2001). For example, it is possible to show how South African and Northern Irish capitalism took advantage respectively of racial and religious segregation to seg-ment and maintain dominance over the labour force, even though such segregation in itself contradicts market principles—segregation con-stituting a political interference in the free market for labour. These were therefore cases of complementarity rather than *Wahlverwand-schaft*. It would however be an error to move from that observation to the thesis that segregation was functionally necessary to capitalism—though South African and Irish Marxists used to make such an analysis. Capitalists were certainly able to *make use* of racial or religious discrim-ination and to bind it into their economic system, but this was the result of skilful action, not system requirements. And eventually they were able to shed their dependence on these forms of labour control when their negative features outweighed their (for them) positive ones.

7.2. Modelling Similarity and Complementarity

We can model similarity and complementarity in the following way. Institutions can be seen as endowing actors within them with certain capacities. The number of capacities relevant to a particular activity is an empirical question, but whether a particular capacity is present is a simple binomial matter: it is present or absent, 1 or 0. These capacities exist across various different fields. Where there is similarity, the pattern of capacities is the same across different fields. Where there is perfect complementarity, the pattern in the complementary set of fields is exactly the reverse of that in the initial set. Where there is partial complementarity, the pattern in the complementary set merely varies in some manner from the initial set, but it has to be a manner that actors find useful, otherwise the linked demand for the two sets of institutions necessary to the economist's concept would not be found. For example: assume that ten different capacities are relevant to performance in Context I.

Context I' capacities	1	2	3	4	5	6	7	8	9	10
Field $F1$	1	1	0	0	1	1	0	0	1	1
Field $F2$	1	1	0	0	1	1	0	0	1	1
Field $F3$	1	1	0	0	1	1	0	0	1	1
Field $F4$	1	1	0	0	1	1	0	0	1	1
. . .										
Field Fj	0	0	1	1	0	0	1	1	0	0
. . .										
Field Fk	1	1	0	1	0	1	0	0	1	0

Here, field Fj provides perfect complementarity in the sense of compensation for fields $F1$–4. Field Fk provides partial complementarity if actors find it useful to combine it with fields $F1$–4. If they do not find it useful, it may nevertheless be a redundant resource that becomes part of a future complementarity.

7.2.1. *Links and barriers*

In the interests of parsimony, and in keeping with the logic of ideal type construction, we start a modelling process by hypothesizing a strain towards isomorphism—and not complementarity—across fields and subfields within an identifiable context. Such an hypothesis is plausible if we can demonstrate the existence of unifying factors working to achieve institutional homogeneity within a bordered framework. In the case of presumed 'national systems', the main examples of bordered frameworks used in the literature, state policy and national legal institutions provide such plausibility (see Whitley, Chapter 8). These unifying factors produce strong links between institutional forms: for example, ensuring that a neoliberal corporate governance system is paralleled by a neoliberal labour market regime. It follows from this hypothesis that complementary institutions, those following a different structural logic and providing different patterns of competences, can exist only when there are identifiable barriers which protect them from the dominant linking, homogenizing forces.

We cannot predict a priori where links will be at their weakest, or where barriers will exist; they may be quite arbitrary, historical, accretions. But we can specify some likely sources, and identify both diffusion mechanisms and barriers. First, to the extent that we can order fields of institutions as being at some kind of 'distance' from each other, we can hypothesize that diffusion is more likely between proximate complexes than remote ones. (For example, we should expect to find more strains towards similarity between the structure of the financial system and that of the labour market than between the former and the structure of religious life.) Second, if it can be established that the patterns found in some fields (or even subfields) are more 'powerful' than those in others, we should expect pressures for diffusion from the powerful to the powerless. 'Power' might here refer to the resources that can be wielded by the interests dominant in certain (sub-)fields, or it might refer to majority against minority situations. For example, behaviour favoured by the authorities within stock markets is likely to be more influential than that favoured by sports authorities.

To model this more formally, let us assume that, in a particular case, all fields share some patterns of capacities, but they vary across others. All fields $F1-n$ share pattern P' (1 1 0 1 1 1 0 0 0 1) across capacities $C1-f$; but while fields $F1-i$ continue with this pattern for capacities $Cg-j$, fields $Fd-k$ here follow pattern P'' (1 1 0 1 1 0 1 1 1 0). To simplify, where $C1-f = C1-5$, $Cg-j = C6-10$, $Fn = F10$, $Fi = F5$, and $Fd-k = F6,7$:

Context I' capacities	1	2	3	4	5	6	7	8	9	10	
Field $F1$	1	1	0	1	1	1	0	0	0	1	
Field $F2$	1	1	0	1	1	1	0	0	0	1	Linked by diffusion
Field $F3$	1	1	0	1	1	1	0	0	0	1	mechanism 1
Field $F4$	1	1	0	1	1	1	0	0	0	1	
Field $F5$	1	1	0	1	1	1	0	0	0	1	
											Institutional barrier
Field $F6$	1	1	0	1	1	0	1	1	1	0	Linked by diffusion
Field $F7$	1	1	0	1	1	0	1	1	1	0	mechanism 2

In this case P' is dominant, but P'' survives—as a potentially—*but only potentially, not necessarily*—complementary institutional form—because of certain barriers around the fields containing it. The barriers that protect such deviant components may take many empirical forms. An example would be the community mechanisms that sustain the religious norms of an ethnic minority; these then make it possible for that minority to sustain strong family authority in defiance of majority practice, which in turn sustains forms of family business which are not possible for the majority community (examples of this could be some minority ethnic businesses in the UK, and Chinese family businesses in pacific Asia). On the other hand, the lack of strong family norms in the majority may give it different kinds of advantage; for example, it may make possible high levels of geographical and social mobility. A very different example would be the formal provisions that prevent the manufacture and sale of nuclear weapons from being subject to the same rules as the rest of a market economy, and make their manufacture a monopoly of certain states. This enables a form of state involvement that assists large-scale investment in this sector, without any spillover into many other parts of the economy that are governed by market criteria. It may well be of course that dominant interests in fields $F1$–5 are quite happy to accept this diversity of norms. There is not necessarily conflict around the deviance.

7.3. **The Role of Governance**

The mechanisms by which the predictability and regularity fundamental to institutions are ensured are their governance mechanisms (Crouch 2004; see also Lütz 2003). I understand governance in the sense that has been developed by Hollingsworth and Boyer (1997), and by Hollingsworth et al. (2002). Unlike some recent, mainly British, authors, this school does not distinguish governance from government, but sees government (or the state) as one form that can be taken by governance, within a list, the main elements of which are: market, hierarchy, association, community, network, and state. Following Van Waarden (2002), I distinguish further between two different state governance forms: the substantive state (which develops its own policies for intervening directly in economic processes), and the procedural state (which maintains and enforces a system of private law whereby social actors can enforce contract procedures on each other).

We first hypothesize that different governance modes are associated with specific sets of capacities. If, as above (see p. 177), $C1$–j is a series of combinations of positive and negative positions (P') on a number of potential capacities within a given field $F1$, we may treat form of governance G' in the same way that we did institutional context I' at the outset: as a coherent and enduring guarantor of a certain structure of capacities. Looked at another way, it is the fact that I' is dominated by G' that it possesses P'; and the fact that I'' is dominated by G'' that it possesses P'':

	1	2	3	4	5	6	7	8	9	10
Context I'										
Governance mode G'										
Field $F1$	1	1	0	1	1	1	0	0	0	1
Context I''										
Governance mode G''										
Field $F1$	0	1	0	1	0	1	0	1	1	0

We need next to analyse each governance mode itself. We can do this: (1) by defining these in terms of certain abstract characteristics, which they either possess or not (i.e. a binomial approach to definition); and (2) by hypothesizing that, where a specific form of governance exists, it operates over all fields. Therefore the set of capacities becomes a set of binomial possibilities, and if a pattern is valid for one field, it is valid for all, leading to:

Context I'	**Characteristics of governance mode**									
	1	2	3	4	5	6	7	8	9	10
All fields	1	0	1	0	1	0	1	0	1	0	1	0	1	0	1	0	1	0	1	0

In a separate exercise, these characteristics need to be linked theoretically to hypothesized capacities, which can then be subjected to empirical test. There is no space here to spell out this model in full (see Crouch 2005), but the most striking conclusion of any such account of the diversity of governance modes can be stated: hardly any of them is likely to be fully autonomous, certainly not in dealing with economic relations of any complexity. They are all therefore unlikely to be found alone, but will exist in combinations that offer some degree of complementarity to 'compensate' for their exaggerated pedigree characteristics. For example, some modes display a rigidity of resource allocation across all aspects that makes it difficult for them to respond to changing demand among consumers (the substantive state, association, community). In practice, these modes are likely to exist alongside the neoclassical market. This happens either openly and willingly, or in the form of black markets. If we are considering only capitalist economies, then the market is by definition always present to some degree, even when other governance modes are also active. Some governance modes lack autonomous enforcement capacity (networks, markets), and are almost certain to co-opt external agencies, in particular the procedural state. In fact, in anything beyond a very primitive system, what is called the free-market economy is always really a hybrid between the pure market and the procedural state. Further, unless an economy consists mainly of autonomous small firms, what passes in common discussion for the 'market economy' is really a compound of market, procedural state, and corporate hierarchy. Virtually all large firms constitute hierarchies, and hierarchy differs considerably from market as a form of governance.

Our starting hypothesis, based on the principle of similarity, that individual modes of governance would extend across a whole social formation unless specific barriers existed to limit their jurisdiction, therefore needs early amendment. We need at least the further hypothesis that strategically located and powerful actors will be able to note where one form of governance can benefit from reinforcement by another. They therefore reach across the institutional barrier, as it were, and combine modes. In other words, the principle of complementarity is almost always found alongside that of similarity. The result is a set of compound empirical forms, sometimes combining opposed principles to comprise their whole, in the way that salts combine acids and alkalis.

These empirically observable compounds must never be confused with ideal types, as they embody more than one logic of governance, and the exact form of the compromise, or structure of the complementarities, among them might vary considerably. If we were to develop a full research programme, we should after a time be able to estimate the relative importance of all the different modes within an individual national economy. To give a more accurate account still, this would need to be nuanced according to sector and locality. For example, in sectors and areas dominated by small firms, corporate hierarchy obviously plays a smaller role relative to the market and possibly networks; in sectors dominated by government contracts (aerospace, some aspects of computers, and information technology), the active state is more important. In several high-tech sectors networks play a stronger role than elsewhere.

Realization that virtually all empirical cases are hybrids brings us to the hypothesis: *that institutional heterogeneity will facilitate innovation, both by presenting actors with alternative strategies when existing paths seem blocked and by making it possible for them to make new combinations among elements of various paths.* A nice example of this is Höpner's (2003b) account of how German Social Democrats seem to have been tougher than Christian Democrats in breaking down associational links in German business that inhibited competition.

This hypothesis can be set against those that point to the advantages of institutional similarity, but it does not dispose of the logic of the rival principle; nor can it cope with the problem that incoherence may create confusion, institutional waste, and loss of efficiency as well as opportunities for fruitful creativity. Can we say anything about the kinds of conditions likely to be associated with each? We can possibly make some progress if we can predict ways in which a particular governance mode might make it difficult for a firm within it to tackle certain kinds of task, any potentiality for functional equivalents being inadequate for solving the problem within the terms of the mode. Adoption of elements of a different mode more adept at performing the task in question would then enable the firm to solve this problem. If the second mode is simply different from the first, but not necessarily in ways likely to assist the firm solve its problem, it might be more likely to create confusion and therefore inefficiency.

7.3.1. *Functional equivalence*

But how good is our knowledge of the capacity of different governance forms? Some authors make strong claims. For example, several assert that the pure market is superior to most other forms of governance in stimulating radical innovation. Our analytical, not to mention prescriptive, capacity would increase considerably if we could confidently make statements of this kind. As Regini (1996) has demonstrated well, the existence of functional equivalents raises considerable difficulties for such simple means-ends associations: actors are able to bend governance mechanisms to carry out surprising tasks. In Regini's own main example, Italian machine-tool firms have demonstrated a capacity to provide training for a skilled workforce, even though the existing literature had argued that provision of such skills required forms of associational governance that Italy lacked.

Functional equivalence, if it is strategically achieved by institutional entrepreneurs, can be described as a situation where actors within I'' refashion G'' so that, while retaining its own characteristics, it gives the same substantive outcome as G'.

This does not mean that anything is possible, and that we should therefore abandon all attempts at institutional analysis. The Italian machine-tool industry found a solution to its governance problem in the provision of machine-tool skills; but their British equivalents did not do so (Crouch and O'Mahoney 2004). On the other hand, the British did solve the governance problem of providing collective training for new film and television skills despite being apparently in a market governance regime (Baumann 2002), while the Italians have not solved the problem of how to build an effective computer industry. Different forms of governance are associated with different capacities, but knowledge of this cannot be derived in a mechanistic, a priori way. We are dealing with creative human actors who, faced with an institution that does not 'work' in a certain way, will sometimes fashion it until it does. But sometimes they will fail.

Combining the apparently irreconcilable is a major form of innovation. We can take the analogy of experimental fruit growers. If there seems to be a clear biological choice between a tomato that is sweet to taste and one that has a robust skin for transport, it can be guaranteed that in some tomato grower's laboratory there is a project for producing a sweet but robust tomato. (Höpner's (2001) account of how, contrary to initial expectations, the German codetermination system (associational governance) seems to have become compatible with shareholder corporate governance would be an institutional example.) Of course, the search is not guaranteed success. And if the sweet robust tomato finally appears, its invention does not suddenly render *retrospectively* false the knowledge that had previously shown these two characteristics to have been incompatible in the past. That knowledge had indeed served as a spur to the research that found a way, creating new knowledge. Research on governance and institutions should operate in the same way. The capacity of humans to learn means that, where there is knowledge of the past (even inaccurate knowledge), there is no pure repetition of an action. As is well known, the repeatability of an experiment, said to be fundamental to the scientific character of knowledge, is not possible when creative human actors are involved.

7.4. Modelling Governance for Complementarity

We can express the main points from the above as follows. When a number of governance patterns is available to them, and assuming that the power relations within which they are embedded do not inhibit them, actors seek out those elements of one governance mode that seem to be associated with certain desired outcomes, and elements of others that give different ones, in order to maximize their performance as defined by particular institutional standards and logics. Let us assume that there are three governance modes, which seem to be associated perfectly complementarily with capacities as follows:

Context I'	1	2	3	4	5	6	7	8	9	10
Governance mode G' Field $F1$	1	1	1	0	0	0	0	0	0	0
Governance mode G'' Field $F1$	0	0	0	1	1	1	0	0	0	0
Governance mode G''' Field $F1$	0	0	0	0	0	0	1	1	1	1

Actors in context I' therefore try ideally to achieve the following:

Context I'	1	2	3		4	5	6		7	8	9	10
Governance mode		G'				G''				G'''		
Field $F1$	1	1	1		1	1	1		1	1	1	1

Several devices might be available to recombine governance modes in this way. First, they might make searches back into their own past experience, trying to use hidden or dormant alternatives within their own repertoires (Crouch and Farrell 2004). Here, we can envisage dormant alternatives as a kind of palimpsest; in terms considered immediately above, modes G'' and G''' had been present in I' before, but had become obscured by G', perhaps by the latter's more frequent use or by its role in a dominant power coalition.

Second, agents might operate simultaneously in different arenas, enabling them to transfer experience from different action spaces, or secure access to the arenas of others, to enable them to transfer experience from other agents through networks of structured relationships (ibid.). This has been already anticipated in the idea of segregated zones within an institutional context, within which other patterns of capacities, and hence other forms of governance, are found. An important aspect of the costs of transferring experience here comprises the barriers that exist to 'protect' the various governance modes and the ease of negotiating them.

A further possibility is that, of several viable alternatives, only one is discovered, leading to possibly false 'one best way' solutions. This can be easily accommodated to the concept of the search for recombinant elements of governance, but it also directs our attention to an issue that until now we have neglected: exogeneity and the strength of the boundary around an 'institutional context'. Just as, between fields within an institutional context, we have to account for both boundaries and their absence, we need to do the same to boundaries that define those contexts themselves. The contexts with which we usually work may well be set within wider ones: national systems may be set within world-regional or global ones. This is then a matter of a wider system within which I', I'', etc. are located (e.g. an international regime within which national systems are located). It is possible that within such a wider system (W) particular governance modes are dominant which clash with those within I' or I''. As these are drawn within W (i.e. their external barriers melt), their locally dominant patterns might weaken; though they may remain concealed as redundant capacities, available for future use. This may well be happening, for example, as the German and Japanese corporate governance systems are forced to change in line with the requirements of the Anglo-American form which is globally dominant (Dore 2000).

In the simplest case we have an impermeable context: no knowledge, learning, action, or power relations enter it from outside or (for simplicity) leave it to move outside. At the other extreme would be a case so thoroughly open to external influence that it has no barriers at all. But this is a limiting case, as by definition this cannot constitute a discrete context or system able to be studied; it has become part of whatever context(s) permeated it. In between we have contexts with various patterns of openness and boundaries. These boundaries can be permeated in a number of different ways: for example, by knowledge diffusion and/or by power relations (Crouch and Keune 2005); and these can flow through actual movement of personnel or the transfer of ideas and/or control mechanisms by themselves. In relation to each identified potential influence source, we need to identify its potential forms of transmission and the boundaries it will encounter.

A research programme based on these principles provides a richer description of an institutional configuration than do standard accounts, and makes it possible to study action and structure interactively as commended by Sewell (1992). It provides a full analysis of the state of governance in a particular context, and of the scope for change and blockages of change to be found within it. It will lack the neatness and capacity for easy classification of national cases afforded by allocative approaches. However, it is not a lapse into description, as it has used generalizable, theoretically derived categories and theories of relations among categories in producing its accounts. The resulting accounts can therefore be used in comparative studies without difficulty, as different cases will be analysed in the same terms.

It is also necessary to develop an approach to modelling that can cope with incremental change within an institution without having difficulties in deciding whether an institution is still 'the same' or has changed into something else. The strategy proposed above, whereby phenomena are seen as comprising varied elements in varied proportions, rather than as being either 'this' or 'that' enables us to do this—again in a manner that avoids lapsing into mere empiricism and that retains a theory-driven analysis with flexibility.

When we study complex macro-social phenomena like the wider institutional structure of an economy we often have to accept that, despite their theoretical identity, explanation and prediction are very different activities, and we may often have to limit ourselves to the former. When an event has already taken place it is possible with various methodologies to reconstruct how and why it occurred, and to delve back into the *ensemble* of wider institutional processes involved. It is not possible to do this for future events, because researchers cannot tell which surprising combinations of institutional resources will in practice be used by creative, entrepreneurial actors (Garud and Karnøe 2001)—if they can, the changes are not surprising.

We shall therefore continue to be taken by surprise by acts of true Schumpeterian entrepreneurialism as opposed to incremental ones. We can however at least conceptualize the likelihood of these occurring in terms of risk taking. Schumpeterian actions can be conceived of as being those which make unexpected and daring leaps in innovation. If we retain the basic assumption of the theory, that even such leaps as these have to draw on knowledge that is somehow already available, an innovative leap can be theorized. Typical costs of such leaps will be lack of knowledge about whether the innovation will work, because the idea for it has been pulled from such a remote and unfamiliar institutional location. It is therefore reasonable to predict that most such attempts will fail, but a small but finite number will succeed.

REFERENCES

Amable, B. (2000). 'Institutional Complementarity and Diversity of Social Systems of Innovation and Production'. *Review of International Political Economy* 7(4): 645–87.

—— (2003). *The Diversity of Modern Capitalism*. Oxford: Oxford University Press.

Aoki, M. (1994). 'The Contingent Governance of Teams: Analysis of Institutional Complementarity'. *International Economic Review* 35(3): 657–76.

Baumann, A. (2002). 'Convergence Versus Path-Dependency: Vocational Training in the Media Production Industries in Germany and the UK'. Ph.D. thesis, Florence: European University Institute.

Boyer, R. and Saillard, Y. (eds.) (1995). *Théorie de la régulation: L'état des savoirs*. Paris La Découverte.

Calmfors, L. and Driffill, D. G. (1988). 'Bargaining Structure, Corporatism and Macro-Economic Performance'. *Economic Policy* 6: 14–61.

Campbell, J. L. and Pedersen, O. K. (2001*a*). 'The Second Movement in Institutional Analysis'. In: Campbell and Pedersen (2001*b*), q.v.

—— and —— (eds.) (2001*c*). *The Rise of Neoliberalism and Institutional Analysis*. Princeton, NJ: Princeton University Press.

Carruthers, B. G., Babb, S. L., and Halliday, T. C. (2001). 'Institutionalizing Markets, or the Market for Institutions? Central Banks, Bankruptcy Law, and the Globalization of Financial Markets'. In: Campbell and Pedersen, q.v.

Crouch, C. (2005). 'The Role of Governance in Diversity and Change Within Contemporary Capitalism'. In: M. Miller (ed.), *Worlds of Capitalism: Institutions, Economic Performance, and Governance in the Era of Globalization*. London: Routledge.

—— and Farrell, H. (2004). 'Breaking the Path of Institutional Development? Alternatives to the New Determinism'. *Rationality and Society* 16, 1: 5–43.

—— and Keune, M. (2005). 'Rapid Change by Endogenous Actors: The Utility of Institutional Incongruence'. In: W. Streeck and K. Thelen (eds.), *Continuity and Discontinuity in Institutional Analysis*, forthcoming.

—— and O'Mahoney, J. (2004). 'Machine Tooling in the United Kingdom'. In: Crouch et al. (2004), q.v.

——, Le Galès, P., Trigilia, C., and Voelzkow, H. (2004). *Changing Governance of Local Economies: Response of European Local Production Systems*. Oxford University Press.

Dore, R. (2000). *Stock Market Capitalism: Welfare Capitalism*. Oxford: Oxford University Press.

Drago, M. E. (1998). 'The Institutional Bases of Chile's Economic "Miracle": Institutions, Government Discretionary Authority, and Economic Performance under Two Policy Regimes'. Ph.D. thesis, Florence: European University Institute.

Ebbinghaus, B. and Manow, P. (2001*a*). 'Introduction: Studying Varieties of Welfare Capitalism'. In: Ebbinghaus and Manow (eds.) (2001*b*), q.v., 1–24.

—— and —— (2001*b*). *Comparing Welfare Capitalism*. London: Routledge.

Esping-Andersen, G. (1990). *The Three Worlds of Welfare Capitalism*. Cambridge: Polity Press.

Fioretos, O. (2001). 'The Domestic Sources of Multilateral Preferences: Varieties of Capitalism in the European Community'. In: Hall and Soskice (eds.) (2001*b*), q.v., 213–45.

Gamble, A. (1988). *The Free Economy and the Strong State: The Politics of Thatcherism*. Basingstoke: Macmillan.

Garud, R. and Karnøe, P. (2001). 'Preface'. In: Garud and Karnøe (eds.), *Path Dependence and Creation*. Mahwah, NJ: Lawrence Elbaum Associates.

Goodin, R. (1996). 'Institutions and Their Design'. In: Goodin (ed.), *The Theory of Institutional Design*. Cambridge: Cambridge University Press.

——, Headey, B., Muffels, R., and Dirven, H.-J. (1999). *The Real Worlds of Welfare Capitalism*. Cambridge: Cambridge University Press.

Hall, P. A. (1999). 'The Political Economy of Europe in an Era of Interdependence'. In: Kitschelt et al. (eds.) (1999*b*), q.v.

—— and Gingerich, D. W. (2004). 'Varieties of Capitalism and Institutional Complementarities in the Political Economy: An Empirical Analysis'. MPIFG Discussion Paper 04/5, Cologne: Max Planck Institut für Gesellschaftsforschung.

—— and Soskice, D. (2001*a*). 'Introduction'. In: Hall and Soskice (eds.) (2001*b*), q.v.

—— and —— (eds.) (2001*b*). *Varieties of Capitalism: The Institutional Foundations of Comparative Advantage*. Oxford: Oxford University Press.

Hollingsworth, J. R. (2002). 'On Institutional Embeddedness'. In: Hollingsworth, Müller, and Hollingsworth, q.v., pp. 87–107.

—— and Boyer, R. (1997). 'Coordination of Economic Actors and Social Systems of Production'. In: Hollingsworth and Boyer (eds.), *Contemporary Capitalism*. Oxford: Oxford University Press, pp. 1–47.

——, Müller, K. H., and Hollingsworth, E. J. (eds.) (2002). *Advancing Socio-Economics: An Institutionalist Perspective*. Lanham: Rowan and Littlefield.

Höpner, M. (2001). *Corporate Governance in Transition: Ten Empirical Findings on Shareholder Value and Industrial Relations in Germany*. MPIfG Discussion paper 01/5. Cologne: Max Planck Institut f. Gesellschaftsforschung.

—— (2003*a*). 'What Connects Industrial Relations with Corporate Governance? A Review on Complementarity'. Paper prepared for first Complementarity Workshop.

—— (2003*b*). *European Corporate Governance Reform and the German Party Paradox*. MPIfG Discussion paper 03/4. Cologne: Max Planck Institut f. Gesellschaftsforschung.

King, D. and Wood, S. (1999). 'The Political Economy of Neoliberalism: Britain and the United States in the 1980s'. In: Kitschelt et al. (eds.) (1999b), q.v.

Kitschelt, H., Lange, P., Marks, G., and Stephens, J. (1999a). 'Convergence and Divergence in Advanced Capitalist Democracies'. In: Kitschelt et al. (eds.) (1999b), q.v.

——, ——, ——, and —— (eds.) (1999b). *Continuity and Change in Contemporary Capitalism*. Cambridge: Cambridge University Press.

Kristensen, P. H. (1997a). 'National Systems of Governance and Managerial Prerogatives in the Evolution of Work Systems: England, Germany, and Denmark Compared'. In: Whitley and Kristensen (eds.) (1997b), q.v.

Lütz, S. (2003). *Governance in der politischen Ökonomie. MPIfG Discussion paper 03/5*. Cologne: Max-Planck-Institut für Gesellschaftsforschung.

Parsons, T. and Bales, R. F. (1955). *Family, Socialization, and Interaction Process*. New York: Free Press.

Powell, W. and DiMaggio, P. (eds.) (1991). *The New Institutionalism in Organizational Analysis*. Chicago: University of Chicago Press.

Regini, M. (1996). 'Le imprese e le istituzioni: domanda e produzione sociale di risorse umane nelle regioni europee', and 'Conclusioni'. In: Regini (ed.), *La produzione sociale delle risorse humane*. Bologna, Il Mulino.

Sewell, W. H. (1992). 'A Theory of Structure: Duality, Agency, and Transformation'. *American Journal of Sociology* 98(1): 1–29.

Shalev, M. (2001). 'The Politics of Elective Affinities: A Commentary'. In: Ebbinghaus and Manow (eds.) (2001b), q.v., 287–303.

Steinmo, S., Thelen, K., and Longstreth, F. (eds.) (1992). *Structuring Politics: Historical Institutionalism in Comparative Analysis*. Cambridge: Cambridge University Press.

Streeck, W. (2001). 'Introduction: Explorations into the Origins of Nonliberal Capitalism in Germany and Japan'. In: Streeck and Yamamura (eds.) (2001), q.v.

—— and Yamamura, K. (eds.) (2001). *The Origins of Nonliberal Capitalism: Germany and Japan in Comparison*. Ithaca: Cornell University Press.

Thelen, K. (1999). 'Historical Institutionalism in Comparative Politics'. *Annual Review of Political Science* 2: 369–404.

Van Waarden, F. (2002). 'Market Institutions as Communicating Vessels: Changes Between Economic Coordination Principles as a Consequence of Deregulation Policies'. In: Hollingsworth, Müller and Hollingsworth (eds.) (2002), q.v., 171–212.

Whitley, R. (1997). 'The Social Regulation of Work Systems: Institutions, Interest Groups, and Varieties of Work Organization in Capitalist Societies'. In: Whitley and Kristensen (eds.) (1997), q.v.

—— and Kristensen, P. H. (eds.) (1997). *Governance at Work: The Social Regulation of Economic Relations*. Oxford: Oxford University Press.

Wood, S. (2001). 'Business, Government, and Patterns of Labour Market Policy in Britain and the Federal Republic of Germany'. In: Hall and Soskice (eds.) (2001*b*), 247–74.

Yamamura, K. and Streeck, W. (eds.) (2003). *The End of Diversity? Prospects for German and Japanese Capitalism*. Ithaca, NY: Cornell University Press.

8

How National are Business Systems? The Role of States and Complementary Institutions in Standardizing Systems of Economic Coordination and Control at the National Level

RICHARD WHITLEY

8.1. Introduction

A central tenet of economic sociology is that cultural values and regulatory institutions help to constitute the nature of economic actors and guide their actions, thus affecting economic outcomes (see, for example, DiMaggio 1994; Smelser and Swedberg 1994). As socially organized agents operating in different kinds of societal contexts, firms and other actors are inevitably influenced by the dominant norms and conventions governing the formation of collective actors and how competition and collaboration between them is to be structured. Different societal 'rules of the game' governing the organization of firms and interest groups and how they interact can be expected to result in contrasting patterns of economic organization and change (Whitley 1999).

The institutionalization of separate economic arenas with their own distinct regulatory norms during the development of industrial capitalism, does not, in this view, negate the socially constructed nature of firms and markets (Polanyi 1957). Rather, it highlights the need to study how differently organized societies and institutional frameworks develop distinctive kinds of market rules and actors, such that they manifest varied patterns of economic organization and generate different outcomes. The extent and mode of separation of the economic sphere from the rest of a social system are seen here as varying between capitalist societies, reflecting broader institutional structures.

Although the role of institutions in structuring economic activities can, in principle, be analysed at a variety of territorial levels, most studies of the social construction of economic phenomena have focused on national institutional frameworks and forms of economic organization (see, for example, Hollingsworth et al. 2002). This is because: (1) the structures and actions of nation states have been crucial influences on the sorts of market economies that became institutionalized in contrasting ways in the twentieth century; and (2) many of the key institutions that govern the constitution and behaviour of economic actors have been nationally specific.

In addition to political competition and mobilization being predominantly organized nationally, and so the structure and behaviour of interest groups being primarily nationally specific, the nation-state has been, and remains, the dominant territorial unit governing the definition and enforcement of private property rights, and so the nature of owner–manager relationships and corporate governance more broadly. It is also the primary agent regulating the conditions for market entry and exit, dispute resolution and competitive behaviour, and so structuring markets (Herrigel 1994).

Furthermore, the organization and control of labour markets are often governed by national institutions such as labour law and court systems, regulations specifying the nature, functions, and organization of labour representation, as well as the system of wage bargaining and employer–employee relations more generally. The training and certification of practical skills are also more likely to be organized nationally, although considerable differences may occur between types of skills—for example, professional and manual skills—and industrial sectors in some countries.

However, as Nettl (1968) pointed out many years ago, the state is a variable phenomenon. Its societal significance, form, and behaviour have varied over time and geographical regions, as has the extent to which the key institutions governing economic relationships are nationally specific and variable. Equally, the institutionalization of coherent forms of economic organization as distinctive kinds of business system, varieties of capitalism, or social systems of production at the national level is a contingent, not necessary, phenomenon (Hall and Soskice 2001; Hollingsworth and Boyer 1997; Whitley 1999). They could, and have been, established at sub-national levels in

Germany, Italy, and elsewhere (Braczyk et al. 2003; Crouch et al. 2001; Herrigel 1996).

As a result, not all states can be expected to establish a single kind of business system throughout all regions and sectors of an economy, and not all cohesive and stable business systems are nationally specific and bounded. The nature of firms, their strategies, and capabilities frequently vary between sectors, technological regimes, and regions within countries, and can also overlap across national boundaries (Breschi and Malerba 1997; Whitley 1999, 2003b).

Such variable connections between national boundaries and forms of economic organization raise questions about how and why do distinctive business systems, social systems of production, and varieties of capitalism become established and reproduced at the national level? More generally, how do different kinds of institutional arrangements at different levels of social organization help to constitute economic actors and regulate their behaviour in contrasting ways, and what are the consequences of changes in such arrangements, especially for economic performance?

In dealing with these kinds of questions, there are two aspects of the key institutions governing property rights, capital, labour, and product markets that are particularly important. First, their relative strength and stability at different levels of collective organization. Under the post-war Bretton Woods' regime, for instance, national controls over financial flows dominated, and nationally specific labour market institutions—especially skills formation and control systems—dominated regional ones in most industrialized economies.

Second, the coherence and complementarity of institutions vary with respect to their encouragement of particular economic rationalities and patterns of behaviour in different spheres of action. Institutional arrangements in, say, labour markets are complementary with those in capital markets if they reinforce actors' preferences for specific strategies and actions in those domains, such as relational financing (Aoki 2001: 310–26). As Deeg suggests in his contribution (Chapter 2, this volume), complementarity implies a logic of synergy whereby the influence of institutions in one domain of action is strengthened by institutional arrangements in another one.

The establishment and reproduction of distinctive and cohesive varieties of capitalism, social systems of production, or business systems at any one territorial level depends, then, on the strength and complementarity of the key institutions governing economic activities at that level. This suggests that when some national institutions become less dominant relative to cross-national ones, as in the European Union, the national specificity of economic systems may be reduced. Their cohesion and distinctiveness are especially likely to decline when the governing principles of institutional arrangements at the national and international levels are contradictory in their implications for economic actors, as may be the case in coordinated market economies such as Germany (see Chapters 2, 4, and 5 by Deeg, Lane, and Sorge, respectively, in this volume).

In attempting to understand how and why different patterns of economic organization, firm type and organizational capabilities become established and reproduced at different levels of collective organization, then, key issues are how strong and complementary governing institutions are at those levels and how much they generate similar kinds of actors to manage their interrelationships in similar ways across sectors, regions, and size classes of firms. At the national level, this involves consideration of the nature and role of states, especially their internal cohesion and ability to pursue consistent policies regarding the organization and regulation of capital and labour markets.

In addition to providing a stable and predictable environment for economic actors to make strategic decisions, an important feature of states concerns the extent of their involvement in the development and organization of economic actors. As Evans (1994: 9–10) points out, most, if not all, states in industrial capitalist societies, are involved in improving national competitive advantages, often by encouraging the development of particular kinds of firms and capabilities. They differ, though, in how they attempt to do this, and in their capacity to implement their policies effectively. These differences affect the extent to which distinctive kinds of national business systems become institutionalized in contrasting types of states.

As a contribution to clarifying the conditions in which nationally distinct and cohesive business systems, social systems of production and varieties of capitalism are likely to become established and reproduced, this chapter considers how different kinds of states with complementary institutions can be expected to lead to contrasting varieties of firm governance structures, authority sharing, and organizational capabilities becoming institutionalized throughout their economies. These characteristics of firms help to explain differences in patterns of sectoral and technological development and specialization between countries with different institutional environments, such as those highlighted by Casper et al. (1999), Soskice (1999), and Tylecote and Conesa (1999) among others.

At least four ideal types of states that combine with particular features of allied institutions to constitute particular institutional regimes can be identified. These differ significantly in how much they organize and develop economic actors, and standardize business system characteristics, across sectors and regions within national boundaries. In general, the more states organize and homogenize economic actors, the rules governing their interaction, and the organization of interest representation, the more we would expect them to develop nationally distinctive business systems.

In the next section of the chapter, I summarize the key features of four kinds of states that vary considerably in the extent to which, and ways in which, they promote specific paths of development. Such broad contrasts between types of states do downplay the significance of internal conflicts and susceptibility to fragmentation between political factions, bureaucratic elites, and other groups within states, as well as differences in electoral systems and the organization of political parties. However, this seems to me justified for the purposes of considering how different kinds of states are likely to affect the establishment of contrasting kinds of business systems at the national level.

Subsequently, I suggest how these different kinds of states and national institutional arrangements are likely to encourage varying degrees of standardization of firm governance structures and strategies across sectors, and how these in turn generate nationally distinctive forms of authority sharing, commitment, and organizational capabilities in different kinds of firms. Finally, I discuss how the changing international business environment and growing internationalization of trade and investment can be expected to impinge upon these kinds of nationally distinctive business systems and companies.

8.2. Types of States and Complementary National Institutions

The development of cohesive business systems at the national level depends, *inter alia*, on states establishing stable rules of the game governing economic decision-making. However, how they do so varies considerably between different kinds of states as the extensive literature on comparative political economy illustrates (see, for example, Amable 2003; Hart 1992; Schmidt 2002). In considering how different kinds of states are likely to: (1) encourage the establishment and reproduction of distinctive national business systems; and

(2) help to standardize these across sectors and sub-national regions, at least two features are critical.

First, the extent to which the state is actively involved in coordinating and steering economic development, especially in helping to construct particular kinds of organizational capabilities, varies greatly between the arm's length approaches of most liberal market economies and the dirigiste policies of highly active states. While the former focus on establishing clear rules of the competitive game within which varied kinds of economic actors are free to pursue their objectives as they wish, the latter are more concerned to develop particular kinds of actors and sectors. In Evans' (1994: 77–81) terminology, 'arm's length states' perform custodial roles that concentrate on establishing and applying rules as remote policing agents, while more 'promotional states' take active steps to develop new industries and skills as direct producers, midwives, and supporters. These often involve providing financial and other types of assistance and sanctioning failure of specific firms and groups, as well as organizing markets to support entry into new industries.

Second, states differ greatly in the extent to which they actively encourage and structure independent intermediary associations representing the interests of different groups that become involved in policy formulation and implementation. While arm's length states typically leave it up to individual firms, unions, and other groups to organize as they wish, more promotional ones tend to standardize interest group representation in particular ways that facilitate the state's coordinating role. These latter do, however, vary greatly in: (1) how they do so; (2) for which interests, and (3) how autonomous such associations are from the state, as the extensive literature on corporatism illustrates (see, for example, Hart 1992; Katzenstein 1985; Streeck and Schmitter 1985). Where states are quite constrained in their attempts to construct national competitive advantages by powerful and relatively autonomous social groupings, as perhaps is the case in Denmark (Karnoe 1999; Kristensen 1992, 1994), the less likely they are to develop nationally specific and homogenous business systems with similar characteristics throughout the country and across all sectors.

Variations in states' developmental policies suggest at least three major varieties of promotional states can be distinguished in terms of the extent to which they standardize interest group representation and involve independent associations of different kinds of interest groups in economic policy development and implementation. In what might be termed *dominant developmental states* such as South Korea since 1961 or France up to the 1980s, industry associations and similar groupings do sometimes form, but these usually function as agents of the state rather than as autonomous representatives of distinct interests (Fields 1995; Kim 1997; Schmidt 2002; Woo 1991). On the whole, such states do not support the establishment of independent peak associations that could challenge its decisions or interfere with its direct links with owners and top managers.

More collaborative developmental states, on the other hand, do support intermediary associations with greater autonomy, often by delegating some powers to them and granting them representational monopolies in dealing with state agencies, either on a formal or informal basis. However, they differ in terms of their recognition and involvement of labour union federations in economic policy-making. *Business corporatist states* tend to work most closely with associations of large companies, such as the *keidanren* in Japan (Eccleston 1989; Pempel 1998; Samuels 1987), and rarely encourage peak associations of labour unions to become involved in policy-making. *Inclusive corporatist states*, on the other hand, are more concerned to mobilize unions at the national level to deal with distributional issues and manage incomes policies. In both cases, the active involvement of business associations by the state tends to encourage their standardization as state agencies seek predictable and reliable partners for achieving their development goals.

A further logically possible kind of state that combines a regulative, arm's length approach with highly centralized economic policy-making and implementation seems both empirically and theoretically unlikely. Since arm's length states are primarily concerned to establish formal rules of the game that are neutral between economic actors and outcomes, they are not inclined to build direct links on a continuing basis to particular firms or to encourage business dependence on state agencies, except perhaps in areas such as defence where state procurement policies inevitably affect firm development. On the whole, then, effective arm's length states do not seek to structure firms' strategies or behaviour, but prefer to operate remotely and allow 'market forces' to determine outcomes.

These four ideal types of states, arm's length, dominant developmental, business corporatist, and inclusive corporatist, develop different kinds of approaches to the regulation and management of capital and labour markets, as well as institutionalizing varied political cultures and legal systems. These different approaches lead to variations in the standardization of interest group formation, labour relations, and skill formation systems. When combined with particular kinds of complementary institutions, such states form distinctive institutional regimes that encourage different kinds of business systems to become established and reproduced at the national level with relatively homogenous characteristics across regions and sectors. The key features of these states and their complementary institutions are summarized in Table 8.1 (p. 198) in terms of the degree to which they are likely to become established and reproduced in different kinds of states, from *low* to *limited* to *some* to *considerable* to *high*, and will now be further discussed.

Since states are political entities, they institutionalize particular conceptions of power and authority that impinge upon relations of subordination elsewhere in market economies, particularly within firms. While, then, cultural norms governing authority are not always standardized within national boundaries, and are often shared between liberal democratic societies, the ways in which state elites justify their status and claims to subjects' loyalty are often specific to particular countries. In particular, the extent to which relations between politicians, and the state more generally, and the public are understood in largely contractual terms, as distinct from paternalistic or communitarian ones, differs considerably between societies.

The more that political authority is seen to rest on services rendered between equal and remote transacting partners who do not directly share collective interests, the more likely that authority within other organizations will also be viewed as primarily contractual. Conversely, political and bureaucratic elites in more promotional states often justify their roles in paternalistic terms that encourage paternalism within companies. Inclusive corporatist states, however, are more likely to invoke communitarian norms that treat citizens as equals and emphasize the common interests of all members of the polity.

Similarly, where states are trusted by most citizens to follow the 'rule of law' and pursue the collective interests of society as a whole rather than those of the political class or individual politicians, trust in other institutional arrangements is likely to be high, including those dealing with economic transactions and disputes. Since the legal and justice systems of states remain the central institutions regulating economic activities, their efficacy, and reliability are critical factors governing the management of transactional uncertainty and the longevity of investment horizons, as well as the nature of employer–employee commitments. National variations in these systems affect the ways in which owners deal with managers and other employees, as well as economic opportunism more generally. While most OECD countries

Richard Whitley

Table 8.1 *State types and complementary institutions*

Key characteristics	State types			
	Arm's length	Dominant developmental	Business corporatist	Inclusive corporatist
Active involvement in economic development	Low	High	Considerable	Considerable
Active encouragement of business associations	Limited	Limited	Considerable	Considerable
Active encouragement of labour associations and organization of representation	Limited	Low	Limited	Considerable
Complementary institutions				
Prevalent norms governing subordination	Contractual	Paternalist	Paternalist	Communitarian
Reliability of legal system and formal institutions	Considerable	Varied	Varied	Considerable
Strength of minority property rights	Considerable	Limited	Limited	Limited
Strength of arm's length competition policies	Considerable	Limited	Limited	Limited
Market segmentation and entry constraints	Limited	Considerable	Considerable	Considerable
Standardization of interest group representation	Low	Some	Some	Considerable
Standardization of labour relations	Limited	Varied	Varied	Considerable
Standardization of skill formation system	Low	Varied	Limited	Considerable

have developed relatively effective legal systems, how these operate in practice and how willing firms are to rely on them for settling disputes vary considerably across countries in ways that affect firm governance and behaviour. In particular, their autonomy, cost, speed, and reliability differ.

States with predictable legal systems develop varied relationships with different kinds of institutions governing financial markets and competition that often complement and reinforce their encouragement of economic opportunism or commitment and cooperation between particular groups of economic actors. Three aspects of these institutions are especially important: their protection of minority shareholders, their facilitation of trading ownership and control of companies in a largely anonymous market, and their regulation of competition. While these are often correlated in terms of their impact on firm structures and behaviour, they arc not necessarily so. It is quite possible, for example, to have a financial system with formally equal shareholders, as in post-war Japan, that has a very weak market for corporate control because of limited mechanisms reinforcing this formal 'constitutional' governance regime (Aguilera and Jackson 2003).

On the whole, arm's length states seem more likely to establish relatively transparent capital markets, in which all participants are formally equal and funds are priced and allocated through market processes, than are promotional ones seeking to mobilize capital for specific goals. They should, then, be more concerned to protect the rights of minority sharcholders, while the latter develop close links to major block holders who can cooperate effectively in achieving state policy goals. Similarly, while arm's length states typically insist that firms are distinct, legally separate entities competing in a large anonymous market, and legislate against collusion and cooperation, promotional ones often encourage them to collaborate and share risks in developing new markets, skills, and technologies. Even where anti-cartel legislation promoting competition has been passed, such countries differ considerably in the vigour with which they enforce it, as the cases of Germany and Japan show (Berghahn 1986; Gao 2001: 144–9; Johnson 1982).

In addition to such norms encouraging flexible trading relationships, states vary in the extent to which they regulate market entry and exit and encourage collective means of settling disputes through trade associations. Segmented markets with strong industry and trade associations are less likely to be developed in arm's length states because they will be seen as preventing market forces acting throughout an economy, while encouraging collusion that may be against the perceived public interest. Conversely, some promotional states often view such groupings as essential to risk sharing and technological progress, as well as being important agencies for state-backed economic growth. By organizing market entry and exit for developmental goals, such states are able to structure incentives for firms to develop effective capabilities in new industries and to exit old ones with limited losses.

The organization and standardization of interest group representation, as well as the nature of the skill formation system, can additionally complement the effects of state types and policies on the organization of economic activities and encouragement of opportunistic behaviour. Considering first business associations, these vary in their domination of different sectors, their national heterogeneity and the scope of services that they provide for their members. On the whole, arm's length states leave the organization and roles of such associations to individual companies, and rarely support attempts to establish monopolistic groupings in each sector that could coordinate training initiatives, diffuse new technologies, and set standards. As a result, business associations in these kinds of market economies often compete for membership, rarely represent all the leading firms in an industry or other unit of collective organization, and are usually unable to discipline their membership or guarantee their support for agreed policies. They are therefore usually unable to provide distinctive collective benefits and control opportunism.

Dominant developmental states are often suspicious of independent intermediary associations that could compete with state authority in developing and implementing economic policies, and so rarely support their development by delegating substantial powers to them. Where they exist then, such groupings are typically weak and unable to coordinate activities independently of state direction. Authority sharing between firms is unlikely to be high in countries dominated by such states, and opportunism in seeking state support considerable.

More collaborative developmental states, on the other hand, actively enlist business association support in carrying out economic policies, and often delegate substantial powers and resources to organizations that monopolize representation and other roles. Because such states encourage firms to join particular organizations and to form federations that unite major interest groups, these associations are usually able to exert considerable influence over their members and to constrain opportunistic behaviour. Authority sharing within such groupings is therefore much greater than that between firms in countries with other kinds of states, especially where companies that remain outside them are seen as weak and/or exploitative and so most firms join them for reputation effects (Culpepper 1999, 2001).

Considering next the institutions governing labour unions, these vary greatly in their homogenization of forms of representation within a country and the extent to which they encourage workers to join them. Again, arm's length states rarely specify the particular forms that labour representation should take, or support their attempts to monopolize membership in particular industries or crafts. Beyond specifying the rules governing labour relations, especially strike actions, most such states restrict their regulation of labour representation. As a result, this is often quite heterogeneous, especially between skilled trades and unskilled workers, between sectors, especially between public and private employers, and manufacturing and service industries, and between professional highly qualified labour and manual workers.

Dominant developmental states usually take more active measures to discourage and/or control union organization, particularly when that would threaten state development policies, and sometimes attempt to structure union organization by forbidding certain forms. The South Korean state, for example, at one time encouraged enterprise unions and prohibited industrial ones. Mostly, such states either attempt to prevent them being formed at all or else ensure that they do so under state tutelage and in effect become an arm of the state's development policy (Deyo 1989; Kim 1997; Woo 1991). In either case, they rarely influence firms' strategies very much and, when independent, often oppose owners and managers in a zero-sum approach.

More collaborative developmental states often, but by no means always, encourage more positive union attitudes and delegate certain welfare functions to them, thus increasing union membership. Business corporatist ones do, however, differ from inclusive corporatist states in the degree to which they support particular forms of labour representation and involve them in policy development and implementation. In the former countries, the state delegates most aspects of labour management and social welfare to private companies, especially the largest ones, and does not usually encourage the formation of national union federations or standardized systems of labour representation throughout the economy. The coordination of wage bargaining across firms and sectors is here left to privately organized groups, albeit, no doubt, with considerable informal state assistance to ensure that developmental objectives are not compromised.

As a result, the national standardization of labour representation and bargaining systems across sectors and firm type remains restricted, and the involvement of labour unions in economic policy-making and implementation remains low. In Japan, for example, after the strikes of the early 1950s, the state encouraged enterprise-based unions rather than industrial and craft-based ones and did not involve national union federations in policy discussions (Cusumano 1985; Gao 2001; Garon 1987).

In many of the European corporatist states, on the other hand, unions are more standardized in their organizational basis and form strong federations that negotiate with both employer' associations and state agencies. Inclusive corporatist states establish formal mechanisms to coordinate wage bargaining and economic policy development. Typically organized through national employers and union federations such public–private collaboration is often quite centralized and based upon relatively formal, standardized systems of labour representation, both within enterprises and sectors. Consequently, these kinds of states develop quite nationally cohesive and distinctive patterns of labour organization that encourage firms to work together as well as to engage in continuous discussions with unions and state agencies. Employment and labour relations more generally are, then, quite systematically organized throughout the economy in ways that encourage cooperation within the overall framework of competitive markets.

Similar differences can be found in the skill formation systems of different states. Arm's length states tend to develop rather heterogeneous and changeable ways of developing, assessing, and certifying practical skills and expertise, often relying on 'market forces' to guide the establishment of training programmes and evaluation of their outputs. Whether these are organized around apprenticeships, professional examinations, or educational establishments, the state here usually prefers to delegate skill formation processes to a variety of groups and organizations, with little attempt to establish a nationally standardized system. As a result, flexibility and responsiveness to market changes are often high, but signalling of competences in labour markets is difficult and time consuming, often leading to high rates of labour turnover (Crouch et al. 1999; Marsden 1999).

Dominant developmental states often take a more active part in organizing skill formation processes, but usually within the state system. Standardization of training in state technical schools and similar organizations is therefore considerable in such countries, but resources are not always substantial and the prestige of the expertise gained may be limited. Since neither employers nor unions are usually involved in these processes, the practical utility of the skills produced may be restricted, and again, firms have to find out through experience how to assess and use them. Additionally, since the state here typically monopolizes the provision and assessment of practical skills, the speed with which training programmes respond to market changes is often limited.

More collaborative developmental states are more willing to involve companies directly in skill formation, usually with state agencies playing a coordinating role, for example through a national skills testing and certification system as in Japan (Crouch et al. 1999). Again, though, they differ in how much they involve labour representatives and standardize training provision. In the business corporatist countries, states tend to delegate most training provision to employers and do not standardize training programmes. Such 'segmentalist' skill formation systems typically rely on public schools and universities to produce a highly educated workforce that can be trained for company purposes in house (Thelen and Kume 2001). Since the larger firms can invest more resources in such training and offer more credible commitments to long-term employment, their staff tend to become more highly skilled and to contribute more to firm-specific knowledge and competences.

Inclusive corporatist states, on the other hand, develop relatively homogenous skill formation systems that integrate state schools with employer provided training, usually with the active participation of labour unions, and workplace representatives. While the extent of employer provided training varies between, say, Germany and Sweden, it is usually cooperatively planned and monitored by representatives of employers, unions, and state agencies. Skills are therefore quite highly standardized and well understood by firms and unions. Such cooperation may limit the speed of response to market changes but does ensure rapid introduction of new standards and courses once they have been agreed. Furthermore, it encourages the generation of relatively broad skills that enable future learning, rather than those that are limited to the performance of specific tasks.

In general, then, skill formation is quite standardized in these kinds of societies and is built upon considerable employer–union collaboration. Again, opportunism in labour markets is constrained by complementarities between state policies, the nature of the institutions governing financial flows and bargaining systems that encourage commitment between economic actors.

8.3. States, Complementary Institutions, and the National Homogeneity of Business Systems and Kinds of Firm

The combination of these institutional features with the four ideal types of states constitute particular kinds of institutional regimes that govern economic activities within their national borders in different ways, and so can be expected to generate nationally distinct business systems and firm types. However, although such institutional regimes generally encourage particular kinds of governance structures and firm strategies, they do vary in the extent to which these are standardized systematically throughout the economy, especially across industrial sectors and between firms of different sizes.

It is also worth emphasizing that national institutions in particular countries often differ considerably in their complementarity in reinforcing certain forms of economic organization and firm behaviour, and discouraging others. Relatively arm's length relations between large banks and companies, for example, can be combined with a legislative framework that severely restricts the market for corporate control and grants the incumbent top management considerable protection, as in the Netherlands (van Iterson and Olie 1992).

Together with largely corporatist public–private relationships and strong unions, this tends to encourage authority sharing and employer–employee commitment in that country, despite some limited institutional pressures towards arm's length contracting. Similar sorts of variations in the extent of institutional complementarity between state strength and promotional policies, bank–firm connections and the organization of labour markets seem to explain differences in the cohesion and homogeneity of Finnish and Danish business systems and firms in much of the post-war period (Kristensen 1992, 1994, 1996; Lilja and Tainio 1996; Lilja et al. 1992).

In any empirical case, then, contradictions between dominant institutional arrangements can be expected with respect to firm governance, strategies, authority sharing, and employer–employee commitments, and their associated organizational capabilities (Whitley 2003b), but these vary in their strength and scope over time and between countries. Generally, the greater they are, the more opportunity that firms' top managers have for developing idiosyncratic characteristics and distinctive strategies and capabilities (Hancké and Goyer, Chapter 3; Herrigel and Wittke, Chapter 11, this volume). When these kinds of contradictions are considerable and linked to powerful competing socio-economic groups, the likelihood of institutionalizing a distinctive and cohesive national business system within particular kinds of state seems limited.

Bearing such possible empirical contradictions between institutions within national boundaries in mind, I now consider how these four distinct kinds of ideal states and their complementary institutions can be expected to establish and reproduce nationally distinct standardized forms of economic organization and firm behaviour. The kinds of governance structures, inter-firm and employment relations and organizational capabilities that are likely to become established in these states, as well as their variability across sectors, are summarized in Table 8.2, and will now be further discussed.

Examining first arm's length states with complementary institutions limiting commitments between economic actors, these establish

Table 8.2 *Types of states, associated business system and firm characteristics*

Associated business system and firm characteristics	Types of states			
	Arm's length	Dominant developmental	Business corporatist	Inclusive corporatist
Governance structures				
Fragmentation of large firm ownership	High	Low	Limited	Limited
Commitment of largest shareholders	Low	High	Considerable	Considerable
Strategic autonomy of large firms	Considerable, within capital market constraints	Limited by state	Considerable, limited by business partners and state	Some, limited by business partners and employees
Inter-firm relations				
Extent of authority sharing with other firms	Limited to short term alliances	Limited, except for state-coordinated alliances	Considerable amongst large firms, limited in SMEs	Considerable
Employment relations				
Authority sharing with skilled staff	Varies between sectors and firm types	Generally limited	Some in larger firms	Considerable in most firms
Long-term employer/ employee commitments	Low	Some for managerial staff, limited otherwise	Considerable in larger firms, limited elsewhere	Considerable in most firms
Organizational capabilities				
Variability across sectors	Considerable	Considerable	Limited	Limited
Prevalent types	Coordinating, reconfigurational in some firms	Coordinating in state-supported firms	Coordinating and learning in large firms	Coordinating and learning

formal rules of competition and cooperation without greatly restrict-
ing and standardizing the nature of economic actors, the organization
of interest groups or the movement of resources and skills between
markets. Such rules are usually generic across markets. They impose
few limits on the kinds of owners or managers that can enter particular
kinds of markets, or on the kinds of strategies they follow and how
they implement them. Equally, the structure and boundaries of interest
groups, as well as their relationships with their members, are typically
not specified, so that employers' groups, unions, and professions are
heterogeneous in their governance and operations. This means that
the relative influence of such groups on firms' priorities and strategies
can vary within and between such countries, as can their pursuit of
growth or profit goals and investment in developing different kinds
of organizational capabilities.

Within the broadly arm's length relationships between major economic actors in these kinds of societies, for example, the autonomy of
managers from shareholders to invest in the development of routines
and collective expertise to realize economies of scale and scope can
differ considerably over time and across sectors. As Lazonick and
O'Sullivan (1996, 1997) have pointed out, for much of the twentieth
century the capital markets of the United States provided relatively
patient capital to large companies able to pay out steady dividends.
This enabled many of them to develop substantial managerial hierarchies and invest in innovative capabilities until increasing inflation
and the rise of the junk bond market stimulated the market for corporate control. Subject, then, to the general constraints of capital market
expectations and market for corporate control, senior managers in
these kinds of states can have considerable freedom to determine
strategies and change direction.

Additionally, the organization of labour relations is often left open
in such societies, with multiple possibilities available to firms. Heterogeneity in employer–employee relationships is therefore quite high,
especially between sectors and firms of different sizes. As a result,
market economies dominated by these kinds of institutions exhibit
a preference for arm's length relationships between owners, managers, and employees, but permit a wide variety of firm type and
commitment within this general framework.

Consequently, while the overall extent of authority sharing between
business partners, employers, and most employees tends to be limited
in such societies, sectoral differences as well as changes over time
in particular industries, can be considerable, as Herrigel and Wittke

suggest elsewhere in this volume (Chapter 11). This is especially likely when different technological regimes encourage contrasting patterns of managerial behaviour and the state pursues particular policy 'missions', in areas such as defence and healthcare. Even within the same sorts of industries, distinct differences in economic organization can develop between regions with contrasting histories and environments, as Saxenian (1994) has emphasized in her discussion of Route 128 firms and Silicon Valley (see also, Kenney 2000).

Given the heterogeneity of skill formation systems and labour representation characteristics of such societies, it is not surprising that considerable variations occur in the organization of, say, financial and professional service companies, capital-intensive industry, high technology new firms, and light industry. The extent to which countries such as the United Kingdom and United States have established nationally standardized and stable forms of owner control, inter-firm relations, and employment policies across all sectors remains, then, questionable, despite their overall tendency to favour an arm's length version of industrial capitalism (Dobbin 1994; Hollingsworth 1991).

Turning now to consider countries where the state has tended to follow more active promotional policies and organize interest groups more directly, these establish a 'thicker' institutional environment for companies that encourages greater similarity in many aspects of economic organization (Hollingsworth and Streeck 1994). However, the considerable differences between types of promotional states and associated institutional arrangements affect the degree of standardization of economic organization patterns and firm strategies across sectors and regions, especially inter-firm collaboration and employment relations.

In state dominated institutional regimes there are likely to be considerable differences between companies and sectors supported by the state and those that are relatively neglected. While the former are often able to obtain cheap credit for expansion in line with state objectives, and so to grow without diluting owners' control, the latter usually have to rely on their own resources and so typically are unable to compete in capital-intensive sectors. Similarly, while the state may assist the former to obtain licences for new technologies and import scarce components, the latter are likely to experience much greater difficulty in accessing key resources for entering new industries. As a result, state supported firms and sectors will probably grow faster in the more capital-intensive and innovation-based industries, be able to attract better educated staff and invest in developing distinctive organizational capabilities. They will therefore tend to be larger, more diversified, and have stronger coordinating abilities than less favoured companies.

However, their high level of dependence upon state agencies and susceptibility to changes in state policies and personnel mean that such firms have to deal with high levels of political risk and often develop quite particularistic relations with the political executive and bureaucratic elite. These can be more personal than organizational and encourage strong levels of owner control over firm strategies and behaviour. Who owns and controls these companies matters to the state in such societies, as does which industries they enter and on what conditions. An important characteristic of successful companies is therefore their ability to develop and maintain close connections with political, and perhaps bureaucratic, elites, and to fulfil their objectives.

Because of continued access to cheap credit, at least during periods of rapid growth, continuing direct owner control is facilitated in these state supported enterprises. Given the dominant role of the state and its predominantly top down, if not paternalistic, pattern of political control and mobilization, their internal authority relations are also likely to be centralized with little authority sharing, especially over issues of finance, strategy, and personnel. Collective learning and continuing incremental innovation based on individual employee problem solving and knowledge enhancement are limited in these circumstances. Equally, competition for state support between these companies is likely to restrict their ability to cooperate with each other, and thus authority sharing between business partners will also be restricted in these sectors. Inter-firm connections are therefore more limited and short-term than in more decentralized economies.

In the less favoured sectors, firms are likely to be smaller, slower growing, and owner dominated. As the history of the *chaebol* in South Korea shows, much of their growth has been achieved through acquiring SMEs with the help of state subsidized credit and many smaller firms have been subjected to predatory behaviour by them (see, for example, Fields 1995; Woo 1991). This uncertain and unsupportive environment seems likely to encourage opportunism by economic actors as well as strong owner control of most companies and a reluctance to share authority, even with managers who might develop coordinating capabilities. Consequently, the establishment of managerial hierarchies and distinctive organizational capabilities in these enterprises will remain limited.

Business corporatist states develop considerable collaboration between state agencies, the banking system, and large companies in managing economic development, as in the post-war Japanese developmental state (Aoki and Patrick 1994; Gao 2001; Johnson 1982; Okimoto 1989; Samuels 1987). Individual shareholder interests are typically weakly represented in large companies' dominant coalitions in these kinds of societies relative to those of top managers and other long-term core employees. Additionally, state supported and strong business associations encourage cooperation between many of the larger firms, who also are not prevented from forming alliances within and across sectoral boundaries to block hostile takeovers and share investments in new developments. Growth goals correspondingly dominate profit ones in most large companies.

Although such states may support some small businesses, as did the Japanese in the pre-war period, albeit somewhat ineffectually (Friedman 1988: 162–6), and more systematically with specialized financial institutions in the 1950s and 1960s (Patrick and Rohlen 1987), promotional states in general find it easier to work with large companies and cohesive associations that can implement agreed policies effectively. As Patrick and Rohlen (1987: 369) suggest: 'government economic policy makers (in Japan) apparently see small and medium-size-enterprise more as a problem than as a source of economic growth and vitality ... on the whole ... MITI's policy approach (to SMEs) is defensive'. There are often therefore considerable differences in the degree of collaboration between companies and opportunism more generally between large and small firms in such countries, especially where the more conservative political parties do not rely greatly upon small business owners' support.

This is especially so in employment relations and labour representation practices that are largely left up to individual firms and business groups. While firms do often develop common norms about poaching skilled workers and exchange information on wage rates, sometimes encouraged by state agencies seeking to limit 'excessive' competition (Gao 2001), they are much more able to pursue idiosyncratic labour management practices than their counterparts in collaborative regimes. Consequently, inter-firm differences tend to be stronger in this regard, especially since unions are less standardized in their organizational forms and more enterprise specific. It should be noted, though, that in Japan at least, what Clark (1979) terms the 'society of industry' exerts quite strong institutional pressures on the larger firms to conform to dominant norms of employment policy.

State coordination of large firms' strategies and restriction of opportunism by employers here encourages them to invest more in training and long-term commitments to skilled employees than do most small firms. Consequently, significant variations in employment policies and bargaining procedures develop between firms of different sizes in these kinds of market economy. While large employers tend to pay higher wages than their smaller competitors in most economies, this is especially likely in business corporatist states where bargaining and many other aspects of labour relations are decentralized to individual companies, and firms attempt to retain scarce skilled workers.

Such variation in labour management practices between employers is further reinforced by the lack of a state supported and standardized skill formation system in these kinds of economies. The development and evaluation of practical skills are essentially in the hands of individual firms, who vary in the resources they can devote to training as well as their ability to retain staff. Large firms are more able to attract better educated workers by offering long-term career prospects, higher pay, and more training in a variety of roles. Because skills are highly firm specific here, they restrict labour mobility, which in turn further enhances employer–employee commitment. As a result, employees are more willing to contribute to long-term organizational learning on a continuous basis, thus further improving collective capabilities and knowledge in ways that smaller firms find difficult to imitate.

Inclusive corporatist states, on the other hand, encourage the institutionalization of common kinds of employment relations, workplace representation, and skill formation systems across sectors and regions so that companies tend to follow similar procedures and deal with similar types of unions, works councils, etc. The management of labour relations is, therefore, quite highly structured by collective rules and norms in such institutional regimes. This means that most companies are enmeshed in collaborative relationships with competitors, suppliers, and customers, as well as with unions and other labour groupings.

Consequently, they are encouraged to develop relatively long-term commitments to established business partners, including skilled workers, that favour growth goals, and incremental rather than radical innovation. However, because skills are developed, assessed, and certified by joint public–private agencies, and standardized around particular technologies and sectors rather than being largely idiosyncratic to firms, commitment to individual employees tends to be less than in countries that delegate more to firms. In the case of countries such as Germany where sectoral bargaining systems and strong employers' associations restrict both employer and employee opportunism, these standardized skills and occupational identities have not led to as much labour mobility as is common in the fluid labour markets of arm's length business environments, and so organizational learning tends to be greater (Marsden 1999; Soskice 1999; Streeck 1992).

As in other credit-based financial systems with limited protection of minority shareholder rights, these kinds of institutional arrangements facilitate the continuation of large blockholder control of companies as they grow, as well as close, relatively long-term, relationships between banks and other financial intermediaries and firms. Together with weak enforcement of any competition legislation that might prevent alliances and cooperation between companies, often because of a history of effective cartelization and rationalization through cooperative agreements as in Germany (Berghahn 1986; Djelic and Quack, Chapter 6, this volume; Herrigel 1996), these interconnections encourage considerable collaboration between companies and the pursuit of long-term growth goals rather than short-term profitability. However, these states often also develop specialized agencies and programmes to support small firms and protect them against predatory actions of large competitors, especially by limiting price competition and supporting technology transfer and cooperative research and development in 'diffusion-oriented' technology policies (Abramson et al. 1997; Ergas 1987). Such efforts limit the differences between large and small firms and further the homogeneity of firm type and behaviour in these kinds of societies.

Overall, then, the more corporatist is the political system, the more owners, managers, and employees are likely to be organized in similar ways and deal with each other according to relatively standardized procedures. Firms in highly corporatist environments will be more constrained to follow institutionalized conventions and should vary less in their governance structures, priorities, and capabilities than those in less organized societies. Sectoral, regional, and size differences between companies should be less marked in these kinds of regimes than in other ones. Because the institutions governing labour and capital markets typically encompass small and medium-sized firms as well as large ones here, more companies are likely to follow similar policies and practices—and so develop similar kinds of organizational capabilities than where states focus on larger firms and do not establish stable mechanisms for managing labour relationships.

It is particularly in such societies, then, that nationally distinctive patterns of economic organization are most likely to be developed and reproduced, and that most firms are likely to follow similar patterns of authority sharing and employer–employee commitment, including the sorts of employment practices identified by Marsden (1999) as key features of employment systems. The national specificity and cohesion of business systems should be greatest in societies where the state takes a leading role in orchestrating economic development with systematic-ally organized and standardized forms of interest group representation and bargaining on a continuing basis.

8.4. The Impact of Internationalization on National Business Systems and Firm Characteristics

These relationships highlight the importance of complementary rela-tions between strong national institutions for cohesive and distinctive business systems to become established and reproduced at the national level. The growing internationalization of markets and economic coordination since the 1960s has, however, been seen as reducing the strength and the complementarity of national institutions, especially in the more coordinated market economies such as Germany and Japan (Lane, Chapter 4, this volume; Streeck and Yamamura 2003). Together with the growth of international regulation—both public and private—and interstate political arrangements such as the European Union, increasing cross-national economic integration threatens the autarky and dominance of national regimes and can enhance the freedom of action of investors and managers from national institutions (Hancké and Goyer, Chapter 3; Herrigel and Wittke, Chapter 11; Moen and Lilja, Chapter 12, this volume).

Compared to the heyday of the Bretton Woods' regulatory system when national control of financial flows was considerable, if not overwhelming, there seems little doubt that international trade and investment flows—both portfolio and strategic—have grown signi-ficantly (Held et al. 1999). Whether they are qualitatively greater than those in the gold standard period before the First World War remains, much debated, however, as do their implications for national autonomy and institutional convergence (Djelic and Quack 2003a; Hirst and Thompson 1996). Similarly, while some have suggested that global business regulation has increased considerably since the 1980s, and is increasingly governed by the institutions of the currently dominant nation-state, it is not at all obvious that this is irreversible or that it signifies the decline of national institutional regimes (Braithwaite and Drahos 2000; Djelic and Quack 2003*b*; Whitley 2003*a*).

Insofar as the internationalization of ownership, managerial coordination, and regulation has greatly increased since the 1970s, we would expect this to reduce the relative strength of national agencies and institutions, especially where these are weakly established and contradictory in their implications for firms. However, the extent to which firms' governance structures, strategies and capabilities, and national business systems more generally, do in fact alter as a result of increased cross-border investment, competition, and regulation varies across institutional regimes and the nature of the changes being considered. In this section I first consider the significance of the growth of international institutions and agencies, before examining the likely impact of inward and outward FDI on different kinds of host and home economies.

8.4.1. *The growth and nature of international institutions and agencies*

Considering initially the significance of international institutions governing economic actors and their behaviour, it is important to note that the establishment of interstate agencies does not necessarily imply that they constitute a distinctive set of global institutions regulating international economic transactions and competition that are separate from national interests and institutions. Despite the importance of the BIS, the IMF, the World Bank, WTO, and similar agencies for the development of the post-war financial system and liberalization of trade, it would be difficult to claim that they are autonomous international organizations able to pursue their own distinct goals independently from those of the strongest states. Just as some EU commissioners appear to behave as national politicians when their domestic interests are perceived to be threatened, so too the willingness and ability of those leading the major international agencies to implement decisions contrary to the interests of the United States and other powerful states seem quite limited, not least by the voting structures of these organizations.

Moreover, in many instances these organizations rely on national courts and justice systems to enforce their rulings, and so remain dependent on nation states for their effectiveness. Most attempts to enforce anti-trust and anti-cartel competition norms, for instance, depend on national legislation and state agencies rather than upon international law and courts. Growing interdependence between states, and their joint establishment of cross-national agencies, may herald some development of governance without government at the international level, as may also the growth of international epistemic communities, pressure groups, and private regulatory bodies such as the ratings agencies and accounting standards boards, but implementation of their judgements and application of their norms usually requires state acquiescence, if not active participation (Furger 2001; Martiny 2001). The critical role of the US SEC in legitimating the leading ratings agencies and judgements of the International Accounting Standards Board reveals the continued significance of national bodies, as do the policies of many regulatory agencies governing securities' exchanges (Porter 1993; Ventresca et al. 2003).

Additionally, because the legitimacy of most cross-national regulation rests upon the national delegation of powers, creating transnational institutions that have equivalent political legitimacy to most democratic states has proved difficult, as the record of EU agencies suggests, and there are few instances of distinctive international political cultures that institutionalize novel forms of authority. Instead, many transnational agencies and organizations function as arenas in which national representatives compete for authority and influence, as in many of the international standards setting bodies (Braithwaite and Drahos 2000; Murphy 1994), and their internal labour markets are as much structured by national interests and identities as by autonomous bureaucratic elites.

At the regional interstate level of political organization, the most important development has been the creation and expansion of the European Union. However, while it has established a number of pan-European regulations dealing with economic activities, especially through the European Court of Justice (Stone Sweet and Caporaso 1998), its weak political legitimacy relative to member states has limited its ability to homogenize and standardize rules governing capital and labour markets throughout Western Europe, let alone to act as a developmental state (Held et al. 1999: 74–7; Katzenstein 2003). Despite the establishment of the Single European Market and the European Central Bank, it would be difficult to argue convincingly that the European Union is a strong state in the sense of being able to impose its rules as an autonomous political entity on member states and major economic actors (Evans 1994; Plehwe and Vescovi 2003). While many European states now share power and authority with each other through EU institutions, they remain the primary unit of political action, competition, and legitimacy.

Turning to discuss the institutions that govern international capital and labour markets more specifically, there are few global regulatory bodies that attempt to control cross-border capital flows, to standardize shareholder rights in different capital markets or to establish credible international rules controlling banks and financial markets. Despite various efforts to institutionalize common regulations for securities markets across the world and establish liquid cross-national capital markets, significant variations in how such markets are regulated remain, and there are few signs of a transnational market for corporate control with fragmented shareholdings and a large liquid transfer market becoming established (Barca and Becht 2001; Morgan and Quack 2000; Porter 1993). Indeed, as the recent attempts of the European Union to establish common financial markets and a 'level playing field' for mergers and acquisitions across Europe illustrate, strong opposition to such a regulatory approach to capital markets remains, and it is not at all clear that an integrated financial market along 'Anglo-Saxon' lines will develop in Europe. Given the prevalence of credit-based financial systems and large block shareholdings in much of Europe, such an outcome is improbable.

There are also few international institutions and organizations able to regulate labour markets and skill formation systems in different countries. Insofar as cross-national labour markets do exist, and these seem to be restricted to business and professional elites, on the one hand, and unskilled labour, on the other hand, they are unregulated and composed largely of ad hoc transactions. While the European Union has developed some mechanisms for mutual recognition of qualifications, these do not appear to have led to substantial cross-border migration and remain subject to considerable national variability in implementation. MNCs therefore have few constraints from international agencies and organizations on how they manage their employees and equally limited pressures to standardize employment practices across subsidiaries.

Additionally, in considering the organization of cross-border interest representation, since there are no international institutions prescribing how groups should be formed, or that delegate particular powers to them in systematic ways, we would not expect much homogeneity in the organization and strategies of international business associations, employers' groups, and labour unions. Given that there is considerable variability in patterns of interest group formation across countries, any transnational pressure groupings that do develop are more likely to resemble the pluralist, competitive lobbying organizations characteristic of many arm's length institutional regimes than the standardized federations of functional monopolies found in many corporatist societies.

Insofar as any international institutions governing capital markets have become established and significant in the last quarter of the twentieth century, it is notable that they are mostly focused on developing common standards for trading financial assets transparently so that no investor is disadvantaged, and prices are set through publicly visible market processes. The general purpose of establishing cross-national rules for financial markets has been to create large and liquid capital markets with many, mostly anonymous, participants that reduce transaction costs and hence the cost of capital. Efficient pan-European markets are advocated by the European Commission in largely arm's length terms to increase liquidity and competition, reduce transaction costs, and so, it is claimed, boost the whole European economy.

While this may be partly a consequence of the dominance of the US economy, and its investment banks, it also reflects the concerns of international investors more broadly who require reliable institutions that can provide a level playing field for all market participants and ensure liquidity if they are to commit capital across national boundaries. If foreign capital markets are to be made safe for US and other international investors, similar institutions to those established in arm's length regulatory regimes are needed to govern cross-border capital flows so that returns can be reliably predicted.

Irrespective of their national provenance, then, groups pressing for international regulation of financial flows and investment norms are more likely to want minority shareholder protection and market transparency than institutions encouraging owner–manager commitment and lock-in since they are relatively remote from companies' decisions. Any international institutions that do become established as effective regulators of financial markets and standardizers of property rights in different countries are therefore likely to be more 'Anglo-Saxon' than 'Rhenish'.

In sum, the regulation and coordination of cross-border economic activities remains largely ad hoc and decentralized to individual companies and their major shareholders. At the global level, the international business environment is more anomic than institutionalized, with weak international institutions and organizations dependent on national agencies to implement decisions. Opportunism by economic actors is therefore relatively unconstrained across borders.

Where effective cross-national institutions have become established, these are usually more concerned with ensuring a transparent and reliable environment for trading assets than coordinating technological and/or sectoral development, or restraining market opportunism. Insofar as they do become significant, cross-national institutions seem likely to reinforce arm's length, opportunistic relationships between variously organized owners, managers, and employees. As a result, they may reduce the complementarity of institutions governing cooperation and competition between economic actors in the more highly coordinated market economies.

This suggests that internationalizing firms and other collective actors are likely to continue to pursue highly individual policies and practices across borders, with few supra-national constraints on how they do so. Just as the reconstruction of post-state socialist societies in Eastern Europe, and elsewhere, generated high levels of uncertainty and freedom of action for many existing and nascent socio-economic groups, the limited cross-border institutionalization of norms governing economic behaviour, coupled with the predominantly arm's length nature of those international agencies and regulations that have become established, are likely to encourage relatively opportunistic relationships with business partners and employees across national borders. They also imply that MNCs are more influenced by the nationally specific institutions governing capital and labour markets in their home and host societies than by transnational ones. As these vary, so too should authority sharing and commitments between owners, managers, and employees (Whitley, Chapter 8, this volume).

8.4.2. *Consequences of inward FDI on host economy business systems*

Turning to consider the broad effects of increasing inward foreign portfolio and strategic investment flows on host economy commitments between economic actors, these points suggest that they are likely to reduce the overall level of authority sharing and commitment between investors and firms, as illustrated by the Vodafone takeover of Mannesman that was facilitated by the considerable number of foreign shareholders of the latter, and encourage more opportunistic behaviour between companies and employees. As complementary changes to arm's length institutional regimes, they should reinforce actors' short-term and narrow goals in these kinds of society, although such regimes do permit a wide range of labour management practices within the dominantly low commitment culture. This means that investors seeking to generate continuous improvements and employee contributions to firm-specific knowledge through authority sharing and long-term organizational careers have few constraints in doing so. As contradictory influences in more promotional states, on the other hand, they may well facilitate firms' autonomy from domestic institutional pressures and enable top managers of host economy companies to pursue more opportunistic strategies.

The extent to which such opportunism does develop depends on the relative concentration of votes controlled by foreign investors compared to domestic ones, and the nature of host economy institutions governing capital and labour markets. The stronger and more complementary these are in generating commitment between economic actors, the less foreign investors, on their own, are likely to encourage opportunism. While this is obvious in countries that enable block holders to limit minority shareholder influence, it also reflects general state effectiveness in coordinating economic development, sharing information and risks, and restraining opportunistic behaviour, as well as institutional arrangements supporting collaboration between companies and inhibiting labour mobility.

The success of the electronics and telecommunications sector in Finland for instance, especially Nokia's transformation, seems to have been highly dependent on the state's ability to coordinate the activities and strategies of key actors in the late 1980s and early 1990s, and represents more a continuation of the post-war pattern of state-enabled capitalism than a radical break from it (Moen and Lilja, Chapter 12, this volume). Similarly, it is possible that the success of Vodafone's bid for Mannesman intensified German opposition to the EC's proposals to create a more level playing field for foreign investors and cross-border mergers and acquisitions, rather heralding the break-up of Rhineland capitalism.

Such limitation of opportunism is even more apparent for employer–employee relationships in corporatist societies that have strong and complementary institutions encouraging cooperation and commitment. While some US companies did not join sectoral wage setting bodies and similar employer–union negotiating arrangements when they first made substantial investments in Germany, most have since followed dominant norms governing employer–employee relationships (Ferner and Quintanilla 1998). Similarly, few foreign strategic investors in Japan have been able to flout the institutionalized conventions encouraging long-term commitment if they wished to attract the best staff and be regarded as trustworthy employers, despite some recent evidence of foreign banks helping to develop a distinct occupational labour market for investment analysts (Morgan and Kubo 2002). Where, then, national institutional regimes are cohesive and mutually reinforcing in encouraging authority sharing and commitment, foreign investment seems unlikely to change dominant patterns of labour relations, especially when firms are keen to take advantage of a highly skilled labour force rather than simply gain market access (Crouch et al. 1999).

Insofar as foreign portfolio and strategic investment does weaken commitment between owners, managers, and employees, then, this is most likely to occur in economies where dominant institutions are contradictory in their implications for authority sharing and/or strategic managers are already attempting to distance themselves from domestic institutional arrangements and develop more international capabilities. Such attempts may be more effective in gaining the support of other groups during periods of weak economic performance. Employers seeking to decentralize wage bargaining and increase their flexibility in managing wage costs, as well as to internationalize their operations and pressure the state on regulatory and tax measures, may invoke the interests of foreign investors and 'global' business practices more generally in order to gain their objectives.

However, given the continued significance of the nation-state in coordinating economic development in many collaborative institutional regimes, and the predominantly national basis of political competition and mobilization, the impact of foreign investors may be less than is sometimes claimed, especially when the fate of leading companies is threatened, as is illustrated by the actions of the French, Japanese, and Korean states in the late 1990s and early twenty-first century. Since much foreign portfolio investment is opportunistic, it is likely to leave when financial results are disappointing, thus reducing share prices. In the absence of a flourishing market for corporate control in most economies, continuing corporate decline in those dominated by promotional states seems likely to lead to a reaffirmation of previous ties and commitments, as has occurred in many Japanese companies in the late 1990s and early twenty-first century, often through state coordinated restructuring involving management changes, rather than to foreign acquisition or bankruptcy and break up. While, then, substantial inward FDI in CMEs may well weaken commitments between investors, managers, and employees, as well as increasing the pluralism of governance structures and capabilities, without additional institutional changes and the support of major interest groups within the host economy, its impact on dominant business systems will probably be limited.

8.4.3. *Consequences of outward FDI on home economy business systems*

Similar sorts of results are likely when firms from different kinds of institutional regimes make substantial foreign investments. Although opportunistic companies from low commitment regimes may have to adapt employment and labour management practices to host economy regimes in strong developmental and collaborative societies, they are unlikely to change their domestic practices or those in weaker institutional environments given the generally arm's length nature of institutions in the international business environment. Investor–manager relations will not alter greatly in these kinds of MNCs and their relationships with employees in different countries will simply display increased variety (Whitley 2001, 2003*a*, and Chapter 9 in this volume). As a result, their overall degree of authority sharing and commitment is unlikely to change very much and their organizational capabilities at the international level should remain similar to their domestic ones.

On the other hand, internationalizing companies from developmental and collaborative institutional regimes, have to deal with quite a different kind of business environment in coordinating their foreign operations and may change their relationships with business partners and employees as a result. This is more likely when top managers are concerned to gain autonomy from the constraints of their domestic environment and to develop novel organizational capabilities than when FDI is primarily made in order to gain market access and/or capital flexibility. If they issue substantial numbers of shares on the Anglo-Saxon stock markets and engage in cross-border mergers and acquisitions in addition, such firms may, of course, begin to be pressured to improve short-term shareholder returns, as has Daimler Chrysler. The effects of such pressure does, however, depend on the relative importance of foreign and domestic shareholders and the level of home economy institutional support. Furthermore, in the cases of firms that have a fragmented international shareholder base but strong domestic barriers to takeovers, such as Shell and Unilever, the impact of declining share prices and short-term owner pressures will be more limited than for companies incorporated entirely in the United Kingdom or United States.

While such companies may well exhibit lower levels of authority sharing and commitment with employees in arm's length economies than in their domestic units, this is unlikely to lead to major shifts in the latter unless there are concomitant institutional changes in their home economies. Experimenting with new kinds of work organization and learning from foreign employment practices, as some German firms have done (Lane 1998, 2001; Müller and Loveridge 1997), will prob ably not result in the transformation of collaborative organizations into more opportunistic ones with radical reconfigurational capabilities unless top managers are willing and able to reject their 'administrative heritage' and the constraints of domestic institutions and interest groups. Integrating highly novel kinds of collective competences from arm's length environments into strong corporate cultures based on long-term employer–employee commitments is fraught with difficulties, as Eisai found out when it invested in British academic research in London (Lam 2003).

The impact of FDI on domestic companies is even more limited when their home economies and customers are much more important for their revenues than foreign ones, as in the case of most internationalizing Japanese banks (Morgan et al. 2003; Sakai 2000; Whitley et al. 2003). Here, quite different relationships have been developed with foreign employees to those with Japanese ones, and often the business partners of manufacturing firms' overseas subsidiaries are treated differently to their first tier Japanese suppliers (Dedoussis 1994). While the domestic Japanese business system, and political economy more generally, may have altered somewhat in the 1990s (see, for example, Gao 2001; Pempel 1998), its key characteristics have not radically shifted to an arm's length regulatory regime of market economy, despite the urgings of many foreign and political commentators (Dore 2000).

Overall, then, the increasing internationalization of capital markets and companies, as well as some regulation of cross-national economic activities, can be expected to reinforce the general arm's length nature of relationships between owners, managers, and employees in market-led institutional regimes. They may also reduce the influence of some national institutional arrangements on companies' governance structures and strategies in more collaborative societies as top managers become more able to access foreign capital markets, engage in foreign takeovers and reduce their dependence on their domestic markets. MNCs from such economies that gain investors from outside their national economy and invest considerable resources in different environments to gain strategic assets, are able to become more detached from home economy institutions than their more nationally restricted counterparts, as well as developing international careers that expose managers to different ways of organizing economic relationships.

It is doubtful, though, whether this increased managerial autonomy from home economy institutions for the largest and most internationalized enterprises heralds the widespread restructuring of promotional states and allied institutions, or even the transformation of such firms into novel hybrids. Most bankers, managers, and unions in developmental and collaborative institutional regimes are likely to feel threatened by changes that would institutionalize an effective market for corporate control and arm's length contracting between companies, and it is improbable that the German or Japanese states would restructure their financial systems to suit UK and US investment bankers. The apparent growing differentiation of the German banking system may herald a separation of a few large banks from 'Modell Deutschland' rather than its radical transformation (Jackson 2003; Vitols 2003). If a unified European capital market ever does become established, it seems more likely to combine features from the different national financial systems than to be a simulacrum of the UK or UK ones (Djelic and Quack 2003b).

Equally, the continued influence of labour unions in many European countries, and the preference of most employers to engage in incremental reform of labour market institutions than to insist upon their radical reorganization, have limited the effects of internationalization on national labour markets and skill formation systems. The advantages of continued employee commitment to firm-specific problem solving, continuing incremental innovation, and functional flexibility seem to outweigh the disadvantages of limited numerical flexibility and employer independence in labour relations, especially in the corporate welfare society of Japan (Thelen and Kume 2003).

8.5. Conclusions

This outline of how distinctive national business systems might arise and be reproduced has emphasized a number of points. First, the establishment of cohesive and distinctive business systems at the national level is greatly affected by the degree to which the national institutions governing capital and labour markets dominate those at other levels, and are complementary to state structures and policies in their implications for the constitution of key economic actors and the prevalent ways in which owners, managers, and employees deal with each other. Especially important here is the extent to which they reinforce tendencies to opportunism and adversarial competition between discrete actors or constrain such behaviour and encourage long-term commitments.

Second, the homogeneity and national distinctiveness of economic coordination and control patterns across technologies, markets, and localities reflects the standardization of key institutions within national borders and differences between countries. The more that the formal institutions governing economic transactions, interest group formation, employment relations, skill development, etc. apply throughout an economy, the more likely that the nature and behaviour of economic actors will be similar in different industries and regions.

Such institutional standardization is linked, third, to the nature of the state and the economic policies followed by its elites. The more active and cohesive is the state in organizing and mobilizing major interest groups in the formulation and implementation of economic policies, the more likely that forms of representation and political–economic bargaining processes will become relatively standardized, particularly the ways that owners, managers, and employees compete and cooperate. Corporatist states encourage and legitimate certain kinds of group formation and collective action to a greater extent than do arm's length ones, and so build more stable and common patterns of interaction between major economic actors.

Fourth, the growing internationalization of investment and managerial coordination may weaken the national specificity of business systems in general, especially institutional constraints on opportunism, but can be expected to have varied consequences in contrasting institutional contexts. Given the weakly institutionalized nature of the international business environment at the global level, the organization of most cross-border transactions is likely to remain more influenced by home and host economy institutions than by international ones, as well as by the individual characteristics of the companies concerned that can often pursue more idiosyncratic strategies internationally than they would at home. While growing cross-national investment in the more coordinated market economies may well attenuate the interdependence of owners, managers, and employees, and perhaps reduce their mutual commitment, strong national corporatist institutions will limit such changes. This is especially so for labour relations, which remain largely governed by local and national institutions in most of the OECD countries.

In sum, the national specificity and distinctiveness of business systems depends on the extent to which characteristics of states and related institutions are complementary in their implications for firms and markets, as well as the active structuring and coordination of interest groups and their interrelationships by state agencies. As long as the nation-state remains the primary unit of political competition, legitimacy, and definer and upholder of private property rights, in addition to being the predominant influence on labour market institutions, many characteristics of business systems will continue to vary significantly across national boundaries, albeit not always constituting highly integrated and consistent coordination and control systems.

REFERENCES

Abramson, H. Norman, Encarmacao, Jose, Reid, Proctor R., and Schmoch, Ulrich (eds.) (1997). *Technology Transfer Systems in the United States and Germany*. Washington, DC: National Academy Press.

Aguilera, Ruth and Jackson, G. (2003). 'The Cross-National Diversity of Corporate Governance: Dimensions and Determinants'. *Academy of Management Review* 28: 447–65.

Amable, Bruno (2000). 'Institutional Complementarity and Diversity of Social Systems of Innovation and Production'. *Review of International Political Economy* 7: 645–87.

—— (2003). *The Diversity of Modern Capitalism*. Oxford: Oxford University Press.

Aoki, Masahiko (2001). *Toward a Comparative Institutional Analysis*. Cambridge, MA: MIT Press.

—— and Patrick, Hugh (eds.) (1994). *The Japanese Main Bank System: Its Relevance for Developing and Transforming Economies*. Oxford: Clarendon Press.

Barca, Fabrizio and Becht, Marco (eds.) (2001). *The Control of Corporate Europe*. Oxford: Oxford University Press.

Berghahn, Volker (1986). *The Americanisation of West German Industry 1945–1973*. Leamington, Spa: Berg.

Braczyk, Hans-Joachim, Cooke, Philip, and Heidenreich, Martin (eds.) (2003) *Regional Innovation Systems: The Role of Governance in a Globalized World*. London: Routledge.

Braithwaite, John and Drahos, Peter (2000). *Global Business Regulation.* Cambridge: Cambridge University Press.

Breschi, Stefano and Malerba, Franco (1997). 'Sectoral Innovation Systems: Technological Regimes, Schumpeterian Dynamics and Spatial Boundaries'. In: Charles Edquist (ed.), *Systems of Innovation.* London: Pinter, pp. 130–56.

Casper, S., Lehrer, M., and Soskice, D. (1999). 'Can High-Technology Industries Prosper in Germany? Institutional Frameworks and the Evolution of the German Software and Biotechnology Industries'. *Industry and Innovation* 6: 6–23.

Clark, Rodney (1979). *The Japanese Company.* Yale University Press.

Clarke, Michael (1999). 'The Regulation of Retail Financial Services in Britain: An Analysis of a Crisis'. In: Glenn Morgan and Lars Engwall (eds.), *Regulation and Organizations: International Perspectives.* London: Rout ledge, pp. 211–29.

Crouch, Colin, Finegold, David, and Sako, Mari (1999). *Are Skills the Answer? The Political Economy of Skill Creation in Advanced Industrial Countries.* Oxford: Oxford University Press.

——, le Gales, Patrick, Trigilia, Carlo, and Voelzkow, Helmut (2001). *Local Production Systems in Europe: Rise or Demise?* Oxford: Oxford University Press.

Culpepper, Pepper D. (1999). 'Individual Choice, Collective Action, and the Problem of Training Reform: Insights from France and Eastern Germany'. In: Pepper Culpepper and David Finegold (eds.), *The German Skills Machine: Sustaining Comparative Advantage in a Global Economy.* New York: Berghahn Books, pp. 269–325.

—— (2001). 'Employers' Associations, Public Policy and the Politics of Decentralised Cooperation'. In: Peter Hall and David Soskice (eds.), *Varieties of Capitalism*, pp. 275–306.

Cusumano, M. A. (1985). *The Japanese Automobile Industry: Technology and Management at Nissan and Toyota.* Harvard University Press.

Dedoussis, Vagelis (1994). 'The Core Workforce—Peripheral Workforce Dichotomy and the Transfer of Japanese Management Practices'. In: N. Campbell and F. Burton (eds.), *Japanese Multinationals.* London: Routledge, pp. 186–217.

Deyo, F. C. (1989). *Beneath the Miracle: Labour Subordination in the New Asian Industrialism.* Berkeley: University of California Press.

DiMaggio, Paul (1994). 'Culture and Economy'. In: N. Smelser and R. Swedberg (eds.), *The Handbook of Economic Sociology.* Princeton: Princeton University Press, pp. 27–57.

Djelic, Marie-Laure and Quack, Sigrid (2003a). 'Introduction: Governing Globalization-Bringing Institutions Back In'. In: Djelic and Quack (eds.), *Globalization and Institutions: Redefining the Rules of the Economic Game.* Cheltenham: Edward Elgar, pp. 1–14.

Djelic, Marie-Laure and Quack, Sigrid (2003*b*). 'Conclusion: Globalization as a Double Process of Institutional Change and Institution Building'. In: M.-L. Djelic and S. Quack (eds.), *Globalization and Institutions: Redefining the Rules of the Economic Game*. Cheltenham: Edward Elgar, pp. 302–33.

—— and —— (eds.) (2003*c*). *Globalization and Institutions: Redefining the Rules of the Economic Game*. Cheltenham: Edward Elgar.

Dobbin, Frank (1994). *Forging Industrial Policy: The United States, Britain, and France in the Railway Age*. Cambridge: Cambridge University Press.

Dore, Ronald (2000). *Stock Market Capitalism: Welfare Capitalism*. Oxford: Oxford University Press.

Eccleston, B. (1989). *State and Society in Post-War Japan*. Cambridge: Polity Press.

Ergas, Henry (1987). 'Does Technology Policy Matter?' In: Bruce R. Guile and Harvey Brooks (eds.), *Technology and Global Industry: Companies and Nations in the World Economy*. Washington, DC: National Academy Press.

Evans, Peter (1994). *Embedded Autonomy: States and Industrial Transformation*. Princeton, NJ: Princeton University Press.

Ferner, Anthoy and Quintanilla, J. (1998) 'Multinationals, National Business Systems and HRM,' *International Jounal of Human Resource Management*, 9(4): 710–31.

Fields, Karl J. (1995). *Enterprise and the State in Korea and Taiwan*. Ithaca, NY: Cornell University Press.

Friedman, David (1988). *The Misunderstood Miracle*. Ithaca, NY: Cornell University Press.

Furger, Franco (2001). 'Global Markets, New Games, New Rules: The Challenge of International Private Governance'. In: R. Appelbaum, W. Felstiner and V. Gessner (eds.), *Rules and Networks: The Legal Culture of Global Business Transactions*. Oxford: Hart, pp. 201–45.

Gao, Bai (2001). *Japan's Economic Dilemma: The Institutional Origins of Prosperity and Stagnation*. Cambridge: Cambridge University Press.

Garon, Sheldon (1987). *The State and Labor in Modern Japan*. Berkeley, CA: University of California Press.

Hall, Peter and Soskice, David (eds.) (2001). *Varieties of Capitalism: The Institutional Foundations of Comparative Advantage*. Oxford: Oxford University Press.

Hart, Jeffrey A. (1992). *Rival Capitalists: International Competitiveness in the United States, Japan, and Western Europe*. Ithaca, NY: Cornell University Press.

Held, David, Anthony, McGraw, David, Goldblatt, and Jonathan Perraton, (1999). *Global Transformations*. Cambridge: Polity Press.

Herrigel, Gary (1994). 'Industry as a Form of Order'. In: R. Hollingsworth, P. Schmitter, and W. Streeck (eds.), *Governing Capitalist Economies*. Oxford: University Press.

—— (1996). *Industrial Constructions*. Cambridge: Cambridge University Press.

Hirst, Paul and Thompson, Grahame (1996). *Globalisation in Question*. Oxford: Polity Press.

Hollingsworth, J. Rogers (1991). 'The Logic of Coordinating American Manufacturing Sectors'. In: J. L. Campbell, J. R. Hollingsworth and L. Lindbergh (eds.), *Governance of the American Economy*. Cambridge: Cambridge University Press.

—— and Streeck, Wolfgang (1994). 'Counties and Sectors: Concluding Remarks on Performance, Convergence and Competitiveness'. In: J. Rogers Hollingsworth et al. (eds.), *Governing Capitalist Economies*. Oxford University Press.

—— and Boyer, Robert (eds.) (1997). *Contemporary Capitalism: The embeddedness of institutions*, Cambridge: Cambridge University Press.

——, Müller, Karl H. and Hollingsworth, Ellen Jame (eds.) (2002). *Advancing Socio-Economies: An Institutionalist Perspective*, Lanham, Maryland: Rowman and Littlefield.

Iterson, A. van and Olie, R. (1992). 'European Business Systems: The Dutch Case'. In: R. Whitley (ed.), *European Business Systems: Firms and Markets in their National Contexts*. London: Sage.

Jackson, Gregory (2003). 'Corporate Governance in Germany and Japan: Liberalization Pressures and Responses During the 1990s'. In: Yamamura and Streeck (eds.), *The End of Diversity?* Ithaca, NY: Cornell University Press, pp. 261–305.

Johnson, C. (1982). *MITI and the Japanese Miracle*. Stanford University Press.

Karnoe, Peter (1999). 'The Business Systems Framework and Danish SMEs', In: P. Karnoe, P. H. Kristensen, and P. H. Andersen (eds.), *Mobilizing Resources and Generating Capabilities*. Copenhagen: Copenhagen Business School Press, pp. 7–72.

Katzenstein, P. (1985). *Small States in World Markets*. Ithaca, NY: Cornell University Press.

—— (2003). 'Regional States: Japan and Asia, Germany in Europe'. In: Yamamura and Streeck (eds.), *The Origins of Nonliberal Capitalism: Germany and Japan in Comparison*. Ithaca, NY: Cornell University Press, pp. 115–46.

Kenney, Martin (ed.) (2000). *Understanding Silicon Valley: The Anatomy of an Entrepreneurial Region*. Stanford, CA: Stanford University Press.

Kim, Eun Mee (1997). *Big Business, Big State: Collusion and Conflict in South Korean Development, 1960–1990*. Albany, NY: State University of New York Press.

Kristensen, Peer Hull (1992). 'Strategies Against Structure: Institutions and Economic Organisation in Denmark'. In: R. Whitley (ed.), *European Business Systems*. London: Sage, pp. 117–36.

—— (1994). 'Strategies in a Volatile World'. *Economy and Society* 23: 305–34.

—— (1996). 'On the Constitution of Economic Actors in Denmark: Interacting Skill Containers and Project Coordinators'. In: R. Whitley and

P. H. Kristensen (eds.), *The Changing European Firm: Limits to Convergence*. London: Routledge, pp. 118–58.

Lam, Alice (2003). 'Organisational Learning in Multinationals: R&D Networks of Japanese and US MNEs in the UK'. *Journal of Management Studies* 40: 673–704.

Lane, Christel (1998). 'European Companies Between Globalization and Localization: A Comparison of Internationalisation Strategies of British and German MNCs'. *Economy and Society* 27: 462–85.

Lane, Christel (2001). 'The Emergence of German Transnational Companies: A Theoretical Analysis and Empirical Study of the Globalization Process'. In: G. Morgan, P. H. Kristensen, and R. Whitley (eds.), *The Multinational Firm: Organizing Across Institutional and National Divides*. Oxford: Oxford University Press, pp. 69–96.

Lazonick, W. and O'Sullivan, Mary (1996). 'Organization, Finance and International Competition'. *Industrial Corporate Change* 5: 1–49.

—— and —— (1997). 'Big Business and Skill Formation in the Wealthiest Nations: The Organizational Revolution in the Twentieth Century'. In: A. D. Chandler, F. Amatori, and T. Hikino (eds.), *Big Business and the Wealth of Nations*. Cambridge: Cambridge University Press, pp. 497–521.

Lilja, Kari, Rasanen, Keijo and Tainio, Risto (1992). 'A Dominant Business Recipe: The Forest Sector in Finland'. In: R. Whitley (ed.), *European Business Systems*. London: Sage, pp. 137–54.

—— and Tainio, Risto (1996). 'The Nature of the Typical Finnish Firm'. In: R. Whitley and P. H. Kristensen (eds.), *The Changing European Firm*. London: Routledge, pp. 159–91.

Marsden, David (1999). *A Theory of Employment Systems*. Oxford: Oxford University Press.

Martiny, Dieter (2001). 'Traditional Private and Commercial Law Rules Under the Pressure of Global Transactions: The Role for an International Order'. In: R. Appelbaum, W. Felstiner, and V. Gessner (eds.), *Rules and Networks: The Legal Culture of Global Business Transactions*. Oxford: Hart, pp. 123–55.

Morgan, Glenn (1997). 'The Global Context of Financial Services: National Systems and the International Political Economy'. In: G. Morgan and D. Knights (eds.), *Regulation and Deregulation in European Financial Services*. London: Macmillan, pp. 14–41.

—— and Quack, Sigrid (2000). 'Confidence and Confidentiality: The Social Construction of Performance Standards in Banking'. In: S. Quack, G. Morgan, and R. Whitley (eds.), *National Capitalisms, Global Competition and Economic Performance*. Amsterdam: Benjamins, pp. 131–58.

—— and Soin, Kim (1999). 'Regulatory Compliance'. In: G. Morgan, and L. Engwall (eds.), *Regulation and Organizations: International Perspectives*. London: Routledge, pp. 166–90.

—— and Kubo, Izumi (2002). 'Beyond Path Dependency? Constructing New Models for Institutional Change: The Case of Capital Markets in Japan'. Unpublished paper, Warwick Business School.

Morgan, Glenn, Whitley, Richard, Kelly, William, and Sharpe, Diana (2003). 'Global Managers and Japanese Multinationals: Internationalisation and Management in Japanese Financial Institutions'. *International Journal of Human Resource Management.*

Mueller, Frank and Loveridge, Ray (1997). 'Institutional, Sectoral and Corporate Dynamics in the Creation of Global Supply Chains'. In: R. Whitley and P. H. Kristensen (eds.), *Governance at Work.* Oxford University Press, pp. 139–57.

Murphy, Craig (1994). *International Organization and Industrial Change.* Cambridge: Polity Press.

Nettl, Peter (1968). 'The State as a Conceptual Variable'. *World Politics* 20: 559–92.

Okimoto, Daniel (1989). *Between MITI and the Market: Japanese Industrial Policy for High Technology.* Stanford, CA: Stanford University Press.

Patrick, Hugh and Rohlen, Thomas (1987). 'Small-Scale Family Enterprises'. In: K. Yamamura and Y. Yasuba (eds.), *The Political Economy of Japan Volume 1: The Domestic Transformation.* Stanford, CA: Stanford University Press, pp. 331–84.

Pempel, T. J. (1998). *Regime Shift: Comparative Dynamics of the Japanese Political Economy.* Ithaca, NY: Cornell University Press.

Plehwe, Dieter and Vescovi, Stefano (2003). 'Europe's Special Case: The Five Corners of Business–State Interactions'. In: M.-L. Djelic and S. Quack (eds.), *Globalization and Institution: The Rules of the Economic Game.* Cheltenham: Edward Elgar, pp. 193–219.

Polanyi, Karl (1957). *The Great Transformation.* Boston: Beacon Press.

Porter, Tony (1993). *States, Markets and Regimes in Global Finance.* London: Macmillan.

Sakai, Junko (2000). *Japanese Bankers in the City of London.* London: Routledge.

Salomon, Danielle (1997). 'The Problematic Transformation of the Banking Sector in France: The Case of Consumer Credit'. In: G. Morgan and D. Knights (eds.), *Regulation and Deregulation in European Financial Services.* London: Macmillan, pp. 133–53.

Samuels, R. J. (1987). *The Business of the Japanese State.* Ithaca, NY: Cornell University Press.

Saxenian, Annalee (1994). *Regional Advantage: Culture and Competition in Silicon Valley and Route 128.* Cambridge, MA: Harvard University Press.

Smelser, Neil and Swedberg, Richard (1994). 'The Sociological Perspective on the Economy'. In: N. Smelser and R. Swedberg (eds.), *Handbook of Economic Sociology.* Princeton: Princeton University Press, pp. 3–26.

Schmidt, Vivien A. (2002). *The Futures of European Capitalism*. Oxford: Oxford University Press.

Soskice, D. (1999). 'Divergent Production Regimes: Coordinated and Unco-ordinated Market Economies in the 1980s and 1990s'. In: H. Kitschelt et al. (ed.), *Continuity and Change in Contemporary Capitalism*. Cambridge: Cambridge University Press.

Stone Sweet, Alec and Caporaso, James (1998). 'From Free Trade to a Supra-national Polity: The European Court and Integration'. In: W. Sandholtz and A. S. Sweet (eds.), *European Integration and Supranational Governance*. Oxford: Oxford University Press, pp. 92–133.

Sturdy, Andrew, Morgan, Glenn, and Daniel, Jean-Pierre (1997). 'National Management Styles: A Comparative Study of a Strategy of *Bancassurance* in Britain and France'. In: G. Morgan and D. Knights (eds.), *Regulation and Deregulation in European Financial Services*. London: Macmillan, pp. 154–77.

Streeck, Wolfgang (1992). *Social Institutions and Economic Performance: Studies of Industrial Relations in Advanced Capitalist Economies*. London: Sage.

—— and Schmitter, Philippe (eds.) (1985). *Private Interest Government: Beyond Market and State*. London: Sage.

—— and Yamamura, Kozo (2003). 'Introduction: Convergence or Diversity? Stability and Change in German and Japanese Capitalism'. In: K. Yamamura and W. Streeck (eds.), *The End of Diversity?* Ithaca, NY: Cornell University Press, pp. 1–50.

Thelen, Kathleen and Kume, Ikuo (2001). 'The Rise of Nonliberal Training Regimes: Germany and Japan Compared'. In: W. Streeck and K. Yamamura (eds.), *The End of Diversity?* Ithaca, NY: Cornell University Press, pp. 200–28.

—— and —— (2003). 'The Future of Nationally Embedded Capitalism: Industrial Relations in Germany and Japan'. In: K. Yamamura and W. Streeck (eds.), *The End of Diversity?* Ithaca, NY: Cornell University Press, pp. 183–211.

Tylecote, Andrew and Conesa, Emmanuelle (1999). 'Corporate Governance, Innovation Systems and Industrial Performance'. *Industry and Innovation* 6: 25–50.

Ventresca, Marc, Szyliowicz, Dara, and Dacin, M. Tina (2003). 'Innovations in Governance: Global Structuring and the Field of Public Exchange-Traded Markets'. In: M.-L. Djelic and S. Quack (eds.), *Globalization and Institution: The Rules of the Economic Game*. Cheltenham: Edward Elgar, pp. 245–77.

Vitols, Sigurt (2003). 'From Banks to Markets: The Political Economy of Liberalization of the German and Japanese Financial Systems'. In: K. Yamamura and W. Streeck (eds.), *The Origins of Nonliberal Capitalism: Germany and Japan in Comparison*. Ithaca, NY: Cornell University Press, pp. 240–60.

Whitley, Richard (1999). *Divergent Capitalisms: The Social Structuring and Change of Business Systems*. Oxford: Oxford University Press.

—— (2001). 'How and Why are International Firms Different?' In: G. Morgan, P. H. Kristensen, and R. Whitley (eds.), *The Multinational Firm*. Oxford: Oxford University Press, pp. 27–68.

—— (2003a). 'Changing Transnational Institutions and the Management of International Business Transactions'. In: M.-L. Djelic and S. Quack (eds.), *Globalisation and Institutions: Redefining the Rules of the Economic Game*. Cheltenham: Edward Elgar, pp. 108–33.

—— (2003b). 'The Institutional Structuring of Organisational Capabilities: The Role of Authority Sharing and Organisational Careers'. *Organization Studies* 24: 667–95.

——, Morgan, Glenn, Kelly, William, and Sharpe, Diana (2003). 'The Changing Japanese MNC'. *Journal of Management Studies* 40: 613–72.

Woo, Jung-en (1991). *Race to the Swift: State and Finance in Korean Industrialization*. New York: Columbia University Press.

PART II

CHANGING FIRM CAPABILITIES WITHIN AND ACROSS INSTITUTIONAL FRAMEWORKS

9

Developing Transnational Organizational Capabilities in Multinational Companies: Institutional Constraints on Authority Sharing and Careers in Six Types of MNC

RICHARD WHITLEY

9.1. Introduction

Recent work on the role of institutional frameworks in structuring firms' strategies and competences has shown how variations in the organization of capital and labour markets, and institutional arrangements more generally, can affect the sorts of organizational capabilities that leading firms develop, and consequently help to explain differences in patterns of technological change and industrial specialization between market economies (see, for example, Amable 2000; Bassanini and Ernst 2002; Casper 2000; Casper and Whitley 2004). Such collective capabilities constitute key sources of competitive advantage for companies that are difficult to imitate, especially perhaps the more 'technical' competences concerned with developing and delivering goods and services (Teece et al. 1994). They take time to build and typically involve relatively 'low powered' incentives to encourage employees to work together over some time in generating firm-specific knowledge. Three major kinds of dynamic capabilities have

Earlier versions of this chapter were presented to seminars at ERIM, Erasmus University, Rotterdam in April 2002, the Institute of International Business, Stockholm School of Economics in May 2002 and the Department of Business Studies, Uppsala University in March 2003, as well as to the 2002 EGOS Colloquium, Barcelona, July. I am grateful to the participants and discussants at these meetings for their comments and suggestions.

been distinguished by Teece et al (2000): Coordinating, learning, and reconfigurational.

Coordinating capabilities involve the development of integrative routines that, for example, gather and process information about internal and external processes, connect customer experiences with engineering design choices, and link production facilities with suppliers. *Organizational learning* capabilities involve joint problem solving and improvement of production and related processes, both through continuing work experience and dedicated projects, as well as developing the firm's understanding of business partners and other external agents. Firms with strong learning skills rapidly codify, diffuse, and apply throughout the organization new knowledge that is developed by individuals and groups, so that routines and procedures are continuously being updated in a process of cumulative improvement. *Reconfigurational* capabilities, in contrast, enable firms to transform organizational resources and skills to deal with rapidly changing technologies and markets. They often involve the radical restructuring of operations and routines as knowledge changes, sometimes by acquiring new skills and competences through hiring on external labour markets or buying newly formed firms, as in the case of Cisco (Lee 2000).

Developing these kinds of organizational capabilities depends on managerial, technical, and other skilled workers being willing to contribute to firm-specific problem solving and knowledge on a continuing basis, even when it may not enhance their own individual worth on external labour markets. Two ways of generating such commitment are authority sharing and organizational careers (Whitley 2003*b*). By authority sharing I mean the delegation of considerable discretion over work performance and organization to skilled staff such that they become involved in problem solving activities and are regarded as authoritative contributors to organizational issues. In general, the more employers are willing to involve employees in complex problem solving and encourage their participation in the collective development of organizational knowledge, the more likely they are to become committed to contributing their experience and learning to organization-specific competence development.

Authority sharing can also occur between companies in variously organized networks and associations. This enables firms to learn from each other and develop common competences, often within professional and technical communities such as those described in the Danish furniture and machinery industries (Andersen and Christensen 1999;

Hendriksen 1999). However, the extent and longevity of such authority sharing, and hence contribution to developing distinctive organizational capabilities, tend to be lower than that in most employment relations, except perhaps in clusters of small firms governed by strong coordinating institutions, as in some Italian industrial districts.

Establishing organizational careers also encourages employee commitment by rewarding continuing contributions to collective problem solving through long-term employment and promotion. They provide strong incentives for staff to work together in dealing with firm-specific issues and opportunities over substantial periods of time, rather than concentrating on enhancing their individual skills that may be more tradable on external labour markets. Firms that offer long-term careers for many groups of skilled staff are more likely to gain continuing employee investment in organization-specific knowledge and skills than are those that restrict careers to only a few staff and/or where such commitments lack credibility.

Employers differ considerably in the extent to which they invest in these ways of developing employee commitment, partly as a result of their institutional environments, and so build varied kinds of organizational capabilities. For example, companies whose owners share authority with senior managers, but not the nonmanagerial workforce, will tend to be slower to learn from the work experiences of most employees and to adapt to technical change, as well as discouraging them from contributing to more general organizational problem solving. Consequently, most staff, including some technical experts, have little incentive to contribute to the development of firm-specific competences at the expense of developing their own skills, and will need considerable persuasion to commit large amounts of time and energy in resolving problems that require organizational cooperation and collaboration across functional boundaries.

In contrast, firms that develop more extensive forms of authority sharing are able to incorporate individual learning and skill development into organizational routines. This often involves engaging core employees in continuous improvement activities and codifying their suggestions so that these can be systematically incorporated into work processes throughout the organization—including suppliers and customers where appropriate, as at Toyota (Fujimoto 2000). Organizational learning occurs on a much broader scale here because it builds on the contributions of all long-term employees and closely allied business partners, and is diffused to a much wider range of groups within and beyond the formal boundaries of the firm. As a result, both coordinating and learning capabilities of these kinds of firms are considerable.

Increasing the longevity of career commitments, and the range of employees to whom they are offered, further encourages long-term commitment to improving organization-specific knowledge and skills, although such commitments may well limit employers' ability to reconfigure capabilities radically. Employers who invest in long-term commitments to skilled staff are, then, likely to develop considerable coordinating and learning capabilities. However, firms that organize such careers primarily around functional departments and business divisions may have difficulty in generating strong company-wide learning capabilities, especially where that involves considerable interdepartmental coordination and cooperation.

On the other hand, where long-term organizational careers involve considerable mobility across functions and departments, and reward employees who learn new organization-specific knowledge and skills in a variety of jobs over the course of their working lifetime, capabilities are likely to be less departmentally focused. Comparing the more organizationally generalist careers in many Japanese firms with the more functionally specialized ones typical of many German firms, for instance, Sorge (1996: 82) suggests that: 'The Japanese engineer is more of a multi-specialist, the German engineer a specialist who extends his domain into other specialisms'.

These sorts of differences in authority sharing and organizational careers are strongly influenced by the nature of the dominant institutions governing opportunism and commitment in capital and labour markets. Particularly important are the overall reliability and efficacy of formal institutions, the role of the state, the nature of the financial system, the power of intermediary associations, and the efficacy of the skill formation system (Whitley 2003*b*). As a result, differences in institutional frameworks affect the kinds of organizational capabilities that leading firms in a market economy are encouraged to develop, and so patterns of sectoral and technological development in differently organized societies (Casper and Whitley 2004; Whitley 2002), as numerous contributions to the comparative business systems, varieties of capitalisms, and social systems of production literatures have shown (see, for example, Casper et al. 1999; Hall and Soskice 2001; Hollingsworth and Boyer 1997; Hollingsworth et al. 1994)

However, most studies of how institutional frameworks affect the development of different organizational capabilities and economic performance have focused on nationally-specific ones. Rather less

attention has been devoted to the kinds of idiosyncratic competitive competences that firms operating in diverse institutional contexts
are able to generate. In particular, the extent to which, and ways in
which, multinational companies (MNCs) develop distinctive kinds of
organizational capabilities at the international level remain relatively
unexplored from a comparative institutionalist perspective, despite
the growth of interest in MNCs as international knowledge generating
and transferring firms (Kogut and Zander 1993; Yamin 2002).

As Solvell and Zander (1998) have pointed out, the ability of such
firms to integrate new knowledge and skills across national subsidiaries is often assumed rather than demonstrated (see also, Arvidsson
1999; Szulanski 1996), and there are significant difficulties in transferring situationally-specific innovation capabilities between countries
with contrasting institutional frameworks. Especially important in this
regard are labour market institutions, which encourage varied levels
of commitment to employers and to the development of organization-
specific knowledge. Where these institutions differ significantly, as in
post-war Germany, Japan, and the United States, generating similar
levels of commitment to long-term organizational problem solving
and developing international capabilities across subsidiaries will be
difficult, particularly from middle and lower level staff.

Even within a single national culture, such as that of the United
States, ensuring sufficient positive commitment to organizational
problem solving among a relatively small group of senior managers to
achieve innovation and growth goals is difficult enough, as Freeland's
(2001) study of General Motors illustrates. When institutional contexts diverge as much as they do in many MNCs, such active consent
to formal managerial authority cannot be assumed, and nor can
MNCs' ability to develop distinctive cross-national capabilities on the
basis of this commitment. Rather, the extents to which they attempt
to do so, and are successful, remain variable (Zander and Solvell
2002).

The comparative institutional analysis of firms' competences in
market economies raises, then, a number of questions about MNCs as
international organizations with firm-specific transnational collective
capabilities, which are distinct from those of their national subsidiaries.
These have become more critical as MNCs are portrayed as international learning systems, differentiated networks, and so on that rely
extensively on subsidiaries' contributions to their global competences
and knowledge (Birkinshaw and Hood 1998; Hedlund 1993; Holm and
Pedersen 2000; Nohria and Ghoshal 1997). In particular, to what extent,

and how, do different kinds of MNCs generate firm-specific organizational capabilities through long-term employee commitments? Given the considerable variety of institutional arrangements governing economic activities in market economies, that is, to what extent and how do international employers develop distinctive transnational competences that are difficult to imitate through employee contributions to long-term cross-national skill and knowledge development when labour markets and skill formation systems vary significantly?

Furthermore, if long-term competitive advantages depend on the development of idiosyncratic firm-specific capabilities that result from managers and skilled workers contributing to organizational problem solving and growth over a considerable time in more than a perfunctory and routine manner, then what kinds of MNCs develop different sorts of competences and how do they do so? This point emphasizes that not all international firms do in fact generate distinctive transnational capabilities (Hu 1992), and that the extent to which they do develop firm-specific competitive advantages on the basis of such capabilities can vary considerably (Whitley 2001).

This variability in kinds of MNCs and their transnational organizational capabilities suggest it would be useful to consider how firms from different institutional frameworks are likely to develop particular competitive competences by coordinating economic activities in differently organized market economies. Central to this analysis is the study of how contrasting institutional arrangements governing capital and labour markets encourage international firms to generate different levels of employee commitment to continuing parent company organizational problem solving, as distinct from commitment to their national employer and labour market. In particular, how do MNCs operating in contrasting types of home and host economy vary in the kinds of international, firm-specific capabilities they develop through sharing authority with foreign employees and by providing international organizational careers for them?

Accordingly, in this chapter I suggest how the institutionalist analysis of organizational capabilities could be extended to MNCs by analysing how international companies from different kinds of market economy are likely to develop varied patterns of employer–employee commitment and so generate different cross-border capabilities. This involves, first, summarizing the general connections between institutional arrangements in a society and prevalent patterns of authority sharing and career provision in companies. Here, I do this by contrasting four ideal types of institutional regime that have distinct implications for authority sharing and career structures. I then consider how MNCs from these kinds of home economies are likely to share authority with, and provide organizational careers for, foreign managerial and skilled employees in the relatively weakly institutionalized international business environment (IBE). In the fourth section of this chapter, I suggest how we can identify six types of MNC in terms of the different levels of international authority sharing and organizational careers that result from varied kinds of home and host economies, and their likely kinds of transnational capabilities.

9.2. The Development of Employer–Employee Commitment and Organizational Capabilities in Four Institutional Regimes

To analyse how MNCs from different kinds of market economy are likely to develop distinctive kinds of transnational organizational capabilities through cross-national authority sharing and careers, it is first necessary to outline the general links between institutional regimes and employer–employee commitment. Four distinct ideal types of institutional regimes that encourage firms to develop quite different kinds of authority sharing and organizational careers are: *particularistic, arm's length, solidaristic collaborative, segmented collaborative* (Whitley 2003*b*). These vary in the extent to which they encourage employer–employee commitment through constraining opportunism and developing trust as well as structuring intra- and extra-organizational careers in different ways. As a result, companies in these kinds of societies are likely to differ in the extent to which they develop particular kinds of organizational capabilities that are difficult to imitate and provide competitive advantages.

Particularistic institutional regimes discourage extensive delegation and employer–employee commitment, primarily because of the low level of trust in the operation and predictability of formal institutions that characterize such societies (Whitley 1999). This means that owners feel unable to rely on the legal system, accounting conventions, and formal systems for assessing competence and ensuring contractual compliance in order to control the behaviour of customers, suppliers, and employees in predictable ways. Consequently, they tend not to delegate substantial amounts of authority to relative strangers with whom they do not have strong personal bonds. Additionally, in paternalist political cultures that justify leadership more in terms of elites' superior abilities to look after the best interests of the population than through their formally credentialled expertise, or by success in formally governed electoral competitions (Beetham 1991), owners tend to consider employees as unqualified to exercise discretion.

Such low levels of trust in formal institutions are often associated with predatory states and unpredictable financial systems. Where state elites are unwilling to allow the growth of large concentrations of privately controlled capital and/or seek to extract substantial amounts of surplus for their own benefit, owners are faced with a highly uncertain political and economic context in which personal connections are often the only reliable means of ensuring trust and predictable behaviour. The legal system in such countries is either very limited in its ability to resolve disputes, or liable to render capricious and unpredictable judgements.

Many industrializing countries, and those undergoing radical institutional change such as the former state socialist societies of Eastern Europe in the early 1990s, exemplify this kind of institutional context (Fafchamps 1996; Humphrey and Schmitz 1998; Menkhoff 1992; Whitley and Czaban 1998; Whitley et al. 1996). In these kinds of institutional frameworks, authority tends to remain highly concentrated and personal, and commitments to impersonal collective enterprises very limited. Organizational structures are often fluid, without a stable set of positions that could constitute a career for ambitious skilled workers and managers, and highly dependent on the personal decisions and judgements of the owner–manager, as in many Chinese family businesses in Hong Kong, Taiwan, and South East Asia (see, for example, Redding 1990; Silin 1976). Incentives for long-term organizational commitment are dependent on personal ties and often restricted to the immediate family or those with whom family-like connections have been developed. Collective problem solving is therefore dependent on the direct authority of the owner–manager, and limited to a small proportion of the workforce.

Arm's length institutional regimes, on the other hand, combine much greater trust in formal institutions with relatively few constraints on opportunistic behaviour by economic actors beyond the formal, legal framework governing market transactions. Here, the largely regulatory state concentrates on maintaining a stable and predictable framework for managing economic activities and limiting transaction costs in labour and capital markets in general. Such states are more concerned to develop efficient markets in general rather than encourage particular industries and do not play a major role in coordinating firms' decisions or sharing investment risks. Often, they legislate against cooperation between companies and encourage arm's length relationships between them.

A complementary feature of these sorts of frameworks that also limits cooperation between economic actors is the capital market based financial system, which facilitates an active market for corporate control. Here, large and liquid capital markets allocate investment funds largely by price competition, and investors typically favour liquidity over commitment and manage assets through diversified portfolios. The combination of liquid capital markets, legal restrictions on managers' ability to develop strong defensive measures against hostile takeovers, and fragmented shareholdings in these kinds of financial systems limits investor–manager commitments and reduces the credibility of long-term career incentives. Where capital is impatient and volatile it is difficult to convince skilled employees to become committed to the long-term development of a particular firm's organizational capabilities.

Arm's length frameworks are also characterized by heterogeneous and relatively weakly organized employers' associations and labour unions. Together with decentralized wage bargaining and fragmented patterns of labour relations management, these features limit inter-firm cooperation and do not support long-term employer–employee commitments. Additionally, these kinds of societies often develop unstandardized and diversely controlled skill formation systems in which general educational success is more valued than the acquisition of practical skills. Certified practical skills tend to be 'owned' and developed by individuals who invest in particular training programmes provided by relatively autonomous educational institutions without much involvement of employers or unions.

Skills are here typically generic across firms, and sometimes industries as in the case of accountancy and some other business services, and are rarely tied to specific organizational arrangements. In terms of the problems they deal with, though, they can be quite specialized, especially when controlled by practitioners. In such cases, workers identify strongly with their professional expertise, particularly when occupational associations combine trade union functions with those of technical societies, as in the United Kingdom. Societies with these kinds of skill formation systems tend to generate strong occupational labour markets in 'codified' expertise that often dominate internal organizational careers (Marsden 1999; Tolbert 1996).

Considering next more collaborative institutional regimes, these are characterized by stronger constraints on opportunistic behaviour by economic actors. They typically have promotional states that encourage firms to share risks, sometimes by providing direct support for new investments and/or technology development, and to work together to develop new industries and markets (Evans 1994; Whitley (see Chapter 8, this volume)). Sometimes, states delegate considerable authority to business associations to organize research projects and gain access to public support for technology development on behalf of their members, as in Germany (Abramson et al. 1997). The more states encourage such collaborative development and sharing of technical and market risks, the more owners and managers are likely to share more authority between themselves and reduce risks of opportunistic behaviour. This provides a relatively stable basis for establishing organizational careers for skilled staff and investing in their training. Because the state here encourages cooperation and mutual commitment between firms, they are more likely to feel able to enter into commitments with many employees than do firms in societies where the state operates more at arm's length from companies and there are few restrictions on opportunistic behaviour.

These kinds of societies also tend to have credit based financial systems with relatively small and illiquid capital markets and considerable concentrations of shareholder control over large companies. The market for corporate control is limited here, especially if significant proportions of firms' shares are held by strategic investors and/or are effectively controlled by top managers, as is the case in many European countries (Barca and Becht 2001) and Japan (Sheard 1994). Such stability of ownership also encourages longer term employer–employee commitments, and indeed other long-term strategies. In general, where firms are committed to long term alliances with suppliers, customers, and other members of enterprise groups through mutual shareholdings, links with banks, and other financial institutions, and regular exchanges of information and personnel, as in the alliance capitalism of Japan (Gerlach 1992), they are more likely to make credible long-term commitments to employees.

Strong business associations, particularly employers' associations, are also significant features of the business environment in these regimes that encourage employer–employee commitment, as Soskice (1999) has emphasized. As well as controlling opportunistic behaviour by member companies, and so encouraging longer term investments in technology and employees, such organizations restrict employee opportunism, whether collective through unions or individual. Where wage rates and other aspects of employment relationships are agreed centrally with strong labour unions organized on a sectoral rather than craft basis, either at the industry or national level, and firms are constrained from poaching skilled staff by offering higher wages, employers are encouraged to develop quite long-term commitments to employees (Dore 2000; Lehmbruch 2001).

There are, however, significant variations in skill formation systems and the organization of labour markets between two ideal types of collaborative institutional regimes. These differences affect the ease with which MNCs develop transnational organizational capabilities. Solidaristic collaborative ones combine relatively strong labour unions, typically organized around industries, with highly organized bargaining systems and strong public training systems that usually involve collaboration between state agencies, employers, and unions. Segmented collaborative societies, in contrast, have weaker unions that are primarily enterprise based, mostly decentralized wage bargaining arrangements and largely privately organized skill formation systems (Thelen and Kume 2001).

In the former kind of collaborative regime, employers, unions, and state agencies together organize and control skill formation, and develop highly valued standardized skills for a majority of the labour force. These form the basis for strong occupational identities in both large and small companies (Crouch et al. 1999; Marsden 1999). Here, pride in one's publicly certified expertise is considerable, and encourages loyalty as much to horizontally defined occupational groups as to vertical authority hierarchies constituting firms. Such skills additionally facilitate mobility between companies and the institutionalization of active labour markets within particular occupational boundaries (Hinz 1999).

However, in many continental European countries this mobility is restrained by strong employers' associations and centralized wage bargaining organized on a sectoral basis, as well as by legal constraints on unilateral employer actions. Together with barriers to firing staff in market downturns, and industry wide barriers to hiring new skills from competitors, these factors mean that both firms and workers here have strong incentives to improve individual and collective skills within current technological trajectories and industry boundaries. Organizational careers are here encouraged by extensive employer–union collaboration within each industry that ties firms and workers into a common destiny.

Employers in these circumstances are encouraged to establish organizational career paths for skilled employees to advance along building firm-specific knowledge and skills on top of their standardized expertise. Careers and identities are accordingly structured by both certificated skills and organizational hierarchies. Because of the widespread diffusion of new knowledge, technologies, and skills throughout each sector, firms in these kinds of coordinated market economies seek to differentiate themselves in terms of products and market niches, and to construct distinctive competences through the organizational coordination and development of skilled staff. They therefore invest considerably in developing skilled workers' commitments to construct such capabilities, but the strong commitment to certified professional expertise in these societies often restricts the amount of job rotation across major departments and cross-functional integration that can be implemented easily.

In segmented collaborative regimes, on the other hand, the general educational system strongly selects children and young adults for different positions in the labour market through academic examinations, and the public training system is relatively poorly developed and/or low in prestige. Here, skill-based occupational identities are weaker and occupational labour markets less important. Firms, especially larger ones, here rely on the educational system to select and train workers in general competences that they can build upon during the course of a working lifetime. Because the strong business associations characteristic of such societies restrict poaching and limit free riders' ability to appropriate skills developed by competitors, both employers and employees make considerable investments in collective competence development through organizational careers. Authority sharing in large firms in these kinds of collaborative institutional frameworks is considerable because both managers and workers are highly dependent on the growth of the firm, and jointly develop distinctive competitive capabilities. Such interdependence is, however, often lower in smaller firms where labour turnover is greater and skills less organization-specific.

The lack of strong horizontal occupational identities based on certified expertise in these kinds of societies facilitates job rotation across functional groups, as well as cooperation between them, so that innovation development and implementation are, in principle, faster and more effective than where functional boundaries are reinforced by publicly standardized skills. Expertise therefore becomes highly firm-specific in large companies in such economies as both managers and core workers invest in the long-term development and improvement of distinctive organizational capabilities. Firms thereby develop strong cultures but also share authority with business partners and other organizations to ensure continuous acquisition and use of new knowledge and cooperation with firms possessing complementary capabilities. Their organizational capabilities can, then, be expected to be considerable.

9.3. Institutional Regimes, Cross-National Authority Sharing, and Organizational Careers in MNCs

These connections between different kinds of institutional regimes and levels of employer–employee commitment have a number of implications for MNCs. First, MNCs with major facilities in different kinds of market economy are likely to develop varying forms of authority sharing and careers in contrasting institutional contexts. As a result, second, the kinds of collective capabilities they develop at different levels of the organization can differ greatly, and may well conflict in their basic principles, as highlighted by Kristensen and Zeitlin (2001) in their study of APV. Third, MNCs will also vary in the extent to which they share authority with, and establish cross-national careers for, foreign employees as a result of variations in their domestic institutional environment and in those of their major subsidiaries. Thus, fourth, they differ in the extent to which they develop distinctive international organisational capabilities. Additionally, the institutional features of the IBE, particularly those that govern transactions and disputes, can be expected to impinge upon the extent to which MNCs are willing to delegate discretion to foreign employees and gain their commitment through providing organisational careers, as well as affecting such employees' responses to these opportunities.

While the role of different institutional environments in developing varied subsidiary competences in MNCs has become more widely discussed in recent years (see, for example, Birkinshaw 2001; Westney 1993), rather less attention has been paid to how national and international institutions affect the development of cross-national commitments and capabilities. In this section, I suggest how features of different national and international institutional environments can be expected to affect employer–employee commitments in MNCs, and so their development of distinctive transnational organizational capabilities.

In considering first the nature of the IBE, it is important to note that most international institutions governing economic activities are less firmly established than many national ones. Where they have developed, most resemble regulatory institutions in arm's length regimes and few, if any, of them encourage investment in employer–employee commitment on a long-term basis (Whitley, Chapter 8, this volume). Constraints on both employer and employee opportunism are typically lower across national borders than within most OECD countries, and hence the extent and longevity of employee commitments to MNC corporate goals and success are likely to be less than those to national employers, especially among middle managers and professionals.

Pressures from international institutions, then, are unlikely to lead many MNCs to engage in the sorts of extensive authority sharing with, and long-term career commitments to, foreign employees that firms in collaborative market economies often develop with their domestic staff. As British employees of Japanese banks found out in the 1990s, the norm of long-term employment for male Japanese staff did not apply to them (Sakai 2000; Whitley et al. 2003). In general, then, the lack of strong international institutions encouraging long-term loyalties between business partners suggests that the degree and scope of cross-national authority sharing and organizational careers within MNCs will not be particularly high, and usually less than occurs in their home organizations.

There remain, however, considerable variations in patterns of authority sharing and career commitments across national borders. These result mostly from domestic and host economy institutional differences, as the large literature on Japanese US and MNCs illustrates (see, for example, Beechler and Bird 1999; Dunning 1993; Kogut and Parkinson 1993; Tolliday 2000). In particular, the circumstances in which companies became established and developed distinctive competences are likely to have substantial influence on when and how they internationalize their operations and manage foreign subsidiaries. As Kogut (1993: 137) has suggested: 'Even as the firm internationalises, it remains imprinted by its early developmental history and domestic environment', especially how it learns and innovates (cf. Doremus et al. 1998).

Additionally, as some MNCs invest more in foreign environments to acquire strategic assets and skills, rather than simply to reduce costs and access markets (Rugman and Verbeke 2001), they can be expected to share authority more with foreign employees, especially in dealing

with complex problems across borders, and try to elicit their commitment on a longer term basis. Such attempts are clearly going to be
affected by the nature of host economy institutions, particularly those
governing skill formation and labour markets, and will vary considerably between subsidiaries, as has been emphasized by Nohria and
Ghoshal (1997).

I turn now to explore how firms from different institutional regimes
are likely to encourage varying degrees of employee commitment
in foreign subsidiaries, and so their probable development of distinctive firm-specific international organizational capabilities. These
are summarized in Table 9.1. First I discuss the probable patterns of
international authority sharing and careers of firms from particularistic business environments. Since owners in these kinds of market
economies remain reluctant to share authority with employees in
their domestic location because of unreliable formal institutions and
an unpredictable political environment, they seem unlikely to trust
foreign employees a great deal, and so delegate much discretion to
them. The combination of a low trust home economy with weak
transnational institutions is unlikely to encourage much authority
sharing with foreign managers and staff.

Table 9.1 *International authority sharing and careers in MNCs from different
institutional regimes.*

	Home Economy Institutional Regime			
International authority sharing and organizational careers	Particularistic	Arm's length	Solidaristic collaborative	Segmented collaborative
Extent of cross-border authority sharing	Low	Varies, but rarely extended beyond managers and experts with codified skills	Some, but limited to managers and experts with codified skills	Limited
Longevity and scope of cross-national organizational careers	Low	Varies, but long-term career opportunities rarely extended beyond managers in most MNCs	Limited	Low

Equally, the common restriction of long-term career opportunities to relatives and others with whom family-like relationships have been developed in these frameworks suggests that few firms will offer organizational careers to foreign employees. As a result, hardly any subsidiary staff are likely to become so committed to the parent company that they will invest their energies in improving firm-specific knowledge and skills on a medium to long-term basis. This means that enterprises from such environments are unlikely to develop strong international organizational capabilities, as distinct from those based on predominantly individual relationships and qualities.

In contrast, owners of firms from liberal or arm's length market economies that share authority with, and develop organizational careers for, senior managers and some professional staff domestically could be expected to delegate rather more discretion to those in charge of foreign subsidiaries where formal institutions are considered reliable. They may also involve foreign managers and professional staff in cross-national problem solving teams when their specialist expertise is highly valued. This is especially likely when dealing with complex problems that require knowledge of different business environments, as in many professional service companies such as those discussed by Morgan and Quack in their contribution to this book.

Authority sharing with foreign professionals will depend on MNC managers' knowledge of their expertise and the reputation of national skill formation systems. Given the importance of technical knowledge and specialist skills in dealing with complex and uncertain tasks, domestic managers of MNCs are unlikely to share much authority with foreigners unless they are convinced that they are highly skilled and able to contribute to current problems. This will be greatly facilitated by skills being standardized through professional associations that operate in similar ways in different countries, and so is more straightforward between arm's length economies that have flexible labour markets and similar institutional arrangements for developing high-level expertise.

It is also worth noting that constructing and changing expert teams for accomplishing complex and risky short-term projects requires efficient signalling of expertise and achievements. This means that firms will not find it easy to delegate authority to deal with complex cross-border problems to employees from economies without strong public credentialling systems and where expertise tends to be highly organization-specific, as in Japan. As a result, authority sharing with foreign employees in cross-national problem solving teams is likely to be greater in economies that share strong transnational technical communities and common ways of certifying skills.

In general, though, any such authority-sharing by firms from arm's length economies is unlikely to extend much beyond professional staff and managers, given similar limitations at home and the lack of strong international institutions that might restrain employer and employee opportunism. While their subsidiaries located in economies with strong collaborative institutions may develop greater levels of authority-sharing with skilled workers, this seems likely to be limited to local operations given the arm's length nature of the parent MNC's domestic business environment.

Similarly, few firms from these kinds of institutional frameworks are likely to make long-term career commitments to foreign employees, especially at the international level. Since commitments in general are short term in such economies, most employers will not feel able to offer cross-national organizational careers to more than a few senior foreign managers, nor would such offerings be viewed as highly credible. Again, where host economy institutions encourage high levels of employer–employee commitment and firms have to offer organizational careers to skilled staff in order to attract the most capable, MNCs may well enter into long term employer–employee commitments at the local level, as do many foreign firms in Japan, but such commitments are unlikely to be extended internationally.

Overall, then, we would not expect long-term commitment to building and improving cross-national problem solving capabilities and skills, as opposed to extending domestic ones, to be high in most foreign subsidiaries of MNCs from arm's length economies. Loyalty to the parent company and investment in the enhancement of its knowledge and capabilities will be no more extensive than in its domestic operations, and so continuing organizational learning at the international level probably restricted to senior managerial levels.

In contrast, MNCs based in more collaborative market economies are embedded in a number of relatively long-term obligations with particular business partners, including skilled employees. However, few of the institutions leading to such commitments transcend national boundaries and so foreign employees are not as locked into the fate of MNCs from these kinds of societies as are many domestic ones. This means that both employer and employee opportunism is likely to be less constrained across borders than within such economies. As a result, long-term employee willingness to invest in enhancing the capabilities of the MNC will probably be lower in foreign subsidiaries than in the domestic organization.

Furthermore, where such firms consider that their core capabilities are substantially derived from these long-term commitments and are highly-specific to their home business environment, they will be reluctant to invest much in authority sharing with foreign staff. The more MNCs see their distinctive competences as being generated by their domestic organization and its particular pattern of employment relations, the less they are likely to involve foreign staff from quite different environments in substantial international problem solving activities. This seems to be the case for many Japanese MNCs (see, for example, Kopp 1999; Pucik 1999).

However, some companies from collaborative institutional frameworks have become more willing to delegate considerable discretion to foreign managers and professionals in some subsidiaries, and to involve them extensively in international problem solving teams as they seek to acquire new kinds of capabilities that their domestic business system appears unable to provide. In situations where the lock-ins encouraged by home economy institutions are seen to be inhibiting radical innovation and limiting growth, such MNCs may deliberately use foreign subsidiaries to try novel practices with the different kinds of approaches and skills developed in societies with contrasting institutional frameworks, such as Japanese investments in UK and US biotechnology facilities (Kneller 2003; Lam 2003). Some German companies seem to have tried to do this in the 1990s, although such plans have not always been realized in practice, particularly in the car industry (Fleury and Salerno 1998; Jürgens 1998; Lane 2001).

MNCs from solidaristic collaborative frameworks that organize careers and identities around specialist skills and activities may well find this kind of authority sharing and joint problem solving with foreign employees easier to accomplish than do those from segmented ones whose internal labour markets are more structured around generalist competences. This is because their home and host economy professional staff are more likely to share a common cognitive framework and approach to problem understanding than are employees in MNCs where engineers and other highly educated employees are encouraged to become organizational generalists.

This contrast in ease of collaboration in dealing with cross-border problems will be especially marked when professionals from collaborative economies are working with those in arm's length ones, since these latter tend to be more specialized and focused on their professional identity rather than that of their current employer. We would expect, then, MNCs from solidaristic collaborative institutional frameworks to be more willing to share authority with managers and professionals in arm's length economies than those from segmented ones, and to be more effective in managing international problem solving teams.

They may also be more willing to develop long-term career commitments to foreign staff because of a greater specialization of organizational careers around professional expertise. However, for many MNCs from collaborative institutional frameworks, the importance of their considerable commitments to domestic skilled workers for the development of their firm-specific competences, and the lack of strong international institutions encouraging similar commitments to foreign staff, mean that extending long-term organizational careers abroad will be difficult, especially to workers in arm's length economies. Indeed, some may not wish to do so in order to increase their flexibility and ability to change competences in foreign subsidiaries at short notice. In effect, these kinds of MNCs develop contrasting employment relations in different environments in order to generate varied kinds of capabilities, as have perhaps some continental European investors in new technology firms in the United States.

Multinational companies from segmented collaborative institutional frameworks are particularly unlikely to establish credible long-term organizational careers for foreign employees since their distinctive organizational capabilities are often generated by generalist career structures that reward long-term contributions to the organization as a whole rather than those to particular specialisms. Weak professional identities and the highly firm-specific nature of careers and skills in such economies enable extensive rotation across functions and divisions facilitating organization-wide communication and learning. Incorporating foreign employees into such career structures will clearly not be easy, especially if they have developed distinctive specialist identities in nationally well-regarded training systems. As a result, many large Japanese firms have become noted for relatively limited career opportunities for foreign staff including managers, especially when they remain heavily dependent upon domestic customers as do most banks (Morgan et al. 2003; Sakai 2000; Whitley et al. 2003).

These points suggest that firms from arm's length economies could find it easier to develop multinational career structures for key foreign managers and technical experts than do MNCs originating in collaborative ones because their competitive capabilities are not so closely tied to home economy employee involvement in joint problem solving and knowledge development. Insofar, then, as the former companies do establish long-term organizational careers for key employees to gain their continuing commitment to organizational-specific problem solving and knowledge development, they may extend them to some senior staff in overseas subsidiaries to a greater extent than would firms from collaborative business environments.

However, this does not imply that most MNCs from arm's length economies are likely to share authority with foreign managers or to provide long-term organizational commitments for them. Indeed, some US firms have been as 'ethnocentric' (Perlmutter 1969) in these respects as Japanese ones (Malnight 1995), as the example of Henry Ford imposing his American manufacturing and pricing model on his British subsidiary in the 1920s and 1930s graphically illustrates (Tolliday 2000). The variety of cross-border authority sharing and career commitments to foreign employees in MNCs from these kinds of institutional frameworks is, then, likely to be considerable.

These institutional influences on MNCs' varied patterns of international authority sharing and career commitments affect the extent to which, and how, they develop distinctive cross-national capabilities and competitive competences, as opposed to those generated by national and regional units. I now turn to consider in a little more detail the connections between varieties of employer–employee commitment in MNCs and the sorts of distinct transnational competences they develop through an analysis of six types of MNC, which combine different degrees of authority sharing with foreign employees with varied kinds of international organizational careers.

9.4. International Authority Sharing, Careers, and Capabilities of Six Types of MNC

In considering how MNCs, varying in the extent to which their authority sharing and provision of careers across national boundaries develop different kinds of international organizational capabilities, it is helpful to distinguish three levels of cross-national authority sharing by drawing on Malnight's (1995) contrasts of 'appendage', 'participant', and 'contributor' roles of major MNC subsidiaries. The lowest degree of authority sharing occurs in firms that are so home-centred (Westney and Zaheer 2001) as to regard domestically developed knowledge and skills as always being superior to those of foreign units. The core competences and business success of the MNC are seen as deriving almost entirely from the domestic organization, such that foreign subsidiaries have to follow its policies and procedures. In these sorts of MNCs, most, if not all, host economy units are treated as appendages to the domestic organization that are given little discretion over what activities they carry out or how they manage them. Equally, they are rarely expected to contribute to problem solving or decision-making in any other units.

Somewhat greater authority sharing of the more significant subsidiaries with foreign managers and staff occurs in more decentralized MNCs that grant them limited discretion to deal with local markets and provide resources to develop local capabilities. In his account of globalization at Eli Lilly, Malnight (1995) characterizes this delegation as participation in meeting local needs and describes how the parent firm provided resources for European subsidiaries to conduct clinical trials and marketing activities at the local level. However, such investments were centrally coordinated and controlled by a special unit at head office to ensure that they followed established procedures and were compatible with domestic practices. Authority sharing in this situation, then, is typically restricted to local issues and does not extend to decisions beyond subsidiary boundaries. It is often limited to subsidiaries that have demonstrated their reliability and/or are situated in clearly differently organized kinds of markets and societies, such as Japanese units of US firms.

Higher levels of authority sharing are involved when MNCs encourage managers and technical staff in major subsidiaries to develop capabilities and knowledge that contribute to international problem solving and strategies, and assess their performance partly in terms of such contributions. Here, successful local units are more able to experiment with alternative ways of doing things and develop novel approaches without needing to obtain prior approval from the parent company. Through membership of international project teams they diffuse these innovations to other units and head office. In Malnight's (1995) terminology, they become *contributors* to the international parent firm and other subsidiaries by, for instance, providing clinical data for regulatory processes in different countries and developing marketing practices that can be used elsewhere. Such contributions involve extensive information exchange, use of international project teams to deal with worldwide issues and considerable staff mobility across national and regional boundaries. In ABB, for instance, the extensive use of 'best practice' benchmarking in the 1990s enabled a number of subsidiaries to contribute significantly to process improvements in the power transformers business area (Belanger et al. 1999).

The significance of international organizational careers in MNCs can similarly be distinguished in terms of the longevity of employer–employee commitments and the range of groups to whom they are extended. These kinds of careers are built around success in dealing with problems and issues in different national and regional locations as well as contributing to cross-national ones. In contrast, more domestic careers are focused on problem solving within the home organization. While this may include some foreign postings in subsidiaries that are closely integrated with the parent firm, success in these is typically regarded as being less important than domestic contributions in home-centric MNCs, and such mobility represents an extension of domestic career patterns more than constituting a distinct international structure.

Three patterns of international careers in MNCs can be distinguished in these terms. First, the least developed international career structure occurs in MNCs that offer few long-term commitments to foreign employees beyond their national subsidiaries, and usually rely on home country nationals to run them. Insofar as long-term careers are established in such firms, then, they are primarily organized within subsidiary boundaries, and expatriate postings form part of the domestic promotion system rather than constituting a separate international one. These can be described as *domestically extended* career structures.

Second, more established cross-national career patterns have developed in MNCs that encourage both foreign and domestic managers to move between subsidiaries and reward contributions to international corporate goals by promoting them abroad. However, such opportunities are usually restricted to senior foreign managers who rise to the top of host economy operations and then transfer to similar posts in other countries before joining the international managerial elite. They are not usually extended to middle managers and technical staff, and can be termed elite international career structures.

Third, more transnational career structures encourage long-term employer–employee commitment at the international level for a larger proportion of managers and professional employees by promoting them across subsidiaries and countries as much as within them and without privileging home country nationals. Here, successful organizational careers involve mid-career international mobility and the global internal labour market dominates local subsidiary ones. They encourage contributions to cross-national problem solving and the development of international organizational capabilities as much as, if not more than, national ones.

While some combinations of international authority sharing and cross-national organizational careers are quite feasible in MNCs, others are less so. For example, companies that offer long-term organizational careers to foreign managerial and technical staff seem likely to grant them considerable discretion and expect them to contribute to global problem solving once they have demonstrated their competence and commitment. As a result, not many MNCs will establish international managerial careers without some authority sharing with foreign employees, or reward long-term organizational commitments by foreign managers and professionals without involving them in cross-national decision-making and development. This suggests that the combination of transnational career paths with low subsidiary discretion is empirically improbable.

However, high levels of authority sharing can be combined with limited organizational commitments to long-term careers, as we have seen with small firms in some industrial districts and new technology start-ups. Substantial delegation to foreign units and employees is quite consonant, then, with limited international career opportunities, especially in international project based firms and professional service companies. Combining the three levels of authority sharing across borders in terms of the roles of major subsidiaries with three kinds of international organizational careers enables us to identify six types of MNC with varied levels of cross-national employee commitment to the parent organization. These are listed in Table 9.2. below:

Table 9.2 *Six types of MNC with different degrees of cross-national authority sharing and organizational careers.*

International authority sharing: the role of major foreign subsidiaries			
Types of international organizational careers	**Appendage**	**Participant**	**Contributor**
Domestic extended	Colonial	Domestically dominated	Delegated professional
Elite	Unlikely	Managerially integrated	Delegated managerial
Transnational	Unlikely	Unlikely	Highly integrated

In broad terms, we would expect MNCs that share authority with foreign subsidiary managers and experts, and provide them with international career opportunities, to elicit greater cross-national employee commitment to MNC problem solving and competence development than those that do not. They are more likely, then, to generate firm-specific international organizational capabilities as distinct from national ones. These involve novel routines and knowledge at the international level rather than simply extending domestic ones across national borders.

In this sense, international coordinating capabilities enable firms to integrate knowledge about internal and external processes throughout all major units, linking information about customer needs with development choices across national borders, and ensuring that inputs and outputs are coordinated cross-nationally. International learning capabilities similarly transcend local boundaries and enable companies to codify, integrate, and diffuse new understandings and approaches to problem solving across subsidiaries without privileging those from the home economy.

Equally, international reconfigurational capabilities involve the ability to restructure resources, skills, and knowledge across national boundaries, rather than within them, and generate new kinds of products and services at the international level. They go beyond simply buying and selling businesses or hiring and firing employees in different countries to encompass the integrated cross-national development of new kinds of competences through, for instance, organizing international project teams of experts to work on new technologies and markets.

Developing these kinds of firm-specific international organizational capabilities—as opposed to more generic portfolio management skills—depends on quite high levels of employee commitment to the MNC. Consequently, we would not expect many of the six types of MNC listed above to generate them to any great extent. I now turn to consider their key characteristics and likely cross-national organizational capabilities, summarized in Table 9.3, in a little more detail.

First, the *colonial* MNC keeps key decision-making over resources, skills, and knowledge production at home, similarly to Perlmutter's (1969) ethnocentric MNC. Whether run as a highly centralized and personally controlled business from a particularistic institutional environment or a home-focused hierarchy from a more stable society, these kinds of MNCs function as national companies with foreign operations

Table 9.3. *International commitment and organizational capabilities in six types of MNC*

Characteristics	Type of MNC					
	Colonial	Domestically dominated	Managerially integrated	Delegated professional	Delegated managerial	Highly integrated
Level of foreign employee commitment to MNC	Low	Low, except for a few senior managers	Some managerial, otherwise low	Considerable in the short term for project teams	Considerable amongst managerial elite	Considerable
Extent of firm-specific cross-national organizational capabilities						
a) Coordinating	Low	Extensions of domestic routines	Some managerial routines	Considerable in project teams, low otherwise	Considerable	High
b) Learning	Low	Limited to domestic organization	Limited to managerial elite	Considerable in project teams, limited otherwise	Considerable amongst senior managers	Considerable
c) Reconfigurational	Low	Limited	Limited to portfolio management skills	Considerable in societies with strong codified skills	Some, especially in arm's length regimes	Some, but radical changes limited by transnational routines and skills

that are highly subservient to the head office. Consequently, their capabilities will be largely those developed domestically, with few if any new ones being generated from their cross-border activities.

In some of these kinds of MNCs, career success is tied to the long-term cultivation of, and services for, large domestic customers. As a result, managers and other staff who work abroad can become regarded as second rate and become less successful in promotion tournaments, as in a number of Japanese banks in the 1980s and 1990s (Sakai 2000). Knowledge and skills obtained from such assignments are not highly regarded and rarely impinge greatly on domestically developed capabilities. Such relegation is, of course, even more marked for foreign workers who rarely deal with home-based customers and are typically excluded from parent company based organizational careers (Morgan et al. 2003). Consequently, foreign-based capabilities are poorly developed, except perhaps for some projects involving highly paid foreign experts, and rarely make any impact on the parent company. As international companies, then, they are unlikely to generate any distinctive kinds of collective competences that distinguish them from their domestic competitors.

Second, in *domestically dominated* MNCs some authority sharing with foreign managers over local issues is combined with few, if any, international careers for foreigners. Here, the home economy and employer are dominant, with overseas subsidiaries either seen as peripheral in terms of collective competences and learning, or else built upon the domestically developed recipe. These firms tend to view their foreign operations as extensions of their domestic ones, and careers in the worldwide organization are largely based on success in the domestic business. Foreign managers may be involved in developing local business strategies, as well as being entrusted with handling personnel matters, but this is often after they have fully imbibed the parent firm's philosophy and can be trusted to follow the x company's 'way'. Such firms are unlikely to come from particularistic environments.

In the case of many Japanese car assembly MNCs in Europe and the United States, the 'hard side' of the production system, that is, equipment, technical processes, and standard operating procedures, is often transferred as a standard package with little flexibility for local staff to alter specifications or practices, although other features are adapted to local circumstances (Abo 1994; Botti 1995; Brannen et al. 1999; Kenney and Florida 1993). Authority sharing with foreigners is often considerably circumscribed by expatriate 'coordinators' who are in daily contact with head office (Pil and MacDuffie 1999). Although improvements to manufacturing processes in these companies derive from foreign operations as well as domestic ones, they are usually planned by engineers and managers in Japan on the basis of continuous feedback from overseas and home plants without much foreign involvement (Whitley et al. 2003).

Most managerial careers in these kinds of MNC remain predominantly national, or perhaps regional. Furthermore, domestically based career success dominates foreign performance since the domestic operations remain the primary source of collective competence development and location of the key succession tournaments. Even when foreign production exceeds domestic output, and successful domestic careers increasingly include some foreign experience, long-term contribution to organizational problem solving, and success in the home economy usually remains more important than foreign success in such MNCs. As a result, foreign staff have limited incentives to invest in long-term MNC-specific knowledge and skill development, and are more likely to focus on demonstrating their expertise and effectiveness at a national or maybe regional level in ways that are externally visible.

Developing new and distinctive capabilities in foreign subsidiaries will not, then, be encouraged in domestically dominated MNCs, and any international competences they do generate will be highly dependent on those developed in their home economy. Strong coordinating and learning capabilities in these kinds of MNCs are more derived from their home economy than from their international operations as a whole, and so they are unlikely to develop separate transnational collective competences that are specific to the company as an international firm.

Third, *managerially coordinated* MNCs combine some authority sharing with foreign managers to deal with local needs and opportunities with the establishment of international careers for some foreign top managers. Commitments by leading subsidiary managers to such parent companies can thus be expected to be greater than in domestically dominated MNCs, and the creation of a more international managerial elite should help to develop distinctive routines for coordinating activities across national borders. However, the largely local focus of most subsidiary managers and professionals, coupled with their lack of involvement in cross-national problem solving in these kinds of firms limit the extent of international integration of knowledge and skills.

Most cross-national coordination, planning, and innovation is accordingly based on home country routines and competences in these kinds of MNCs, with little input from foreign subsidiaries. However, the growth of a multinational managerial elite may encourage some cross-national learning as foreign managers become assimilated into the top management ranks and seek to build on their foreign experiences. This possibility will, though, be restricted by the strong pressures for conformity to the domestically dominated culture and domestically derived operating procedures. The opening of some senior MNC posts to foreign employees in these kinds of firms does not alter their largely ethnocentric nature, as Perlmutter (1969) emphasises. Similarly, while the limited extent of authority sharing enables the top managers of such companies to restructure subsidiaries relatively easily and speedily, especially those in arm's length institutional regimes, the lack of involvement of most foreign employees in cross-national activities means that reconfigurational capabilities are more derived from domestic practices than from international ones.

The limited autonomy granted to some foreign subsidiaries in these kinds of MNCs does, however, allow them to develop more varied approaches to some organizational issues at the local level. As a result, local institutional environments can affect the nature of loyalties and commitments in subsidiaries. Employees in collaborative market economies, for example, may well be more loyal and committed to the success of their national organizational unit than to the parent company because there is only limited international authority sharing and long-term commitment. Equally, organizational careers and commitments to dealing with organizational problems will be more focused on the national or regional employer than the parent one. Problem solving efforts and collaboration are accordingly more likely to be easier to manage within these units than internationally, and so collective coordinating and learning capabilities more developed at the national level.

In contrast, employees of managerially coordinated MNCs in more arm's length market economies will limit their commitment to organization-specific problem solving at both national and international levels, and so restrict the development of distinctive, continually improving employer-specific competences. However, formal coordination of generic skills nationally and internationally should be relatively straightforward in these subsidiaries, and flexibility in changing direction considerable. Skilled staff here are likely to prefer to work on project-based problem solving activities that enhance and display technically specialized expertise and so managerial integration of such projects across national labour markets should not be too difficult. They will not be encouraged, though, to commit considerable time and energy to learning about, and contributing to, MNC-wide activities on a long-term basis, and thus building organization-specific capabilities.

The variety of organizational commitments in different subsidiaries of such MNCs, then, can be considerable, but at the worldwide level they are unlikely to develop firm-specific collective competences through long-term cooperative problem solving and learning. Instead, the international managerial elite may well prefer to focus on refining formal coordination and control systems for realizing the benefits of integrating diverse national and regional capabilities, as well as dealing with international capital markets, suppliers, and customers on a cross-national basis. A key 'global' organizational capability of such MNCs, then, may well be their ability to develop and implement standard routines and procedures for integrating diverse operations and competences located in different kinds of business environments, often building on those developed domestically.

The final three kinds of MNC to be discussed here share considerable authority with foreign employees over local and international issues and involve them extensively in cross-national problem solving, such that subsidiaries are expected to develop strong capabilities for contributing to global strategies. They differ in their willingness to establish long-term international careers for managers and professionals, and hence in the likely longevity of their commitment to developing MNC-specific competences and knowledge.

Considering first *delegated professional* MNCs, these share considerable authority with a number of foreign employees and delegate high levels to discretion to them, but limit the extent and scope of international careers. They mobilize managers and professionals from around the world to work on highly complex and often risky problems, as in, for instance, many business services, but are unable to offer long-term organizational commitments to most staff. This is often because they undertake highly uncertain activities that have unpredictable and risky outcomes, and so flexibility in developing and using skills is more important than the long-term development of organization-specific knowledge.

A major capability of such firms, then, is the capacity to create and direct cross-national project teams for specific, discrete problems with finite outcomes and clear performance criteria. International coordination is achieved primarily through such project teams that combine relatively standardized sets of expertise for dealing with particular, one-off problems. Long-term integration of activities and skills leading to the development of international organization-specific capabilities tends to be limited in such companies, especially their cross-national coordinating and learning capabilities. Although teams may contribute codified information to a central database, as in some consultancy firms, their short-term nature limit the extent to which the organization as a whole can build firm-specific knowledge internationally.

Since authority sharing with foreign managers and professionals is typically quite high in these companies, we would expect them to develop quite varied ways of dealing with the local environment and to innovate in ways that differ from the home economy. This is especially likely when the major institutions governing labour and capital markets vary significantly between countries so that the organizationally-specific nature of skills and careers differs across subsidiaries. Given the disparity of commitments, skills, and capabilities between teams in different kinds of market economies, such MNCs may well experience considerable coordination difficulties and effectively decentralize decision making to national subsidiaries to a high degree, as in franchise-based professional service organizations.

However, their flexibility and ability to mobilize highly skilled staff to work on complex and risky problems can enable them to develop strong international abilities to transform key assets and skills. These kinds of MNCs should be able to adapt rapidly to changing circumstances particularly where there are strong technical communities and fluid labour markets across national boundaries, and their reconfigurational capabilities can be expected to be considerable, as in some business service companies. This is less likely in highly regulated professional service firms where skills and technologies are more standardized and problem solving is more a matter of applying current skills to particular client problems than inventing new technologies.

Next, *delegated managerial* MNCs combine considerable delegation of authority to managers and professionals in many foreign subsidiaries with international careers for senior subsidiary managers. These kinds of MNCs encourage foreign subsidiaries to develop distinctive capabilities that contribute to international strategies as well as meeting local targets. By delegating considerable discretion to local managers and professionals they enable them to innovate and adapt to local conditions, and so generate varied capabilities at the local level. By also involving them in international teams to deal with more global issues, they are able to draw upon these different backgrounds and expertise. The establishment of international managerial careers here should ensure that commitments to the long-term development of the parent MNC is greater than in delegated professional MNCs and integration of activities through managerial routines and controls correspondingly more developed.

In the case of ABB in the 1990s, for instance, considerable local diversity in one division was combined with extensive use of benchmarking and imposition of common improvement programmes from the centre to upgrade process efficiencies and learn from the better performers (Belanger et al. 1999). Here, a cadre of international managers was developed by rotating successful plant executives across countries and continents, and eventually to leading positions in global divisions. They transferred effective recipes and processes between subsidiaries and so were key components of the MNC's learning activities. Committed to the success of the parent company, these elite managers contributed to the development of its international knowledge and capabilities on a continuing, long-term basis.

The predominantly national nature of organizational careers for most foreign employees, however, means that their loyalties will be more focused on national labour markets than the parent company. This means that local institutional differences are likely to affect levels and foci of long-term commitments such that significant variations can be expected between, say, R&D teams in the United Kingdom and Japan that affect cross-national organizational learning, as some Japanese pharmaceutical firms have found out (Lam 2003; Methe and Penner-Hahn 1999).

While the international coordination of technology development activities through project planning and regular communication may be relatively straightforward when problem solving activities follow relatively predictable trajectories, it becomes more difficult as the importance of tacit knowledge increases and technical uncertainty grows (Cantwell 2001). Long-term international cooperation to develop organization-specific knowledge and skills in situations of considerable uncertainty is obviously not easy to accomplish when labour market institutions in some countries discourage long-term organizational commitments—whether national or international—and key staff are as much concerned with enhancing their external reputations and generic skills as developing firm-specific knowledge.

Finally, *highly integrated* MNCs develop organizational careers and commitments that dominate those within national and regional subsidiaries, and reward both managerial and professional employees who demonstrate success in dealing with international problem solving and commitment to the parent organization. As a result, these firms develop distinctive knowledge and skills at the international level, and their organizational capabilities are transnational rather than national. In particular, complementary activities are here integrated across borders by technical experts, as well as by managers, whose loyalties and identities are as much focused on the MNC as a whole as on national subsidiaries or local labour markets. Technical careers are as international as senior managerial ones, and depend on internationally visible success in solving organization-specific problems cross-nationally.

Ambitious foreign professionals and managers in these kinds of MNCs seek to demonstrate their success cross-nationally in contributing to major parent company issues rather than focusing on enhancing their reputations in local labour markets. This should generate strong international coordinating and learning capabilities as professional and managerial elites compete in the transnational organizational labour market on the basis of their success in dealing with major MNC problems. Because international careers dominate purely national ones, complex and tacit knowledge is more likely to be transferred and built upon by technical experts across national units than in delegated managerial MNCs.

The more international nature of commitments and loyalties in highly integrated MNCs additionally encourages the development of customer-specific knowledge at the international level. While the lack of strong cross-national institutions encouraging authority sharing between suppliers and customers limits the extent of such cross-national linkages compared to those in collaborative institutional frameworks, the primacy of international careers and problem solving in these MNCs means that any investments in dealing with customers' problems will be cross-national rather than national. Similarly, they are as likely to compete with other MNCs at the international level as nationally, and so collectively develop an international competitive system that can, in some industries such as oil exploration, refining, and distribution dominate local markets.

For firms to be able to make credible commitments to key members of their international labour force such that they are encouraged to invest in long-term, firm-specific problem solving and knowledge development, they need to be large and stable enough to maintain employment over business cycles and to offer international promotion prospects that greatly exceed domestic ones. MNCs are only likely to want to develop distinctive transnational capabilities through such commitments when they have strong international coordination and learning needs that far outweigh national and regional market variations and labour costs considerations. These points suggest that the relatively few MNCs that do develop long-term international careers for key experts and managers will be in capital intensive industries with systemic technologies and worldwide markets for standardized products dominated by a few vertically integrated companies, such as the oil extraction, refining, and distribution industry.

The primacy of international careers and commitments in such companies suggests that they may be more difficult to establish in collaborative economies than in arm's length ones because domestic organizational loyalties and authority sharing are greater in the former societies. Separating a relatively small group of highly trained employees for international careers from local colleagues, and rewarding cross-national competence development more than focusing on nationally-specific issues is likely to be more difficult in these kinds of market economy. In contrast, because arm's length institutional regimes discourage high levels of employer–employee interdependence with the bulk of the workforce, they may enable MNCs from such domestic economies to provide organizational careers for technical and managerial staff. Additionally, low levels of authority sharing with business partners in these kinds of societies enables MNCs to develop a variety of linkages with customers and suppliers on a worldwide basis without having to integrate these with home economy ones.

Insofar, then, as companies are able to establish such integrated international organizations that generate distinctive cross-national capabilities—and I suspect that this is less common than much of the literature celebrating transnational MNCs suggests—they are more likely to originate in arm's length economies than in collaborative ones. It is also worth pointing out that companies based in these kinds of economies will have had more experience of dealing with arm's length investors and capital markets than those from more collaborative regimes. Such MNCs may, then, be more adept at managing relations with international investors.

9.5. Conclusions

This analysis of the organizational capabilities of MNCs in the light of differences in the institutional frameworks of home and host economies suggests a number of conclusions about their development of transnational competences. First, while many companies with major facilities in different countries may develop distinctive collective capabilities at the national and regional levels, by no means all of them do so internationally. Because of the relative weakness of international institutions governing employer and employee opportunism, belief in the superiority of domestically developed competences and the variable nature of institutional frameworks across market economies, many companies are often reluctant to share authority with foreign managers and professionals or to offer them long-term organizational commitments. This means that their organizational capabilities as MNCs are little different from those of their domestic organization, together perhaps with those generated separately by some subsidiaries. The coordination of economic activities in different countries does not, then, necessarily produce distinctive cross-national collective capabilities, and so MNCs as such do not constitute a distinctive kind of company from the point of view of the competence-based view of the firm.

Second, the variety of organizational capabilities in MNCs reflects the varied nature of institutional regimes across market economies, and the resultant differences in kinds of firms that develop in them. Arm's length institutional frameworks may, for example, encourage firms to develop the ability to manage varied kinds of businesses through managerial procedures and routines that do not involve the bulk of the workforce. This in turn leads MNCs from such backgrounds to extend these control and planning systems to operations in different countries, limiting any authority sharing and career commitments to senior managers. The kinds of international organizational capabilities that they develop are therefore likely to be quite similar to domestic ones.

Similarly, MNCs from highly coordinated economies that have developed strong organizational learning capabilities through considerable authority sharing with, and career commitments to, many domestic employees are likely to restrict such commitments to foreign staff because the institutions that constrained opportunism in the home economy are often missing in their societies. This is particularly probable when long-term careers in the domestic organization are both highly firm-specific and general across specialisms, as in many MNCs from segmented collaborative regimes.

Additionally, the impact of host economy institutions governing skill formation and labour markets can affect the development of cross-national capabilities by varying in their standardization and certification of practical expertise, as well as in their control over employer and employee opportunism. In general, the more fluid are external labour markets in an economy, and the more standardized are skills through educational and/or professional development and certification, the more difficult it becomes to develop long-term employee commitment at both national and international levels. While such institutional arrangements do facilitate employers' ability to hire and fire staff with varied kinds of skills, and so rapidly transform their knowledge and expertise base, they limit employees' willingness to invest in developing firm-specific capabilities on a continuing basis.

This suggests, third, that cross-national problem solving and learning should be easier when skill boundaries, knowledge bases, and organizational structures in different countries overlap. When they do, careers in both internal and external labour markets are likely to reward comparable kinds of technically specialized contributions, and externally certified skills are sufficiently standardized across labour markets to provide common languages for joint problem solving. Even when commitments to developing employer-specific knowledge and skills differ considerably between national subsidiaries, continuing communication, and gaining the cooperation of specialists across border on a long-term basis will be greatly facilitated by organizational career structures that reward expertise-based performance, as distinct from broader contributions to general organizational success. However, such specialist careers can, of course, inhibit cross-functional collaboration.

These kinds of expertise-based career structures are in turn encouraged by similar kinds of public skill formation and evaluation systems that generate social identities and loyalties around certified skills. For MNCs to develop distinctive cross-national learning capabilities that enable different kinds of knowledge production and problem solving to be transferred between subsidiaries—as opposed to the codified results of such activities—careers and commitments have to overlap across organizational subunits.

Overall, the more varied are subsidiaries' environments and their organization of careers, especially the kinds of contributions and skills that they reward, the more difficult it is likely to be for MNCs to develop distinctive international learning capabilities, particularly for developing new knowledge that is not readily codified. Establishing a common cross-national career structure for some middle managers and professionals will contribute to the generation of these kinds of capabilities, but this requires the MNC to be able to offer credible commitments over business cycles and national differences.

Fourth, the few MNCs that do develop strong coordinating and learning capabilities across borders through long-term international employer–employee commitments are less likely than delegated professional MNCs to be able to reconfigure their skills and competences radically to deal with rapidly changing circumstances. This is because of their dependence on current employees' skills and their establishment of transnational integrating routines. Building and maintaining long-term firm-specific organizational capabilities at the international level usually involves considerable investments in cross-national procedures, routines and competences. These are unlikely to encourage rapid and radical transformation of key skills and technologies that would enable firms to move effectively into quite novel industries with discontinuous technological trajectories and markets.

Delegated professional MNCs, in contrast, are more flexible, especially when their major operations are in fluid external labour markets, but tend to limit the international coordination of knowledge and skill development to cross-national teams working on discrete, one-off problems (Morgan and Quack, Chapter 10, this volume). They are therefore able to adjust relatively quickly to changing technologies and markets, particularly when there are highly organized markets for technical specialists, but key competences are as much individual and team-based as organizationally-specific. International capabilities here involve coordinating teams of specialists across countries on a largely ad hoc opportunistic basis with little employer or employee commitment to organizational careers. Mobilizing and controlling such teams are here central organizational competences that depend on considerable knowledge of local labour markets and reputational networks, further encouraging authority sharing and delegation of operational control, as in many project-based firms in emerging industries (Grabher 2002a,b).

REFERENCES

Abo, Tetsuo (ed.) (1994). *Hybrid Factories: The Japanese Production System in the United States*. Oxford: Oxford University Press.

Abramson, H. Norman, Encarmacao, Jose, Reid, Proctor R., and Schmoch, Ulrich (eds.) (1997). *Technology Transfer Systems in the United States and Germany*. Washington, DC: National Academy Press.

Amable, Bruno (2000). 'Institutional Complementarity and Diversity of Social Systems of Innovation and Production'. *Review of International Political Economy* 7: 645–87.

Andersen, P. H. and Christensen, P. R. (1999). 'Internationalization in Loosely Coupled Business Systems: The Danish Case'. In: P. Karnoe, P. H. Kristensen, and P. H. Andersen (eds.), *Mobilizing Resources and Generating Competencies*. Copenhagen: Copenhagen Business School Press, pp. 205–31.

Arvidsson, Niklas (1999). *The Ignorant MNE: The Role of Perception Gaps in Knowledge Management*. Stockholm: Stockholm School of Economics.

Barca, Fabrizio and Becht, Marco (eds.) (2001). *The Control of Corporate Europe*. Oxford: Oxford University Press.

Bassanini, Andrea and Ernst, Ekkehard (2002). 'Labour Market Regulation, Industrial Relations and Technological Regimes: A Tale of Comparative Advantage'. *Industrial and Corporate Change* 11: 391–426.

Beechler, S. L. and Bird, A. (eds.) (1999). *Japanese Multinationals Abroad: Individual and Organizational Learning*. Oxford: Oxford University Press.

Beetham, David (1991). *The Legitimation of Power*. London: Macmillan.

Belanger, Jacques, Berggren, Christian, Bjorkman, Torsten, and Kohler, Cristoph (eds.), (1999). *Being Local Worldwide: ABB and the Challenge of Global Management*. Ithaca, NY: Cornell University Press.

Birkinshaw, Julian (2001). 'Strategy and Management in MNE Subsidiaries'. In: A. Rugman and T. Brewer (eds.), *The Oxford Handbook of International Business*. Oxford: Oxford University Press, pp. 380–401.

—— and Hood, Neil (eds.) (1998). *Multinational Corporate Evolution and Subsidiary Development*. London: Macmillan.

Botti, Hope (1995). 'Misunderstandings: A Japanese Transplant in Italy Strives for Lean Production'. *Organization* 2: 55–86.

Braithwaite, John and Drahos, Peter (2000). *Global Business Regulation*. Cambridge: Cambridge University Press.

Brannen, Mary Yoko, Liker, Jeffrey K., and Fruin, W. Mark (1999). 'Recontextualization and Factory-to-Factory Knowledge Transfer from Japan to the United States: The Case of NSK'. In: J. K. Liker, W. M. Fruin, and P. S. Adler (eds.), *Remade in America: Transplanting and Transforming Japanese Management Systems'*. New York: Oxford University Press, pp. 117–53.

Cantwell, John (2001). 'Innovation and Information Technology in the MNE'. In: A. Rugman and T. Brewer (eds.), *The Oxford Handbook of International Business*. Oxford: Oxford University Press, pp. 431–56.

Casper, Steven (2000). 'Institutional Adaptiveness, Technology Policy and the Diffusion of New Business Models: The Case of German Biotechnology'. *Organization Studies* 21: 887–914.

Casper, Steven and Whitley, Richard (2004). 'Managing Competences in Entrepreneurial Technology Firms: A Comparative Institutional Analysis of Germany, Sweden and the UK'. *Research Policy* 33: 89–106.

——, Lehrer, M., and Soskice, D. (1999). 'Can High-Technology Industries Prosper in Germany: Institutional Frameworks and the Evolution of the German Software and Biotechnology Industries'. *Industry and Innovation* 6: 6–23.

Crouch, Colin, Finegold, David, and Sako, Mari (1999). *Are Skills the Answer? The Political Economy of Skill Creation in Advanced Industrial Countries.* Oxford: Oxford University Press.

Dore, Ronald (2000). *Stock Market Capitalism: Welfare Capitalism.* Oxford: Oxford University Press.

Doremus, P. N., Keller, W. W., Pauly L. W., and Reich, S. (1998). *The Myth of the Global Corporation.* Princeton, NJ: Princeton University Press.

Dosi, Giovanni, Nelson, Richard, and Winter, Sidney (eds.) (2000). *The Nature and Dynamics of Organisational Capabilities.* Oxford: Oxford University Press.

Dunning, John (1993). 'The Governance of Japanese and US Manufacturing Affiliates in the UK: Some Country-Specific Differences'. In: B. Kogut (ed.), *Country Competitiveness.* New York: Oxford University Press.

Evans, Peter (1994). *Embedded Autonomy: States and Industrial Transformation.* Princeton, NJ: Princeton University Press.

Fafchamps, Marcel (1996). 'The Enforcement of Commercial Contracts in Ghana'. *World Development* 24: 427–48.

Fleury, Alfonso and Salerno, Mario Sergio (1998). 'The Transfer and Hybridization of New Models of Production in the Brazilian Automobile Industry'. In: Robert Boyer, Elsie Charron, Ulrich Jurgens, and Steven Tolliday (eds.), *Between Imitation and Innovation: The Transfer and Hybridization of Productive Models in the International Automobile Industry.* Oxford: Oxford University Press, pp. 278–94.

Freeland, Robert F. (2001). *The Struggle for Control of the Modern Corporation: Organizational Change at General Motors, 1924–1970.* Cambridge: Cambridge University Press.

Fujimoto, T. (2000). 'Evolution of Manufacturing Systems and *Ex Post* Dynamic Capabilities'. In: G. Dosi et al. (eds.), *The Nature and Dynamics of Organizational Capabilities*, pp. 244–80.

Gerlach, Michael (1992). *Alliance Capitalism.* Berkeley, CA: University of California.

Grabher, Gernot (2002*a*). 'Cool Projects, Boring Institutions: Temporary Collaboration in Social Context'. *Regional Studies* 36: 204–14.

—— (2002*b*). 'Fragile Sector, Robust Practices: Project Ecologies in New Media'. *Environment and Planning A* 34: 1911–26.

Hall, Peter and Soskice, David (eds.) (2001). *Varieties of Capitalism: The Institutional Foundations of Comparative Advantage.* Oxford: Oxford University Press.

Hedlund, Gunnar (1993). 'Assumptions of Hierarchy and Heterarchy, With Applications to the Management of the Multinational Corporation'. In: S. Ghoshal and E. Westney (eds.), *Organization Theory and the Multinational Corporation*. London: Macmillan, pp. 211–36.

Hendriksen, Lars Bo (1999). 'The Danish Furniture Industry: A Case of Tradition and Change'. In: P. Karnoe, P. H. Kristensen, and P. H. Andersen (eds.), *Mobilizing Resources and Generating Competencies*. Copenhagen: Copenhagen Business School Press, pp. 233–58.

Hinz, Thomas (1999). 'Vocational Training and Job Mobility in Comparative Perspective'. In: P. D. Culpepper and D. Finegold (eds.), *The German Skills Machine*. New York: Berghahn Books, pp. 159–88.

Hollingsworth, J. Rogers and Boyer, Robert (eds.) (1997). *Contemporary Capitalism: The embeddedness of Institutions*. Cambridge University Press.

——, Schmitter, Philippe, and Streeck, Wolfgang (eds.) (1994). *Governing Capitalist Economies*. Oxford: Oxford University Press.

Holm, Ulf and Pedersen, Torben (eds.) (2000). *The Emergence and Impact of MNC Centres of Excellence: A Subsidiary Perspective*. London: Macmillan.

Hu, Y.-S. (1992). 'Global Firms are National Firms with International Operations'. *California Management Review* 34: 107–26.

Humphrey, John, and Schmitz, Hubert (1998). 'Trust and Inter-Firm Relations in Developing and Transition Economies'. *Journal of Development Studies* 34: 32–61. 0

Jurgens, Ulrich (1998). 'Implanting Change: The Role of "Indigenous Transplants" in Transforming the German Productive Model'. In: Robert Boyer et al. (eds.), *Between Imitation and Innovation*. Oxford: Oxford University Press, pp. 319–60.

Kenney, M. and Florida, R. (1993). *Beyond Mass Production*. Oxford: Oxford University Press.

Kneller, Robert (2003). 'Autarkic Drug Discovery in Japanese Pharmaceutical Companies: Insights into National Differences in Industrial Innovation'. *Research Policy* 32: 1805–27.

Kogut, Bruce (1993). 'Learning, or the Importance of Being Inert: Country Imprinting and International Competition'. In: S. Ghoshal and E. Westney (eds.), *Organization Theory and the Multinational Corporation*. London: Macmillan.

—— and Parkinson, David (1993). 'The Diffusion of American Organizing Principles to Europe'. In: B. Kogut (ed.), *Country Competitiveness: Technology and the Organising of Work*. New York: Oxford University Press, pp. 179–202.

—— and Zander, Udo (1993). 'Knowledge of the Firm and the Evolutionary Theory of the Multinational Corporation'. *Journal of International Business Studies* 24: 625–45.

Kopp, R. (1999). 'The Rice-Paper Ceiling in Japanese Companies: Why it Exists and Persists'. In: S. L. Beechler and A. Bird (eds.), *Japanese Multinationals Abroad: Individual and Organizational Learning*. New York: Oxford University Press, pp. 107–28.

Kristensen, Peer Hull and Zeitlin, Jonathan (2001). 'The Making of a Global Firm: Local Pathways to Multinational Enterprise'. In: G. Morgan, P. H. Kristensen, and R. Whitley (eds.), *The Multinational Firm: Organizing Across Institutional and National Divides*. Oxford: Oxford University Press, pp. 172–95.

Lam, Alice (2003). 'Organizational learning in Multinationals: R&D Networks of Japanese and US MNEs with UK.' *Journal of Management Studies*, 40: 673–704.

Lane, Christel (2001). 'The Mergence of German Transnational Companies'. In: G. Morgan, P. H. Kristensen, and R. Whitley (eds.), *The Multinational Firm*. Oxford: Oxford University Press, pp. 69–96.

Lee, Chong-Moon (2000). 'Four Styles of Valley Entrepreneurship'. In: Chong-Moon, Lee, William F. Miller, Marguerite Gong Hancock, and Henry S. Rowen (eds.), *The Silicon Valley Edge: A Habitat for Innovation and Entrepreneurship*. Stanford: Stanford University Press, pp. 94–123.

Lehmbruch, Gerhard (2001). 'The Institutional Embedding of Market Economies: The German 'model' and its Impact on Japan'. In: W. Streeck and K. Yamamura (eds.), *The Origins of Nonliberal Capitalism: Germany and Japan in Comparison*. Ithaca, NY: Cornell University Press, pp. 39–93.

Malnight, Thomas W. (1995). 'Globalization of an Ethnocentric Firm: An Evolutionary Perspective'. *Strategic Management Journal* 16: 119–41.

——(1996). 'The Transition from Decentralised to Network-Based MNC Structures: An Evolutionary Perspective'. *Journal of International Business Studies* 27: 43–66.

Marsden, David (1999). *A Theory of Employment Systems*. Oxford: Oxford University Press.

Menkhoff, Thomas (1992). 'Xinyong or How to Trust Chinese Non-Contractual Business Relations and Social Structure: The Singapore Case'. *Internationales Asienforum* 23: 261–288.

Methe, David P. and Penner-Hahn, Joan D. (1999). 'Globalization of Pharmaceutical Research and Development in Japanese Companies'. In: S. L. Beechler and A. Bird (eds.), *Japanese Multinationals Abroad: Individual and Organizational Learning*. Oxford: Oxford University Press, pp. 191–210.

Morgan, Glenn, Kelly, Bill, Sharpe, Diana, and Whitley, Richard (2003). 'Global Managers and Japanese Multinationals: Internationalisation and Management in Japanese Financial institutions'. *International Journal of Human Resource Management*: 389–407.

Nohria, Nitin and Ghoshal, Sumantra (1997). *The Differentiated Network: Organizing Multinational Corporations for Value Creation*. San Francisco: Jossey-Bass.

Perlmutter, Howard (1969). 'The Tortuous Evolution of the Multinational Corporation'. *Columbia Journal of World Business* 4: 9–18.

Pil, Frits and MacDuffie, John Paul (1999). 'Transferring Competitive Advantage Across Borders: A Study of Japanese Auto Transplants in North America'. In: J. K. Liker, W. M. Fruin, and P. S. Adler (eds.), *Remade* in America: *Transplanting and Transforming Japanese Management Systems*. New York: Oxford University Press, pp. 39–74.

Pucik, Vladimir (1999). 'When Performance Does Not Matter: Human resource management in Japanese-owned US affiliates'. In: S. L. Beechler and A. Bird (eds.), *Japanese Multinationals Abroad*. Oxford: Oxford University Press, pp. 169–88.

Redding, S. G. (1990). *The Spirit of Chinese Capitalism*. Berlin: de Gruyter.

Rugman, Alan and Brewer, Thomas (eds.) (2001). *The Oxford Handbook of International Business*. Oxford. Oxford University Press.

——and Alain, Verbeke (2001). 'Location, Competitiveness and the Multinational Enterprise'. In: A. Rugman and T. Brewer (eds.), *The Oxford Handbook of International Business*. Oxford: Oxford University Press, pp. 150–77.

Sakai, Junko (2000). *Japanese Bankers in the City of London*. London: Routledge.

Sheard, Paul (1994). 'Interlocking Shareholdings and Corporate Governance in Japan'. In: M. Aoki and R. Dore (eds.), *The Japanese Firm: The Sources of Competitive Strength*. Oxford: Oxford University Press, pp. 310–49.

Silin, R. H. (1976). *Leadership and Values: The Organisation of Large Scale Taiwanese Enterprises*. Harvard University Press.

Solvell, Orjan and Zander, Ivo (1998). 'International Diffusion of Knowledge: Isolating Mechanisms and the Role of the MNE'. In: A. D. Chandler, P. Hagstrom, and O. Solvell (eds.), *The Dynamic Firm: The Role of Technology, Strategy, and Regions*. Oxford: Oxford University Press, pp. 402–16.

Sorge, Arndt (1996). 'Societal Effects in Cross-National Organizing Studies: Conceptualizing Diversity in Actors and Systems'. In: R. Whitley and P. H. Kristensen (eds.), *The Changing European Firm: Limits to Convergence*. London: Routledge, pp. 67–86.

Soskice, David (1999). 'Divergent Production Regimes: Coordinated and Uncoordinated Market Economies in the 1980s and 1990s'. In: Herbert Kitschelt, Peter Lange, Gary Marks, and John Stephens (eds.), *Continuity and Change in Contemporary Capitalism*. Cambridge: Cambridge University Press, pp. 101–34.

Szulanski, G. (1996). 'Exploring Internal Stickiness: Impediments to the Transfer of Best Practices Within the Firm'. *Strategic Management Journal* 17: 27–44.

Teece, David, Rumelt, Richard, Dosi, Giovanni, and Winter, Sidney (1994). 'Understanding Corporate Coherence: Theory and Evidence'. *Journal of Economic Behavior and Organization* 23: 1–30.

——, Pisano, Gary, and Shuen, Amy (2000). 'Dynamics Capabilities and Strategic Management'. In: G. Dosi et al. (eds.), *The Nature and Dynamics of Organizational Capabilities*. pp. 334–62.

Thelen, Kathleen and Kume, Ikuo (2001). 'The Rise of Nonliberal Training Regimes: Germany and Japan Compared'. In: W. Streeck and K. Yamamura (eds.), *The Origins of Nonliberal Capitalism: Germany and Japan in Comparison*. Ithaca: Cornell University Press, pp. 200–28.

Tolbert, Pamela S. (1996). 'Occupations, Organisations, and Boundaryless Careers'. In: M. B. Arthur and D. M. Rousseau (eds.), *The Boundaryless Career*. New York: Oxford University Press, pp. 331–49.

Tolliday, Steven (2000). 'Transplanting the American Model? US Automobile Companies and the Transfer of Technology and Management to Britain, France, and Germany, 1928–1962'. In: J. Zeitlin and G. Herrigel (eds.), *Americanization and its Limits: Reworking US Technology and Management in Post-War Europe and Japan*. Oxford: Oxford University Press, pp. 76–119.

Westney, Eleanor (1993). 'Institutionalisation Theory and the Multinational Corporation'. In: S. Ghoshal and E. Westney (eds.), *Organization Theory and the Multinational Corporation*. London: Macmillan, pp. 53–76.

—— and Zaheer, Srilata (2001). 'The Multinational Enterprise as an Organization'. In: A. Rugman and T. Brewer (eds.), *The Oxford Handbook of International Business*. Oxford: Oxford University Press, pp. 349–79.

Whitley, Richard (1999). *Divergent Capitalisms: The Social Structuring and Change of Business Systems*. Oxford: Oxford University Press.

—— (2001). 'How and Why are International Firms Different?' In: G. Morgan, P. H. Kristensen, and R. Whitley (eds.), *The Multinational Firm*. Oxford: Oxford University Press, pp. 27–68.

—— (2002). 'Developing Innovative Competences: The Role of Institutional Frameworks'. *Industrial and Corporate Change* 11: 497–528.

—— (2003a). 'Changing Transnational Institutions and the Management of International Business Transactions'. In: M.-L. Djelic and S. Quack (eds.), *Globalisation and Institutions: Redefining the Rules of the Game*. Cheltenham: Edward Elgar, pp. 108–33.

—— (2003b). 'The Institutional Structuring of Organisational Capabilities: The Role of Authority Sharing and Organisational Careers'. *Organization Studies* 24: 667–95.

—— and Czaban, Laszlo (1998). 'Institutional Transformation and Enterprise Change in an Emergent Capitalist Economy: The Case of Hungary'. *Organization Studies* 19: 259–80.

——, Henderson, J., Czaban, L., and Lengyel, G. (1996). 'Trust and Contractual Relations in an Emerging Capitalist Economy'. *Organization Studies* 17: 397–420.

——, Morgan, Glenn, Kelly, William, and Sharpe, Diana (2003). 'The Changing Japanese MNC'. *Journal of Management Studies* 40: 639–68.

Yamin, Mohammed (2002). 'Subsidiary Entrepreneurship and the Advantages of Multinationality'. In: V. Havila, M. Forsgren and H. Hakansson (eds.), *Critical Perspectives on Internationalisation*. Oxford: Pergamon, pp. 133–50.

Zander, Ivo and Solvell, Orjan (2002). 'The Phantom Multinational'. In: V. Havila, M. Forsgren, and H. Hakansson (eds.), *Critical Perspectives on Internationalisation*. Oxford: Pergamon, pp. 81–106.

10

Internationalization and Capability Development in Professional Services Firms

GLENN MORGAN AND SIGRID QUACK

10.1. Introduction

Over the last two decades, the service sector has become increasingly internationalized. As well as exporting services to other countries, firms have established a variety of organizational forms and networks in order to enable themselves to deliver services across national borders. Whereas some consideration has been given to understanding strategic issues (Aharoni 1993; Baden-Fuller 1993; Dezalay 1993; Dezalay and Sugarman 1995; Dunning 1993), very little is known about the internationalization of service sector firms at the level of organization, management, and work processes. This is particularly true for what in the literature have been referred to as 'professional services firms', characterized by the knowledge intensity of their services, their dependency on highly skilled employees (often but not always accredited professionals) and the intangibility and customization of solutions delivered to their customers (Alvesson 2001; Empson 2001a,b; Greenwood and Lachman 1996; Greenwood et al. 1999; Løwendahl 2000; Maister 1993; Morris and Empson 1998; Rose and Hinings 1999). Most discussions of the internationalization of professional services firms have been limited to a small number of empirical

Earlier versions of this chapter have been presented at the ERIM Workshop at the University of Rotterdam in January 2003 and the conference on National Business Systems in the New Global Context at the University of Oslo in May 2003. We would like to thank the participants of these meetings for critical discussions and suggestions. We are particularly grateful to Ariane Berthoin Antal, Tim Morris, Laura Empson, Christoph Dörrenbächer, Bart Noteboom, and Richard Whitley for their constructive comments which helped to frame the paper in its current form. Sigrid Quack would like to thank Emily Richards for the careful language editing of her parts of the text.

studies of accounting, law, management consultancy, and investment banking industries. These highlight the need for professional services firms to reconfigure existing structures and develop new mechanisms of organizational coordination as they expand across national borders—a process which, given the complexity and velocity of change in international business environments, appears to involve a considerable amount of experimentation.

Most of such studies have developed from debates on professional services firms rather than the analysis of internationalization and multinationals. They are therefore limited in the degree to which they specifically address the questions posed by the more recent contributions emerging from the institutionalist analysis of multinational firms and transnational processes (e.g. Djelic and Quack 2003; Morgan 2001; Morgan et al. 2001), especially the extent to which and ways in which multinational firms develop distinctive sets of competences that enable them to outcompete nationally based firms. Much institutionalist analysis has suggested that multinationals frequently attempt to transfer their home-based practices to their subsidiaries, often making only minor adaptations (see, for example, the contributions in Morgan et al. 2001; Geppert et al. 2002). The degree to which they develop more novel transnational organizational capabilities is unclear. Generalization of home country practices has two consequences depending on the host country context. First, it leads to conflicts with local employees and managers' models of organizing work. Second, it contributes to the destruction of locally embedded skill systems by imposing global benchmarks that ignore local specificities. The overall result is that many multinationals become sites of conflict between different competing rationalities which is managed through an unstable combination of market mechanisms (those subsidiaries which win internal competition games grow by being provided with additional resources from the head office, while those that 'fail' simply wither away) and bureaucratic procedures (setting performance goals based on financial and other targets) (see, for example, Bélanger et al. 1999; Kristensen and Zeitlin 2001). As Whitley demonstrates in Chapter 8 on multinationals in this book, the ability of multinationals to achieve distinctively cross-national capabilities is limited by the complexities of coordinating across national boundaries. In reality, many firms themselves recognize this and often limit their exposure to the uncertainties and costs of internationalization in the ways which he describes. The model of the 'global firm' that has been presented in some contexts is then a myth; knowledge, people, technologies, etc. do not flow 'frictionlessly' across national borders, creating a whole that is greater than the sum of its parts. On the contrary, it may be that some MNCs are less than the sum of their parts because centralizing mechanisms actually detract from the value of the 'parts', that is, the subsidiaries.

These issues are relevant for the analysis of professional services firms (hereafter PSFs). The internationalization of these activities is on the increase and the WTO and other interested parties have been debating for some time how to remove what are seen as constraints on trade by making it easier for international professional services firms to gain access to national markets that have previously been closed to them. Such arguments are based on just the sort of optimistic, naïve view of the benefits of the 'global firm' that institutionalists have been trying to deconstruct in the sphere of manufacturing multinationals. Indeed when we look at how the real world of professional services firms is evolving we can see that the globalization of these firms varies significantly across sectors and does not have the force of a generalized and universal move to a global firm model. For example, in the area of law, the process of internationalization of firms is slow and variable. The most 'global' law firm is generally considered to be Clifford Chance which has offices in only nineteen countries (compared, for example, to the big four accountancy firms which have offices worldwide in over 150 countries). Even in the accountancy area, the collapse of Arthur Andersen which had previously billed itself as the global professional services firm par excellence reveals that this process of internationalization is by no means without its difficulties.

Such variations highlight the different degrees and modes of internationalization of PSFs and suggest it would be useful to examine in more detail the different organizational forms that professional services firms develop in order to become international. In this chapter we consider the nature of the organizational arrangements developed in order to coordinate professionals and their knowledge across national boundaries, given that they come from historically distinct national systems of professional knowledge, norms, and values. Additionally, what limitations are placed on these organizational arrangements by particular institutional contexts, and how does this affect the form which such firms take? As Whitley describes in his chapter, international professional services firms have to rely on delegating responsibility to foreign employees because of the nature of the tasks which they perform for clients and because of the local nature of the explicit and tacit knowledge which they require for successful completion of tasks. However, the loyalty and willingness of employees to commit to the parent organization, and in particular, to participate effectively in cross-national projects and teams, is affected by their own local circumstances. International firms will seek to align these conflicts through mechanisms of rewards, career development, and responsible autonomy over work tasks but their degree of manoeuvre in these areas may be limited according to their basic structural design. Firms may either accept these structural limitations in return for their advantages or they may seek to change form and thus transform from one set of limitations and advantages to another. Either way, they do not resolve their problems but rather reconstitute them as new tensions between national institutional settings and global firm structures. In this sense, our chapter emphasizes the necessity of understanding firms in relation to the different institutional settings within which they are located. The self-proclaimed identity of 'global firms', whether in the professional services sector or in other sectors, needs to be critically examined in the light of the continued importance of national and other institutional contexts.

The chapter proceeds as follows. In the next section, we discuss in more detail the nature of professional services firms and the problems that their specific characteristics raise in broad terms for the processes of internationalization. In the following section, drawing on existing literature and our own exploratory work, we construct four ideal types (or models) of organizational form which professional services firms may use in order to coordinate across borders. In the final section, we analyse the strengths and weaknesses of these different organizational models with regard to their ability to develop three key organizational capabilities: coordination, learning, and reconfiguration (Teece et al. 2000).

10.2. The Internationalization of Professional Services Firms

Professional services firms primarily deliver problem solving to their customers. This problem solving can involve the application of standardized solutions but also the development of customized solutions (Hansen et al. 1999). Thus, processes of knowledge transfer and knowledge creation are central to professional services firms (Dierkes et al. 2001; Empson 2001a). Such processes, however, are highly context-specific and often involve a complex interaction between explicit and tacit forms of knowledge (Nonaka and Takeuchi 1995; Polanyi 1966; Robertson et al. 2003; Werr and Stjernberg 2003: 902). As a consequence, professional services firms need to coordinate and manage work processes in which people possessing the relevant knowledge cooperate in applying and developing this knowledge in order to meet the demands of their clients. Professional services firms also need to develop various forms of boundary-spanning activities in order to coordinate their own specific knowledge and skills with external resources (Böhling 2002). Fosstenløkken et al. (2003), for example, have suggested that the development of tailored problem solutions involves a strong element of knowledge development through client interaction. This creates the need for various forms of organized boundary-spanning activities between the professional services firm and the client firm.

The delivery of complex problem solutions furthermore often requires access to highly specific knowledge that the firm may either possess internally or may gain more simply and easily through (partial or temporary) cooperation with other professional services firms. This is Richardson's (1972) well-known argument about firms engaging in collaborative arrangements because of their need to combine their own specific resources with different but complementary resources possessed by other firms in order to create a new product or service. Such combination can occur between potential competitors as well as between firms operating in distinct but complementary and overlapping markets.

The professional services firm, therefore, is usually more than just an aggregation of the knowledge of its individual professionals. What any individual professional can achieve for the corporate client is necessarily limited and as problems become both more extensive and more complex, a key issue for the professional services firm is how can it deliver the coordinated teamwork approach that is necessary. What set of organizational arrangements enable the effective combination of varying forms of knowledge and expertise in ways that contribute to the identification and solution of clients' problems?[1] Thus the nature of the firm, how it is governed, how funds for investment and reward are managed, how work activities are organized and coordinated, how employees are incentivized

[1] It is obviously the case that all 'problems' are socially constructed. Professional services firms are instrumental in 'helping' their clients define what their problem is as the first step in selling their own skills in solving it. They are purveyors of 'legitimate' problems and 'appropriate' solutions (see especially the work of Alvesson 2001).

to share knowledge and expertise are clearly central to understanding organized professional activity. The development of models of organization that enable core assets (in this case, professional knowledge and expertise) to be effectively utilized is essential, yet by no means fully understood or theorized in the case of professional services firms.

As previously stated, this is even more the case where such firms are becoming involved in international business. There are two main reasons for this. First, internationalization—as a firm or as a network of firms—usually requires an increase in the number of interfaces between a growing number of professionals, clients, and competitors in order to manage the knowledge development of the organization successfully. In the course of this process, professional services firms often recognize the limits of the informal and highly personalized forms of coordination that hitherto dominated in their industries. The second factor is the increasing heterogeneity of the knowledge bases of the firm. Numerous studies on the problems of cross-border knowledge transfer (Dörrenbächer 2003; Marchazina et al. 2001; Szulanski 2000) indicate that perceptions of what constitutes relevant knowledge and appropriate processes for knowledge creation are likely to differ considerably between countries. As professional services firms expand abroad they can no longer expect the same degree of common understanding of rules, norms, and behaviours among professionals, clients, competitors, and regulators that they have been used to in their home jurisdiction. In particular, they have to resolve how to share authority across national jurisdictions and, related to this, how to encourage employees to commit to the development of firm-specific knowledge. These issues first relate to governance: how does the firm create a system of cross-national governance, particularly as professional services firms have traditionally operated 'partnership' governance mechanisms for reasons to do with the nature of their activities (Greenwood and Empson 2003)? Second, these issues relate to skills: in contexts where professional skills have traditionally been defined in nationally distinctive ways and where barriers between national labour markets for professionals are still high, how does the firm create a system that enables coordinated cross-national activity and learning? Our argument is that far from assuming a 'frictionless' solution to these problems reflected in a shift to a 'global firm', internationalizing professional services firms take a variety of shapes and structures, with varying advantages and disadvantages.

10.3. A Typology of Forms of International Coordination of Professional Services Activities

In this section of the chapter, we outline four basic structural models which allow firms to resolve these problems and establish a framework for internationalization. The models that we present offer distinctive ways of managing the interactions between governance structures, diverse skill sets and modes of coordinating knowledge and resources. They represent, in that sense, organizational forms where there is complementarity and coherence between the various elements but also limitations and tensions as to what can be achieved within a particular structural form.[2] Three of the forms which we identify are different types of legally unified entities (the collegially coordinated, the hierarchically controlled, and the financially controlled international firm). The fourth type that we label the reciprocity-based international network of firms is based on an alliance of legally independent firms. In the following discussion, we begin by considering an internationalization process constrained by more traditional professional partnership consideration (the collegially coordinated international PSF) and then move progressively away from this form with our analysis of the 'hierarchically controlled' and 'financially controlled' international PSF. We reserve our analysis of the network model to the end. A summary of the types which we identify is presented in Table 10.1 (on p. 284).

10.3.1. *The collegially coordinated international professional services firm*

The model of the collegially controlled firm[3] builds most directly on traditional models of professionalism. In this type of firm, the basic decision-making element consists of the partners themselves. In the partnership form of the PSF, partners receive rewards both as

---

[2] The factors which condition which 'type' particular firms resemble is not our main issue here though it is clearly a crucial next step in our broad research agenda. Obvious features would be the nature of client demand within sectors, the type of regulation of the professional service, the power and politics of particular firms, and the influence of national institutional contexts.

[3] Our first two ideal models, the collegially coordinated and the hierarchically controlled firm correspond in many respects to Greenwood et al.'s (1990) unitary and confederation model. From an institutionalist view, however, the different type of authority sharing appears more relevant with regard to the development of organizational capabilities than variation in organizational form. Whereas hierarchical coordination is unlikely to occur in the confederation model, collegial coordination is in principle possible in both, a legally unified international partnership firm as well as in a confederation model consisting of legally independent national firms.

Table 10.1. *Forms of international coordination in four types of professional services firms*

	Collegially coordinated international firm	Hierarchically controlled international firm	Financially controlled international firm	Reciprocity-based international networks of firms
Ownership	Standard partnership form in national contexts; committee to run international level	Partnership (increasingly Llp status); incorporated private company governing international level	Publicly owned and quoted on stock exchange	Dispersed; member firms are partnerships or publicly owned companies
Authority sharing	Collegial persuasion in lateral decision-making at international partner meetings and boards	Hierarchical authority of strong international executive management committee	Financial control of national units through international head office and shareholders	Dispersed authority; some degree of authority sharing between member firms in project teams
Training	Training directed towards international promotion of consistent services, but decentrally organized	Centralized training aiming at diffusion of firm-specific technical and behavioural standards	Limited training, often technical and ad hoc	Very few common training initiatives with focus on network building
Routines and information systems	Heterogeneous routines and practices; information systems used as a pathfinder to personalized knowledge necessary for customized solutions	Management and organizational culture supporting standardization of routines and practices; information systems used as basis for application of ready-made solutions	Standardization of procedures likely to be limited by interest of individual professionals to maintain their valuable individual knowledge; client and product-specific information systems	Heterogeneity of routines and practices of member firms; low investment in joint information systems with pathfinder function to knowledge of member firms
Career systems	Firm-specific internal labour market with up- or out-system; predominantly national careers; becoming a partner the main goal and determinant of reward	Firm-specific internal labour market with up- or out-system; both, international and national careers; importance of achieving partnership position	Industry specific professional labour markets; national and international careers; high mobility across firms; financial rewards determined short-term performance	Career opportunities arise within individual member firms; international careers very rare

employees (they generate fee income and receive salaries and bonuses based on this) and as 'owners' of the firm. As a collective, partners decide on what to do with the surplus over and above salaries and bonuses. They may decide to keep the surplus low and distribute most of it through salaries and bonuses (either primarily to themselves or more equitably across the firm); alternatively they may decide to build the surplus up in order to provide for insurance against possible future liabilities or more positively for future new investment (as their organizational form precludes them from going to the capital markets for funds for this purpose). These processes are highly invisible to the outside world. The partnership has only to justify its activities to itself and nobody else. The partnership form is a way of locking individuals into the firm. It gives them a share of the overall profits of the firm and it gives them a substantial say over how the firm runs and thus on how they themselves work.

In general, it may be argued that one consequence of the partnership form is that it is likely to lead to risk aversion. Partners want to make sure that they can meet any future claims against them. They also want to make sure that any new investments do not dilute their earnings as decisions to invest in new activities are, in effect, taking from the partners' current rewards. They are therefore reluctant to agree to new initiatives. On the other hand, because there is no outside scrutiny, it is also unlikely that highly structured investment decision-making processes such as are demanded in public companies will take place and some significant decisions may be made on the basis of personal authority, reputation, and networks.

Broadly speaking, the overall strategy of the firm tends to be the sum of the outcomes of the decisions of individual partners, and their skill, knowledge, and networks supplemented by some partnership level initiatives.[4] But these partnership level initiatives tend to be limited in scale and scope (as partners are reluctant to invest highly in what they consider speculative ventures). The authority to follow them through is not strong, being primarily dependent on the interest and commitment of the managing partner (who may be simply serving a compulsory period in this role before returning to the 'real business' of being a partner).

---

[4] These issues have been well explored in the debate on the movement from the P2 (partnership and professionalism) model to the managed professional business model in the writings of Greenwood, Hinings, and colleagues, for example, Hinings et al. (1999); also Greenwood and Empson (2003); Pinnington and Morris (2002, 2003).

Going international, however, inevitably has the potential to disrupt this model. On the one hand it is an attraction (broadening the market, access to new fees etc.) as well as a necessity (clients may require an international service and thus change their professional advisers if they cannot get it). On the other hand, it raises coordination issues and the question of associated costs. One solution may be just to keep the national partnership and create a set of branch offices which employ locally qualified professionals on salaries. These are then supervised by a small number of partners from the home base, some sent out on semi-permanent assignment to the branch, others coming in on a short-term basis to manage certain projects. However, this clearly has significant limitations in terms of what can be done in branches and how this impacts on the main home base. The other solution involves the creation of an international firm with a number of nationally based partnerships. In such a firm, the main decision-making element remains at the national partnership level but inevitably there has to be a tier of authority and governance above the national level to deal with issues of cross-national working. Traditionally it appears that this was constituted by a committee of the senior partners in the national partnerships negotiating and bargaining about how to maximize the advantages from the international form without fundamentally threatening their national identities (and control over revenue). The international committee is here given limited resources and authority to establish 'international' policies.

This is reflected in the way in which the collegially coordinated international professional services firm manages the coordination of skills and competences across national boundaries (Lazega 2001; Lazega and Pattison 1999). Training is directed towards the international promotion of consistent service methods but nevertheless is often organized in a decentralized way that allows for local adaptation. Lateral decision-making structures, right up to the international committee or board of partners, are based upon discussion, negotiation, and voluntary acceptance rather than the mandatory adoption of international practices (Greenwood et al. 1999: 285). The collegially coordinated international professional services firm would tend to have only a small international administration with support functions. Among this type of professional services firms, the main initiative for developing common organizational routines may come less from strategic decisions made by the international board of partners and more from the pressures at levels of practice to improve lateral cross-border communication and decision-making structures leading, for example, to global practice groups with a mandate to develop common procedures and standards for service provision.

Collegially coordinated international professional services firms may make considerable investments in the development of international firm-specific information management systems. However, given the greater heterogeneity of practices and the higher autonomy of national and regional offices, these information management systems rarely reach the same degree of unified codification as in the hierarchical firms that we discuss next. As a consequence, global information management systems are less frequently used to apply standardized solutions. Instead, they are more often employed as pathfinders to the personalized and often implicit knowledge of colleagues in other offices of the firm.

Although the collegially coordinated firm usually operates an internal labour market on the up-or-out principle, careers are, except for international secondments for junior staff, predominantly national careers. There are only very few senior partners whose careers are truly international. Collegially coordinated firms offer their professionals the autonomy regarded as necessary for the creation of highly customized services and complex problem solutions for customers. The cross-border cooperation of professionals in international project teams is supported by financial rewards at partnership and project level as well as a strong culture of professional collegiality and gradually built up relational networks to colleagues in the various national offices of the international firm. It remains a question, however, whether these incentives are strong enough to enable such collegially coordinated firms, particularly those that take the form of a loose confederation, to create the commitment to knowledge sharing in international teams necessary to generate complex problem solutions.

In sum, our model of the collegially coordinated firm shows low investments at both the national and the international level in complementary organizational assets such as training, information management systems, and the development of unified organizational routines. The cooperation of professionals on the international level builds to a large attempt on the actual or assumed common values of an international professional community and tends to arise on the basis of specific needs. Such cooperation will be ad hoc, though certain contexts may encourage more formalization and joint activity. Strategic investment in building mechanisms and processes of international cooperation will be limited not least by national partnerships' reluctance to relinquish control over significant portions of revenues and fees. This reluctance may be overcome as the advantages of strategic international cooperation are perceived to be increasing but a delicate balance remains between the national partnerships where power resides and the international coordinative level.

The greater autonomy of the individual professional, the emphasis on dialogue between highly skilled professionals and the importance given to lateral and consensual decision-making between partners all favour what Hansen et al. (1999: 110) refer to as the logic of 'expert economics': the creation of services and problem solutions that are rich in tacit knowledge and depend on a personalization strategy for knowledge creation and development. Such strategies neither need, nor do they allow for a highly leveraged firm.

In terms of the other models which we discuss, they tend to be characterized by a higher number of partners to salaried professionals as fees are predominantly earned by partners using their specific skills on distinctive and unique problems. Expenditure on overhead and management costs is also kept low and national partnerships retain authority over the bulk of the revenues that they generate. Such firms do create some firm-specific knowledge and complementary assets at the international level, for example, some shared training and information systems. In general, however, they continue to rely to a major extent on their individual partners within particular national contexts to bring in and manage international business. The ability of the partners to develop their own professional networks within the firm across national boundaries is central. Knowing who can be relied on in other parts of the firm is a function of personal knowledge and experience of working across borders. The firm does not expend large effort and resources on standardizing its members and their behaviours through an international programme of recruitment, training and development, and reward and appraisal systems. Instead it relies on professionals in different countries finding their way to each other and to modes of working together by networks and experience. This is why the partnership principle and the strategic control exercised by partners remains so strong. If it were to be sacrificed, for example, by giving more hierarchical authority to the international committee, there would be a danger that the partners would leave the firm and set up their own organization. The firms would thereby loose the social capital which such partners have generated internally through their networks and experience because the complementary and firm-specific assets that are developed and held in such firms is low. If the firm loses a lot, there is an asymmetrical loss on the part of the partner who leaves.

The partner takes the client list (subject to various forms of constraining agreements) and although he/she may lose the specific contacts inside the firm, the experience of developing such cross-national linkages is transferable and useful in the new context. This means that the key problem for such firms is retaining their high performing professionals. Attempts to either limit their control over their own work (by establishing more standardized operating procedures) or to constrain their earnings (by 'taxing' them more to support an international office) would undermine the partnership mechanism that holds people in the firm.

The drawbacks of this model of collegial coordination reflect these tensions and become more visible as the firm expands internationally and in staff numbers. The model relies on personal networks where colleagues are known to each other, or at least know their most important colleagues, and this becomes more difficult as the company expands across the globe and employs an increasing number of staff. Therefore, the need for a sphere of formal coordination beyond the national partnership level increases. Also the idea of serving international clients assumes some sort of standardization of practice, knowledge, procedures, or processes across national boundaries that can be leveraged to develop economies of scale and scope. Such standardization implies the production of firm-specific assets and investment in such a process of production. All this points to a potential diminution in the power and significance of individual national partners and a growing emphasis on the identity of the firm per se at the international level, a process that is inevitably accompanied by a formalization of the international sphere of governance within the firm, for example, away from an international committee system towards the creation of a formal legal entity that links the national partnerships. Depending on demand pressures and the decisions of the senior partners, then, collegially coordinated international firms may begin to gravitate to a more hierarchical model of organization. It is this model which we discuss next.

10.3.2. *The hierarchically controlled international professional services firm*

In governance terms, the hierarchically controlled firm has moved further towards establishing a distinctive sphere of control above the partnership level as a way of establishing a firm-specific set of assets that can have value across national boundaries. As Greenwood et al. (1999) describe in their discussion of national partnerships, this involves the emergence of a strategy at firm level that goes beyond a simple aggregation model of individual professionals' workload. The development of the strategic level implies first of all, a recognition of the need to look beyond existing practices to new possibilities in the light of changing environments; secondly, the delegation of authority to an executive charged with developing the strategy and thirdly the provision of resources to this level enabling it to actually achieve its goals. In this sense, collegiality becomes gradually replaced by hierarchy with stronger efforts to capture knowledge and problem solving at the firm level, for example, through increased standardization of procedures and models built out of collective training efforts and feedback mechanisms to knowledge databases. However, professional partnerships and claims to professional autonomy remain in existence and act as limitations on the ability of 'managers' to exercise hierarchical authority in order to enforce both the standards themselves and the process of developing them and sharing them.

In the international context, this form reveals two interesting features. On one hand, professional services firms find themselves moving towards increased cross-national coordination. In this process, they move towards first, increased standardization of practices, procedures, and underlying knowledge-based expertise and second, increased teamwork across borders, all of which is facilitated by strong cross-national networks, shared training, and development facilities and common technological interfaces. On the other hand, the legal status of the firm is defined primarily by the national incorporation of each of its national partnerships. This has the strong advantage of limiting the contagion that can arise when liabilities exceed assets. National partnerships may be liable but the global firm (and the national partnerships not directly involved) cannot be held liable.

In the hierarchically coordinated firm, however, more authority and more revenues are controlled by the international level. Increasingly, the international level itself is constituted as a separate legal entity, usually as a limited company or, in some circumstances, as a limited liability partnership. Its relationship with the constituent national partnerships is more formalized than in a situation where there is a management committee coordinating the joint activities. This reflects both the higher significance of this tier of authority and the greater sums of revenue passing through its hands. This model of the firm is more highly formalized in all respects than the collegially coordinated international PSF where personal ties between senior partners from different national partnerships are crucial to resolving potential conflicts. Issues such as what the international level of the firm 'owns' (e.g. the 'brand', the company methodologies, the common stock of knowledge), become important. How do the constituent companies relate to this? How is it valued and how do the national partnerships pay for this? How does the international firm generate consent and legitimacy for its use of authority and its demand for payment from the constituent companies for access to these? How does the international company 'leverage' these assets in order to improve the markets for the national partnerships? These become central issues for debate. In effect, the firm is developing more firm-specific assets and more complementary assets that increase the value of professional knowledge per se.

In the hierarchically controlled international firm, centralized training (at an international level) is regarded as a key factor for the development and dissemination of common technical and behavioural standards among all professionals of the firm—independently of their national origin and the locality of their current position within the firm. Upon recruitment, young employees usually pass through extensive training courses at internal teaching facilities, where they are socialized into a collective sense of identity (see, for example, the discussion in Greenwood et al. 1999). This sense of identity comes partly from the experience of working together in a cross-national environment. It is further strengthened by the firm's attempt to demonstrate its (verbal) commitment to a strong central mission statement, the facilitation of cross-national problem solving teams and management development programmes, and the organization of conferences and other informal activities which provide multiple forms of lateral communication across national boundaries.

In addition to training and socialization, hierarchically controlled international professional firms attempt to coordinate their staff to a considerable degree through the standardization and routinization of procedures. This is supported by efforts to develop coherent documentation and comprehensive information management systems in order to make the most effective use of the firm's knowledge. The creation of international information management systems, however, is a difficult and cumbersome process: the codification of tacit, experience-based knowledge requires the active cooperation of the professionals who possess this knowledge. Even though the hierarchical firm encourages knowledge sharing through firm-specific socialization and culture, as well as financial rewards, these mechanisms are often not sufficient to overcome the knowledge-hoarding strategies of the individuals and subgroups in the organization (Empson 2001*b*; Gammelgaard et al. 2003).

This process, in turn, is influenced by national labour markets and the degree to which professionals see alternative futures for themselves outside the firm. In active professional labour markets, such as characterize what Whitley refers to as arm's length economies, the partnership is the means of tying-in professionals who have the opportunity to go elsewhere. However, as this is not guaranteed to all, knowledge hoarding may still occur especially where it can become an added selling point for the individual on the labour market. In collaborative economies (in Whitley's terms), there are more incentives to share knowledge than just those arising from individual benefit, though the degree to which professionals from different national contexts can make sense of such knowledge varies on the degree of 'cognitive distance' (Nooteboom 2000) and associated with this, the amount of effort put in by the organization into narrowing the gap, for example, by international training systems, etc.

In sum, the hierarchically controlled firm undertakes high investments in 'non-productive' activities in the sense that the hours spent in training and documentation activities cannot be billed to clients, while central facilities such as the staff in information technology and human resources departments need to be paid out of the income generated from clients. The creation of these 'complementary assets' (Teece 1986: 288) becomes an overhead, a 'tax' on the earning activities of employees and subsidiaries. In general, the higher the cost of these complementary assets, the more the pressure on the partnership form itself as the main source of funding for such activities comes out of the partners' profits. Simultaneously the growth of the business, particularly across borders, increases the risk of liability claims against the firm. In such circumstances, the temptation to shift from a partnership structure (even a limited liability partnership mode) to a public limited company status increases, as PLC status can improve access to capital for growth and limit personal liabilities for failure.

If hierarchically coordinated firms wish to stay as partnerships or are constrained to do so by legislative requirements, they can compensate for the increasing cost of overheads in two ways. First, they may develop a higher leverage, that is, having a larger number of junior staff working for one partner. Due to the intensive socialization and the standardization of some of the work processes, junior staff can be trusted to undertake more of the work than in contexts where such a culture is absent. As leverage is so important and senior positions are rationed, hierarchically controlled firms are also likely to be characterized by high levels of performance monitoring and up-or-out systems of promotion and career development in order to keep some of the operational costs low while encouraging the search for new talent (on these processes in law firms see Morris and Pinnington 1998, 1999; Pinnington and Morris 2003). High leverage, however, clearly brings with it issues of monitoring to ensure that liabilities are not incurred because junior staff make wrong decisions.

Second, such firms may be able to produce more standardized packages of solutions to a wider range of problems than other firms; and these solutions can also be learnt and implemented by junior professionals. Creating cross-national teams is facilitated by the existence of common standards and procedures as well as by shared socialization on company training schemes. Unlike the collegially controlled firm, this is not dependent on personal networks which can be lost when individuals leave the firm. It is a property of the firm, constituted by the actions of the firm itself—a firm-specific asset that adds to the value of the firm. Large international professional services firms which aim to focus on what Hansen et al. (1999: 100) have called the 'economics of reuse', that is, the application of codified knowledge to a range of similar problems, require high levels of stable revenue-generating activities to sustain their considerable investments in these organizational complementary assets. However, the problem with this strategy is that market competition tends to erode profit margins for standardized solutions. Thus, firms will be pushed to compete for client assignments in higher valued market segments, for example, in the classic case of accounting and auditing firms moving into other 'business services' such as management consultancy. This in turn opens up obvious 'conflicts of interest' questions within the firm and increases the tension between the pressure for expansion and growth and the potential new liabilities taken on in the process (e.g. as in Arthur Andersen's strategy and demise in the aftermath of Enron). The complex regulatory issues arising from such tensions are reflected in current debates in the United Kingdom and the United States over what are termed Multidisciplinary Professional Practices as well as in legislation such as the Sarbanes–Oxley Act in the United States in 2002.

This leads us to the underlying tension alive in the hierarchically controlled firm. The principle of hierarchical control itself stands in contradiction to the demands of professionals for autonomy in organizing their work. The resulting tensions are to some degree smoothed over by up-or-out career systems which offer those who have worked themselves up through the ranks to the level of partner access to ownership, greater autonomy in doing their work and more influence on decision-making. High leverage, however, makes the chances of achieving full partnership status more remote and instead leads to a more stratified structure including the introduction of the salaried partnership status. Even if a person makes it to full partner level, different hierarchies of partnership and position (within national structures and particularly in relation to international forms of governance) make participation in broader strategic decisions unlikely for a long time. It is more difficult to use the promise of full partnership status as a form of control for all professional employees. However, the up-or-out system makes professional employees desperate to carry strong cv's and references with them when they either voluntarily or involuntarily exit the firm. As Grey and colleagues demonstrate (Anderson-Gough et al. 2000; Grey 1994, 1998), the combination of highly selective recruitment procedures for new entrants, intensive socialization and training in the early years together with the promise of partnership to the few and a comfortable landing for the many when they are 'let go' by the firm is sufficient to ensure that there is a strong 'commitment to the firm' and a downplaying of issues of professional identity. Thus in contrast to the collegial firm, the basis is set for an organization within which individuals are both highly motivated to cooperate across borders and helped in doing so by shared experiences and the existence of an infrastructure of shared information.

Attempts to establish matrix management structures (see, for example, the discussion in Baron and Besanko 2001) which delegate a certain amount of authority from the central office to lateral decision-making structures, such as globally oriented practice groups, further facilitate these processes. Such organizational structures which transcend national boundaries can make it easier to create cross-national teams which can work on both standardized and on more complex problems solutions. As long as these lateral structures remain subordinated to the overall centralized and hierarchical control of organizational resources, however, the economics of the *modus operandi* of hierarchically controlled international professional services firms tend to push the latter back towards standardized solutions and stable areas of business that can cover core costs.

In conclusion, these firms aim to develop more firm-specific knowledge and complementary assets so that they are ultimately less dependent on individual partners than the collegially coordinated firm. They can afford to lose partners and other professionals more easily as clients require the range of related services and not just the personal attention of the partner. Creating firm-specific assets is, however, a complex process that requires resources and effort at the international level that in some ways detracts from national partnerships. In this respect it is interesting to note that it seems as though the international tier of governance is likely to be run and controlled by powerful national partners (often drawn mainly from the biggest market, that is, in many cases the United States). Therefore, it may be that the balance between national and international interests may need to be thought of not just in these terms but also in terms of how one particular national partnership interacts with and dominates the rest of the national partnerships within the international organizational form.

10.3.3. *The financially controlled international professional services firm*

Our model of the third type of international professional services firms, which we call the *financially controlled firm* sacrifices the partnership principle in favour of limited company status. This has significant implications for how it controls and manages its professionals and its firm-specific assets. The financially coordinated PSF is likely to be a limited company with shares owned by outsiders. In the case of the larger companies, this is likely to mean that shares are quoted and traded on stock exchanges. The pressures on senior managers are those common to all such firms, that is, managers in incorporated professional services firms tend to be exposed to much stronger shareholder pressure than managers in partnership firms (Pinnington and Morris 2002). This affects both the way in which strategies are formulated (with higher transparency, accountability, and 'objectivity') and the sorts of strategies that are formulated (i.e. to meet market expectations of growth). It also clearly affects the resources that can be placed behind strategies as the firm does not have to rely on internally accumulated funds but can go to the capital markets.

Why should professional services firms make this move? Essentially the logic is that the more the key assets of the firm become not the knowledge of individual professionals per se but the competence of the firm itself to bring together firm-specific assets and complementary assets that enable clients' problems to be solved, the more attention must be paid to the management of these assets. They must be nurtured, developed, and invested in by the firm. The individual knowledge assets of the professional only work in conjunction with these existing assets. One key asset, for example, may be capital. In partnership forms, capital comes from the partners themselves forgoing current income and current consumption. In contexts, however, where demands for capital are extremely high, this is no longer viable and outside capital must be sought. Demands for capital vary between sectors and over time. For example, as investment banking has become more subject to capital adequacy requirements or trading becomes more dependent on funds to make markets so the partnership form has been of declining significance in these sectors. Demand for capital may also be a function of technological change and the need for huge levels of investment in global trading systems or global knowledge databases, as Nightingale and Poll (2000) suggest, again a factor leading to the decline of partnership in investment banking. As processes become increasingly standardized, the overheads for creating these standards, communicating them, inculcating them, and monitoring them also increase. There is a limit to how much this can be controlled within the partnership form, even when it has become hierarchical.

The financially driven firm resolves these pressures by abandoning the partnership status and becoming incorporated. In doing so it develops a new relationship between the individual professionals and the assets of the firm per se. Individuals and their knowledge and networks remain central in this process but the firm is no longer their property. Similarly the professionals are not the 'property' of the firm. Rather the labour market becomes the central mechanism through which these relationships are negotiated. Along with this, rewards and economic incentives are increasingly tightly linked to performance on actual tasks. Recruitment to and layoffs from the firm are determined according to product and labour market demand and supply. Individual rewards are strongly linked to performance. Employees bring professional skills and knowledge into the firm but use them in conjunction with firm-specific assets in order to solve clients' problems. Thus, clients 'belong' both to individuals (star performers) and their teams and to the firm. This dynamic lies behind the fear of firms that they will lose clients if they lose specific star performers and their teams (Lorsch and Tierney 2002). However, this is quite a subtle mechanism and the value that clients place on the 'firm' as opposed to the 'star' depends on the specific nature of the task and the degree to which the service is reliant on the complementary assets of the firm rather than just the knowledge and networks of the 'star' (cf. advertising agencies). Thus when 'star' fund managers or traders leave financial institutions, they do not automatically carry their clients with them as clients may be sceptical of the ability of the new firm to provide the same levels of service as the firm which has been left.

Firms will rely predominantly on highly differentiated financial reward packages to retain highly valuable employees. They will be less concerned to provide for firm-internal careers at least in part because they may want to retain the flexibility to thin down their organization depending on market conditions and thus are reluctant to enter into long-term credible commitments with employees no matter how valuable their skills and knowledge are perceived to be at a particular time. Firms from arm's length contexts are particularly likely to take this view; they will tailor their rewards systems strongly to performance so that when downturns happen, their costs are cut. They are also likely to take this further by reducing headcount where demand falls below a certain level, as has happened in many investment banks following the dot.com collapse. On the other hand, firms from collaborative economies may be slower to cut bonuses and numbers, partly in order to sustain existing skills but also partly as a way of avoiding overpaying for skills when the upturn comes and the labour market becomes tighter. However, this may be most relevant to home-based employees, and employees of firms from collaborative economies in host contexts may find themselves no more protected than they would be in firms from that home base, for example, as bankers working in Japanese banks in the City of London have found.

In international terms, an incorporated structure resolves (at least theoretically) issues of national partnership autonomy. The senior management is free to develop its own global firm-specific assets (in terms of technologies, and knowledge bases) so long as it convinces shareholders. However, because the firm wishes to retain flexibility to respond to market changes, it is likely to invest less in global systems of training and development than the hierarchically coordinated firm. Instead individuals invest in building their own skills, knowledge, and networks, often through moving between and within companies. The professionals then learn the best way to put these skills and networks to use quickly and effectively with the specific firm-level assets of the company that they have joined. Frequently the key to this cooperation across national boundaries to create solutions for clients is a clear shared incentive structure based on visible financial performance in relation to the project goals of clients.

The standardization of procedures and processes in terms of relations to clients is likely to be resisted in these circumstances where it is the expertise of individuals and their networks and contacts in particular national contexts that have to be coordinated in order to achieve the clients' goals. On the other hand, there will be high levels of standardization and routinization across borders in all the 'back office' functions which make the relationship with the client work, for example, in banking, global trading networks, settlement systems, etc. (see, for example, Nightingale and Poll 2000), all of which in turn require high levels of capital. In terms of client facing activities, however, incentives for knowledge sharing in international project teams consist predominantly of financial rewards that are supported by a professional culture of a 'give and take' exchange of individual favours in terms of knowledge exchange and helping each other with providing contacts to relevant people.

Careers in financially controlled professional services firms are embedded in industry-wide professional labour markets. Within the firm, national and international careers are oriented towards financial rewards. Careers, however, are not confined to a single firm but are likely to involve high mobility between firms within a particular sector. Particularly during periods of high market demand, career movements between the largest firms on the basis of the most advantageous financial packages for individuals and teams tend to increase considerably. From an organizational point of view, the key weakness for such firms is the problem of retaining the professionals possessing the necessary knowledge. On the other hand, this problem is cyclical because it occurs predominantly in times of high market demand for such professionals. When such demand slackens off, it becomes advantageous to the firm as first, its outlay on bonuses to such staff reduces and second, these employees can be laid off from the firm. As market demand rises, it is possible to recruit from the external labour market though, as previously discussed, firms may tend to hoard labour during downturns in the belief that this retains skills and knowledge in the firm in the long term at a cheaper cost than bidding for professionals at a time of rising demand would.

10.3.4. *Reciprocity-based international networks of professional services firms*

Finally in contrast to these varying forms of firms, we wish to draw attention to another pattern of international coordination that can be characterized in terms of reciprocity-based networks. International inter-firm networks are common among nationally based professional services firms, particularly in law, where firms and professionals do not want to give up their independence either to processes of international standardization or to becoming a subsidiary office of an international firm. At the same time, nationally based professional services firms do increasingly recognize the importance for their clients, and indeed for their own survival, of being able to access cooperation in other jurisdictions. Reciprocity-based international networks of professional services firms are formed on a voluntary basis between firms that retain their legal independence. Over time these networks often evolve from loose referral practices into more exclusive business relations with one 'best friend firm' in each specific jurisdiction. The key principle for cooperation in these networks is reciprocity. Within the network, firms refer business opportunities to each other and/or seek cooperation with each other on specific projects with the expectation that favours will be returned by the other partners at a later stage, but without calculating a strict relation between the services given and the services to be expected in return.

The evolution of reciprocity-based networks relies to a large extent on the long-term development of generalized trust between firms (Lane and Bachmann 1995; Nooteboom 2000). In professional services firms, such trust has been built (possibly even more than in other sectors) on personal relations between key representatives, for example, senior partners, of the member firms of these networks. In the past, such networks used to be effective and simple to use for referral business. A professional services firm would refer one of its clients, whose problem it could not solve on the basis of its own specific competence, to another member firm of the network (mostly in a different country) which had the necessary complementary competence. This situation involved a minimum of competition between member firms of the network, very low coordination costs and did not require any changes in the organization of the individual member firms. The more attractive and rewarding international business became, the more complex became the relations of professional services firms in such inter-firm networks. Member firms were no longer operating on an entirely national basis. As they started to engage in international business, and some of them even established offices in selected locations abroad, the members of the international inter-firm networks started to compete with each other in identical markets. Tendencies towards the standardization of some international business services increase the potential for economies of scale and thus may undermine the logic of reciprocity-based network cooperation. The provision of complex advice in such a context now requires considerable efforts of entrepreneurship among the senior partners of some firms in order to develop a coordinated strategy for expanding the networks' business and to become proactive in searching for clients and tasks that can only be accomplished by the coordinated action of members of the network.

Within the network, this is mirrored by the evolution of organizational arrangements aimed at nurturing common orientations. These include joint training and exchange of junior staff; information management systems to be used by professionals in the different member firms as pathfinder to both the codified and personalized knowledge in other partner firms; the formalization of fee-sharing agreements; and the creation of organizational arenas, such as international management committees and/or practice groups, in which a wider range of professionals from the different firms can come to know each other as a basis for potential knowledge sharing in future joint international project teams. As networks move towards more coordinated forms, the costs of governance, both financial and managerial (in terms of limiting the autonomy of national members) increase, as do potential rewards. Clearly, therefore, at some point such developments will inevitably lead to the question of whether the amount of managerial coordination and governance being expended requires that the network evolve to the structure of a firm and if so, what type of firm. In order to stabilize on a more long-term basis, reciprocity-based international networks of professional services firms need to achieve a difficult balance between cooperation and competition, trust and distrust, knowledge sharing, and knowledge hiding between the member firms. Whatever action they take to achieve this balance, it is likely to introduce new dysfunctions and new sources of instability (Hirsch-Kreinsen 2002; Podolny and Page 1998).

10.3.5. *Organizational capabilities of different types of international professional services firms*

What are the consequences of these patterns for the capabilities of firms? Drawing on Teece et al. (2000), Whitley (Chapter 8, this volume) refers to three particular capabilities of international firms—their ability to coordinate across national boundaries, their ability to learn across boundaries and their ability to reconfigure themselves quickly in response to changing environmental circumstances. He comes to the conclusion that the capabilities of what he terms 'delegated professional MNCs' (within which professional services firms are one category) rely entirely on project teams for cross-border coordination, and that these firms have limited capabilities for organizational learning but considerable capabilities for reconfiguration. The essential problem is whether firms have the capacity to set in place organizational mechanisms which facilitate these different types of international capabilities. Our argument is that as they make choices about their structures and strategies in the light of the type of knowledge which they have and the type of clients which they seek to attract, they build up differential capabilities. They cannot solve all their problems at once and therefore they satisfice by developing some capabilities while sacrificing others. Table 10.2 (p. 302) summarizes our basic argument in relation to the four organizational structures which we have identified.

Taking first the issue of coordination of skills and knowledge, collegially coordinated firms draw on informal and personal networks of knowledge within the international firm to create cross-national solutions for clients. They rely on the development of such networks among key senior partners. In this respect, they become even more reliant on not losing partners whose knowledge and reputation through the firm is the primary lubricant of international activities. The emphasis on the partner and sustaining the position and status of the partner militates against high managerial control and high overheads. This in turn means that it is unlikely that such firms will be effective in delivering large-scale worldwide standardized services. By contrast, in the hierarchically controlled firm, the balance turns in the other direction. Cross-border coordination is embedded in a culture of centrally steered training and socialization, as well as considerable top-down efforts to establish common routines and information systems. This specific combination of complementary assets leads the hierarchically controlled firm over time to build up organizational capabilities which allow it to produce, more easily than other types of professional services firms, standardized services at an internationally identical high level of quality. This does not mean that the hierarchically controlled firm is not able to generate other types of services. For the reasons described above, however, the hierarchically controlled firm's organizational capabilities to generate highly complex and customized services on a large scale are limited.

Table 10.2. *Organizational capabilities likely to be developed by four types of international professional services firms*

	Collegially coordinated international firm	Hierarchically controlled international firm	Financially controlled international firm	Reciprocity-based international networks of firms
Coordination of skills and competences at international level	Managed through personal linkages between senior partners; not embedded strongly in organizational mechanisms. Works for complex customized cross-national client projects but weak with regard to provision of standardized services	Based on shared procedures, processes, and knowledge, reinforced by commitment to the firm. In a long-term perspective works well with regard to the delivery of standardized services but limited with regard to generation of highly complex services	Coordination achieved through financial mechanisms based on observable performance criteria. More effective where services can be evaluated with market-based standards	In a medium to long-term perspective low for standardized services, medium to high for customized services and highly complex problem solutions
Organizational learning	Learning predominantly by the senior partners; no real organizational mechanisms for identifying and codifying learning across national contexts reflecting low degree of organizational integration across borders and highly specific nature of each problem solution	Enabled by organizational structures and culture; high emphasis on capturing knowledge for the firm and ensuring that it is accessible to all members. Useful for standardized problems but less valuable for complex projects	Differentiated learning; firm attempts to capture learning in back office facilities; client facing activities dominated by 'stars' and firms try to retain 'stars' through financial performance measures rather than incentivizing them to share information and aid in organizational learning	Very limited as result of competitive tensions within the network and the structural instability of the networks as such
Organizational reconfiguration	Possible through new member firms joining and/or old member firms leaving; principle of consensual decision-making favours slow and gradual reconfiguration	Difficult, time-consuming and costly; dissolution of firm more likely	Possible through acquisition of new and/or selling off of current national subsidiaries; authority of head office allows radical reorientation as far as financial resources are available	Changes in individual member firms as well as dissolution of overall network are relatively easy, quick and low cost due to high flexibility of networks; major reconfiguration of overall network aggravated and slowed down by conflict avoidance and need to reach consensus

The financially controlled firm has a somewhat more clearly separated profile of collective skills and competences. The organizational devices of this type of firm allow a high level of coordination across borders in areas where the value of services can be measured entirely according to the standards of the market and therefore professionals can clearly see the gain from their commitment to coordination. Its focus on financial performance indicators, however, makes it difficult to expand into fields where the output is measured by multidimensional standards, as in legal advice or consulting, for example. Reciprocity-based international networks of firms clearly lag behind in the development of coordinative organizational capabilities if compared with the three other forms of professional services firms previously discussed. Their strengths lie in referral business and the ad hoc organization of project-centred international teams. International networks tend to find it difficult to provide highly coordinated and standardized services on a permanent basis. Their potential to develop highly customized international service solutions for their clients is more developed but it remains unclear to what extent their abilities are ad hoc abilities or abilities which can be maintained over a longer time period through shared organizational routines and practices within the network.

As far as organizational learning is concerned, this varies across the four types. The collegially coordinated firm tends to have few mechanisms for capturing learning within the firm. It is the senior partners who learn from international activities and this becomes the basis for their growing position and status within the firm. The firm is reliant on them for developing this learning and putting it to use on behalf of the firm. As the firm itself is controlled by the partners, there is no clear mechanism for leveraging this knowledge out of the individual and into the organizational domain. Hierarchically coordinated firms are much more likely to invest in the complementary assets that make learning possible. These include the development of knowledge management databases, intensive shared training and development, structured mentoring and appraisal systems, and incentive systems for sharing knowledge. Investment in these systems is highly expensive and the degree to which individuals actually commit to them or have the time to involve themselves when they are part of high intensity work teams will vary. Financially controlled firms can be divided into the professional client-facing part and the back-office servicing part of the operation. In the latter, the firm is continually trying to upgrade its performance and learn from its interaction with clients. This is an area in which firm-specific capabilities are developed and enhanced through learning. In the former, the individual professional has the key role. Because the individual professional in these firms is predominantly incentivized through financial performance rewards, there are restraints on the willingness of individuals to share knowledge and skills beyond a rather narrowly defined team that directly support the client-facing activities. Thus, it is easy to lose any learning if the individual leaves. Firms are reluctant to resolve this by tying people in too strongly other than by creating a powerful cash nexus for loyalty by offering huge performance bonuses. They do not spend large amounts of effort trying to socialize these employees into the values of the firm and trying to win commitment to organizational loyalty and teamwork. This is for two reasons. First, because ultimately there tends to be an open labour market in these areas and other people with equally relevant experience can, at a price, be bought into the firm if a particular individual or team leaves. Second, clients are attracted not just by the 'star' but also by the reliability of the back-office which in many of these firms is absolutely essential to successful client service. Finally, the ability of reciprocity-based networks to learn is extremely limited as a result of competitive tensions within the network and the structural instability of the networks. Again, a small number of senior professionals may learn about the trials and tribulations of international work and they may develop strategies, tactics, and personal networks that resolve these difficulties but in these cases, the learning is again at the individual not the organization (and certainly not the network) level.

Finally, considerable differences between these four types of international professional services firms are found in their potential for organizational reconfiguration. The collegially coordinated firm can in principle, through accommodating new national offices and/or separating from old national offices, change its configuration relatively easily and at low cost. But the need to reach consensus among partners on such changes is likely to slow down the speed at which this occurs. Hierarchically controlled professional services firms are less flexible. Due to their more unified governance structure at the international level and their high reliance on standardized socialization, these firms will find it more difficult, time-consuming and costly to radically reshape their international organizational configuration. In periods of severe crisis, these firms may actually be more likely to dissolve than to reconfigure—the case of Arthur Andersen may be seen as just one example of these difficulties in reacting as a unified organization to drastically changing environmental conditions.[5] The hierarchically organized firm may have the highest learning capacities but it is certainly the most vulnerable to regionally specific crises of legitimation.

As long as it has the necessary financial resources at its disposal, the authority of the head office in the financially controlled firm allows for relatively radical reorientations through firstly rapid closure or restructuring of businesses when they fall below satisfactory performance levels, and secondly rapid growth patterns through mergers and acquisitions in favourable market contexts. Reciprocity-based international networks of firms find it relatively easy to change individual member firms in response to changing market conditions. They can also dissolve at low cost if necessary. Since cooperation partners in networks tend to develop behaviours of conflict avoidance (Hirsch-Kreinsen 2002) and a basic reconfiguration of such a network would require a consensus of the major member firms, such a process may prove to be as slow and as difficult as in collegially coordinated international professional services firms. In relatively stable periods, the flexibility of networks might compensate for their relatively low organizational capabilities in the areas of coordination and organizational learning. In periods of crisis, however, it might prove difficult for this type of organization to react constructively to the parasites of network communication: unspecific non-knowledge, distrust, and countervailing powers may become predominant and erode the basis for cooperation within the network (Strassheim, forthcoming).

10.4. Conclusions

The purpose of this chapter has been to clarify the different organizational forms that professional services firms develop as they become

---

[5] On one hand, the model of the hierarchically controlled professional services firm worked well in the case of Arthur Andersen in that the structure of national partnerships meant that there was no financial contagion across national boundaries. The liabilities belonged to the US office. But on the other hand, the international level of the firm was not able to simply sever the diseased limb and cauterize its effects with the rest of the body carrying on as before. On the contrary the whole body of the firm was contaminated; every national partnership lost in reputational terms and the investment which had gone into building the international brand was destroyed. The international firm dissolved, as individuals left the sinking ship and groups of partners within national partnerships sought to gain some advantage from their collective expertise, networks, and clients by arranging deals for their absorption within other big firms.

international. We have argued that this involves an understanding of the interaction between the professional and the knowledge that the professional has and the structures of governance, authority, and coordination that the firm develops. The framework illustrates both the variety of organizational forms that exist within a particular set of activities and the fragility and experimental nature of such forms. Internationalization of professional services firms is, in the terms in which we have phrased it, a relatively recent phenomenon and there are no certain recipes.[6] Easy claims to the label of a 'global firm', which many such firms use, conceal a variety of organizational forms as well as a range of problems to do with providing 'international' services to clients.

Clearly these tensions need more systematic empirical research both to reveal their underlying sources and to understand how and why firms move between these different structural forms. Out of the factors which induce such moves, we anticipate that three will prove to be of outstanding importance and in themselves deserve more detailed investigation in future research. These are, first, demand differences (explicable in terms of the nature of clients and the services being produced), second, the sort of the knowledge being used (its degree of predictability, complexity, and codification) and third, the way in which both link to regulatory constraints. Combining a thorough analysis of demand-side developments and the regulatory processes in which they are embedded with a differentiated look at the structures of governance, authority, and coordination which professional services firms develop as they internationalize constitutes a promising research programme.

What are the wider implications of this chapter for a book of this kind? First, the variety of organizational forms that exist within a particular set of activities links in to the broader institutionalist argument that some of these forms might be more akin to certain patterns of institutional resources in a particular society than others. This is certainly an important research question that requires more studies with a stronger empirical and comparative approach, and with a tighter focus on specific sorts of professional services sectors and their national institutional embeddedness than we have espoused here.

---

[6] We do not deny that from the nineteenth century at least there have been networks of lawyers, accountants, and investment bankers and that we can learn much from the study of these forms. However, the internationalization of such firms since the 1970s takes a much more formally organized form and is much less particularistic and family based than during earlier periods.

Second, we would like to highlight the role that these firms have in constructing the social, political, and economic infrastructure of global capitalism. Previous chapters in the first half of this book have emphasized that national systems are more complex and diverse than may sometimes be thought. Some of them have also indicated the need to study how international orders are being constructed. Professional services firms are central to both of these processes, opening up ambiguities in national systems and working with them across national boundaries and within international regulatory setting organizations. They therefore need special attention. But we also want to emphasize linkages to the second part of this book. International professional services firms are not unproblematic organizational constructs, simply responding to market demand. They are fragile and ambiguous entities that struggle to bring order into settings that are complex, divided, and conflictual. The ideal types that we have constructed are means to understanding this complex reality. They are not a substitute for such detailed understanding. If they teach us one thing it is that there is no single model of an international professional services firm but rather multiple models responding to complex variations in the international environment. We need look no further than the spectacular and surprising fall of Arthur Andersen to see that as researchers we have a long way to go in catching up in our understanding with what is occurring in the external world being constructed by these firms.

REFERENCES

Aharoni, Yair (1993). 'Ownership, Networks and Coalitions'. In: Yair Aharoni (ed.), *Coalitions and Competition. The Globalization of Professional Business Services*. London: Routledge, pp. 121–42.

Alvesson, Mats (2001). 'Knowledge Work: Ambiguity, Image and Identity'. *Human Relations* 54(7): 863–86.

Anderson-Gough, Fiona, Grey, Christopher, and Robson, Keith (2000). 'In the Name of the Client: The Service Ethic in Two Professional Services Firms'. *Human Relations* 53(9): 1151–74.

Baden-Fuller, Charles (1993). 'The Globalization of Professional Service Firms: Evidence from Four Case Studies'. In: Yair Aharoni (ed.), *Coalitions and Competition. The Globalization of Professional Business Services*. London: Routledge, pp. 102–20.

Baron, David P. and Besanko, David (2001). 'Strategy, Organization and Incentives: Global Corporate Banking at Citibank'. *Industrial and Corporate Change* 10: 1–37.

Bélanger, Jacques, Berrgren, Christian, Bjorkmann, Torsten, and Kohler, Christoph (eds.) (1999). *Being Local Worldwide: ABB and the Challenge of Global Management*. Ithaca, NY: Cornell University Press.

Böhling, Kathrin (2002). 'Learning from Environmental Actors about Environmental Developments. The Case of International Organizations'. Wissenschaftszentrum Berlin für Sozialforschung, FS II 02-110, Berlin.

Dezalay, Yves (ed.) (1993). *Batailles territoriales et querelles de cousinage. Juristes et comptables europeens sur le marche du droit des affaires*. Paris: Librairie Generale de Droit et de Jurisprudence.

—— and Sugarman, David (1995). *Professional Competition and Professional Power. Lawyers, Accountants and the Social Construction of Markets*. London, New York: Routledge.

Dierkes, Meinolf, Antal, Ariane Berthoin, Child, John, and Nonaka, Ikujiro (2001). *Handbook of Organizational Learning and Knowledge*. Oxford: Oxford University Press.

Djelic, Marie-Laure and Quack, Sigrid (2003). *Globalization and Institutions. Redefining the Rules of the Economic Game*. Cheltenham: Edward Elgar.

Dörrenbächer, Christoph (2003). *Modelltransfer in multinationalen Unternehmen. Strategien und Probleme grenzüberschreitender Konzernintegration*. Berlin: Edition Sigma.

Dunning, John H. (1993). 'The Internationalization of the Production of Services: Some General and Specific Explanations'. In: Yair Aharoni (ed.), *Coalitions and Competition. The Globalization of Professional Business Services*. London, New York: Routledge, pp. 79–101.

Empson, Laura (2001a). 'Introduction: Knowledge Management in Professional Service Firms'. *Human Relations* 54(7): 811–17.

—— (2001b). 'Fear of Exploitation and Fear of Contamination: Impediments to Knowledge Transfer in Mergers between Professional Service Firms. *Human Relations* 54(7): 839–62.

Fosstenløkken, Siw M., Løwendahl, Bente R., and Revang, Øivind (2003). 'Knowledge Development Through Client Interaction'. *Organization Studies* 24(6): 859–80.

Gammelgaard, Jens, Husted, Kenneth, and Michailova, Snejina (2003). 'Probleme des Wissenstranfers nach Akquisitionen: Wissenhortung und Wissenzurückweisung. In: Christoph Dörrenbächer (ed.), *Modelltransfer in multinationalen Unternehmen. Strategien und Probleme grenzüberschreitender Konzernintegration*. Berlin: Edition Sigma, pp. 13–28.

Geppert, Mike, Matten, Dirk, and Williams, Karen (2002). *Challenges for European Management in a Global Context*. Basingstoke: Palgrave Macmillan.

Greenwood, Royston and Empson, Laura (2003). 'The Professional Partnership: Relic or Exemplary Form of Governance?' *Organization Studies* 24(6): 909–33.

—— and Lachmann, Ran (1996). 'Change as an Underlying Theme in Professional Service Organizations'. *Organization Studies* 17: 563–72.

——, Hinings, Christopher R., and Brown, John L. (1990). "'P2-Form" Strategic Management: Corporate Practices in Professional Partnerships'. *Academy of Management Journal* 33: 725–55.

——, Rose, Teresa, Brown, John L., Cooper, David J., and Hinings, Christopher R. (1999). 'The Global Management of Professional Services: The Case of Accounting'. In: Stewart R. Clegg, Eduardo Ibarra-Colado, and Luis Bueno-Rodriguez (eds.), *Global Management: Universal Theories and Local Realities*. London: Sage, pp. 265–96.

Grey, Christopher (1994). 'Career as a Project of the Self and Labour Process Discipline'. *Sociology* 28(2): 479–97.

—— (1998). 'On Being a Professional in a Big Six Firm'. *Accounting, Organisations and Society* 23(5/6): 569–87.

Hansen, Morten T., Nohria, Nitin, and Tierney, Thomas (1999). 'What's Your Strategy for Managing Knowledge?' *Harvard Business Review* 77(2): 106–18.

Hinings, Christopher R., Greenwood, Royston, and Cooper, David J. (1999). 'The Dynamics of Change in Large Accounting Firms'. In: David M. Brock, Michael J. Powell, and Christopher R. Hinings (eds.), *Restructuring the Professional Organization: Accounting, Health Care and Law*. London: Routledge, pp. 131–53.

Hirsch-Kreinsen, Hartmut (2002). 'Unternehmensnetzwerke—revisited'. *Zeitschrift für Soziologie* 31(2): 106–24.

Kristensen, Peer Hull and Zeitlin, Jonathan (2001). 'The Making of a Global Firm: Local Pathways to Multinational Enterprise'. In: Glenn Morgan, Peer Hull Kristensen, and Richard Whitley (eds.), *The Multinational Firm: Organizing Across Institutional and National Divides*. Oxford: Oxford University Press, pp. 172–95.

Lane, Christel and Bachmann, Reinhard (1995). *Risk, Trust and Power: The Social Constitution of Supplier Relations in Britain and Germany*. Cambridge: Centre for Business Research.

Lazega, Emmanuel (2001). *The Collegial Phenomenon. The Social Mechanism of Cooperation Among Peers in a Corporate Law Partnership*. Oxford: Oxford University Press.

—— and Pattison, Philippa E. (1999). 'Multiplexity, Generalized Exchange and Cooperation in Organizations: A Case Study'. *Social Networks* 21: 67–90.

Lorsch, Jay and Tierney, Thomas J. (2002). *Aligning the Stars: How to Succeed when Professionals Drive Results*. Boston, MA: Harvard Business School Press.

Løwendahl, Bente R. (2000). *Strategic Management of Professional Service Firms*, 2nd edn. Copenhagen: Copenhagen Business School Press.

Marchazina, Klaus, Oesterle, Michael-Jörg, and Brodel, Dietmar (2001). 'Learning in Multinationals'. In: Meinolf Dierkes, Ariane Berthoin Antal, John Child, and Ikujiro Nonaka (eds.), *Handbook of Organizational Learning and Knowledge*. Oxford: Oxford University Press, pp. 631–56.

Maister, David H. (1993). *Managing the Professional Services Firm*. New York: Free Press.

Morgan, Glenn (2001). 'The Multinational Firm'. In: Glenn Morgan, Peer Hull Kristensen, and Richard Whitley (eds.), *The Multinational Firm: Organizing Across Institutional and National Divides*. Oxford: Oxford University Press, pp. 1–24.

——, Whitley, Richard, and Kristensen, Peer Hull (2001). *The Multinational Firm: Organizing Across Institutional and National Divides*. Oxford: Oxford University Press.

Morris, Timothy and Empson, Laura (1998). 'Organisation and Expertise: An Exploration of Knowledge Bases and the Management of Accounting and Consulting Firms'. *Accounting, Organizations and Society* 23: 609–24.

—— and Pinnington, Ashly (1998). 'Promotion to Partner in Professional Service Firms'. *Human Relations* 51: 3–24.

—— and —— (1999). 'Continuity and Change in Professional Organizations: Evidence from British Law Firms'. In: David M. Brock, Michael J. Powell, and Christopher R. Hinings (eds.), *Restructuring the Professional Organization: Accounting, Health Care and Law*. London: Routledge, pp. 200–14.

Nightingale, Paul and Poll, Robert (2000). 'Innovation in Investment Banking: The Dynamics of Control Systems within the Chandlerian Firm'. *Industrial and Corporate Change* 9: 113–41.

Nonaka, Ikujiro and Takeuchi, Hirotaka (1995). *The Knowledge-Creating Company: How Japanese Companies Create the Dynamics of Innovation*. Oxford: Oxford University Press.

Nooteboom, Bart (2000). *Learning and Innovation in Organizations and Economies*. Oxford: Oxford University Press.

OECD (1996). *International Trade in Professional Services. Assessing Barriers and Encouraging Reform*. Paris: OECD.

Pinnington, Ashly and Morris, Timothy (2002). 'Transforming the Architect: Ownership Form and Archetype Change'. *Organization Studies* 23(2): 189–210.

—— and —— (2003). 'Archetype Change in Professional Orgnizations: Survey Evidence from Large Law Firms'. *British Journal of Management* 14: 85–99.

Podolny, Joel M. and Page, Karen L. (1998). 'Network Forms of Organization'. *Annual Review of Sociology* 24: 57–76.

Polanyi, Michael (1966). *The Tacit Dimension*. New York: Anchor Books.

Richardson, George Barcley (1972). 'The Organization of Industry'. *Economic Journal* 82: 883–96.

Robertson, Maxine, Scarbrough, Harry, and Swan, Jacky (2003). 'Knowledge Creation in Professional Services Firms'. *Organization Studies* 24(6): 831–57.

Rose, Teresa and Hinings, Christopher R. (1999). 'Global Clients; Demands Driving Change in Global Business Advisory Firms'. In: Michael J. Powell,

David M. Brock, and Christopher R. Hinings (eds.), *Restructuring the Professional Organization: Accounting, Health Care and Law*. London: Routledge, pp. 41–67.

Strassheim, Holyer (2004). 'Power in intercommunal knowledge networks: On the endogenous dynamics of network governance and knowledge creation'. WZB Discussion paper sp111, 2004–104, Berlin: Social Science Research Centre.

Szulanski, Gabriel (2000). 'The Process of Knowledge Transfer: A Diachronic Analysis of Stickiness'. *Organizational Behavior and Human Decisions Processes* 82(1): 9–27.

Teece, D. J. (1986). 'Profiting from Technological Innovation: Implications for Integration, Collaboration, Licensing and Public Policy'. *Research Policy* 15: 285–305.

Teece, David, Pisano, Gary, and Shuen, Amy (2000). 'Dynamics Capabilities and Strategic Management'. In: G. Dosi et al. (eds.), *The Nature and Dynamics of Organizational Capabilities*, pp. 334–62.

Werr, Andreas and Stjernberg, Torbjörn (2003). 'Exploring Management Consulting Firms as Knowledge Systems'. *Organization Studies* 24(6): 881–908.

11

Varieties of Vertical Disintegration: The Global Trend Toward Heterogeneous Supply Relations and the Reproduction of Difference in US and German Manufacturing

GARY HERRIGEL AND VOLKER WITTKE

As is well known, there is a global trend toward vertical disintegration in many manufacturing industries. Large manufacturing firms are radically reducing the amount of their product that they both produce and design themselves. Instead they are turning to suppliers for key design, component, and even system inputs. This shift has created a great deal of business for specialized suppliers in a vast array of areas throughout the global manufacturing economy. But it has also created an entirely new and challenging—often quite contradictory—terrain of relations between suppliers and their customers. Our claim in this chapter is that relations between suppliers and customers in manufacturing are becoming systematically more heterogeneous within all advanced industrial societies. Further, this global trend is exacerbated by the diversity of institutional architectures and production practices in different political economies. In making this argument, we show that neither neoliberal nor particular forms of institutionalist arguments (in particular the Varieties of Capitalism, VoC, perspective) adequately capture current global dynamics in manufacturing.

The chapter is in three sections. The first describes the changing dynamics in the purchasing strategies of large manufacturers in the

We thank the editors and workshop participants for this volume and Jonathan Zeitlin, Charles Sabel, Tim Sturgeon, Mari Sako, Josh Whitford, Hyeong ki Kwon, and Hans Joachim Sperling for very useful comments on this chapter. We also thank the Alexander v Humboldt Foundation's Trans. Coop. Program and the Alfred P. Sloan Foundation for generous funding for our research.

advanced industrial countries. The second section then constructs a typology of the range of supplier–customer relationships that seem to be emerging in the contemporary global manufacturing environment. The third section then moves to a discussion of the way in which these relationships are being realized in different national market contexts, in particular the United States and Germany.[1]

11.1. Changing Dynamics in the Purchasing Strategies of Large Manufacturers

For over a decade now, the literatures on the automobile and electronics industries have been preoccupied with the process of vertical disintegration in production (Borrus and Zysman 1997; Clark and Fujimoto 1991; Liker et al. 1999; McKendrick et al. 2000; Sturgeon 2002; Womack et al. 1990). Recently, observers of lower volume sectors of manufacturing, such as the production of agricultural equipment, construction machinery, and other forms of industrial machinery have also been describing this phenomenon (Mesquita and Brush 2001; Whitford 2003). The contemporary logic of vertical disintegration is the following. Due to intensifying global competition, rapid technological change, shortening product life cycles, and greatly variegated consumer demand for product customization, the spatial, financial, manpower, and organizational resources of firms become overtaxed and cannot respond efficiently. In order to save time and resources, diversify exposure to risk and enhance flexibility, Original Equipment Manufacturers (OEMs) concentrate their activities on so-called 'core competence' areas—that is, on particular functions, such as marketing or overall styling and product design, and/or on particular aspects of the manufacturing process in which they hold a competitive advantage or have valuable, difficult to replicate, expertise (Prahalad and Hamel 1990). In all other areas outside core competences, OEMs rely on suppliers to contribute essential components, systems, and aspects of product development.

This change in the purchasing strategies of OEM firms has not simply increased the amount of business available to component

---

[1] The primary empirical foundation for this chapter is nearly 100 interviews conducted by the authors at manufacturing firms, trade unions, regional governments, and trade associations in the United States and Germany since the year 2000. All references in the text to case examples not otherwise indicated stem from this research.

suppliers and other specialists. Rather, it has also dramatically changed the kinds of demands that OEMs place on them. Suppliers are now expected to

(1) provide their customers with significant know-how (in the form of product design and/or manufacturing expertise);
(2) produce at extraordinarily high levels of quality (fewer than 100 defective parts per million is increasingly standard);
(3) provide a variety of services for the customer (in the shape of logistics and subassembly);
(4) all while continuously reducing the cost at which they provide these things.

Moreover, customers do not simply trust that their suppliers are doing these things. Even long-time customers are now subjecting their traditional suppliers to constant benchmarking procedures, which place their performance in comparison to 'best practice' in their market. Importantly, this is not simply a disciplining tactic on the part of newly dependent OEMs to protect against potential supplier opportunism (though it can have that effect). Rather, even in cases where there is extensive collaboration and mutual dependence between customer and supplier, constant benchmarking, and comparison of supplier performance and capabilities stems from the OEMs' urgent need for information about new developments in technology and manufacturing practice. Because they are increasingly dependent on outside knowledge of these things, and because their future technological and manufacturing needs are uncertain and always subject to change, the process of surveying suppliers has become a crucial mechanism for learning for the customer firm (Helper et al. 2000; Sabel 1995).

As a result of all of this surveying, benchmarking, and comparison on the part of OEMs, suppliers, as we shall see below, must learn to live with the paradoxical reality of customers becoming both more reliant on them for know-how and manufacturing input, while they simultaneously become more demanding and actively survey (and contract with) the suppliers' competitors for newer, better, and lower cost alternatives.

Finally, it is important to emphasize that even though the trends toward vertical disintegration just described are unmistakable, the practices of OEMs in manufacturing are far from uniform. There are at least three significant aspects of the situation in which OEMs find themselves that produce broad heterogeneity in their practices in production and in relationship to suppliers (Herrigel 2004).

First, many OEMs are very large multinational corporations with far-flung operations involving multiple plants and production facilities in many locations. Moreover, such firms produce a broad and wide array of products and models across those far-flung plants. Companies of this scale and complexity do not vertically disintegrate massively, all at once, and in toto. Instead, they seek to do it piecemeal in locations where it is very easy to do, or where it is most urgently needed—or they introduce new models as 'experiments' with disintegrated production in locations where there will be no entrenched in-house opposition. In other production locations, or with respect to a particular product model, where internal resistance to disintegration is great or where in-house production continues to be profitable or where suitable suppliers are unavailable, vertical disintegration does not occur.

Second, even in cases where it is clear that an OEM does not view a particular aspect of production as possessing special long-term competitive advantage for the firm, it may nonetheless retain some internal production capacity in that area simply to retain some in-house know-how and enhance its ability to engage in knowledgeable collaboration with (and evaluation of) outside suppliers. In-house production facilities can be made to bid on projects against outsiders to facilitate this. In some cases the supplier could win the bid and be brought intimately into the development process of a model, while in other cases the in-house unit is the victor. This kind of competition between in-house and external suppliers can exist for extended periods of time, with the outcomes continuously changing and unpredictable (Bradach and Eccles 1989).

Third, heterogeneity in practice with respect to suppliers arises out of the sheer complexity of the contracting that vertical disintegration in production produces for any given model or product—and the content of heterogeneity changes over time. OEMs seek to gain cost savings and know-how from their suppliers. But it is not necessarily true that the OEM seeks to maximize both of those goals in every contract with every supplier every time. For example, a buyer for an OEM may need to achieve certain aggregate cost reduction targets on a particular model and he/she can achieve those targets by using leverage with one or two suppliers (or helping them achieve leverage) or by bidding out a relatively standard or mature component or subassembly that had been designed and until then produced by a particular specialized supplier. This move to push a supplier further away, however, can be undertaken to create space for OEM engineers to engage in a valuable but relatively expensive collaboration with another supplier of a different component or subassembly for the same product.

Thus, the same OEM on the same product model may be engaging in a variety of different sorts of relations with suppliers simultaneously. And, as the product is redesigned, OEM behaviour toward suppliers may change—those pushed away may be offered greater intimacy (and better margins), while the intimate partners of the past suddenly find themselves having to bid on their own designs against competitors. As we will see, suppliers learn to participate in this kind of waltz with their customers, often agreeing to (or offering) a cost reduction that ruins the margin of profit on one contract in exchange for future business with the customer, at a better rate.

All of these examples are intended to show that although the evidence is incontrovertible that there is a secular trend toward vertical disintegration in manufacturing across industries world wide, this has in no way produced uniformity in the practices of OEMs across industries, within industries or even within single firms and plants. There are multiple and changing strategic calculations in play. In the following sections, we will attempt to outline the range of relationships that seem to be emerging and the differing contributions of national context in their emergence and governance.

11.2. Typology of Emerging OEM–Supplier Relations

These changes in the kinds of demands that are being placed on suppliers have given rise to a great deal of turbulence in the way in which relationships between OEMs and suppliers are constituted. We suggest that vertical disintegration can produce (at least) five ideal typical forms of customer–supplier relations in manufacturing:

- arm's-length/spot market relation
- autocratic or captive supplier relation
- contract manufacturing
- collaborative manufacturing
- sustained contingent collaboration.

These differ in terms of the division of labour between design and production on the one hand and in the roles that customers and suppliers play in the relationship over time. The first four types all involve supplier production, all have clear role divisions between customer and supplier over time, but they vary in the amount of design the supplier engages in and the production the customer engages in.[2] The fifth type has neither a stable division between design and production, nor a clear role division between customer and supplier over time. Our claim is that the environment is such that it is possible to find each of these relationships in practice today, but that types 3, 4, and 5 are the most historically distinctive, and type 5 in particular seems to be rapidly emerging as the most stable and modal relation.

11.2.1. *Type 1: arm's-length /spot market relation*

For much of the twentieth century in many of the most developed industrial economics, vertical integration was a dominant strategy in capital intensive manufacturing industries. In this context, the typical supplier relationship was an arm's length one in which the price mechanism in the market governed the logic of exchange. In this kind of relationship, suppliers either constructed complex parts according to designs made by the OEM, or they sold commodity or standardized products to the OEM. In both cases, the relationship was characterized by a strict division between product development and production and by a strong emphasis on price. Contracts went to the lowest bidder.

These relationships continue to exist in the current environment of increasing vertical disintegration, though now they exist as one of several different kinds of ties between suppliers and customers, and tend to appear under relatively specific and quite constrained conditions. In all cases of spot market subcontracting, the competences between customer and supplier are very clearly defined and the contours of the desired component are very precisely specified. In particular, no customized design input from the supplier is needed. There is neither ambiguity nor competition between customer and supplier on their respective roles in the process of developing and producing the customer's product. At the margin, components that can be produced within this kind of relationship have a great potential to migrate to low cost production locations. But there are also many countervailing trends such that one still finds significant amounts of this kind of contracting taking place among customers and suppliers in high wage regions.

---

[2] Our first four types are consistent with those developed in Gereffi et al. 2005.

11.2.2. *Type 2: autocratic or captive supplier relations*

This kind of relationship exists in only very specific contexts, quint-essentially within Japanese keiretsu networks. Here, the competences in design and production of the supplier and customer are comple-mentary, but the relationship is hierarchical. The supplier is typically dependent on a single customer, and follows the lead of the customer in design and production. The contours of the product can be uncer-tain at the beginning of the relationship, but the solution to design and manufacture problems follow the lead of the customer and there is no ambiguity on the distribution of returns. In the Japanese case, such relationships are possible because suppliers are integrated in a larger Keiretsu network which structures the flow of resources among a large end assembler and its suppliers (finance, technology, skilled labour, etc.). Cooperation and flexibility among the players within this context is high and improves over time as the constancy of the tie (neither sup-plier nor OEM have alternatives) allows for learning and continuous improvement in the joint undertaking. Moreover, the moral hazard risks typically associated with bilateral mutual dependence are sig-nificantly mitigated due to mutual embedding of the supplier and customer in the keiretsu network (Nishiguchi 1994; Nishiguchi and Brookfield 1997; Smitka 1991).

In many ways, these relationships resemble vertically integrated relations, and as a consequence it is not surprising that they seem to be under significant stress in the contemporary environment (Dyer et al. 1998). One very important limitation in the captive relation is that its practical business ties to specialists and bearers of know-how outside the network of dependent producers, much less outside the industry, is limited. While learning occurs through the process of joint problem solving among the dependent parties, neither party seeks analogous relations with competing specialists or customers in order to survey the terrain of technology and practice.

11.2.3. *Type 3: contract manufacturing*

The distinctive feature of the customer–supplier relation here is a clear and unambiguous separation between processes of product design and product manufacture. OEMs (or 'lead firms') do the design (and also marketing and distribution) and award production con-tracts to sophisticated suppliers who conduct and coordinate all of the production and assembly of the item. There is virtually no supplier input into the design of a product, but there can be interaction and negotiation between supplier and customer in the process of applying designs to manufacturing processes. Customers undertake no production.

As such, there is a strong mutual dependence between customer and supplier within this type and relationships can be long term and grow stronger over time. On the whole, this clean separation is made possible by a far-reaching standardization and modularization in the base technology of the sector. Products are composed out of modules with distinctive content, interlinked by standard interfaces. Indeed, nearly all of the hardware components manufactured by suppliers is in some way standardized—volumes are very high and supplier competitiveness hinges strongly on its capacity to achieve leverage. The quintessential realm for contract manufacture in the contemporary manufacturing environment is product level electronics (computers, consumer electronics, etc.) (Lüthje 2002; Lüthje and Sproll 2002; Sturgeon 2002).

The relationship between OEM and supplier in this relation is very close, but limited. In some ways, the limitation allows for the deepening of the relationship over time. Because suppliers have no ambition to design and customers have no ambition to produce, both have an incentive to work together to exploit one another's strengths. Unpredictability and instability in this relationship is introduced by two factors: the desire on the part of OEMs to avoid capture by powerful contract suppliers and the need on the part of both parties to seek alternative customers and suppliers as a way to survey the relevant terrain in their sector for emergent technological and organizational possibilities (Adler 1995; Chesbrough 2004; Leachman and Leachman 2004; Sturgeon and Lee 2004). Both of these factors push OEMs to limit their commitments to a single supplier or even to a stable pool of suppliers in the interest of gaining technological and cost reduction leverage. For their part, contract suppliers search the terrain for additional technological and organizational possibilities as well, causing them (opportunity cost) to bound their commitments even to their most trusted and reliable customers. In the long run, this search process is not only valuable to the individual development of customer and suppliers; it can also strengthen the ongoing relationship between the parties because what each learns from its relations with others allows them to contribute more creatively to mutual projects. In the short run, however, such mutual searching creates difficulties as finite quantities of work have to be parcelled between traditional and new suppliers (customers). Compromises and concessions on all sides must be made and this can produce considerable heterogeneity in the quality of relationships.

11.2.4. *Type 4: collaborative manufacturing*

This is the limit case in the global trend toward vertical disintegration, if you map the first four types on a power/coordination scale (Gereffi et al. 2005). The relationship differs from the captive supplier relationship in that there is near parity in the power balance between customer and supplier: each depends on the other for the definition and production of the desired part, and both bring know-how to the relationship that neither could nor would be interested in acquiring on its own. Thus, competences are fully complementary and leverage is counterbalancing. Collaborative manufacturing also differs from the contract manufacturing relationship in that the competence and capacities of both parties are jointly indispensable not only for the production of a desired component, but for its design and development as well. In this limiting case, collaboration begins as a joint exploration of the possibilities for the definition of a product between customer and supplier; neither party has a clear idea ex ante what the precise contours of the final product of the collaboration will be, nor of its specific articulation or interface with the overall design of the end product. But both parties recognize that they require the competences of the other and their collaboration defines the content of both design and production. As a result, the collaborating parties view the outcome of their collaboration as a joint product from which equal rents should be drawn.

As a type of relation between customer and supplier, collaborative manufacturing is defined by the systematic integration of development and manufacture between the parties. Both bring competence in both to the joint project. This distinctive characteristic of the relation, however, is also what makes collaborative manufacturing a limiting case in the typology. While it is possible to imagine stable collaborative manufacturing for the life of a particular joint product, it is extremely difficult to identify conditions under which relations between customers and suppliers could be characterized by full integration of production and development capability over multiple contracts over time. In part, the explanation for this is the same one that contributed to creeping heterogeneity within the contract manufacturing relation: the need to enlarge the pool of ties in search of new possibilities is in tension with the reality of a finite amount of work and capacity at any given time. Through their efforts to learn, in other words, customers and producers are forced into trade-offs and compromises in an effort to preserve old ties while developing new ones (Sabel 2004; Whitford 2001). This invariably leads to the separation of development and manufacture between customer and supplier. Customers vary the quality of the contracts they establish with a single customer, some involving full blown collaboration, others involving only manufacture or more limited collaboration on design, in order to expand the number of potential suppliers it has available for collaboration. As such, over time and multiple contracts, collaborative manufacturing as a type has a very strong tendency to degenerate into our fifth and final type, sustained contingent collaboration.

11.2.5. *Type 5: sustained contingent collaboration*

If the collaborative relation is the limit case in the current environment, sustained contingent collaboration is the modal one. This relationship can only be understood as a tie that exists between customer and supplier over time. It emerges under conditions where both customer and supplier have important capabilities in both design and production. This makes role definition a central point of negotiation between the contracting parties. As we saw above, collaboration is one limiting—and reproducible—moment within a sustained contingent collaboration. But the definition of roles turns out to be much more heterogeneous within a relationship of sustained contingent collaboration due to two factors (both already mentioned) in the current global competitive environment:

(1) the tendency of both customers and suppliers in the process of searching their environments for new technological and organizational capacities to vary the quality and character of their relations with even their most valued partners in the interest of expanding the size of their pool of ties/partners;

(2) the fact that the volatile, complex, and non-simultaneous character of product change in the current environment leads OEM firms to separate their aggregate goals for the outside acquisition of know-how and cost reduction from the particular relationship that they establish with individual suppliers.

The mutual desire for access to outside capability results in variation in the intensity of the tie between customer and supplier over time and across projects. Because both customer and supplier have both development and manufacturing capabilities, the parties can negotiate on the definition of the roles they will play in each contract round. A customer and supplier involved in intense and intimate collaboration on one project may opt for a more limited relation (perhaps the supplier manufactures a component according to someone else's designs) for a different project on a different product. The variation allows each party to seek rewarding ties to others without exhausting their own capacities and while also avoiding the possibility that their relations will be entirely severed once the older, very intimately collaborative, project runs out. The more flexibly partners can vary the roles they play, the greater is their capacity to search their environment for innovation and the more enduring can their relations with any particular partner be over time.

Thus, the first factor above explains how a relationship between a single customer and supplier that is variously constituted over time can nonetheless be thought of as a sustained collaboration. The second factor helps to elaborate how such collaboration can also be contingent. OEMs maximize the know-how gains and cost reduction contributions they receive from suppliers at an aggregate level, rather than at the level of each individual supplier relation, because it gives them more flexibility. In many cases, they attempt to realize both cost reductions and know-how gains in the same relationship through collaboration with the supplier. But in other cases, circumstances may be such that the OEM would like to lure an attractive specialist into its pool of suppliers, so it will be willing to pay a premium for that specialist's know-how. In order to meet aggregate cost targets for the whole product, however, such a move will have to be compensated by significant cost reductions from other suppliers in the pool. The OEM can use its market power, leverage, or very frequently the promise of more lucrative work in a subsequent round to extract extra cost concessions from suppliers.

This kind of multiple goal contracting with suppliers engenders significant role ambiguity and hence contingency and even conflict in the character of relations between suppliers and customers. Suppliers are never sure what role they will play, or even are playing, at any moment in time—will they be courted for their know-how, integrated into a collaborative process of combined development and cost reduction, or will they simply be pressed for cost concessions on components that were once understood to be one of the previous two categories? OEMs foster this ambiguity because it is in their interest to have a supply base with broad capacities. Good suppliers should have both technological know-how and a skilled understanding of how cost can be eliminated from their role in the supply chain. Suppliers, naturally, resent providing cost reductions because it threatens their margins. Hence, they continually resist OEM pressures by attempting to define their role as a know-how-providing, premium-deserving, collaborator. It is in the OEMs interest to allow the supplier to succeed sometimes in their counter-arguments regarding their role (otherwise they risk losing the supplier and its know-how). It is also in the supplier's interest to develop the skill of being able to supply cost reduction when demanded without such reductions irreparably damaging the supplier's margins. If it cannot do this, the OEM is likely to regard the supplier as unskilled and too costly to keep within the pool of suppliers. Strategic interest in the present and concern for future business make customer supplier relations into a sustained contingent collaboration.

11.3. Vertical Disintegration in National Context

In this section, we argue that producers in both Germany and the United States are struggling to construct and govern the array of relations we have outlined in the previous section. In particular, we will focus on efforts to construct our modal type, sustained contingent collaboration, and suggest that this is emerging as the norm in both countries. But the difficulties that firms encounter in constructing and governing these relations, while overlapping, are not identical in each economy. The institutional and experiential resource base (habitus) for producers is different so the distribution of possibilities, strengths, and weaknesses in capabilities and competences, is different (Bourdieu 1977; Dewey 2002). Sustained contingent collaborations are prevalent in both the German and the US political economies, yet they are entwined and enacted quite differently in both societies.

In this sense, we agree with the institutionalist claim, against neoliberalism, that there is variety or diversity in the forms of capitalism in the contemporary world (Berger and Dore 1996; Hall and Soskice 2001; Hollingsworth and Boyer 1997; Whitley 1999; Yamamura and Streeck 2003). Nonetheless, it is important to see that our argument departs quite substantially from the claims of a central school of contemporary institutionalism, the VoC approach pioneered by Peter Hall and David Soskice (2001) and their colleagues and collaborators, in two ways.

First, we reject the strong Hall and Soskice argument that societies are endowed with comparative institutional advantages (Soskice and Hall 2001: 36–44). For Hall and Soskice, successful German OEM manufacturers, because they are embedded in the institutional architecture of a 'coordinated market economy' (cooperative labour relations, corporate governance with labour participation, patient capital, regulatory law), are most likely to construct cooperative (nonmarket) relations with both labour and their suppliers and pursue competitive market strategies that are characterized by product quality and incremental innovation. By contrast, because US OEM producers are embedded in the institutional architecture of a 'liberal market economy' (conflictual labour relations, capital dominated corporate governance, a financial system concerned only with profitable return, and strict contract law), their labour and supply chain relations will be distant and arm's length, characterized by conflict, wage, and price pressure, all of which divert producer attention from gradual improvements and incremental innovation (Casper 1995, 1997, 2001). As section 11.3.1 will report, however, this is not what the available evidence shows regarding supplier relations in both countries.

Second, we also reject the related, but not identical, institutionalist claim that national institutional systems change in path dependent ways. That is, in the absence of a significant exogenous shock such as a war or terrible economic catastrophe, the coherence of institutional complementarities within a national architecture of institutions encourages actors to seek solutions to governance problems that are compatible with (if not reinforcing of) existing arrangements and constrain them from adopting governance solutions that are 'fundamentally' incompatible with those arrangements (Pierson, Mahoney. Also compare Crouch, Deeg, and Hancké and Goyer, Chapters 7, 2, and 3, respectively, this volume).

In what follows (S. 11.3.2), we will show that different kinds of actors in both the United States and Germany are to a surprising extent neither significantly constrained nor especially enabled by the institutional architecture of the political economy. Indeed, in many ways the institutional architectures in both the United States and Germany, as coherent systems, have been overtaken by events and stand awkwardly by, as various actors seek to construct new relations and forms of governance alongside them. This is not to say that there are no efforts to reform or adapt existing institutional arrangements to changing circumstances. There are (Boyer 2003; Jürgens 2003;

Thelen and Kume 2003). Nor do we want to claim that actors are entirely ignorant of the normative dispositions constituting institutional rules. Far from it! In crucial ways we find that they are guided by these dispositions (esp. Dewey 2002: 14–88). But we find both that actors act independently of institutional incentives and constraints *and* that they try to use institutional mechanisms in new or unstandard ways in order to achieve their governance ends—that is, that they try to change the incentives and constraints that institutions provide to make them more suitable to the new context.

Stated in a positive way, rather than looking, as institutionalists do, for structural constraints or enablers, we view the social terrain of the economy in the United States and Germany as peopled by a community of reflexive agents, beset by common problems of their own definition (though not necessarily of their own making), seeking to construct solutions to the problems they encounter in practice. And, rather than looking for institutional complementarities between system parts and greater and less 'coherence' for the system as a whole, we conceive of the (very different) institutional architectures of the political economy in the United States and Germany as constituting sets of resources for actors to use, not use, deconstruct, or redefine in their efforts to contend with the problems of industrial transformation that beset them in practice. In our view, institutions help actors solve governance problems. If they do not solve (or even address) the problems that actors have, then institutions are either ignored or changed.

At the end of the day, experimentation upon the social terrain of OEM supplier relations in both the United States and Germany is very widespread, and there are many different kinds of 'solutions' to the governance problems posed by the new production relations being constructed. In the conclusion, we suggest that this process of experimentation is slowly recomposing the institutional character of the political economies of both Germany and the United States in ways that nonetheless reproduce significant differences between the two political economies.

11.3.1. *Sustained contingent collaboration in Germany and the United States*

We constructed sustained contingent collaboration as a type in section 2 based on qualitative observation of supplier–OEM relations in both the United States and Germany, so we are convinced that this type of relation can be found in both countries. But there is no reason to take our word for it. Indeed, there is a strong presumption within the VoC camp that relations in the United States and Germany will systematically diverge, with German relations likely to be more cooperative and US relations likely to be more arm's length and market defined. Appeal to some neutral and broadly representative data would therefore seem to be in order.

Numerous quantitative studies have been undertaken over the course of the last decade to determine the extent to which supply relations in manufacturing (particularly in the automobile industry) have become more collaborative and structured by the precepts of 'lean manufacturing' (low inventory, low work in process, early supplier involvement in product design, team work, transparency on costs between supplier and customer—etc.). Happily for us, most of the evidence is extremely contradictory. Researchers find conflict and collaboration, trust and distrust almost in equal measure in both societies.

Sue Helper, for example, in studying supplier relations in the US automobile industry, has repeatedly found that many US suppliers are being asked to engage in product development, are being incorporated earlier into the product development process and have adopted a wide array of cost reducing and transparency enhancing arrangements in production (Helper and Sako 1995, 1998; see also Luria 1996*a,b*; Whitford and Zeitlin 2004). In comparison to the conflictual and arm's length practices of thirty and forty years ago in the United States, there is a remarkable amount of cooperation in contemporary US manufacturing. But Helper also finds that US suppliers have a low level of trust in their customers. Many feel that their relationships with customers involve one-way exchanges of know-how. Customers press supplier margins in the name of mutually beneficial cost reduction. Customers solicit innovative design from their suppliers only to shop those designs around to supplier competitors. And, OEM requests for just-in-time delivery are experienced as inventory shifting rather than inventory eliminating moves on the part of the OEM (see Dziczek et al. 2003).

For Helper, the contradictory character of this evidence is viewed as a marker for the incompleteness of the transition to lean production in the United States and above all as an indication of the legacy of arm's length contracting in US manufacturing for much of the twentieth century (Helper 1991; Helper and Sako 1995, 1998; Whitford and Zeitlin 2004). From the perspective of the VoC school, such contradictory data is evidence for the strength of the market tradition in the United States and the absence (or weakness) of institutions capable of sanctioning self-dealing in non-market relations (Casper 2001). From our point of view, however, the contradictory impulses observed in Helper's findings provide evidence for the kind of sustained contingent collaboration relations we believe are being systematically created in today's competitive environment in spite of the institutional arrangements encouraging or discouraging particular forms of behaviour in the particular society (Whitford 2003). The challenge for producers in the United States, we will see, is to create forms of governance that allow them to cope with the contradictory pressures being generated.

Evidence is similarly contradictory in studies of German manufacturing supplier relations. One very extensive study, conducted by three major economic research institutes in Germany at the end of the 1990s of the automobile, electrical, and mechanical engineering industries, found that German suppliers were indeed being asked to participate in product development at much earlier stages than they had been in the past (Fieten et al. 1997). Forty one per cent of automobile suppliers, 44.4 per cent of electromechanical industry suppliers and 47.1 per cent of mechanical engineering industry suppliers indicated that they were involved in intensive cooperation with other firms (though not all of these collaborative ties were with their direct customers) (Fieten et al. 1997: 232–8, table 235). The survey also indicated that production cycle times were drastically declining across the supply base and that suppliers were adopting production level procedures (longer machine utilization rates, cross-functional teams, ISO 9000 certification) to create greater cost transparency, improve quality, and lower inventory (Fieten et al. 1997: 152–75).

Yet, at the same time, the survey also showed that over 91 per cent of all surveyed firms in all surveyed industries ranked price pressure from OEMs as the greatest problem for suppliers; 61.1 per cent said that inconsistent delivery terms were a significant problem and 47.6 per cent said that OEMs were forcing them to hold inventory (rather than seeking to eliminate it from the supply chain) (Fieten et al. 1997: 152 ff.). Of those firms engaged in collaborative research and development with their customers, 57 per cent said that they were partially compensated (as opposed to fully compensated) for their efforts. Nearly 50 per cent of firms with fewer than 100 employees indicated that they typically received no compensation at all for their research contributions (Fieten et al. 1997: 282–3). In addition, the report notes that 42.9 per cent of all German automobile suppliers complain of customers shopping the supplier's designs around to their competitors (Fieten et al. 1997: 289).

As in the American case, the evidence here is strikingly contradictory. German suppliers are engaging in collaborative relations, but there is considerable conflict and struggle among the producers for the rents from the relationship and significant variety in the quality of relations. Seen with the institutionalist lenses of the VoC framework, this kind of contradiction within a coordinated market economy is a sign of systemic distress. The system of constraints and enablers is not functioning in a way that inhibits the diffusion of arm's length market relations in Germany. We agree that the constraints and enablers are not working in this way, though given the fact that there is considerable cooperation in the United States where there are no institutional incentives for it, it is unclear to us that even the cooperation observable in German OEM–supplier relations is in any significant way traceable to the 'beneficial constraints' of the institutional architecture in the German coordinated market economy (Streeck 1997). From our point of view, the evidence fits very well into the logic we have attempted to portray of sustained contingent collaboration. The challenge for German producers is to construct forms of governance that enable them to cope with the contradictory character of the current situation.

Judging by the evidence presented, it seems fairly clear that both German and American manufacturing supplier relations today have strong elements of both conflict and partnership within them. It is also clear that the institutional architectures in each of the political economies are not only achieving the outcomes they are thought to be able to produce; they are also allowing for the achievement of those that they are not supposed to produce. For us, this is a sign that in order to understand the character of practical, relational, and institutional recomposition in Germany and the United States one should not start by observing the performance of institutions. Instead, one must begin by looking concretely at the efforts of both suppliers and OEMs to cope with the contradictory character of their situation.

11.3.2. *Coping with the problem of sustained contingent collaboration in Germany and the United States*

The situation that confronts both US and German suppliers and OEMs in the context of the trend toward vertical disintegration and the emergence of sustained contingent collaboration as the modal relationship between OEMs and suppliers is one of continuous change in the character of relations, technology, specific workplace arrangements, skills, markets, etc. Actors (and regions) unable to cope with this kind of environment are unlikely to reproduce themselves. In this context, there are two different governance problems for which actors in both societies have had to devise mechanisms to cope: the problem of initial learning and the problem of cost reduction.

By initial learning, we refer to the processes by which producers acquire information and know-how in order to be able to participate in the new style of relationship. How do firms learn, for example, about new style production arrangements (team work, cellular manufacturing, low work in process, etc.) and services (just-in-time delivery, subassembly, logistics) that are needed to participate competitively in the new supply chains? How are they able to develop the capacity to participate in collaborative design and product development? By cost reduction, we refer to the strategies and procedures suppliers and OEMs use to organize the generation of continuous cost reductions in production. Analysis of both of these problem areas will reveal some commonalities but also significant differences in the way in which producers in the United States and Germany cope with such demands.

11.3.2.1. *Initial learning*

Prior to the onset of the trend toward vertical disintegration in the 1980s, the majority of supplier and OEM relations in both Germany and the United States were primarily of the type 1 variety: that is, short-term, arm's length relations in which suppliers either produced standardized commodity products or produced overflow capacity for OEMs during periods of peak demand. On the whole, price was the determining factor for sales in old style manufacturing supply chains in the United States and Germany. OEMs were very vertically integrated and supplier structures in both countries tended to be divided between a relatively small number of large standard component producers, such as Robert Bosch or Borg Warner in the automobile industry and multitudes of small and medium-sized contract shops engaged in capacity subcontracting (Birou and Fawcett 1994; Helper 1991; Kwon 2002; Schrader and Sattler 1993).

For the bulk of supplier firms in both economies, the trend of vertical disintegration and the shift toward sustained contingent collaboration has therefore involved significant pressures to upgrade their technological capabilities, production quality, service delivery capacities, and internal cost management procedures. This has pressed suppliers into large investments in new engineering personnel, to profound recomposition of their manpower usage and training practices, and to the reorganization of the work flow in production, forward to the customer and back to their own suppliers. Mechanisms and methods facilitating this adjustment in both the United States and Germany have been parallel but systematically divergent.

Initially in the United States, OEMs themselves invested significant direct effort and cost in the form of 'supplier development' to instruct their suppliers, one by one, in the new techniques (McDuffie and Helper 1997). This, however, is a mechanism that has begun to disappear. Supplier development was always accompanied and supplemented by consulting services that firms could acquire over the market, and these practices continue (though they are often too expensive for many smaller firms to make extensive use of). Additionally, firms with the resources (and some without them) sought to acquire knowledge of the new techniques, and also new competences in technology and service, through the acquisition of complementary firms and/or rivals in the market. The pressures placed on supplier firms by OEMs to enhance their development capabilities has led to significant mergers and organizational recomposition in the industry, at all levels, as actors have sought to create entities capable of efficiently participating in sustained contingent collaborations.

The market is a traditional mechanism for resolving governance problems in the United States, but it has not been the only one in play in the current adjustment period. There has also been a very broad array of public, private, and cooperative experiments attempting to upgrade the capabilities of the supply base in the areas of production quality, service provision, and cost reduction. The experiments can be categorized as consortial, associational, and corporate. In each case, public support may or may not play an important role.

The Wisconsin Manufacturers Development Consortium (WMDC) is an example of a public–private consortium of large OEM firms, public agencies such as the Wisconsin Manufacturing Extension Partnership (WMEP) and technical colleges devoted to the improvement of the capacity of local component manufacturers to compete at the levels of production quality and cost reduction capability that the participating manufacturers require (Erickson 2002; Klonsinski 2002; Rickert et al. 2000; Schmitt 2002; Whitford and Zeitlin 2004). Component supplier firms serving the members of the consortium have their participation subsidized by public money and they gain significant access to OEM know-how through participation in consortia-sponsored courses. A similar programme has been started in Pennsylvania in the United States.

There are two different examples of associational leadership in the provision of service to firms seeking to learn how to square the circle of quality, service, and low cost that is constitutive of sustained contingent collaboration. The first is a programme for supplier training directed by the Industrial Training Program (ITP) in Illinois's Department of Commerce and Community Affairs (Kulek 2002). This programme provides public funds to a variety of Illinois industry associations with membership structures composed primarily of small and medium-sized component manufacturers. In the case of the Valley Industrial Association (VIA) (in the outer western Suburbs of Chicago) (Whalen 2002) or of Norbic (a membership-based industrial development association on the north side of Chicago serving primarily small and medium-sized producers), the ITP awards the associations funds and member firms make specific proposals to the association for training subsidies. Fifty per cent of an individual firm's training expense is paid for by the programme. The Valley Industrial Association encourages members to make use of the funds (which they do in large numbers), but does not give advice or assistance as to the types of training that may be necessary. Norbic provides consulting services to its members to help them optimize the kind of training they utilize and then provides grants to firms for the training (Norbic A and B).

The final variant of governance mechanisms capable of balancing manufacturing quality with continuous cost reduction is a corporate one. Here there are two different kinds of mechanisms: one directed by internal corporate consulting units on operating units that are active as component suppliers; the other directed by OEM firms toward their component suppliers.

The first mechanism can be found among large component and complex subassembly producers such as Emerson Electric, Danaher, GKN, and more specialized component producers such as ITW. These firms operate their own internal organizational consultancies, often through their corporate 'Technology Centers'. Firms such as Danaher are widely known for their uniformly 'lean' production operations and they are able to achieve this across a broad array of operating units and subsidiaries through the use of corporate training programmes for operating unit engineers, managers, and workers (often run through their corporate university) and technical consultants who benchmark subsidiaries within the conglomerate and disseminate information on successful organizational forms. These corporate institutions broker solutions for independent operating units, bringing knowledge and expertise to a local production level which those local units would not have been able to marshal on their own.[3]

The second mechanism is in many ways a variant on the now increasingly discontinued practice of supplier development, although here the aim is to provide training to groups of suppliers to enable them to reorganize rather than to directly reorganize individual suppliers. Moreover, in the most prominent case, this corporate policy is undertaken with local government subsidy. The same Illinois ITP programme mentioned in the discussion of associational initiatives above also makes supplier training money available directly to the three largest manufacturing OEMs in Illinois—Caterpillar, John Deere, and the Ford Motor Company. These firms are charged with using the money to train suppliers that they identify as needing production quality assistance and improved cost reduction capability. In these cases, the large OEM designs the curriculum and offers training that it believes will enable suppliers to consistently achieve quality and cost reduction targets that the firm establishes (DeDobbelaere 2002). In effect, the state of Illinois outsources regional industrial policy to the major actors and shapers of industrial practice in the state. The effect, however, is to ensure that small and medium-sized component suppliers cross the initial learning threshold for participation in the new style subcontracting relations.

In sum, the governance of initial learning on the American side is characterized by processes of merger and firm recomposition guided by the market as well as by an array of non-market experiments: associational, consortial, and corporate. Some of the mechanisms that have been set up (in particular the state sponsored corporate programmes in Illinois) have the traditional character of firm-led or arm's length incentive creating industrial policy for which the United States has long been known. But others are more path breaking: the consortial and associational programmes in Wisconsin, Illinois, and Pennsylvania and some of the intra-corporate consulting agencies are interesting because they are deliberative. They involve systematic contact for information and experience exchange among the principle parties

---

[3] The danger, of course, is that these centralized mechanisms undercut the strengths of the local units in their efforts to impose a unitary idea of best practice. For an extensive discussion and critique of this kind of centralized top down benchmarking in the context of multinational companies, see Kristensen and Zeitlin (2005), Ch 8–13.

(OEM, Supplier, Association, State agency) in both the conception and execution of policy.

In Germany, efforts to help producers to develop the capability to participate in the new subcontracting arrangements also have been quite varied. Different mechanisms have been in play (market, corporate, and associational) and the use and impact of the different mechanisms has been different in different regions. In some ways, the mechanisms observed are quite consistent with the kind of governance that traditionally has existed in industrial Germany, but in other ways the current experiments mark a clear departure from the path.

One traditional mechanism (often underplayed in discussions of Germany) has been the market. Private consultancies, for example, have been very important vehicles for the diffusion of knowledge about the new production and supply relations in Germany (Jürgens 2003). Mergers have also been very prominent in the component supplier market, again at all levels. In Baden Württemberg alone, the largest region of automobile component production in the country, the number of prominent first tier suppliers to OEMs has been consolidated from somewhere between twenty-five or thirty players to less than ten over the course of the last decade. Plainly, in both the United States and Germany, many firms have found it easier to acquire new capabilities by merging with actors who possess them (particularly in the technology and development area) than they have to develop them from scratch in-house.

There have been other efforts, however, involving the cooperation of state, associational, firm, and educational entities, that resemble the kinds of governance arrangement that is extensively discussed regarding the German case in the varieties of capitalism literature. For example, beginning in the mid-1990s, a series of Länder government 'supplier initiatives' were created in the automobile industry (after strong lobbying by component industry associations) which brought together large automobile firms, their suppliers, and local technical universities into a informational network. For several years, these initiatives sponsored regular events in which details about the new production arrangements and supplier relations were extensively discussed. Stronger and more enthusiastically attended in some regions than others, such initiatives made information available to those suppliers interested in receiving it. In large part, such efforts stopped at the boundary of the supplier firm, but they facilitated consulting business for the local technical university experts among member firms in the Initiative. Finally, the traditional German system of codetermination has also played an effective role in helping to diffuse the workplace and production arrangements of 'lean production' (in particular team work, continuous improvement procedures, and cellular production) through the issuance of central guidelines for the adoption of the various elements of lean manufacture (Jürgens 1997, 2003; Roth 1997).

Such reactions to the challenge of the new supplier–OEM arrangements constitute a kind of systemic reflex: the German institutional architecture doing what it can to help producers adjust to a new set of conditions. Such reflexes have been significant, but in crucial ways they have not always been enough for producers. The supplier initiatives had very uneven coverage (in many ways their success depended on the interest of the local OEM). Concretely, they facilitated information exchange and created networks for consultants, but this was often either too little information or too expensive (or both) for many firms to benefit from. The industrial relations system had success with problems related to work organization and production flow within firms, but it was crucially inattentive to the elements of the new system that involved inter-firm relations—logistics, services, cooperation in design, and product development. As a result, many German supplier firms felt left in the cold by the traditional institutional architecture. This opened up a space for very interesting experiments in governance that depart quite dramatically from the German norm.

One remarkable experiment of this kind has been taking place in the Bergisches Land in Nordrhein Westfalen. This region is the second largest centre of automobile components production in Germany and the largest concentration of small and medium-sized component producers in that sector. For traditional reasons, public policy for suppliers has been very underdeveloped in the Bergisches Land (Herrigel 1996). Local banks are overwhelmed and cash poor; larger banks are pulling away from the industrial Mittelstand (SMEs); employers' associations are traditionally fractionalized and as a result passive. In this case, the institutions of German coordinated capitalism are truly in disarray.

Somewhat ironically, it has been the local IG Metall union, the strongest extra-firm institution in the region, that has stepped into the breach and begun pushing firms to upgrade and embrace not only newer forms of work and production organization, but new production services and logistics as well. IG Metall's involvement in restructuring takes place in one of two ways (Janitz 2002). First, in a significant array of cases, agents from the trade union district office in Wuppertal act directly as consultants, offering firms advice on how to restructure their product palette, their labour and production arrangements, and their finances in order to be able to achieve the quality and cost targets demanded by large automobile industry OEMs. Second, and more often, the union acts as an intermediary between the firm and consultants who come in, audit the company and provide advice and consulting on how to restructure the firm to be competitive.

Typically the union becomes involved (in either of the above ways) because it is asked to do so, first by the works council in a troubled firm (either in bankruptcy or in financial trouble) and then by the management itself. The union establishes a set of conditions with the firm on restructuring—that is, they will help with connections and line up consultants as long as the firm agrees to certain parameters (in the interest of IG Metall members) in the restructuring process. With agreement, the union then goes ahead and lines up the consultant. There are a number of very skilled local consultants who have had success in local restructuring. They know the firms, know the regional culture, know the industry, etc. But the union also uses its position to pressure the works council (to the extent it is resistant) to adopt practices in the long-term interest of the competitiveness of the firm (cells, teams, continuous monitoring, benchmarking of best practices in the industry, etc.).

In these ways, IG Metall is playing a pivotal role in the management of small and medium-sized firm adjustment in the region. The union is simultaneously a broker and a conveyor of specialized knowledge. IG Metall mediates consultants who help troubled firms restructure; it establishes guidelines for the general restructuring process with the firm before the consultants are deployed; it engages itself in the internal restructuring discussion and is typically given access to the firms' books. Moreover, due to the structure of the German Federal Works Constitution Act, the union is in a remarkably good position to be able to evaluate the performance of the various actors it engages and sets into action in the restructuring process. Union officials from the local district office sit on the supervisory boards of important megasuppliers (core customers of local SME firms) and hence are privy to very intimate information on the megasupplier's practices and strategies—worldwide. IG Metall knows what the customers of local firms want and is in a position to helpfully convey that information to its clients and critically evaluate management suggestions and the performance of consultants.

It is important to emphasize that this kind of intervention constitutes a dramatic departure from traditional practice for IG Metall. It is improvisation in the context of a failure of the traditional system to provide for area firms. In one sense, the union's actions have a very traditional interest: to protect jobs in the region by enhancing the competitiveness of the firms that are located there. But in order to achieve this goal the union has had to break from the traditional confines of union activity within the German system. In effect they are constructing a system of 'comanagement' within local firms where the trade union and works council deliberate on strategic questions regarding the firm's future and its customer relations that go well beyond the relatively circumscribed work place and labour market arenas demarcated in the system of codetermination and works constitution statutes in German law. At the same time, they are acting as a regional benchmarking agent, distributing information regarding best practice among area firms and even using information about international best practice that they are able to access through other roles they play in the system of codetermination (i.e. sitting on boards of multinational corporations headquartered in the region).

This example for how the process of initial learning is being organized in Wuppertal is dramatic, but there are myriad other forms of departure and innovation occurring across the German industrial landscape as firms and associations seek to cope with the limits of the existing institutional architecture. As in the United States then, the problem of initial learning in Germany is being confronted in ways that both conform with and depart from the traditional path. Crucially, the departures from path in each case do not converge. Although they perform some of the same services and functions, for example, the Wisconsin supplier consortium and the Wuppertal experiment in Union-led restructuring constitute quite distinct and different institutional efforts to cope with initial learning.

11.3.2.2. *Coping with cost reduction pressures in the United States and Germany*

Cost reduction pressure in the current environment stems from the permanent pressure that producers feel to be technologically innovative. Firms must allocate increasing amounts of resources to research and development—and moreover, in areas that are not always part of the traditional strengths of the business (e.g. plastics or electronics for automobile producers). In order to be able to do this, they must withdraw resources from other areas—hence the trend toward outsourcing and a focus on core competences. But in addition to these measures, the pressure to remain innovative imposes permanent pressure on in-house operations and on suppliers continually to reduce costs. As we indicated in our discussion of the sustained contingent collaboration relation, a firm's facility in cost reduction is a major competitive advantage for it in dynamically changing relations.

Being able to cope with this continuous pressure is thus a crucial governance issue in manufacturing today (Herrigel 2004). Firms must develop the in-house procedures to be able to continuously generate and identify cost reduction possibilities. The overarching challenge in achieving continuous cost reduction is to create an organization that encourages all actors in the product design, development, and manufacturing processes to reveal to others what they know about their area of preoccupation. Such organizational transparency facilitates the identification of inefficiencies within functions as well as possibilities for improvement in the interfaces between functions. Actors have to abandon the opportunistic impulse to protect information for local advantage and recognize that transparency is in the interest of everyone in the process.

At the level of work and production organization, the core arrangements of lean production (teams, production cells, kaizen practices) make continuous improvement one of their objectives. Typically these arrangements encourage actors to reveal to one another what they know by grouping all relevant functions in the creation and production of a product together in a governance structure that directs its production—hence, the outcome/reward for each function is dependent on the outcome/reward for all the others. All recognize their common stake in the successful delivery and continuous improvement of the product. Such arrangements seem to have diffused quite broadly in both the United States and Germany at this point, though the transformation continues to be incomplete and the emphases in each political economy differ slightly (Jürgens 2003; Streeck and Yamamura 2003: 29).

Cost reduction is also a key component of the search process that all producers in the sustained contingent collaboration relationship engage in. Firms scan the terrain, both through collaborative benchmarking procedures in the product development process and through serial contracting with specialists, not only for technological know-how, but also for organizational innovation and cost reduction expertise. Practices in the United States and Germany are remarkably convergent along this dimension as well.

Both of these layers of cost reduction practice are limited, however, in that they tend to be focused on particular projects or parts of the production process and as a result lack a sense of the overarching situation of multiple projects and multiple production processes in the enterprise as a whole. But it is precisely at this level that much of the strategic back and forth of cost reduction takes place between firms in sustained contingent collaborations. Consequently, firms have had to develop internal mechanisms which encourage product dedicated teams to reveal to super-ordinate internal scanning actors what they know. This makes it possible for the scanners both to identify cost reduction possibilities throughout the firm (including projects whose profitability can be sacrificed to achieve a customers cost reduction demand in the interest of the extension and development of other very profitable projects) and to help diffuse innovations and practices that product-dedicated teams may be developing. At this level of internal scanning, American and German firms have some similarities, but on the whole they have been developing different sorts of mechanisms.

The similarities can be found in the smallest firms. Here in both countries the super-ordinate monitoring role is frequently assumed by the principle owner of the firm. In both countries, the effectiveness of this role depends very much on the local balance of power: if the owner acts autocratically, based on what she can observe rather than on what is revealed to her by the various product cells, cost reduction is often a battle over givebacks and wages between production workers and management. This kind of arrangement is less successful, in large part because the top down structure of governance does not encourage actors in production to truthfully reveal what they know. If, on the other hand, the owner facilitates exchange between the various parts of his firm and engages in regularized consultation with shop floor personnel—team leaders, project coordinators, etc.—the results are better. Cost reduction is most successful when it becomes a process of collective self-examination across roles and lines of authority in the firm.

An alternative mechanism, found in small firms we visited in both the United States and Germany, involves the creation of actors with roles in the firm that systematically cross functions and stages in the production process. In one small family-owned component producer we interviewed in Germany, for example, the owner described their internal deliberation procedures, in which works councillors and production workers met regularly with management and ownership, was designed to 'systematically produce surprises' about plant layout, machine operation, work organization, material flow, as well as possibilities for new products. The key to the success of this was the existence of toolmakers and set-up personnel who were allowed (expected) to float back and forth between design engineering and machine operators and across product lines. Similarly, one small US deep draw stamping firm in western Michigan that we interviewed organized cost reduction scanning through the construction of dramatically expansive job descriptions for skilled toolmakers in their shop. These skilled workers shepherded projects from beginning design to end manufacture and met regularly with one another as well as plant management and machine operators to discuss progress. In both the German and US cases, the key to success was that management and work teams both identified their success with the improvement of the product and the cost reduction process. Skilled workers who were intimately involved at all stages of the production process act as key integrating figures between the shop floor and firm management.

In larger firms, however, the formation of a super-ordinate internal scanning practice differs between US and German firms. In the United States, two sorts of scanning practices predominate. One is an autocratic role for finance departments in internal deliberations about cost. Because public US firms are required to make costs more transparent to the outside, finance people are able to use the force of accounting and shareholder value arguments to impose particular decisions on multiple projects. The criterion used is purely financial without consideration for the location strategically of particular projects in the historical relationship between the firm and its customer. In this case, the powerful role of finance departments is very much in line with what one would expect from the institutional structure of the US 'liberal market economy'.

A second mechanism, often conceived of as a counterweight to the force of finance departments, has been to establish ongoing inter- and intra-operating unit cost reduction conversations among the relevant actors in the production process. Such conversations (organized in the form of weekly meetings or teleconferences between project teams—often including key subsuppliers) bring together all those responsible for contracts with particular clients to exchange information and discuss collective possibilities for meeting the client's targets. The parties all have an interest in coming up with something to satisfy the client—each recognizes that future business with the client may depend on it. Such meetings tend both to identify best practice within the firm (through self-reporting), and create a forum in which the generalization of such practice can be discussed.

Rather than by hierarchical direction or financial leverage, such mechanisms turn mutual learning and information exchange to the competitive advantage of the firm as a whole. It is in many cases true that the genesis of these institutionalized conversations has occurred because of the unrelenting internal pressure of finance departments in American corporations: the institutional goal of the cross-project and cross-functional conversations is to achieve (or beat) the goals established by finance, but in ways that are consistent with the health of both internal and customer relations as well as long-term efficiency of production within the enterprise. Regardless of how they are generated, the key to their success is that all stakeholders in the products going to a particular client are represented in the conversation. Needless to say, this kind of mutual monitoring and sharing of information, as a form of governance, marks an interesting departure from the 'liberal market' practices associated with VoC characterizations of the American production system.

In the German case, the institutional form of the super-ordinate scanner is different because the basic institutional contour of the firm is different from that in the United States. Many large firms, for example, do not have the same kind of external pressure from finance markets that embolden (and strengthen) the hand of the finance department in US corporations. Engineering and production departments are far stronger within German corporations than in American ones. But cost reduction pressure is just as intense in Germany, so firms have had to develop alternative mechanisms to identify firm-wide cost reduction possibilities. Three different kinds of experiments in this regard suggest the flavour and range of organizational recomposition that is taking place.

The first, currently being developed at a large first tier automobile supplier resembles in some ways the internal consulting groups in American corporations that have played such an important role in initial learning. This is a cross-functional team charged with what the firm calls *Leistungsorientiertes Management* (Performance Oriented Management) whose charge is to monitor operations across the firm seeking efficiencies and cost reduction possibilities that may be neglected by the structure of team projects, for example, material purchases that could be combined, common design possibilities, complementary machine usage rates, etc. These teams are given general cost reduction targets, but they can only achieve them in consultation with project and production teams. In turn, the production teams, who experience direct pressure from their customers for specific give back percentages, view the performance-oriented team as a resource.

The second and third mechanisms seek to achieve the kind of continuous conversation among stakeholders described above in the American context. But the conversations are realized via different institutional actors and catalysing agents. The second mechanism being deployed by many German firms is to redraw the role of logistics departments in extremely expansive ways, such that agents from that department concern themselves with all organizational and product development issues within and across projects. Logistics teams engage with all existing product development and production teams, at all stages of the development and production process, in an effort to generate and diffuse continuous cost reduction throughout the product development and production cycle. The logistics departments also concentrate, in conjunction with purchasing, finance, and development departments, on achieving the flexibility to balance varying intensities of cost reduction pressure across all projects within the firm. In these ways, logistics players have their incentives aligned both with the teams associated with specific projects and with the general cost reduction targets associated with the department as a whole within the enterprise.

A third kind of experiment, at once the most remarkably German, but also perhaps the most at odds with the traditional institutional structure of the German production system, involves the systematic involvement of works councils, in collaboration with plant management, to scan for cost reduction potential. In the case of one large supplier to the mechanical engineering industry, in which the IG Metall is very strongly represented (over 90 per cent workforce organization, including management), the works council pursues an extremely expansive version of German comanagement. Instead of confining their activities to the narrow tasks of workplace training, wages, scheduling, and arbitration, this works council contributes detailed proposals for work, production and product design reorganization to plant management (in most cases themselves IG Metall members).

Initially, the works council became involved in the presentation of proposals for reorganization in an effort to present management with alternatives to proposals developed by outside management consultants. With time, however, as it became clear that pressure for cost reduction was unremitting, the works council devoted an increasing share of its resources to the problem (devoting two full-time members of the works council exclusively to the problem of cost reduction). It has gone so far that the works council has become involved not only in the optimization of organization in the servicing of existing contracts. They have also become actively involved in the way in which the company constructs its bids on new contracts. These activities are in line with the general role of German works councils—to make the employment of its members secure. But it pursues this goal in a very unconventional manner—involving itself with engineering and controlling departments in addition to production level management in an effort to achieve internal efficiencies that allow the firm to meet existing cost reduction targets and to win new contracts.

As in the case of the new style logistics departments (and in some ways, the newly defined boundary spanning toolmakers in the small firm examples), the advantage of the works council in the process is that it is, as an actor, both part of the local level in the plant and involved in super-ordinate scanning. Local players are willing to reveal what they know regarding the strengths and weaknesses of their area because they know that the works council has no incentive to punish them with that information. The result is greater transparency regarding cost throughout the firm.

Many of these German and American examples show that there are clear departures from the traditional path. There are, for example, no constraints or enabling rules in the institutional system in the United States to create cost reduction conversations or boundary-crossing toolmakers; nor are the new style logistics departments or cost reduction oriented works councils enacting a logic prescribed by the German institutional architecture. In all these cases, actors are innovating despite the rules of the game. The institutional arrangements are not so much constraints or enablers as they are resources in the creative process of experimentation.

Nonetheless, although we believe these examples constitute departures from the path, we also believe strongly that they should be viewed as experiments. We do not intend to suggest that the above illustrations constitute the emergence of a new 'system' in either institutional setting. Rather, by outlining an array of experiments, we want to convey the breadth of current experimentation that exists at a local level. We see institutional adaptation through the recomposition of organizational design or the redefinition of roles. Many of the experiments involve departures either from the traditional roles of actors within the institutional architecture of the German and American production systems or from the organizational ecology established by those architectures. All the experiments draw on existing resources, but apply them in new and creative ways.

11.4. Conclusion

In conclusion, we would like to review and underscore three points about the argument and evidence in this chapter. First, we have argued that the process of vertical disintegration and the emergence of sustained contingent collaboration is a global trend. It is occurring in similar ways across different political economies. But unlike neoliberal arguments, ours is not a claim about the diffusion of a single standard of efficiency throughout the global economy. We are not making a 'one best way' argument about institutional convergence. Instead, our argument, embodied in the characterization of OEM purchasing behaviour in Section 11.1 and the typology we develop in Section 11.2, is that there is great heterogeneity of practice in the current global manufacturing environment. OEMs pursue a wide array of practices and strategies even as their commitments to vertical disintegration intensifies. In our view, sustained contingent collaboration as a type of relation between OEM and supplier is emerging across advanced industrial societies as the modal relation, but it remains only one possibility among several others. Finally, we show that even our modal relation, sustained contingent collaboration, is emerging under a broad array of different governance mechanisms in both Germany and the United States. Vertical disintegration and the emergence of sustained contingent collaborations are global trends. But this is not evidence in support of neoliberal claims regarding the economic processes of globalization.

Second, this chapter has been an extended reflection on the limits of contemporary institutional analysis, particularly that of the Varieties of Capitalism School, in accounting for the differences that continue to exist in developed political economies. In insisting on the difference between our argument and the strong convergence claims of contemporary neoliberalism, we are in agreement with much institutionalist writing on the persistence of differences across advanced political economies in the context of contemporary trends. But, in our view, contemporary institutionalism of the VoC variety goes too far in its emphasis on comparative institutional advantage and the path dependent character of systemic change. In a way that is inconsistent with the VoC characterization of the national institutional advantages in the United States and Germany, we have shown that sustained contingent collaborations are emerging in both societies. Germany does not have a greater preponderance of, nor display, any particular advantage in cooperative practices. US firms are neither more invested in arm's length contracting, nor more capable of radical organizational recomposition than their German counterparts. Instead, conflict and cooperation and institutional recomposition and experimentation characterize actors' strategies in both societies.

Similarly, regarding institutionalist claims about path dependence, our evidence shows that with the diffusion of sustained contingent collaboration, actors' efforts to cope with pressures for adjustment are producing a variety of significant departures from the path of action generally thought to be encouraged by either the US or German institutional architectures. The cooperative deliberation within large US firms regarding cost reduction and the collaborative supplier training consortia in the US and Union led restructuring and works council-driven cost reduction in Germany all are significant departures from the path. In some cases, actors are guided by traditional conceptions of their institutional roles, yet find it to be necessary to act in unconventional ways to be able to realize those goals (e.g. the IG Metall in Wuppertal or works councils engaging in systematic scanning for cost reduction). But in other cases, actors respond to challenges posed by the competitive environment in ways that appear to be neither systematically constrained nor encouraged by the institutional architecture in which they are embedded. That is, actors respond creatively to their situation (e.g. the expansive role for logistics departments in Germany or the expansive cross-functional role of toolmakers within US and German small firms).

All of this evidence, in our view, underscores the reflexive character of action within a social economy. Actors are not confined within a rigid institutional system of constraints and incentives, but instead exist within a social system of contingently coupled dispositions and habits (Bourdieu 1977; Dewey 2002). They solve problems through collective self-reflection and experimentation, using and recomposing the resources (institutional and otherwise) that they have on hand. The result, as we have shown, is not only that actors appear at times to be oblivious to the constraints or incentives provided by their institutional surround. They also recreate institutional difference across political economies as actors creatively recompose and even break from the framework for practice that their institutional context provides.

The third and final point we would like to underscore here concerns the experimental and ultimately piecemeal character of change in both the German and US political economies. None of the examples of institutional innovation and recomposition outlined in the second half of the chapter in the areas of initial learning and cost reduction constitutes a dominant form of adjustment within either the United States or Germany. Adjustment in both societies is extremely fractured and driven by local experimentation. It is not for this reason to be taken less seriously. Instead, we believe that the transformation of institutional architectures within contemporary advanced political economies is occurring in precisely this sort of decentralized, local, and piecemeal fashion. Giants are felled by thousands of arrows.

The current character of global competition, characterized as it is by virtually permanent technological change and organizational uncertainty, leads to the following boundedly general consideration. Much of the literature on institutional systems, not least the VoC tradition, discusses the historical development of institutional architectures in the imagery of periods of stability marked by dramatic junctures of upheaval and change followed again by a period of stability. One can be critical of this historical imagery as a general matter (Sabel and Zeitlin 1997), but it seems particularly inappropriate to impose narrative expectations of a coming period of institutional stability (equilibrium) on the current situation. In large part this is because what stands out about the experiments that one observes today is their self-consciously provisional character. They have been brought into being because actors perceive common problems that are not being addressed by the traditional institutional instruments available to them for the purpose of addressing such problems. Actors are not willing to describe what they are doing as a new order because they are too acutely aware of the possibility that they will have to change again in the current turbulent environment. The distinctiveness of current problems is that they are never definitively resolved: Innovation and Cost reduction, and the institutional tinkering and recomposition that they entail are continuous processes. Old institutional rules today are not only being broken, but new ones are continually being defined and then redefined.

REFERENCES

Abbott, Andrew (2001). *Time Matters. On Theory and Method*. Chicago: University of Chicago Press.

346 Gary Herrigel and Volker Wittke

Adler, Paul (1995). 'Interdepartmental Interdependence and Coordination: The Case of Design/Manufacturing Interface'. *Organization Science* 6(2) (Mar.–Apr.): 147–67.

Berger, Suzanne and Dore, Ronald (eds.) (1996). *National Diversity and Global Capitalism*. Ithaca, NY: Cornell University Press.

Birou, Laura M. and Fawcett, Stanley E. (1994). 'Supplier Involvement in Integrated Product Development: A Comparison of US and European Practices'. *International Journal of Physical Distribution and Logistics Management* 24(5): 4–14.

Borrus, Michael and Zysman, John (1997). 'Globalization with Borders: The Rise of Wintelism as the Future of Global Competition'. *Industry and Innovation* 4(2): 141–66.

Bourdieu, Pierre (1977). *Outline of a Theory of Practice*. New York: Cambridge University Press.

Boyer, Robert (2003). 'The Embedded Innovation Systems of Germany and Japan: Distinctive Features and Futures'. In: Kazo, Yamamura and Wolfgang Streeck (eds.), *The End of Diversity? Prospects for German and Japanese Capitalism*. Ithaca, NY: Cornell University Press, pp. 147–82.

Bradach, J. and Eccles, R. (1989). 'Price, Authority and Trust: From Ideal Types to Plural Forms'. *Annual Review of Sociology* 15: 97–118.

Casper, Steven (2001). 'The Legal Framework for Corporate Governance: The Influence of Contract Law on Company Strategies in Germany and the United States'. In: Peter Hall and David Soskice (eds.), *Varieties of Capitalism*. NY: Oxford University Press.

Casper, Steven (1995). 'How Public Law Influences Decentralized Supplier Network Organization in Germany: The Cases of BMW and Audi'. Discussion paper FS I 95-314, Wissenschaftszentrum, Berlin.

—— (1997). 'Nationale Institutionengefüge und innovative Industrieorganisation: Zulieferbeziehungen in Deutschland'. In: Frieder Naschold, David Soskice, Bob Hancke, and Ulrich Jürgens (eds.), *Oekonomische Leistungsfähigkeit und institutionelle Innovation: Das deutsche Produktions-und Politikregime im globalen Wettbewerb*. Berlin: WZB Jahrbuch.

Chesbrough, Henry (2004). 'Towards a Dynamics of Modularity. A Cyclical Model of Technical Advance'. In: Andrea Prencipe, Andrew Davies, and Mike Hobday (eds.), *The Business of Systems Integration*. Oxford: Oxford University Press, pp. 174–98.

Clark, Kim and Fujimoto, Takahiro (1991). *Product Development Performance. Strategy,Organizationand Management in the World Auto Industry*. Boston: Harvard Business School Press.

DeDobbelaere, Donald R. (2002). 'John Deere: Global Learning and Development'. Power point presentations at the conference. *Supply Chain Governance and Regional Development in the Global Economy*.

University of Wisconsin, 10 September. See www.cows.org/supplychain/presentations.asp.

Dewey, John (2002) [1922]. *Human Nature and Conduct*. Mineola, NY: Dover Publications.

Dyer, Jeffrey, Cho, Dung Sung, and Chu, Wujin (1998). 'Strategic Supplier Segmentation: The Next "Best Practice" in Supply Chain Management'. *California Management Review* 40(2): 57–77.

Dziczek, Kristen, Luria, Daniel, and Wiarda, Edith (2003). 'Critical Relationships in Manufacturing'. A special supplement to *Performance Benchmarking*. Ann Arbor, MI, 10 November, p. 1.

Erickson, Paul (2002). 'OEM Leveraged Economic Development'. Paper presented at the conference on 'Supply Chain Governance and Regional Development in the Global Economy'. University of Wisconsin-Madison, 10 September 2002, available at www.cows.org/supplychain/presentations.asp.

Fieten, Robert , Friedrich, Werner, and Lageman, Bernhard (1997). *Globalisierung der Märkte—Herausforderung und Optionen für kleine und mittlere Unternehmen insbesondere für Zulieferer, Gutachten im Auftrag des Bundesministeriums für Wirtschaft*, Schriften zur Mittelstandsforschung, Nr 73 NF. Stuttgart: Verlag Schäffer-Poeschel.

Gereffi, Gary, Humphrey, John, and Sturgeon, Timothy (2005). 'The Governance of Global Value Chains' *Review of International Political Economy*, forthcoming.

Hall, Peter and Soskice, David (eds.) (2001). *Varieties of Capitalism. The Institutional Foundations of Comparative Advantage*. New York: Oxford University Press.

Helper, Susan (1991). 'Strategy and Irreversibility in Supplier Relations: The Case of the US Automobile Industry'. *Business History Review* 65(4) (Winter): 781–824.

—— and Mari Sako (1995). 'Supplier Relations in Japan and the United States: Are They Converging?' *Sloan Management Review* 36(3): 77–84.

—— and —— (1998). 'Determinants of Trust in Supplier Relations: Evidence from the Automotive Industry in Japan and the United States'. *Journal of Economic Behavior and Organization* 34: 387–417.

——, MacDuffie, John Paul, and Sabel, Charles (2000). '"Pragmatic Collaborations"' Advancing Knowledge While Controlling Opportunism'. *Industrial and Corporate Change* 9(3): 443–88.

Herrigel, Gary (1996). *Industrial Constructions. The Sources of German Industrial Power* (Ch. 5). New York: Cambridge University Press.

—— (2002). 'Large Firms and Industrial Districts in Europe: De-regionalization, Re-Regionalization and the Transformation of Manufacturing Flexibility'. In: John Dunning (ed.), *Regions, Globalization and the Knowledge Based Economy*. Oxford: Oxford University Press.

Herrigel, Gary (2004). 'Emerging Strategies and Forms of Governance in the Components Industry in High Wage Regions'. *Industry and Innovation* 11(1–2) (Mar.–June): 45–79.

Hollingsworth, J. Rogers and Boyer, Robert (eds.) (1997). *Contemporary Capitalism*. New York: Oxford University Press.

Janitz, Fritz (2002). Power point presentation at the conference: *Supply Chain Governance and Regional Development in the Global Economy*, University of Wisconsin, 10 September 2002. www.cows.org/supplychain/presentations.asp.

Jürgens, Ulrich (1997). 'Germany: Implementing Lean Production'. In: Thomas Kochan, Russell Lansbury, and John Paul MacDuffie (eds.), *After lean Production. Evolving Employment Practices in the World Auto Industry*. Ithaca, NY: Cornell University Press, pp. 109–36.

—— (2003). 'Transformation and Interaction: Japanese, US and German Production models in the 1990s'. In: Kazo Yamamura and Wolfgang Streeck (eds.), *The End of Diversity? Prospects for German and Japanese Capitalism*. Ithaca, NY: Cornell University Press, pp. 212–39.

Klonsinski, Mike (WMEP) (2002). 'Targeting Supply Chains as Economic Development Policy: Lessons from the WMDC'. Paper presented at the conference on 'Supply Chain Governance and Regional Development in the Global Economy'. University of Wisconsin-Madison, 10 September 2002, available at www.cows.org/supplychain/presentations.asp.

Kristensen, Peer Hull and Zeitlin, Jonathan (2005). *Local Players in Global Games*, Chapters 8–13. Oxford University Press, forthcoming.

Kulek, Carol (2002). 'State of Illinois, Department of Commerce and Community Affairs, Industrial Training Program'. Power point presentation at the conference: *Supply Chain Governance and Regional Development in the Global Economy*, University of Wisconsin, 10 September 2002. www.cows.org/supplychain/presentations.asp.

Kwon, Hyeong-Ki (2002). 'Fairness and Division of Labor in Market Society: A Comparison of US and German Automotive Parts Markets'. Ph.D dissertation, Department of Political Science, University of Chicago, December, chs 2–4.

Leachman, Robert C. and Leachman, Chien H. (2004). 'Globalization of Semi-Conductors: Do Real Men Have Fabs, or Virtual Fabs?' In: Martin Kenny with Richard Florida (eds.), *Locating Global Advantage. Industry Dynamics in the International Economy*. Palo Alto: Stanford Universitiy Press, pp. 203–31.

Liker, Jeffrey K., Fruin, W. Mark, and Adler, Paul S. (1999). *Remade in America: Transplanting and Transforming Japanese Management Systems*. New York: Oxford University Press.

Luria, Daniel (1996a). 'Toward Lean or Rich? What Performance Benchmarking Tells Us about SME Performance, and Some Implications for Extension

Center Services and Mission'. Atlanta: Conference on Manufacturing Modernization: Learning From Evaluation Practices and Results.

——(1996*b*). 'Why Markets Tolerate Mediocre Manufacturing'. *Challenge* 11–16.

Lüthje, Boy (2002). 'Electronics Contract Manufacturing: Global Production and the International Division of Labor in the Age of the Internet'. *Industry and Innovation* 9(3) (Dec.): 227–47.

Lüthje, Boy, Schumm, W., and Sproll, M. (2002). *Contract Manufacturing: Transnationale Produktion und Industriearbeit im IT-Sektor.* Frankfurt, New York: Campus.

Mahoney, James (2002). 'Path Dependence in Historical Sociology'. *Theory and Society* 29: 507–48.

McDuffie, John Paul and Helper, Susan (1997). 'Creating Lean Suppliers: Diffusing Lean Production Through the Supply Chain'. *California Management Review* 39(4)(Summer): 118–51.

McKendrick, David, Doner, Richard, and Haggard, Stephan (2000). *From Silicon Valley to Singapore. Location and Competitive Advantage in the Hard Disk Drive Industry.* Stanford: Stanford University Press.

Mesquita, Luis and Brush, Thomas (2001). 'Relationship Management in Vertical Manufacturing Alliances, Supplier Development and Supplier Performance'. Working paper, Purdue University, Krannert School of Management pp. 1–30.

Nishiguchi, Toshihiro (1994). *Strategic Industrial Sourcing.* Oxford University Press.

——and Brookfield, Jonathan (1997). 'The Evolution of Japanese Subcontracting'. *MIT Sloan Management Review* 39(1) (Fall): 89–101.

Norbic A: activities: www.norbic.org.

Norbic B: industrial training grants: www.norbic.org/industrial_training_program.htm.

Pierson, Paul (2002). 'Increasing Returns, Path Dependence and the Study of Politics'. *American Political Science Review* 94: 251–68.

Prahalad, C. K. and Hamel, Gary (1990). 'The Core Competence of the Corporation'. *Harvard Business Review* 66 (May/June) pp. 79–91.

Rickert, Jeffrey, Zeitlin, Jonathan, Vassina, Darya, and Rogers, Joel (2000). 'Common Problems and Collaborative Solutions: OEM–Supplier Relationships and the Wisconsin Manufacturing Partnership's Supplier Training Consortium'. Draft report produced for the Center on Wisconsin Strategy, January.

Roth, Siegfried (1997). 'Germany: Labor's perspective on Lean Production'. In: Thomas Kochan, Russell Lansbury, and John Paul MacDuffie (eds.), *After Lean Production. Evolving Employment Practices in the World Auto Industry.* Ithaca, NY: Cornell University Press, pp. 109–36.

Sabel, Charles F. (1995). 'Learning by Monitoring'. In: Neil Smelser and Richard Swedberg (eds.), *The Handbook of Economic Sociology*. Princeton: Princeton University Press.

—— (2004). 'The World in a Bottle, or, Window on the World? Open Questions about Industrial Districts in the Spirit of Sebastiano Brusco'. Paper presented to the Conference on Clusters, Industrial Districts and Firms: The Challenge of Globalization, Modena, Italy, September 2003.

Sabel Charless, F. and Zeitlin, Jonathan (1997). 'Stories, Strategies, Structures: Rethinking Historical Alternatives to Mass Production'. In: Charles F. Sabel and Jonathan Zeitlin (eds.), *World of Possibilities: Flexibility and Mass Production in Western Industrialization*. Cambridge: Cambridge University Press, pp. 1–33.

Schmitt, Mike (2002). 'Wisconsin Manufacturing Development Consortium WMDC'. Paper presented at the conference on 'Supply Chain Governance and Regional Development in the Global Economy'. University of Wisconsin-Madison, 10 September 2002, Available at www.cows.org/supplychain/presentations.asp.

Schrader, Stephan and Sattler, Henrik (1993). 'Zwischenbetriebliche Kooperation: Informaler Infomationsaustausch in den USA und Deutschland'. *Die Betriebswirtschaft* (DBW) 53(5).

Smitka, Michael J. (1991). *Competitive Ties: Subcontracting in the Japanese Automotive Industry*. New York: Columbia University Press.

Soskice, David and Hall, Peter (2001). 'An Introduction to Varieties of Capitalism'. In: Hall and Soskice (eds.), *Varieties of Capitalism. The Institutional Foundations of Comparative Advantage*. New York: Oxford University Press, pp. 36–44.

Streeck, Wolfgang (1997). 'Beneficial Constraints: On the Economic Limits of Relational Voluntarism'. In: J. Rogers Hollingsworth and Robert Boyer (eds.), *Contemporary Capitalism*. New York: Oxford University Press.

—— and Yamamura, Kazo (2003). 'Introduction: Convergence or Diversity? Stability and Change in German and Japanese Capitalism'. In: Yamamura, Kazo and Wolfgang Streeck (eds.), *The End of Diversity? Prospects for German and Japanese Capitalism*, p. 29. Ithaca, NY: Cornell University Press.

Sturgeon, Timothy J. (2002). 'Modular Production Networks: A New American Model of Industrial Organization'. *Industrial and Corporate Change* 11(3): 451–96.

Sturgeon, Timothy J. and Lee, Ji-Ren (2004). 'Industry Co-Evolution. Electronics Contract Manufacturing in North America and Taiwan'. Working paper, Industrial Performance Center, MIT.

Thelen, Kathleen and Kume, Ikuo (2003). 'The Future of Nationally Embedded Capitalism: Industrial Relations in Germany and Japan'. In: Kazo Yamamura and Wolfgang Streeck (eds.), *The End of Diversity? Prospects for German and Japanese Capitalism*, pp. 183–211. Ithaca, NY: Cornell University Press.

Whalen, Judy (2002). 'Valley Industrial Association: Multi-Training Grant'. Power point presentations at the conference: *Supply Chain Governance and Regional Development in the Global Economy*, University of Wisconsin, 10 September 2002. See www.cows.org/supplychain/presentations.asp.

Whitford, Josh (2001). 'The Decline of a Model? Challenge and Response in the Italian Industrial Districts'. *Economy and Society* 30(Feb.): 1.

—— (2003). 'After the Outsourcing: Networks, Institutions, and the New Old Economy', Unpublished Ph.D. thesis, University of Wisconsin-Madison.

—— and Zeitlin, Jonathan (2004). 'Governing Decentralized Production: Institutions, Public Policy, and the Prospects for Inter-Firm Cooperation in the United States'. *Industry and Innovation*, 11/1–2, 11–44.

Whitley, Richard (1999). *Divergent Capitalisms. The Social Structuring and change of Business Systems*. Oxford: Oxford University Press.

Womack, James, Jones, Daniel, and Roos, Daniel (1990). *The Machine that Changed the World*. New York: Harper Row.

Yamamura, Kazo and Streeck, Wolfgang (eds.) (2003). *The End of Diversity? Prospects for German and Japanese Capitalism*. Ithaca, NY: Cornell University Press.

12

Change in Coordinated Market Economies: The Case of Nokia and Finland

ELI MOEN AND KARI LILJA

12.1. Introduction

In the late 1990s, Nokia became a global leader in mobile telephones, and Finland one of the most 'technology developed' countries in the world. The success of both Nokia and Finland has startled the surrounding world; Nokia for having overtaken the well-established Motorola and Ericsson, and Finland for having been ranked above the United States, the vanguard of the 'new economy', in terms of competitiveness and future dynamics. The stories of Nokia and Finland are conspicuous due to their point of departure and the abrupt nature of their technological–economic change. Until the early 1990s, Finland appeared to outside observers as a typical raw-material-based economy due to the dominant position of the forest industry, and Nokia was known to consumers for its rubber products. Within a period of five years, Nokia became a global market leader in the mobile phone business, and high-tech industries the dominant sector in the Finnish economy. Finland's foreign trade in high-tech products turned into a surplus. The growth in exports was so strong that Finland overtook Sweden, the European Union, and the United States with respect to the ratio of high-tech exports to high-tech imports.

A radical shift in a country's sector specialization is an interesting case in its own right. From the perspective of the literature on 'varieties of capitalism' and 'national business systems', the Finnish case, as a variant of a coordinated market economy, also represents an unexpected outcome. Research largely agrees that change in both technological regimes and in sector specialization of a nation-state is less likely to take place in coordinated market economies than in liberal ones.

Since liberal market economies, characterized by the arm's length sort of coordination, allow a radical reshuffling of people and resources, rapid adjustments and discontinuous technological innovations are considered more likely in these sorts of economies. In coordinated market economies various societal stakeholders, industrial firms, and banks are strongly interlinked. The nature of these interlinkages and also the complementarities of subsystems are seen to cause inertia (see, for example, Amable 2003; Hall and Soskice 2001: 44; Schmidt 2002: 131–4; Streeck 2001; Whitley 2000: 881).

The main objective of this chapter is to explain the shift in sector specialization in the Finnish economy. According to the popular conception, Finland's performance is a result of Nokia's success. Indeed, the Nokia story is compelling; as a big company in a small country it holds a rare position not only because of its size, but also because it is a technology intensive player. Although it has certainly been an engine in transforming the structure of the Finnish economy, the change in sector specialization is far from being a one-company show. The transformation of both Nokia and the Finnish economy is the outcome of mutually dependent processes. In developing a new specialization, Nokia's role was crucial as it acted as a flagship firm for other Finnish companies (see Rugman and D'Cruz 2000). At the same time public investments in R&D, education, and the telecommunication infrastructure facilitated Nokia's success. In addition, the replacement of bank-group-based finance and governance systems with an internationally open financial market and engagement of international investors facilitated both the transformation of Nokia and the sector specialization.

Nevertheless, despite radical change in several subsystems such as the emergence of a market-driven finance system, Finland is still a coordinated market economy. In different ways this outcome of continuity and change relates to a core topic in the current debate on capitalistic systems: the issue of institutional change and complementarities. How is institutional change brought about and how and to what extent do adjustments in one sphere of a business system affect others (see Deeg, Chapter 2, this volume; Hall and Soskice 2001: 64; Schmidt 2002: 130; Thelen 2003: 209–12). In conceptualizing the intricacy of continuity and change a key question is whether the complementarities of societal subsystems and sector policies can take several forms in collaborated market economies, that they are not only confined to strong lock-ins. Based on the empirical evidence of Nokia and Finland, we will argue that interaction between actors and institutions had the opposite effect. In the Finnish case the critical mediating mechanism is the *horizontal coordination* across sectors.

Variants of institutional theory that ground its frameworks on comparative static often point to the necessity of exogenous shocks in cases of radical breaks. Such an explanatory model would not be far-fetched in explaining the transformation of Nokia and the Finnish economy given the nature of the dramatic events in the early 1990s. The crises of those years certainly impacted on the pace and intensity of reforms. However, in a multi-actor political system such as the Finnish one, the speed and breadth of the changes would not have been possible without a distinct relational policy-making capacity. Above, this sort of capacity was referred to as cross-sectoral horizontal coordination. But the intention of this chapter is to move beyond this generic concept and to identify the quality of the social relationships that provide a strong agency. In specifying the Finnish way of interaction, the chapter makes use of the notions of bonding, bridging, and linking social capital in line with Szreter's (2002) ideal types. The proneness towards the two latter types can constitute a lever for radical change in a coordinated market economy. Bridging and linking social capital can facilitate strategic action between dissimilar and non-symmetric actors.

A relevant question is then what sort of arrangements can facilitate the accumulation of social capital? One answer given has been termed discursive institutions for policy-making (see Hall and Soskice 2001; Schmidt 2002). In the Finnish case, these types of institution have had a critical function in the coordination of political and economic action. At the same time the mediating function of the discursive institutions makes it possible to turn exogenous shocks into endogenous processes of collective sense making and change (see Deeg, Chapter 2, this volume; Sabel 1994; Schmidt 2002: 63). Combined with a temporal dimension, they provide a pertinent framework for analyzing institutional change in the bank-group-based finance and governance systems and the national innovation system. Ultimately, it is the transformation of these subsystems that epitomizes the issue of continuity and change.

The core coordination functions of the bank-group-based finance and governance systems were replaced by new policy-making institutions such as the Science and Technology Policy Council, a body that comprises public as well as private actors. One result of this reconfiguration is that the state's macroeconomic regime and the coordinating functions of the banks have been relegated to the background. Accordingly, the Finnish version of a state-led, coordinated market economy has assumed the character of a 'state-enhanced' system (see Schmidt 2002: 110). The privatization of state-owned corporations and the internationalization of core companies have brought the Finnish development path in line with observed trends in contemporary capitalism; firms have become central players and act as isolated hierarchies (Schmidt 2002; Whitley 1999). But like many other coordinated market economies where firms now play a more prominent role, such as France, neither has Finland become a liberal market economy (Hancké 2002; Schmidt 2002: 111). Coordination and cooperation form a continuing feature of the current Finnish business system. Despite the radical change in banking and corporate governance this mechanism is still to be found especially in the national innovation system but also at all levels and in various spheres and sectors of Finnish society.

For constructing an explanatory model of the change in the Finnish business system, the chapter makes use of analytical narratives (Levi 2002). Interlinked narratives facilitate explication of a layered explanatory model. Hence, the chapter conforms to actor-centred institutionalist approaches that demonstrate how and why strategic actors can mobilize institutional resources for radical change. The chapter is structured as follows: the next section elaborates the theoretical framework for radical change in this specific case. The third section presents a narrative that illustrates the transformation of Nokia and its role in the Finnish ICT cluster. The fourth section delineates the transformation of the different subsystems. The fifth section demonstrates how discursive institutions have emerged, and how the capacity for deliberation has facilitated the formation of new complementary links between subsystems. The concluding section draws together the explanatory layers contained in the three narratives and clarifies the mutual underlying processes between Nokia's ascendancy and the shift in sector specialization.

12.2. Key Features of the Explanatory Model for Change and Continuity

In the case of Nokia and Finland, the concrete outcomes are exceptional. For this reason such empirical observations challenge assumptions of institutional stickiness in coordinated market economies. For constructing an explanatory model for the case at hand it is necessary to exclude the alternative that the outcomes have been determined simply by external shocks. In many institutionalist frameworks, radical changes in coordinated market economies are attributed to external shocks. Given the serious nature of the economic crisis in the early 1990s and the acceleration of the globalization process, there is no doubt that these events triggered reforms. But the histories of Nokia and Finland contradict such a monocausal explanatory mechanism. Nokia's breakthrough in mobile phones, and the shift in sector specialization took place in the 1990s. Processes linked to these outcomes can be traced back to earlier events. To go beyond explanations based on external shocks, we therefore need to construct a multilayered explanation. The explanatory model proposed combines two main elements: a temporal dimension and conceptual tools that capture mediating mechanisms. In multi-actor systems, such as coordinated market economies, change presupposes a strong mediating activity to overcome entrenched interests.

By including the temporal dimension the aim is to show that contingent events in a critical juncture are not only dependent on external shocks, but also on endogenous processes of change. A cause may have long historical roots and their cumulative effect occur at a later point of time (see Pierson 2003: 181). In capturing these intricacies the path dependence framework is pertinent because it problematizes institutional change and continuity as is the case in the present study (Mahoney 2000). Currently the challenge is to develop conceptual tools that distinguish the mechanisms of reproduction from those promoting endogenous institutional change. For explaining the latter, Thelen (2003) proposes two types of mechanisms: institutional layering and conversion.

The call for conceptual tools that can explicate institutional change has in turn placed the importance of agency on the agenda. For this purpose the perspective of actor-centred institutionalism offers a fruitful way to construct how actors can gain agency (Hancké and Goyer, Chapter 3, this volume; Deeg, Chapter 2; Mayntz 2002). As a point of departure, actor-centred institutionalism assumes that institutions are not only constraining but also enabling. Such a perspective implies that institutions contain a repertoire of resources that are latent and that can be mobilized at critical junctures (see Sorge, Chapter 5, this volume). As Deeg puts it, 'institutions evolve, not as a result of some intrinsic law, but as a result of how they are used by relevant actors'. In addition Deeg (Chapter 2, this volume) points out that institutional change requires actor complexity: the interaction of both economic and political actors. Since these actors have a different logic, and it is in general difficult to coordinate increasing numbers of actors, institutional change represents a challenge for any business system. Apparently actors in the Finnish business system have overcome such difficulties. In fact, horizontal coordination has become the hallmark of the Finnish business system. This is also Castells and Himanen's (2002: 150) point: the Finnish model of the information society is uniquely shaped by the interaction between social, political, and economic actors. A key question thus arises, what sort of social interaction provides the Finnish business system with such a high degree of coordination?

For better explaining the dynamics of coordination, and specifying mechanisms that make strategic interaction possible, the chapter introduces concepts that differentiate between various types of social relations and their outcome. Szreter (2002) points out that national institutional configurations differ to a great extent depending on their potential for accumulating various types of social capital. He distinguishes between three main types. *Bonding* social capital consists of knowledge, social relationships, and network positions among *similar* actors. These actors share the same identity and position in the societal division of work. In contrast, *bridging* social capital is based on the encounters of *dissimilar* actors. These actors have different sectoral roots and political orientations, but are nevertheless able to exchange views, learn from each other, and even formulate action programmes that redefine interests and perceived opportunities. This suggests that bridging social capital covers a wide variety as to actors' experience, interests, and aspirations. The third form of social capital is *linking* social capital, and this variant is found where actors are completely dissimilar. Therefore, this form may have various subtypes depending on the nature of exchange relations between actors, ranging from clientelism to a benevolent, altruistic support of resource-weak actors.

Szreter's typology is useful for highlighting a potential variety in coordinated market economies. For predicting either inertia or change in institutional systems the balance between bonding social capital, on the one hand, and bridging and linking social capital on the other could be critical. If the balance is biased in favour of bonding social capital over bridging and linking social capital, institutional change can easily be blocked as strategic actors tend to be myopic, shelter their own interests, and lack the intellectual resources to reframe and initiate systemic modes of action.

In the cold war period, Finland's geopolitical situation was delicate and the national response was to create institutions for cross-sectoral coordination. Since international politics represented the country's main challenge, the state played a key role in such cross-sectoral coordination. These tasks resulted in a state-led tradition that in some ways represented a fit with the business system that evolved in the late nineteenth and early twentieth century. The key components were companies specializing in capital intensive process industries, the emergence of bank-group-based spheres of influence and the importance of state-owned companies in facilitating industrialization and regional development (Lilja and Tainio 1996; Lilja et al. 1992; Moen and Lilja 2001). This institutional legacy enabled strategic actors to accumulate abundant bridging of social capital across sectors. It is a special feature of the Finnish system that special institutions were established to ensure generation of bridging social capital. These institutions, which can be characterized as discursive institutions, comprise the area of policy-making (see Hall and Soskice 2001; Sabel 1994; Schmidt 2002). Discursive institutions serve to enhance actors' political capacity to negotiate reforms in multi-actor political systems. Typically, discursive institutions are established on top of existing systems of governance or as annexes to them. They are thus examples of the layering and conversion of institutions that Thelen has proposed as a potential mechanism for changing institutions.

For analysing the impact of discursive institutions on institutional change, Schmidt (2002) separates ideational and interactive dimensions in policy discourse. The ideational dimension covers the cognitive and normative aspects of generating and justifying core ideas for a policy, and legitimizing them with respect to generally accepted values. The interactive dimension contains two overlapping stages: the coordinative and communicative discourses. This dimension makes it possible to bring different types of actors, their background organizations, and the general public into the analysis. In coordinative market economies the coordinative discourse is more elaborate whereas the communicative discourse is thin. This is connected to the fact that coordinative market economies are multi-actor governance systems. Here, a wide mobilization of different types of actors occurs already during the search phase for new ideas. Due to coordination needs, the most intensive phase is the policy formulation one. When some kind of compromise has been reached, the task of communicating it to the general public is no longer so critical for implementation. By contrast, in liberal market economies, communicative discourse is harder because decisions on policies occur in a single-actor governance system excluding opposition and the wider public.

At some critical junctures in the Finnish case, mobilizations of cross-sectoral elites through discursive institutions were clearly at work.

One important instance was the political process in the late 1970s and the early 1980s that led the government to support a technology-driven development by increasing funding and establishing new policy-making institutions. These organizations institutionalized the interaction between political and economic actor groups that had previously taken place informally or had been more ad hoc in nature. As part of this development, a public debate was initiated and a social movement emerged to reinvent the nation's identity: Finland was to be a knowledge-based society. When external shocks in the early 1990s created pressures to change priorities in sector policies, the existence of this set of discursive institutions was critical for supporting the national system of innovation.

Another important instance occurred in the early 1990s. Due to the bank crisis the bank-group-based governance system evaporated. The transformation of the system of finance and corporate governance clearly had an impact on Finnish sectoral specialization and Nokia's ascendancy. It created space for top management to take action. But the opening of space for new action and practice is not sufficient to explain the shift in sector specialization. Extensive cross-sectoral coordination and new policy institutions were instrumental in bringing about change. This continuity was possible because the new institutions replaced the traditional governance system. The next sections elaborate on how and why cross-sectoral horizontal coordination could survive and facilitate sectoral specialization. For explaining this continuity, we make use of the notion 'discursive institution'. Discursive institutions constitute a vital mechanism for transferring coordination from the bank-group-based governance system to the evolving innovation system. Furthermore, the subsystemic changes caused a reconfiguration of national institutions. The state-led Finnish business system has become more of a 'state-enhanced' system at the same time as firms play a more prominent role (Schmidt 2002: 110). To sum up, radical change in subsystems as well as continuity in cross-sectoral coordination, form key elements in the explanatory model proposed in this chapter.

12.3. Nokia—Institutional Legacy and Strategic Action

Nokia is the undisputed leading firm in the Finnish economy. But it is far from being the only player in the ICT sector. Altogether, there are about 3,000 firms in the cluster, and between 1996 and 2000 these firms experienced an average annual growth rate of 20 per cent (Castells and Himanen 2002: 23). The strong and rapid growth accounts for the shift in Finnish sector specialization. In 1990, the electronic industry accounted for 12 per cent of total commodity exports. By 2000, this share had risen to more than 30 per cent, surpassing that of the former dominating sector, the forest industry (Tainio and Lilja 2003: 84). Although many of the firms in the ICT cluster have developed independently of Nokia (see Ali-Yrkkö et al. 2000: 48–9), Nokia has nevertheless functioned as a flagship company, and in many ways been instrumental in the development of the sector (Rugman and D'Cruz 2000). Nokia has played a key role by outsourcing parts of its production; by diffusing innovation through partnership projects in research and development; and by facilitating internationalization. At the same time, Nokia has benefited from public resources: research funding, the education system, and long-term technology programmes. Public policy and financial resources have facilitated Nokia's development, as have labour market policies, public demand, and public support of related industries.

12.3.1. *How Nokia got leverage for its telecom orientation*

In the early 1990s, Nokia's transformation was sparked off by the collapse of Soviet markets, the deep recession in Europe, and Nokia's own overinvestments in consumer electronics. Nokia's board responded to the crisis by changing management. Immediately after taking office the new CEO, Jorma Ollila, made the strategic decision to create a 'new' Nokia in late 1992. The vision for reinventing the Finnish conglomerate—with roots back to the 1860s—was 'focused, global, telecom-oriented, high value-added products' (Tainio and Lilja 2003: 77).

The focus on telecom represented a break with the conglomerate type of corporation, but Nokia could at the same time rely on a comparatively strong tradition in its new business. First, Nokia itself had a track record in both networks and mobile phones, and could in addition draw on its experience in consumer electronics. Second, the competitive edge of the new business was closely linked to public investments in telecom research and Tele Finland's protracted development work. Third, Nokia could build on a knowledge base developed within the framework of Nordic collaboration dating back to the late 1960s. This publicly funded collaboration, which comprised the participation of industrial players and technical universities in all the Nordic countries, is characterized by some remarkable achievements. One is the development of the Nordic Mobile Telephone System (NMT), the first automatic mobile network in the world covering several countries. The other achievement is the invention of the most advanced second generation (2G) of mobile telecom technology, the Global System for Mobile Communications (GSM) (Hommen and Manninen 2003; Steinbock 2003).

GSM represented the introduction of a digital system in mobile telecom, and when the EC adopted GSM as the industry standard for digital telecommunication in the late 1980s, this decision provided a unique platform for growth in the mobile phone sector. The system became commercially available in the early 1990s, and in fact the GSM became the first commercially operated digital cellular system used on a global scale thus facilitating tremendous business opportunities.

From this perspective, Nokia's timing of its new vision was perfect, and the company mobilized all their efforts to make their products comply with the GSM standard. Typically, Nokia was the first company to deliver a network based on GSM. But in adopting the new technology Nokia added one dimension that strongly widened business opportunities. The company's first step in its design to establish an advantageous competitive position was to redefine the cellular. The stroke of genius was to turn handsets into a consumer product, and to differentiate between various market segments, and using design as a way to approach different segments and geographic markets (Pulkkinen 1997).

In establishing a competitive position Nokia also benefited from the professional labour markets in Finland. The company could draw on a large pool of well-educated people in engineering, science, and design. Technical universities and colleges had for a long time been able to attract talented students, and from an international perspective their scientific standards were high. The egalitarian tradition of incomes policy, favouring low national increases in wages and salaries, had kept the salaries of professionals educated in universities low. This difference increased as a result of the devaluation of the Finnish currency in 1991. Moreover, due to the recession, the unemployment rate rose close to 20 per cent (Lilja 1998). The large and relatively cheap reserve of qualified engineers and other employees could be hired for only one-third of the salaries paid in Silicon Valley. It should be noted that the existence of a highly qualified workforce was the result of the government's long-term policies for promoting technological development in Finland.

12.3.2. *The emergence of collaborative systems in production and innovation*

The first step in developing the ICT network was in the area of production. Faced with the explosive growth in the global telecom market, Nokia chose to outsource parts of the production. In building up a large-scale business, more and more elements were subcontracted. Finnish companies were engaged for customized inputs and services, particularly in electronic manufacturing services, automation, and precision, whereas standardized products were bought globally. However, the explosive growth on the one hand, and changing product demand on the other led to the first profitability crisis of the new Nokia. Competitors started to spread rumours that the Nokia story was over (Tainio and Lilja 2003: 78). By the end of 1995 top management intervened, and had the supply chain streamlined in order to meet the volatile market and changing priorities in product categories.

The reorganizing involved the introduction of assembler services. For Nokia the assembler system involved the reduction of coordination tasks at the same time as it eased the problem of the mismatch between the life spans of products and production technologies. It reduced the number of direct suppliers because a few key suppliers assumed the role of assembler or system suppliers. Instead of delivering products directly to Nokia, subsystem suppliers delivered to assemblers. The new system of logistics—that was expanded worldwide—made Nokia a flagship company of a complex value chain. In order to monitor market trends and take quick action, it depended on transparency and a rapid sharing of information. This requirement induced the development of permanent partners and the globalization of suppliers (see Rugman and D'Cruz 2000).

For Nokia it was advantageous that contract producers and partners coevolved with its own development. To have suppliers and partners in the technical forefront allowed Nokia to concentrate on its own core areas. Cooperation with partners was an important channel for diffusing the latest knowledge and increasing competences. Cooperation took place at either the practical level or through teamwork to solve different problems. At the same time, Nokia encouraged partners in the Finnish ICT cluster to follow its lead and establish operations abroad. In this way Nokia could benefit from highly qualified supply and subcontractor networks worldwide. In this endeavour, partners could also benefit directly from Nokia's support. Nokia either helped them to obtain new customers, 'Nokia has recommended us', or taught companies to understand market requirements better. As a result, some supplier companies have developed their own network, and some have even grown to become big companies in their own right. Elcoteq, Nokia's contract manufacturer, is the largest European electronic manufacturing service company (EMS). At the beginning of the new millennium there were about 240 Finnish EMSs that were diversifying their customers (Ali-Yrkkö 2001; Castells and Himanen 2002).

When Nokia started preparing for the launch of the third generation mobile telecom (3G) in the latter part of the 1990s, this sort of horizontal coordination was also extended to include R&D activities and software development (Ali-Yrkkö 2001: 46). Although this sort of sensitive inter-firm relationship was new at the time, it clearly has a prehistory in the long tradition of formal and informal cooperation in the Finnish business system. This sort of cooperation was facilitated by the public technology programmes and the cooperation clause linked to them (Ali-Yrkkö and Hermans 2002: 18). This clause also included cooperation with universities or public research institutions. And when the partnership mode was taken further to involve the sharing not only of risks, but also of profits, this legacy was highly relevant. Moreover, this perspective also explicates why newly founded software companies can be global right from the start, and why Nokia came to function as an engine for the globalization of the emerging ICT sector in Finland.

Thus, Nokia's role in the shift of sector specialization involves direct action for diffusing knowledge, promoting innovation, and encouraging growth. Cooperation has been promoted at all phases of the innovation chain. For the Finnish, ICT cluster cooperation in R&D has had an overall positive effect on the level of technology. Universities have been helped to acquire the latest technology. Companies have been supported to develop their technology through cooperation at the practical level, through the rotation of employees between companies, and by investing in entrepreneurial firms. Even Nokia's own employees are helped and encouraged to establish their own companies. Through this entrepreneurial strategy Nokia has been creating and offering highly specialized roles for external high-tech companies. The telecom giant incorporates the products of SMEs into its own solutions. To support the creation of new businesses and stimulating renewal, Nokia founded its own funding institution, Nokia Venture Organization. The result of these efforts can be seen in the fact that Finland has become a node in the world's telecom innovation system. Several multinational companies such as Hewlett Packard, Siemens, and Ericsson have established R&D units in the Finnish 'mobile valley'

(Castells and Himanen 2002: 27). Nokia's centrifugal and centripetal functions in this development process are related to its continuous success.

12.3.3. *Moving into software*

By 1998, movement towards the third generation triggered a reorientation of the company. The 3G implies the convergence of mobile phone, internet, media, and PC businesses. Realizing the limits of the growth path of the 2G, Nokia has changed its focus to software development. This represents the second, and ongoing, transformation of its technological regime. Maintaining leadership into the 3G means the capability to set industry standards for a wide variety of technologies. In reaching for this goal Nokia has strongly increased its R&D input. By the end of 2002, 19,500 employees or 38 per cent of its total workforce were engaged in R&D activities worldwide, and 60 per cent of the R&D spending was used on software (Helsingin Sanomat, 13 February 2003). The R&D activities take place in fifty-five research centres in fifteen different countries. Hardly any other multinational company has internationalized R&D to such an extent (IMF 2001), a circumstance that illustrates the limits to growth for a big company in a small country.

To support the new corporate strategy, Nokia has restructured its organization twice in the last couple of years. The motivation for the restructuring is to retain and deepen its decentralized entrepreneurial force, and to be able to move faster and be more flexible. Top management's commitment to renewal is based on the acknowledgement that Nokia is carrying out creative destruction. For this purpose, the former monolithic structure of the Mobile Phone Division was first split into nine separate business centres in 2002. The difficulty in finding the 'right' solution is explicated by the fact that the top management worked on it for half a year in weekly internal debates. The second structural change was announced in September 2003. This time the company was divided into four different divisions: mobile phones, mobile multimedia products, enterprise solutions, and mobile telecom networks (*Financial Times*, 27 September 2003). By way of a matrix organization all the divisions have the same modular business infrastructure that contains R&D, marketing, strategic management, production, logistics, IT, and other support functions. According to the rhetoric, the divisions are responsible for the agility, and the modular infrastructure for the economies of scale. To preserve an entrepreneurial spirit, the divisions are kept relatively small. The divisions' multifunctional competences facilitate cooperation with strategic partners and other players in what Nokia calls the wider ecosystem. This sort of cross-functional cooperation between partners is referred to as the extended firm (see Kodama 2003).

The joint venture company Symbian is an example of operations in the extended firm. In 1998 Nokia, Psion, Ericsson, and Motorola established the new company (*Wall Street Journal*, 22 May 2002). The aim was to speed up the development of software for the 3G, and with the hidden agenda of locking Microsoft out of the mobile phone market. Earlier the same year Microsoft had approached Nokia to sound out the prospects for collaboration in software development, but Nokia turned down the offer. However, Symbian in its turn, proved to be a partial failure. The joint venture failed to make advances in software development due to the bureaucratic structure of this inter-firm collaboration. Nokia chose therefore to bring a core part of the software project back in-house, and left Symbian in charge of the development of the operating system for the 3G multimedia terminal.

The in-house software project comprised the development of parts that control the basic functions of the handset and that takes care of the linkages to other equipment such as internet, PCs, etc. In other words, it was the project that was to take Nokia a step further into the 3G. By managing it in-house, Nokia succeeded quickly in producing the new software, called Series 60, for the use in its 3G multimedia terminals. When Nokia in November 2001 announced that its new software would be available for all, the rest of the industry was taken by surprise. Moreover, the company proclaimed that it would license the software at very low rates and make its source code—which shows how Series 60 is written—available. From Nokia's point of view, the option to keep the software to itself would entail the risk that service providers would not be capable or willing to invest in services that make use of its 3G. The strategy is to opt for a smaller share of a rapidly growing market than to have a dominant share in a slumbering market.

Giving away the most valuable software product to rivals is considered a hazardous game. Nokia's strategic initiative to construct an extended enterprise with organic linkages to its business centres has stunned the business community. Nokia's experiment is being watched with 'a mix of curiosity and dread' (*Business Week*, 1 July 2002). Another example of this strategy is the establishment of the 'Open Mobile Alliance' in 2001. It is a transnational organization of the 300 biggest ICT companies in the world, including Microsoft, as its members. This sort of industry coordination represents in many ways *a replication of the Finnish national business system at the global level.* Nokia's advantage is that it has recruited and educated managers who know how to play this type of collaborative game. The outcome of this extended profit-sharing strategy remains to be seen.[1]

12.4. Contingent Platforms of Change

12.4.1. *The end of the bank-group-based governance system, and the emergence of a stock-market-driven finance system*

Until the early 1990s, leading banks formed hubs of interrelated non-financial companies in the Finnish business system. Through ownership in flagship companies, interlocking directories, and customer relationships the biggest commercial banks had been able to build a strategic position in the economy. The dominant logic of this governance system was based on long-term investments in capital-intensive production systems, and it rested on a system of risk sharing between banks, corporations, and the state. The state had a double role. First, it was the owner of industrial enterprises in several capital-intensive industries as well as of banks. Second, it had tools for macroeconomic regulation. As a final resort to restore the competitiveness of Finnish firms, it could devaluate the currency (Lilja et al. 1992; Moen and Lilja 2001). When Finland decided to join the European Economic and Monetary Union in the 1990s (formally on 1 January, 1995), devaluations were taken out of the arsenal.

The bank-group-based governance system came to an end with the bank crisis in the early 1990s (Tainio et al. 1997). The crisis led to a restructuring process that started with the liquidation of the largest retailing bank. Its operations were divided among the remaining banks. Thereafter, the two leading commercial banks merged. The new organizational unity constituted the Finnish roots of the current pan-Nordic bank, Nordea. In addition, several retail banks, investment banks, and insurance companies merged. On the Nordic level, Nordea represents the start of a consolidation process in the finance sector (Tainio and Lilja 2003).

---

[1] By 2002 three companies, Siemens, Matsushita, and Samsung, have agreed to license the Series 60. The market share of these four companies is about 60 per cent (*Financial Times*, 1 September 2002).

The first steps in the process of loosening ties between national banks and large companies were taken in the early 1980s when the state started to deregulate the financial market. Large industrial companies began experimenting with different types of 'independent' financial operations. The biggest non-financial corporations created the so-called 'grey markets' for overnight lending, and operated as 'industrial bankers'. At the same time, foreign banks entered the Finnish finance market by establishing branch offices, and the Finnish based banks started international operations. Finnish non-financial companies were also able to borrow money directly from the international markets.

The second step was linked to the restructuring in the early 1990s. After the concentration at the national level was finalized, the previous pattern of ownership and customer risks became too high for the remaining banks. To reduce customer risks, lending was limited, and ownership stakes in companies were reduced. Ownership stakes were also sold to international investors through the stock exchange. This was a new phenomenon in Finland, and was introduced in 1993 as a part of Finland's negotiations to join the European Union. At the same time the taxation of company profits and capital incomes were reduced to facilitate the accumulation of own capital in companies, and to activate private investments in stock markets.

The restructuring of the finance sector had two important consequences. First, the bank-group-based spheres of influence withered away, and the systems of finance and corporate governance became separated. Second, the restructuring gave impetus for banks to concentrate on financial services as the main source of their revenue instead of power games for strategic ownership in core companies. At the same time the activation of the Finnish financial markets was reinforced through the entry of international venture capital companies. For start-up companies in the new economy the emergence of a market-driven finance system was important, since they obtained a complementary source of risk capital. In turn the availability of venture capital contributed to the transformation of the financial system from a credit-based to a stock-market oriented system.

The disintegration of the traditional finance and governance system also opened windows of opportunity for managerial strategic action. Previously managerial action had been restrained through negotiation with banks and other owners because in general the solidity of the balance sheets was weak. Even customers could be involved in such negotiations. These linkages promoted strategic initiatives that maximized long-term growth opportunities and value creation. However, this practice was at odds with the managerial doctrines, tools, and fads originating in America that were being continuously introduced through consulting companies, and management education, and not least with expatriots' experience when Finnish firms started to internationalize in the 1980s. When the ties to banks were loosened and alternative sources of equity capital became available, space was created for the board of directors and managerial teams to design corporate and business strategies on their own. As a consequence, Finnish firms started to act as isolated hierarchies in the financial and product markets. However, as to the development of competences the collaborative tradition has prevailed.

The significance of the disintegration of the traditional governance system is illustrative in the case of Nokia. To implement Nokia's new vision the company needed fresh capital. Ollila, who had a background in international banking, managed to sell the vision of the new Nokia to selected American investors. The next step was to list the company on the New York Stock Exchange in 1994. Fresh capital created slack resources for the restructuring of the company and for a transformative innovation strategy. To some extent, Nokia showed the way out of bank control. Due to its exceptional profits, the company served as an eye opener for international investors. Nokia catalyzed their interest in other Finnish-based companies. Sonera, the former state-owned telecom company, is the most visible example of this (Tainio 2003). The cumulative effect was that the Helsinki Stock Exchange (HEX) became the eighth largest in Europe. True, 60 per cent of its market capitalization was and still is based on the shares of Nokia. Nonetheless, the mutually reinforcing dynamics of the restructuring of the finance system and liberated managerial action was instrumental in providing the new Finnish economy with sufficient equity capital.

12.4.2. *Governmental policies and the national innovation system*

The deep economic crisis in the beginning of the 1990s also opened avenues for a new economic policy. Two measures in particular contributed to promote innovation and technical change. The first was the decision to amplify R&D spending in 1993. This policy was taken further in the period 1996–99 when investments in R&D rose and reached above 3 per cent of the GDP and the average growth of the GDP was close to 5 per cent (www.research.fi). The second measure involved the strengthening of the interorganizational linkages in the national innovation system.

The main organizations in what was later to be termed the national innovation system were established in the 1980s. The reason for the institutional innovation was a decision-in-principle by the government in 1982 to support a technology-driven development. Two new institutions in particular were crucial for the development of the new sector specialization: Tekes and the Science and Technology Policy Council. Tekes, The National Technology Agency, was founded in 1983. It complemented the mission of Sitra (the Finnish National Fund for Research and Development) founded in 1967. While Sitra is a think-tank and venture capital investor, Tekes obtained the task of funding the long-term R&D projects of companies, research institutes, and universities. The Science and Technology Policy Council (STPC) was founded in 1987. For enhancing technology policy, it was decisive that this policy area was included in the state's highly prestigious Science Policy Council, which had been in operation since 1963. In establishing a common council for the two policy areas, potential conflicts and rivalries were thereby curbed.

As a political tool to promote innovation and technological change, the STPC adopted the concept of a national innovation system in 1990 (Miettinen 2002: 62). Finland was thus the first country to make use of the concept and to approach innovation processes from a systemic perspective. In fact, key actors of the policy-making organizations of the Finnish innovation system had been part of the researcher group that coined the National Innovation System (NIS) concept (Ormala, interview 30 August 2002). In 1993, when the STPC declared that Finland's future was to become a knowledge-based society, the institutional framework for approaching this goal was already in place.

Parallel with the development of the institutions of the national innovation system, a sector-based policy for supporting competitiveness of companies was designed by the Ministry of Trade and Industry. The main strategy was to promote cooperation between companies and between companies and research institutions. The new focus on clusters was, however, not new in Finland. In fact, the strength of the forest industry sector had been based on cooperation between companies, the supplier industries, research institutes, and universities. The novelty in the beginning of the 1990s was related to the identification of new sectors that had a higher growth potential than the forest industry sector. The ICT sector was given the highest priority.

Public programmes for promoting the development of networks have resulted in a significant increase in the degree of cooperation. In 2000, 80 per cent of projects financed by Tekes were allocated to firms working in networks with business. A comparative survey conducted by the European Union in various member countries shows that by the turn of the century 70 per cent of all innovating companies in Finland had established contact with R&D institutions or educational institutions (EU 2001; Routti 2003). On this indicator Finland had the highest position among EU countries. For this reason the IMD World Competitiveness Index has ranked Finland as the world leader in technological and research cooperation (Asplund 2000: 2; www.research.fi/index_en.html). For the upgrading of the national innovation system the flow of knowledge resulting from cooperation has been vital. As pointed out above, Nokia could successfully reap the fruits of this policy when it started its exceptional growth.

The use of the concept of national innovation system resulted in a widening of the technology policy concept. Traditionally it comprised natural and technical sciences. The new concept technology policy was to include all spheres of the educational system. A feature of the Finnish educational system is that it has a strong technology orientation. This is due to the fact that the German education system served as a model. Between the 1960s and the 1980s the university system was extended to the whole country. When this process was completed, a second initiative was launched to construct a system of polytechnics. The latter initiative was motivated by the need to provide a skilled labour force to knowledge-intensive sectors. Currently the number of university level institutions amounts to twenty, and the number of polytechnics to twenty-nine. Though the system of polytechnics is a rather recent one, the percentage of people between 24 and 64 years of age with a tertiary degree in science is comparatively high. In 2001 the percentage amounted to 32 per cent, a level which matched that of Sweden, but which was somewhat lower than the leading countries Canada (41 per cent), the United States (37 per cent), and Ireland (36 per cent). (www.stat.fi/tp/maailmanumeroina/11_koulutus.xls; see Crouch et al. 1999: 72–3).

12.4.3. *New complementarities between subsystems*

The main conclusion at this stage of the analysis is that cross-sectoral relations did not vanish despite the fact that the bank-group-based governance system dissolved. When this linkage was loosened, the former partners created new links fitting their new strategies. The banks consolidated partly at the national level and partly at the Nordic level. Finland-based companies integrated into international finance markets to finance growth in global markets. At the same time the emergence of a domestic venture capital market has served to support start-ups in the new high-tech sectors.

In a similar vein, the state has created new policy instruments to enhance national competitiveness. Long-term competence development and cross-sectoral collaboration have replaced direct state intervention and macroeconomic regulation to a large extent. In the new policy regime, policy-making institutions, such as the STPC, exercise the new coordinating functions. Their primary coordinating role is linked to the creation of political visions and goals, and to support long-term development of competence for strategic clusters. In this perspective the new coordinating activities correspond well to the perception of a knowledge-based economy. Due to this shift in the locus of the coordination system, the Finnish business system can still be characterized as a coordinated market economy. But a key question remains to be answered: how could the change in coordination practices be orchestrated when the traditional coordinating institutions evaporated? To answer this question, the next section will describe the evolvement of a special institutional layer: over time, special institutions have been formed to strengthen and support the deliberation of cross-sectoral elites.

12.5. Discursive Institutions: Policy-Making and Learning *fora* for Elites

The use of participatory councils and special educational systems for cross-sectoral elites constitutes a key mechanism in the Finnish decision-making system. The Science and Technology Policy Council and a few educational systems are briefly sketched to elucidate their functions. Several of these institutions were created at critical junctures in order to mould the search for ideas and appropriate strategies.

In addition to the Science and Technology Policy Council there is one council for every important policy area such as the National Defence and the Economic Policy Councils. The Prime Minister chairs all these councils, and they have several ministers and representatives from different stakeholders organizations as members. For creating consensus on common policy goals and strategies, these bodies have played a decisive role. When Finland decided to become a leading information society and at the same time joined the European Union, the importance of the STPC was enhanced. This council crosses all kinds of dividing lines in society, and in this capacity it is a unique institution by international standards. The council consists of a mixture of public and private members, and is headed by the Prime Minister. Other members include eight ministers, ten high-ranking representatives from universities, industry, the Academy of Finland, Tekes, and in line with the neocorporate tradition the peak organizations of both employers' and employees' organizations. One of the industry representatives has been Nokia's managing director. In policy-making processes the council constitutes a key institution because it ensures the coordination of decisions between ministries. It can even make de facto decisions above the level of sectoral ministries. Due to its broad representation the issue of technology policy was brought on the agenda to wide circles in the state administration and in society at large.

The events that led to the establishment of the STPC and other key institutions in the Finnish innovation system, took place at the turn of the 1980s. Finland, like other western countries, faced a deep recession. The issue was raised whether the industrial backbone of the economy had to be widened. To suggest measures a state committee was set up to assess the role of technology in societal development, and define key areas for state-funded research and development work. One of the conclusions the committee came up with was that technology creates more jobs than it destroys. This assessment was used to mobilize stakeholders to support a policy for technology-driven development based on high technology. The government followed up the initiative, and in 1982 it made the decision-in-principle to increase investments in R&D. Four technology programmes were launched, three of them in electronics and ICT (Ormala, interview 30 August 2002). Soon after, the debate for turning Finland into a knowledge-based society by investing in R&D started. The then CEO of Nokia, Kari Kairamo, was the most visible figurehead for the policy initiative. Also being elected to the position of the chairman of the Confederation of Finnish Industry, he was able to push the issue to the agenda of the government. The formation of the Science and Technology Policy Council in 1987 was a significant step in this process.

In the deep economic crisis in the early 1990s, the Science and Technology Policy Council was well prepared to play the role as

an advocate for redirecting the focus of the economic policy towards
the national innovation system (Miettinen 2002: 60–3). It was instrumental in creating a coherent policy in the area of R&D. The striking
feature of this policy change was that all sorts of societal stakeholders accepted it (Aho, interview 17 September 2003). Even the trade
unions consented to the reallocation of resources despite an unemployment rate of about 20 per cent. Debates prior to the decision partly
explain why the redefinition of interests and identities could occur
so smoothly.

However, the effect of discussion would not have been sufficient
if it had only been restricted to the top level of decision-makers. For
providing platforms for the ideational and interactive dimension of
policy-making, another type of discursive institutions was instrumental. It consists of special courses that are designed for members of
cross-sectoral elites. All the course institutions have been initiated in
relation to critical junctures, starting with the Ministry of Defence's initiative in 1961. Since then educational courses have diffused to several
policy areas such as forestry, social policy, and healthcare. For changing identities and reinterpreting class and group specific interests,
the economic policy course institution stands out.

Like the roots of Tekes and the STPC, the economic policy courses
had their origin in the recession of the late 1970s. In 1977 the
Government called in a large number of representatives to a seminar to
discuss national economic strategy. The intention was to establish consensus among interest organizations and political parties for measures
to be taken. Although the seminar became a symbol of the consensus
policy, the issue of long-term economic strategy was difficult. For
this reason, a special course for strategic actors in companies, interest
organizations, and the state was initiated. The idea behind the course
was to concentrate on long-term economic issues instead of immediate
policy decisions. The model was educational courses designed for top
management. The practical work of planning and implementation was
given to Sitra. The following year it became a permanent institution. In
2003, after twenty-five years of operation, about 1,800 elite members
have participated in the programme (www.sitra.fi/; Allén and Karhu
2003: 12–41).

In retrospect, the evolution of discursive institutions is remarkable because the Finnish political system was characterized by strong
centralization until the late 1970s. However, the practice of ground-
ing policy-making on a broad societal and political basis started
before this point of time. For dealing with relations between classes

and the division of economic gains Finland copied the centralized system of incomes policy negotiations from the other Nordic countries. The system was introduced and developed during the long presidency of Urho Kekkonen (1956–81). Kekkonen used his constitutional power to form governments that included political parties from the centre to the left. These coalition governments were instrumental in bringing various interest groups into negotiations. One of the main outcomes from this process was the emergence of a strong developmental state. Over time, the negotiations of the state, political parties, and interest groups were extended to almost all policy areas, and eventually led to the formation of the Finnish welfare state. When new linkages between societal subsystems were needed from the early 1990s on, the accumulated bridging social capital was in place due to the discursive institutions. 'National projects' could accordingly be identified and implemented.

To sum up, through councils, committees, and educational institutions the interactive dimension of policy discourse has become exceptionally widespread in Finland. In off-path subsystemic changes, especially in the national innovation system, the STPC constituted a mediating mechanism and a lever. In other sectoral policy-making areas the courses have functioned as a source of new ideas for policy programmes, *fora* for debating conflicting perspectives, and triggers for reinterpretation of interests and identity of strategic actors (see Sabel 1994). Elite members have contributed to policy formation across sectors and bridging social capital has been accumulated at the personal level.

12.6. Conclusion

The analytical narratives constructed in the chapter comprise a complex explanatory model for Nokia's breakthrough as a mobile phone company, and for the change in sector specialization in the Finnish economy. The theoretical thrust of this exercise has been to question the stickiness hypothesis of coordinated market economies. For this purpose, the Finnish case is relevant. It demonstrates that the complementarities of subsystems do not necessary lead to inertia. On the contrary, horizontal coordination provided the Finnish business system with a strong relational policy-making capacity. The particular achievement of this study has been to specify the quality of social relationships that underlies the Finnish way of strategic interaction. In the present case, the accumulation of bridging and linking social capital made possible a swift reshuffling of actors and resources. At the same time the chapter has stressed the interrelation between Nokia's ascendancy and the shift in sector specialization, and the protracted nature of theses processes (see Pierson 2003). In illustrating the complexity of these processes and mediating mechanisms, the analytical narratives in the chapter have highlighted the following interrelated sequences of action.

First, Nokia's breakthrough in mobile phones sparked off a shift in sector specialization in the Finnish economy. Nokia played an important role as a flagship firm. It outsourced parts of its production, promoted common projects in research and development, and supported different types of innovative activities. With the additional support of international investors, companies based in Finland followed Nokia and internationalized their operations. Nokia's success encouraged other Finnish companies to investment more in R&D, and as a result the whole national innovation system was strengthened. These interrelated processes were, however, built on technological capabilities that were developed in the 1970s and the 1980s by the Finnish telecommunication sector. Both public and private investments in R&D were essential. Moreover, even in the 1990s Nokia benefited from public technology and education policies. These investments were paid back in the 1990s with a multiplier that would have been inconceivable at the time the investments were made.

Second, the role of the state diminished as the availability of macroeconomic tools for direct intervention in the economy declined during the 1990s. For this reason, support for the national system of innovation became the Government's main economic policy instrument. In addition, a cluster-based industrial strategy encouraged cooperation across sectors: between companies, and between firms and research institutions. In defining and implementing the new technology-driven development mode, the innovation system in general, and the Science and Technology Policy Council in particular, played a crucial role in coordinating activities. In this capacity, the innovation system has become the most prominent subsystem for cross-sectoral cooperation and coordination, and as such replaced the bank-group-based system.

These event histories cannot be understood without focusing attention on the tradition of cross-sectoral discursive institutions. This layer constituted a participatory channel, and in addition served to accumulate bridging social capital. Cross-sectoral ties facilitated the relocation of horizontal coordination in the national system of innovation. Therefore, Finland still fits the category of a coordinated market economy. The Finnish case thus supports the argument that similar institutional constellations, framed by the concept of coordinated market economies, can lead to radically different outcomes during specific historical periods (see Hancké and Goyer, Chapter 3, this volume). For elaborating the path dependence concept further, the Finnish case is also relevant, because it includes mechanisms of both change and reproduction. In explaining the outcome, the obvious differentiating mechanism is the constellation of social capital. Different constellations of accumulated social capital can constitute the critical differentiating mechanism between coordinated market economies. In order to investigate the role of bridging and linking social capital as a differentiating mechanism, further case studies are needed.

REFERENCES

Interviews

Aho, Esko, Partner, Verbatum Ltd, Prime Minister in 1991–1995, President of Sitra, since the 1st of July 2004; interview in September 17, 2003.
Ormala, Erkki, Technology Policy Director, Nokia Corporation, former secretary general of the Science and Technology Policy Council; interview in August 30 2002.

Newspaper and magazine articles

Financial Times
Helsingin Sanomat
Newsweek
Wall Street Journal Europe

Internet sites

www.research.fi
www.sitra.fi
www.stat.fi/tp/maailmanumeroina/11_koulutus.xls

Literature

Ali-Yrkkö, J. (2001). *Nokia's Network: Gaining Competitiveness from Co-operation.* ETLA B-162. Helsinki: Taloustieto Oy.

—— and Hermans, R. (2002). *Nokia in the Finnish Innovation System*. Helsinki: ETLA Discussion paper No. 811.

——, Paija, L., Reilly, R., and Ylä-Anttila, P. (2000). *Nokia: Big Company in a Small Country*. ETLA B-162. Helsinki: Taloustieto Oy.

Allén, T. and Karhu, M. (eds.) (2003). *Pennejä taivaasta? Talouspolitiikkakoulutusta 25 vuotta*. Helsinki: Edita Prima Oy.

Amable, B. (2003). *The Diversity of Modern Capitalism*. Oxford: Oxford University Press.

Asplund, R. (ed.) (2000). *Public R&D Funding, Technological Competitiveness, productivity, and job creation*. Helsinki: ETLA.

Castells, M. and Himanen, P. (2002). *The Information Society and the Welfare State. The Finnish Model*. Oxford: Oxford University Press.

Crouch, C., Finegold, D., and Sako, M. (1999). *Are Skills the Answer? The Political Economy of Skill Creation in Advanced Industrial Countries*. Oxford: Oxford University Press.

Edquist, C. (2003). 'The Fixed Internet and Mobile Telecommunications Sectoral System of Innovation: Developments in Equipment, Access and Content'. In: C. Edquist (ed.), *Internet and Mobile Telecommunications System of Innovation*. Cheltenham: Edward Elgar, pp. 1–39.

EU (2001). *Towards a European Research Area—Key Figures*, Special Edition. Belgium: EU.

Häikiö, M. (2002). *Nokia. The Inside Story*. Helsinki: Edita.

Hall, P. and Soskice, D. (2001). *Varieties of Capitalism. The Institutional Foundations of Comparative Advantage*. Oxford: Oxford University Press.

Hancké, B. (2002). *Large Firms and Institutional Change. Industrial Renewal and Economic Restructuring in France*. Oxford: Oxford University Press.

Hommen, L. and Manninen, E. (2003). 'The Global System for Mobile Telecommunications (GSM): Second Generation'. In: C. Edquist (ed.), *Internet and Mobile Telecommunications System of Innovation*. Cheltenham: Edward Elgar, pp. 71–128.

IMF (2001). 'Finland: Selected Issues'. IMF Country Report No. 01/215. Washington: International Monetary Fund.

Kodama, M. (2003). 'Strategic Innovation in Traditional Big Business: Case Studies of Two Japanese Companies'. *Organization Studies* 24(2): 235–68.

Levi, M. (2002). 'Modelling Complex Historical Processes with Analytical Narratives'. In: R. Mayntz (ed.), *Akteure—Mechanismen—Modellen*. Frankfurt am Main: Campus Verlag, pp. 108–27.

Lilja, K. (1998). 'Finland: Continuity and Modest Moves Towards Company-Level Corporatism'. In: A. Ferner and R. Hyman (eds.), *Changing Industrial Relations in Europe*. Oxford: Basil Blackwell, pp. 171–89.

—— and Tainio R. (1996). 'The Nature of the Typical Finnish Firm'. In: R. Whitley and P. Kristensen (eds.), *The Changing European Firm*. London: Routledge, pp. 159–91.

Lilja, K., Räsänen K., and Tainio R. (1992). 'A Dominant Business Recipe: The Forest Sector in Finland'. In: R. Whitley (ed.), *European Business Systems*. London: Sage, pp. 137–54.

Mahoney, J. (2000). 'Path-Dependence in Historical Sociology'. *Theory and Society* 30: 507–48.

——and Rueschemeyer D. (eds.) (2003). *Comparative Historical Analysis in the Social Sciences*. Cambridge: Cambridge University Press.

Mayntz, R. (2002) (ed.), Akteure–Mechanismen–Modelle. Zur Theoriefäigkeit makro-sozialer Analysen, Frankfurt/New York: Campus Verlag.

Miettinen, R. (2002). National Innovation System: Scientific Concept or Political Rhetoric. Helsinki: Edita.

Moen, E. and Lilja, K. (2001). 'Constructing Global Corporations: Contrasting National Legacies in the Nordic Forest Industry'. In: G. Morgan, P. H. Kristensen, and R. Whitley (eds.), *The Multinational Firm. Organizing Across Institutional and National Divides*. Oxford: Oxford University Press, pp. 97–121.

Pierson, P. (2003). 'Big, Slow-Moving, and Invisible: Macrosocial Processes in the Study of Comparative Politics'. In: J. Mahoney and D. Rueschemeyer (eds.), *Comparative Historical Analysis in the Social Sciences*. Cambridge: Cambridge University Press.

Pulkkinen, M. (1997). *The Breakthrough of Nokia Mobile Phones*. Helsinki: HSE Series A-122.

Routti, J. (2003). 'Research and Innovation in Finland—Transformation into a Knowledge Economy'. Keynote Speech at Knowledge Economy Forum II. Helsinki, 26–28 March 2003.

Rugman, A. M. and D'Cruz, J. R. (2000). *Multinationals as Flagship Firms*. Oxford: Oxford University Press.

Sabel, C. F. (1994). 'Learning by Monitoring: The Institutions of Economic Development'. In: N. J. Smelser and R. Swedberg (eds.), *The Handbook of Economic Sociology*. New York: Princeton University Press, pp. 137–65.

Schmidt, V. A. (2002). *The Futures of European Capitalism*. Oxford: Oxford University Press.

Steinbock, D. (2003). *Wireless Horizon. Strategy and Competition in the Worldwide Mobile Marketplace*. New York: Amacom.

Streeck, W. (2001). 'Introduction: Explorations into the Origins of Nonliberal Capitalism in Germany and Japan'. In: W. Streeck and K. Yamamura (eds.), *The Origin of Nonliberal Capitalism*. Ithaca: Cornell University Press, pp. 1–38.

Szreter, S. (2002). 'The State of Social Capital: Bringing Back in Power, Politics, and History'. *Theory and Society* 31: 573–621.

Tainio, R. (2003). 'Financialization of Key Finnish Companies'. *Nordiske Organisasjon Studier* 3(2): 61–86.

—— and Lilja, K. (2003). 'The Finnish Business System in Transition: Outcomes, Actors and their Influence'. In: B. Czarniawska and G. Sevón (eds.), *Northern Light—Organization Theory in Scandinavia*. Trelleborg: Liber/Abstrakt/Copenhagen Business School Press, pp. 69–87.

——, ——, and Santalainen, T. (1997). 'Changing Managerial Competitive Practices in the Context of Growth and Decline in the Finnish Banking Sector'. In: G. Morgan and D. Knights (eds.), *Regulation and Deregulation in European Financial Services*. London: Macmillan, pp. 201 15.

Thelen, K. (2003). 'How Institutions Evolve: Insights from Comparative Historical Analysis'. In: J. Mahoney and D. Rueschemeyer (eds.), *Comparative Historical Analysis in the Social Sciences*. Cambridge: Cambridge University Press.

Whitley, R. (1999). *Divergent Capitalism: The Social Structuring and Change of Business Systems*. Oxford: Oxford University Press.

—— (2000). 'The Institutional Structuring of Innovation Strategies: Business Systems, Firm Types and Patterns of Technical Change in Different Market Economies'. *Organization Studies* 21(5): 855–86.

AFTERWORDS

13

Modelling National Business Systems and the Civilizing Process

PEER HULL KRISTENSEN

13.1. What We have Learned from the Comparative Study of National Capitalisms?

During the last couple of decades the comparative study of national business systems has gradually compiled material allowing us to see that neither the social space occupied by the capitalist enterprise in different societies nor its nature as a social entity is given by its universal function as an agency in the market or as an expression of class relations in the capitalist mode of production.

Rather than determining the evolution of other social phenomena, the capitalist enterprise and the market are entangled in a mutual evolutionary development with these other phenomena, which in part follow evolutionary patterns that emerge from endogenous political conflicts, discourses, or institutional preconditions within the spheres or fields themselves. Conversely, Whitley (1992*a,b*, 1999), Whitley and Kristensen (1996, 1997) have emphasized repeatedly that the firm needs to respond to such institutional preconditions in distinct ways in each society in order to make effective social and economic use of institutions. In this way the nature of the firm, for example, must build upon the educational and vocational training system of a country, and must accept to have the characteristics of the resulting career paths of different groups penetrating its organization, if it is to make efficient use of the general labour market. In a similar way the firm must obey the rules that guide behaviour in relation to its financial institutions if it wants access to its particular way of providing cheap financial resources, often tacitly importing distinct governance principles from the larger society. Rather than universalistic capitalist relations of production, this results in complicated and distinct authority relations between different social groups in distinct national and regional contexts. Thus hierarchies within and among firms are constituted in various ways so that cooperation, competition, and rivalry combine in each society in particular ways making distinct processes of evolution possible. In a similar way, the firm's position in state developmental polities and the game of mutual ranking among firms and other forms of organizations influence its social space toward institutional formations of other social spheres, such as the state and the financial system, and not only its capacity to accumulate capital by being competitive in a market.

The emergent understanding of performance criteria differing among countries (Quack et al. 2000) is of particular importance. Western countries tend to measure both firms and nations according to universalistic performance criteria (i.e. profitability, growth of GDP). However, it is obvious from the comparative study of business systems that progress is measured quite differently among countries dependent on how social groups have been composed, how they have constituted their particular and mutual aspirations and on the institutional formations surrounding these groups and which help them direct their search for ways to achieve the fulfilment and wider evolution of these aspirations. Contextual rationalities surrounding firms simply differ widely among countries. Rather than believing institutions in a country to be in the last case measured according to their contribution to the evolution of firms and the economy 'an und für sich', coevolution is taking place in which the firm may continually try to adapt to the changing contextual rationalities of its surrounding formation of institutions and social groupings. Thus these will, as organizational units, interest groups, and regulatory bodies try to achieve their particularistic aspirations in competition, rivalry, or cooperation among themselves and with, among, and within capitalist firms and their internal groupings.

Recently, certain scholars have summarized this debate as 'Divergent Capitalisms' (Whitley 1999) or 'Varieties of Capitalism' (Hall and Soskice 2001) signalling that rather than following a universal path, capitalist nations move along numerous routes of social and economic evolution with a much more complicated and less given relationship to global development than earlier concepts—such as the convergence thesis—or various world systems views made us believe. In particular Whitley (1999, 2000) and Casper (2000) are emphasizing that the institutional structuring of national labour markets makes a difference in relation to which innovations and in which phases of the innovative process different nations hold comparative advantages.

Nations will benefit in differentiated ways from emerging new technologies taking departure from different industrial structures and in effect develop differing industrial structures. Not only has the outcome of capitalist economic history given rise to divergent national business systems, it has also created a certain path dependency that will give distinctiveness to the future development of these national business systems.

13.2. What Does It Take to Make Useful Modelling and Research Practices?

Compared to former habits of universal theorizing, comparative traditions have given rise to much more complex 'modelling'. The 'logic' of firms can no longer simply be deduced from theoretical economic reasoning. It must be recognized by also understanding how distinct labour and financial markets influence the behaviour of firms and the groupings that inhabit them; how economic activity may be subsidized by relations with the state and conversely. One of the great achievements of this tradition is that if a change is reported in one institutional sphere of a National Business System (NBS), the NBS-scholar will immediately question how this change is related to, reinforced, or weakened by the interaction with other institutional spheres. One of the great advantages of having created complex 'mappings' of national business systems is that they provide organization scholars with tools for generating questions about the larger landscape of a distinct society if embarking on and making surprising observations in field studies of particular organizations within a narrow institutional sphere. Given the current post-modern orientation in organization sociology and the tendency to study fields and cases just for the sake of reporting on their particularities, national business systems and varieties of capitalism offer a way of relating such observations to larger societal issues. This style of doing research might come to play a significant role if, in the future, social sciences begin to aspire more to understand how societies construct themselves as complex, systemic worlds, to integrate micro observations with macro-synthesis, and to a more cumulative view of knowledge formation based on induction, rather than simply wanting to deconstruct and tear apart universalistic prejudices or deductively reinforce them with poor reference to what is going on in the world.

For scholars with an interest in institutions, these comparative frameworks have already helped, if not to shape an explicated drive for accumulating knowledge and gradually building a more comprehensive understanding of what happens in societies, then a break with the former habits of institutional sociology and economics. Previously, old or new institutions of a society would be looked upon in isolation and then assessed against how they would modify markets, polities, classes, etc. 'all other things being equal' according to the normative assumptions of general theories. Now we can take a studied novel phenomenon within an institutional sphere and relate it to an accumulated complex knowledge of a given society to assess how it may affect and be affected by the larger particular society. The framework for reasoning is not a theory but gradual systematically generated knowledge of a particular society, characterized by its sameness and differences compared to other societies. Amable's recent work (2003) is a very good example of how complementarity and clusterings can be done and is useful in understanding societies in a more comprehensive way.

To organize this growing body of knowledge, we badly need some guide for modelling that makes it possible to be informed by growing flows of information about a distinct society so that both sharper synthesis and greater detail are able to mutually improve simultaneously. Admittedly it sounds self-contradictory, and from the outset I do not know how such a job could be done. But I find many useful, though partly contradictory, suggestions emerging in Part 1 of this volume and more were discussed during the workshop from which the papers originate. In particular Lars Mjøset (2003) gave a highly informed paper on this issue (see also Mjøset 2002). I think that one of the most important challenges to this form of knowledge formation is to create ways of modelling, typologizing, or plainly synthesizing so that this form of knowledge simultaneously asks to become informed by more details, to discover novel, partly contradictory phenomena and therefore constantly aims at making the initial model obsolete through the search it generates.

For this reason, I also think that a strong warning is required. A potentially strong problem seems to emerge when attempts at synthesis, modelling, or typologizing take on a sort of new dogmatism. Some authors seem to indicate that there are only a few (ideal typical) models of capitalism that are viable in practice, and that this viability is dependent on the internal coherence of these capitalisms as 'real-type' systems. Furthermore, behind this coherence often hides some form of functionality in which institutions, behaviour of groupings, state action, etc. are assessed in terms of how well the distinctive form of capital accumulation is helped to succeed.

Recent contributions in this direction include Hall and Soskice (2001) and Amable (2003), who see the complementarity of institutions as a hallmark for the coming into existence of 'models'. In Hall and Soskice's terms nations are clustering around either 'coordinated market economies' or 'liberal market economies' (ibid.: 18 cont.), whereas Amable identifies five 'clusters': 'the market-based model; the social-democratic model; the Continental European model; the Mediterranean model, and the Asian model' (ibid.: 14). The contributors neatly explain how the complementarity of institutions makes sense and equips the societies grouped this way with a certain evolutionary logic. Both books, so to speak, synthesise and summarize how far comparative studies have moved our understanding.

It seems, however, important to emphasize repeatedly that the current varieties of capitalisms and of National Business Systems are themselves the outcomes of endless, far-reaching, and unpredictable experiments within different nations, regions, etc. to develop their respective societies. Just as these various 'systems' could not have been deduced from the workings of the capitalist logic as theorized by Marx and various economic theories, there were and will probably not be only a few teleological end positions for such systems. And why should some distinct features among which we see complementarity and coherence today be given the position to count as crucial for the future viability of such systems? I doubt that we know what could be theorized to count as criteria for future choice, while it is much easier to make 'post festum' rationalizations.

On the contrary, it is worth emphasizing that distinct modelling of particular national systems circumscribes both their internal complexity, their complementarity and coherence, and also their internal incoherence and conflicts; and, taking into account in consequence, how they give rise to rivalry, competition, and cooperation is, in the current situation, one of the best ways to create a highly calibrated research tool to discover new details or even novel phenomena in such systems.

To be able to do so, it is, however, important to distinguish sharply between 'the things of logic and the logic of things' (Bourdieu 1994) when going about such models. Coherence and complementarity belong to 'things of logic', and it takes—at least—independent and powerful mechanisms of discourses and distinct self-reflection of a society to transform such coherence of logic into the coherence of things. Such mechanisms may be active (e.g. in the way Italian industrial districts have made social use of the social scientific notions

of industrial districts and flexible specialization to reconstruct themselves), but are probably more the exception than the rule within
societies. What researchers can do is to try to equip *the modelling* of
particular capitalisms or business systems with a logic (e.g. of coordination, governance, authority, collaboration, rivalry, competition, etc.
among characterized groupings, institutions, organizations, firms,
and other active or potential agencies each with their behavioural pattern). We can then use this logic to deduce a system of hypotheses as
to how that particular society will meet given challenges (new technologies, global competition, and new forms of corporations, etc.).
This system of hypotheses is not developed to say something con-
clusive about how this or that society will be affected and will adapt.
Rather it serves as a way to generate a comprehensive set of hypotheses
sufficiently sharp as to generate and reveal new information (differences that make a difference) about these societies, when we embark
on careful empirical studies of them. In most cases empirical studies will simply prove our models wrong in accordance with sound
Popperian principles (Popper 1957). In this way we secure the continuous discovery of new important details, which might either reveal
ignored aspects of these societies or reveal that unpredicted changes
and adaptations are going on. This gives us the kind of impetus that we
need as researchers to resynthesize past models into new modelling
attempts. Such a research style is a way of ensuring that the ongoing
experimentalism of the societies we study also enters into the practice of how we work as social scientists. A modelling administered
with scientific openness and experimentalism towards the underlying
societal experimentalism has the chance to reveal new aspects or nov-
elties of these societies that will pressurize us to embark on empirical
investigations guided by the logics of coherence of our models. In this
way we may discover that revealed phenomena are connected to larger complexes of the society. We may need to reform the model, not
just from the point of view of one particular part of the system, but
in terms of a larger set of social relations, culminating in the need to
change the operating logic of the model as a whole.

13.3. What Directs the Experimental Process that Socially Constructs Societies?

At a more metatheoretical level the interesting question that could
guide the experimental search of scholars towards the experimental

processes of societies is of course: What directs the experimental process that shapes and changes the complex institutional construction of national (or other societal) systems?

Despite the fact that neither Whitley in his *Divergent Capitalisms* nor Hall and Soskice in *Varieties of Capitalism* explicitly ask this question, they actually take departure from a similar implicit answer to this problem. In both approaches every institution or institutional change is measured according to its ability to improve the performance of the distinct form of capitalism under study. In this way, the focus of analysis is almost entirely on how forms of capitalism perform in competition with each other, considering them as purely economic phenomena. Amable (2003) is more explicit on this matter as he takes macroeconomic performance in the long run to be determining for whether societies will have to change their 'model': the problem for him is whether a dominant social bloc can be formed as a coalition of social groups that is able to reform the system. This in turn necessitates deconstructing past complementarities of the institutional formation and shaping a new one that can meet the competitive challenges arising in new economic conditions, as different national business systems adapt and change at different rates.

The problem I see is that by using terms such as 'divergent capitalisms' and 'varieties of capitalism' we seem to summarize or synthesize our new discoveries and improved understandings of Western and other societies in a less productive way than the accumulated material allows for. In my view such synthesis implies that there is an overwhelming number of social and institutional sources for variability in how societies become socially constructed. But what these various forms of societies help channel, substantiate, and form are the processes that unfold within merely the economic sphere. In this way there seems to be an unquestioned Marxist thread in our analysis in which the universal mode of production is capitalism, while the social formations in which this mode of production unfolds differ. Or in other terms, we have a capitalist world system that puts distinct societies under a uniform pressure and poses universal challenges to which they must adapt from divergent positions and through distinct capabilities that are inscribed into their respective 'identities'. In effect we can observe national business systems evolving through some mixture of reproduction and non-identical transformations, but always guided by the measures of their relative capitalist economic performances.

The risk is that we subsume most other social processes under the capitalist process, neglecting their own endogenous dynamic and the social interactions through which they are brought about.

One of the great discoveries of our research programmes is that the firm occupies highly different social places in different countries. In some the state has elevated them to a position so that the entire evolution of society follows in the wake of their development. In others, firms have elevated themselves to a position, where a role has been ascribed to the state under their dictatorship, while finally in a third group of countries, firms have developed as underground oppositions to an existing state. In comparing the Middle East with Western democracies, Bernard Lewis (2002) has said that the difference between their respective perspectives on the economy can be measured by the dynamics of corruption in the two types of societies. In the West, money is accumulated in the market sphere and used to buy power and influence in the political sphere. In the Middle East you come to power and use it to earn money. The effects of agency on the economy and the dynamics of society therefore differ substantially. Does this not indicate that, rather than seeing capitalist competition as the very sphere where struggles for social space unfold and determine, on the one hand, the position of nations within a global dynamic and, on the other, the mutual positioning of different social groups within a nation, we should investigate with critical distance how important capitalist competition is in comparison with all the other social spheres in which social groups and nations contest their mutual positioning? The promise of such an approach might also be that the very sphere of capitalist competition breaks up and becomes a whole complex of differentiated spheres with distinct forms of rivalry and competition each governed by their own set of distinct rules of the game. Today such differentiated spheres of various games are often hiding behind the dormant concepts of capitalism, market, and competition rather than being investigated with the open eyes of field researchers.

If we do not break with the habit of automatically evaluating any institution or institutional experiment by its contribution to keeping capitalism viable, we seem to be stuck with a very strange paradox. We focus on institutions because we think markets, competition, and capitalism are simply not 'out there', but are socially constructed and socially embedded. But 'that' which embeds and constructs markets gets it meaning or is 'directed' not by any reference to itself but only from the function which it performs for the reproduction of capitalism. In this way, I think, we will never be able to understand more than one source—or maybe criterion—for institutional experimentalism and modes of constructing and reconstructing societies. The generative processes underlying the experimentalism of societies are concealed from our eyes as long as we focus on the process by which 'capitalism', in exploiting such generative processes, unfolds and becomes distinctively shaped in distinct societies.

I think this generative process of experimentalism is very heterogeneous consisting in the ability to let numerous voices be aired and heard through a language that experimentally changes to allow for new conceptualizations and variations in interpretation. It consists in the experimental construction of polities that helps new publics to form and to be articulated. This in turn enables new institutions to emerge, providing groups with pathways for transforming their lives and careers at work so that new identities and roles get formed, when group aspirations reflexively surpass their former identities and social space.

Societies are not born into a state that allows this to happen. They must be in turn constructed by an experimental process that allows them to continue to sustain this dynamic of change. Many philosophers and social scientists have tried to understand how such an outcome is possible. Hegel saw it as an outcome of the phenomenology and dialectical development of the spirit; Machiavelli through a transition from princedom to republic; whereas Hobbes wanted to free us from a barbarian civilian society by establishing an autarkic kingdom that could rule citizens and protect them from themselves. In retrospect it is possible to see that these social philosophers were a few voices among many in the ongoing 'civilizing process' that might bring societies to a stage where such experimentalist processes become possible, without resulting in everybody being at war with everybody else.

13.4. Capitalisms and the Civilizing Process

Despite possible criticisms, in my view Norbert Elias (1994, first published 1939) in his *The Civilizing Process* gives us the best account from which to imagine what directs ongoing experimental institutional processes. Especially if we read his first book together with his last one on *The Germans* (1996, published in German 1989) it becomes clear that the civilizing process need not be unidirectional or teleological, but rather may lead to decivilization in some societies in some epochs, dependent on the social situation and balances among social classes.

The civilizing process can be seen as the process by which a society gradually civilizes the fight for and over social space, constantly going on among individuals and social groupings in any society (see for instance Hobbes 1968). This civilizing goes on by building formal institutions at the state level (such as the royal court to tame the fight through wars over social space among feudal lords and towards the king; by institutionalizing property laws and protections, by creating institutions for collective bargaining among unions and employers to reduce strikes and lock-outs); by changing manners and by creating individuals with individual responsibilities out of 'mobs', and by finding more civilized arenas for fighting over social space. With this view on the longer historical process Elias was able to criticize Marx and other social scientists for giving too much attention to the economic process.

From this perspective, societies are formations internally circumscribing an endless ongoing fight among social groupings each of which in trying to extend their own social space, comes into conflict with other social groups. Especially in a feudal estate society, taking land over from other feudal lords through brute force may be the only way of accumulating land. Social space in such societies equals geographical space. Externally states are in constant rivalry over social space, and in feudal times and during imperialism this mutual fight over social space takes place by capturing foreign territories, which helps sustain the power of the king as a feudal lord *vis-à-vis* other feudal lords within his realm.

From this perspective, capitalism may be seen as a truly formidable social innovation. Wealth, social space and position could be accumulated without extending geographical space. Wars could be transformed to competition. In certain societies, central rulers advocated capitalism because it would give the King an income independent of his feudal lords. But even more so because it would offer a whole new arena in which social groupings could fight over social space without winding up in situations in which winning estates would challenge the King. Simply in and by capitalism, social space may be extended through capital accumulation without necessarily leading to territorial wars over geographic space, though this might also happen as during the nineteenth century period of European expansion.

In Britain, where the social position as capitalist entrepreneur could be achieved without being dependent on the central state authorities (Wood 1991), capitalism could also be seen as a way to civilize the fight over social space. If we read Adam Smith's two books together, it becomes clear why. In *Theory of Moral Sentiments* (1969) he argues that people of ordinary station by watching the reaction of external spectators to their own behaviour will develop an internal spectator that predicts others' reactions. In this way the individual learns that 'decent' behaviour can be combined with looking after one's self interests. However, this development may be distorted if people know that they may be especially favoured, for instance at the royal court, if they break with the ordinary people's code of honourable conduct and instead search for power and wealth through such connections and privileges. I read Adam Smith's *The Wealth of Nations* (1970) as an argument for getting rid of the access to royal privileges. In his view, the market is a means by which people mutually regulate not only their economic but also their moral conduct through egalitarian social interaction.

British capitalism may in this respect be considered particular, because property was achieved outside the state rather than through the state (Wood 1991). In France, Germany, and other continental European countries, many capitalists for a long period won their position as capitalists by being granted royal privileges, so that the regulation of property became negotiated or inherited through the state and through positioning within the royal court rather than being an issue among private individuals. Thus, capitalism was institutionalized in highly different ways in different countries, each with its particular composition of former status groups and relations and balances between princes, feudal lords, peasants, labourers, the military and civil society, and cities and the land. In terms of which groups benefited and suffered in their struggle for social space through capitalism and markets, each country is an individual story. This is also why different societies seem to invent highly diverse types of institutions during the early phases of capitalism as a way to foster, support, or civilize capitalism itself.

Born under the banner of 'egalité, fraternité, et liberté', capitalisms soon showed signs of decay viewed from the perspective of Adam Smith's moral sentiments and principles of egalitarian mutual regulation in the market. Capitalism separated the working population into workers and capitalists and led to growing inequalities. In place of former feudal status groups that had held monopoly over positions and privileges came monopolies created through the market (Weber 1978: 635–40), dividing the capitalist class itself into those who benefited and those who suffered from a competition that seemed increasingly unegalitarian. In the last decades of the nineteenth and the first half of the twentieth century 'liberalism' proved its failure for many social groups that might have initially shared Adam Smith's hopes. Through political action, each dependent on their particular power and ideological mobilization, different political groups in different countries succeeded in creating institutions that could help them fight for their own social space by modifying the impact and consequences of capitalism on their own groupings.

One way to do this was to build up institutional spheres that gave some groupings a sheltered life and institutions in which they could develop their social space without being destroyed by capitalism.[1] Another alternative was to try civilizing the way in which capitalism functioned. The entrepreneurial middle class in the United States succeeded in creating a regulatory regime against cartels through the Sherman Act, which in consequence, pushed the American economy towards a regime of the large integrated corporations through a process of mergers and acquisitions. But different groups together with social reformers also created cross-Atlantic dialogues on housing, unemployment insurance, pension systems, saving banks, cooperatives, etc. to find ways of making it possible for the poor workers to make a living under capitalism (Rodgers 1998). All these attempts came together when taming and civilizing capitalism became a major business after the Soviet revolution and in the light of the world economic crisis of the 1930s with the rise of the modern welfare states. Ways to regulate general demand, competition, and even business as such through standards for auditing became established at the macro-level, while ways of creating participative influence for employees were created at the micro-level together with rules of the game about how bureaucracies must balance duties and rights so that employees are given some protection within the overall dominance of the logic of capitalist corporations. Scholarly accounts of how modern capitalisms had taken different routes have since emerged. These have focused on different core elements, for example, macroeconomic planning (Shonfield 1965), welfare state systems (Esping-Andersen 1990), industrial relations and forms of corporatism (Crouch 1993; Regini 1991), the organization of labour markets and vocational training, and how work regimes help structure the capitalist enterprise itself in different ways (Maurice et al. 1986).

---

[1] As when under Bismarck, the German *Mittelstand* secured its own institutions and reserved certain types of production for its own members rather than industry (Streeck 1992).

Each of these scholars measured the effectiveness of various capital-isms in different ways. Andrew Shonfield found that French indicative planning had helped achieve the lowest capital/output-ratio. Regini and Crouch showed that the Nordic central bargaining institutions helped create a less conflictual work relation at the shop floor. This led to improved production results through institutions taming some of the market processes that could otherwise sustain worker unrest and hold up production at the workplace. Maurice, Sellier, and Silvestre showed how the function of the German labour market, vocational training, and works councils led to savings on numbers of managers and hierarchical positions, compared to France.

It is very important to stress that these outcomes in terms of per-formance and economic effectiveness were unintended consequences for those who had initially tried to reform their respective capital-isms by proposing the creation of new institutions. Such reforms have generally been met by resistance and criticism from the leading cap-italists of the day, because they rightly saw them as being opposed to their immediate interests. Such criticisms would often try to del-egitimize reform proposals by arguing that the reforms would be counter-productive to the general economic interest. Only when they later included them in their own planning, and strategized accord-ingly, would the reforms have any effects in terms of improving performance measures, even though this was not intended in the first place.

Charles Sabel (1982) stresses correctly how much we reduce our understanding of complicated historical processes when we anticipate reforms to be the outcome of deliberate attempts to create functional efficiency. Thus, he criticizes Dore (1973) for seeing the Japanese *nenko* system of employment as simply a reform to enable a late industri-alizing nation to create a system for developing industrial skills by systematizing on-the-job-training.

In stressing efficiency considerations—on-the-job training as the rational response to the problem of forced-draft industrialization—it underlies the perpetual struggle that Japanese employers have had to wage against crafts-men's efforts to establish associations independent of single employers. The *nenko* was not the result of the straightforward application of old habits to new circumstances. It was deliberately created by skilful reinterpretation of traditional ideas of deference and solidarity, for example, the *oyabata-kotata* relation of master and apprentice. (Sabel 1982: 26)

In retrospect the good news is that societies have been able to civilize capitalism in many experimental ways without necessarily jeopardizing the abilities of capitalism to continuously expand the social space within which individuals and groupings, organizations, and institutions can fight for wealth, status and power. Rather, conversely—as technological innovations, especially when they come in swarms—institutional innovations may furnish the capitalist process with not only a new impetus but also offer it an expansionary option to shift form creating eventually a new long wave of expansion. Whereas capitalism is supreme in its ability to exploit existing frontiers, it takes the much broader cognitive, political, and imaginative faculties of heterogeneous social groupings to make explorations that may discover and define new frontiers—in terms of forging new relations across geographical space, around new technological possibilities, new institutions and new forms of artistic and cultural production.

For that reason it is not only reductionist and functionalist to assess ongoing institutional experimentalism from the standpoint of a given variety of capitalism, but it may also restrict the very mechanisms by which societies gradually discover new frontiers and give their particular capitalisms a new lift, both in terms of economic performance and in degree of 'civilization', or standard of life more generally conceived.

Elias only gives us rough outlines as to how civilizing and decivilizing goes on in history, and what is involved in its progression or diminution. Of course, individuals and social groupings may civilize themselves in order to improve their reputation and position towards others in a given society, but what seems much more important is that social groupings try to mobilize polities to influence and regulate the behaviour of other groups so that they behave less in opposition to their own interests and codes of conduct. This eventual dialectical process is probably without limits and will work continuously with various groups shifting between the role of civilizer and being civilized. As one of the tools to civilize feudal lords, princes mobilized capitalists whose main interest was in peace and the peaceful expansion of markets. According to Hirschman (1977) capitalists tried to reduce the passion for wars among princes by moving capital away from those who indulged their passion for war. In a similar way corporate America in the nineteenth century tried to civilize competition by forming cartels and trusts. However, this had the effect of cutting small businesses off from markets. They, in turn, mobilized their political power to ensure that state action would curb the cartels. This in turn had the paradoxical effect of reinforcing huge monopolistic corporations which overcame the uncertainties of the market not by cartels and price rigging but through the achievement of massive economies of scale (Fligstein 1990: Introduction).

The experimentalist process by which various societies have tried to come to terms with and civilize capitalism has in each of these societies, led to the formation of new institutions that in turn have reshaped and repositioned the social groups to which they connect. In this way different social groupings have created a dialectics of endogenous development among institutions and social groupings constantly reshaping both the aspirations and the identities of the social groupings. Institutions and social groupings cannot engage in such experimental transformation without coming into conflict with other social groupings as they will more or less accidentally come to fight over similar social spaces as new territories open up. How these conflicts among groups are fought out constitute a separate outcome of the 'Civilizing Process'. Crouch (1993) identifies three different ways to 'organize' interest intermediation: contestation, pluralist bargaining, and neocorporatism. Amable (2003: 17) groups Australia, Canada, the United States, the United Kingdom, the Netherlands, and Switzerland as pluralist bargaining; France, Belgium, Spain, and Italy as examples of contestation models; Germany, Austria, and Ireland as models of simple neocorporatism (where unions are relatively weak but endowed with a strategic capacity); while Finland, Sweden, and Denmark are examples of extensive neocorporatism (with strong and centralized unions).

However, in most Western societies after reconstruction had taken place, post World War II, the general adoption of Keynesianism created the opportunity for all types of society, whatever their form of interest mediation, to reduce conflicts by allowing state budgets to be continually expanded. Schools, vocational training centres, universities, scientific bodies, financial institutions, theatre, design, labour market policies, and industrial planning bodies all tried to expand their territories in collaboration or rivalry with the groupings which they helped foster or which helped foster them. The effect which some observers foresaw was the emergence of a fiscal crisis of the state in most countries by the beginning of the 1970s. In retrospect it is difficult to conclude that differences in the type of interest mediation in a society gave any particular society a comparative advantage in resolving such problems. Rather combined with the oil crisis, fast increasing wages and stagflation a growing number of commentators held the view that welfare states, strong unions, etc. had managed to overregulate (or civilize) the economy to the extent that it undermined the 'market' from doing a proper job.

This situation could have been interpreted as a new need for civilizing experimentation. In this context the need to search for new devices could have led to innovative suggestions from groupings as well as institutions. A new discourse around a reformed development project for capitalism could have been constructed and institutionalized even within these highly developed forms of welfare capitalism.[2] Had this discourse been institutionalized, complementarity, and coherence among institutions could have left the 'things of logic' and entered the realm of the 'logic of things'. Ironically it was the combination of Keynesianism and Fordism as general models of how to organize capitalism that had paused the cross-Atlantic discourse on how substantive and diverse social politics could reform and civilize capitalism that had evolved in the first half of the twentieth century (Rodgers 1998). All the old movements and associations that had contributed to the dynamism and diversity of this discourse declined in the post-war period.

Neither social scientists nor political practitioners, thus, succeeded in discovering devices for 'civilizing' and reforming Keynesian states and creating a constitutional framework for their operation before other actors and institutions reacted. Instead a number of international institutions, significant politicians in both the United States and the United Kingdom, and the globalizing financial community used the first oil crisis to initiate a neoliberal turn to reintroduce the market as a regulator of public institutions. Capitalism was now instead civilizing the institutions and organizations that had previously been created to civilize capitalism. It is astonishing to read Rodgers (1998) and compare how the reforms that were carefully implanted (1870–1950), were gradually and systematically rolled back after the first oil-crisis. Countries that did not comply soon learned that global financial capital had strong sticks at hand to punish states unwilling to do so. During this process, capitalism in general subsumed the explorative capabilities and civilizing devices of Western societies under the exploitative mechanisms of capitalism. Ronald Dore (2000: 12) simply called it a 'capitalist-managerial-counter-revolution', but many have discovered that globalization as a discourse of economic necessity and compulsion has become the prime reference in discourses over state budgets.

---

[2] Such devices and a framework for their operation have, in my view, been put forward much later by Dorf and Sabel (1998).

Within the last quarter of the twentieth century financial institutions played themselves into taking on or were given the role of 'civilizing' both welfare states and capitalist corporations. The World Bank and the International Monetary Fund play this role when intervening directly with the policies of a nation. The private financial institutions do it more indirectly by grading the creditworthiness of different nations and corporations, or helping stocks of individual corporations climb up or down the price ladder. In this way financial institutions—in particular in Wall Street and the City of London—have managed to put themselves into a similar position of transforming capitalism as the royal court had in transforming feudal society.

If we want to assess the impact of the current institutional equity nexus (Golding 2001), it might be useful to think back on how authors such as Galbraith (1967) and Baran and Sweezy (1966) narrated the logic of the then 'New Industrial State'. For these authors, the 1960s produced a situation in which a managerial techno-structure had come to power within large organizations in both the private and the public sectors. The actors in this managerial techno-structure secured their own growth by expanding the organizations and number of employees they controlled. They were much more concerned about the expansion of their organizations than about profitability or usefulness for stockowners or the public. By the 1960's managerial bureaucracies, as first discovered by Berle and Means (1932), seemed to have created a novel system of economic organization and power which had no limits. However, much of the legitimacy, which the institutional equity nexus holds today stems from the interpretation that it managed to curb the self-interested growth of managerial techno-structures and bureaucracies—in the interests of both the general public and shareholders. The institutional equity nexus in other words managed to civilize the then 'new industrial state'.

13.5. What Can We Learn from Court Society about the Destiny of the Institutional Equity Nexus?

However, the institutional equity nexus has done much more than curb the 'new industrial state'. The changed situation for business managers today looks, on the surface, very similar to the situation of the nobility in the sixteenth and seventeenth centuries when they discovered that they could improve their standing in society much easier and faster through their relations to the King at the royal court than by either cultivating their estates in novel ways by or going to war with other warrior-noblemen to win land and thereby the resources with which to equip their armies. As Norbert Elias (2000) shows, court society means a huge transition in how positional games in societies take place, as life at court has very different 'rules of the game' from that of warrior-society.

Life in this circle is in no way placid. Very many people are continuously dependent on each other. Competition for prestige and royal favour is intense. 'Affairs', disputes over rank and favour, do not cease. If the sword no longer plays so great a role as the means of decision, it is replaced by intrigue, conflicts in which careers and social success are contested with words. They demand and produce other qualities than did the armed struggles that had to be fought out with weapons in one's hand. Continuous reflection, foresight, and calculation, self-control, precise and articulate regulation of one's own affects, knowledge of the whole terrain, human and non-human, in which one acts, become more and more indispensable preconditions for social success. Every individual belongs to a 'clique', a social circle, which supports him when necessary; but the groupings change. He enters alliances, if possible with people ranking high at court. But rank at court can change very quickly; he has rivals; he has open and concealed enemies. And the tactics of his struggles, as of his alliances, demand careful consideration. The degree of aloofness or familiarity with everyone else must be carefully measured; each greeting, each conversation has significance over and above what is actually said or done. They indicate the standing of a person; and they contribute to the formation of court opinion on his standing. (Elias 2000: 398)

This description of court life explains how the nobility had to become absentee owners to their landholdings, as they had to focus on court life to secure access to the much more important resources that came through the king both in the form of treasures, offices, land, and power. In my view the City and Wall Street have moved CEOs into a similar position as formerly the court did to noblemen. This similarity illustrates why MNC HQs must now pay immense attention to the institutional equity nexus rather than to their businesses and markets.

Ironically, to make his case clear for the court, Norbert Elias compares the royal court with the stock exchange, but indicates some differences, which I think have later faded away.

The court is a kind of stock exchange; as in every 'good society', an estimate of the 'value' of each individual is continuously being formed. But here his value has its real foundation not in the wealth or even achievements or ability of the individual, but in the favour he enjoys with the king, the influence he has with other mighty ones, his importance in the play of courtly cliques. (ibid.)

In court society other subjects would seek the protection of those in good standing with the king in exactly the same way as independent firms now seek the protection of MNCs in with good standing institutional investors, fund managers, and financial analysts in the financial districts of London and New York (Kristensen and Zeitlin 2001, 2005). Such potential 'clients' became another source of power if they were of value in the eyes of other courtiers, whereas bad clients were a disadvantage. In much the same way the City and Wall Street favour CEOs who are approached for mergers by companies that the City and Wall Street approves of, whereas their standing in the positional games suffers, when deemed bad company.

This courtly art of human observation—unlike what we usually call 'psychology' today—is never concerned with the individual in isolation, as if the essential features of his behaviour were independent of his relations to others, and as if he related to others, so to speak, only retrospectively. The approach there was far closer to reality, in that the individual was always seen in his social context, *as a human being in his relations to others, as an individual in a social situation*. (Elias 2000: 401, author's emphasis)

The institutional equity nexus, however, is not bound to a central authority, as is the court with its relation to the King. Golding (2001) describes it as a complex set of institutions and actors that by interacting in self-interested ways create a web of interactions that nobody masters and yet nobody seems to be able to escape. Until recently, role-takers within the institutional equity nexus possessed a set of complementary roles that propelled the system in a certain direction. For instance, pension funds try to escape criticism or the loss of members by contracting out investments to portfolio managers on short-term contracts. These in turn, to increase the probability that they will have their contracts extended, try to reach the general benchmarks on returns by imitating investments of other portfolio managers. This means that demand for and trading in so-called 'liquid', favoured stocks becomes the name of the game. Only corporations with stocks in large quantities qualify, which means that such corporations must always search for growth, for instance through mergers and acquisitions, so that they can keep their position among, for example, FTSE 100. Staying among these top players means access to cheaper capital that makes growth much easier than among smaller corporations, whereas fall from the top of this mountain means a much more difficult life, with the risk of falling victim to hostile takeovers.

CEOs are also rated and a particular individual CEO who shifts from one corporation to another may cause dramatic increases or decreases in stock prices among the corporations that he or she moves into or out of. The game to stay top is not a passive one. The nexus continuously invents new fashions in strategic planning, managerial techniques, incentives, and benchmarks thought to favour stockholders. It gives top managers autonomy to exert a pressure downward inside their corporations, using benchmarks to pit subsidiaries against each other, for example, over the siting of new investment, thus institutionalizing regime shopping, and governance by 'divide and conquer' (Müller 1996; Müller and Purcell 1992).

That the court society was able to develop a figuration capable of rating nobles and their client-networks explains why it developed such a central role in the formation of European societies. And for similar reasons it may be possible for both the City of London and Wall Street to develop assessments that reduce the conflicts within MNCs. But there are good reasons to doubt this process will happen easily. Despite intense intermarriage among the royal houses and courts in Europe, they remained in rivalry for dominance of the entire European landscape for many centuries. Conquering new land was often the most promising way for a king to acquire the treasures with which he could make rich his loyal dependants at court. Thus even at its very peak, in the period of Louis XIV, court society was surrounded by crises of wars, civil wars, and in the period of the associated destruction of wealth and property. This highly volatile situation within European societies was mixed up in religious conflicts between Protestants and Catholics giving every location a specific composition of political forces. It was further aggravated because aristocratic power was waning in the face of emerging new local elites, based on the wealth of trade and cities. These new elites and their local subjects sometimes succeeded in forming large-scale alliances to oppose the huge tax burdens that arose from royal wars and courtly life (Te Brake 1998: 118).

At the very same time as Elias reports the civilizing victory of court society, Wayne Te Brake reports on a European setting in which distinctive local coalitions are being built and being replaced. This process educates the general population to take part in politics—and in effect in the long term to form (with merchants and urban elites) constitutional orderings that would limit the power of both kings and courtiers. The Catalan revolution in 1640–52 is illustrative.

At bottom, the Catalan revolt is familiar because it involves so clearly the triangulated set of political actors that was the characteristic legacy of dynastic or composite state formation. . . . national or princely claimants to power (plus their agents), indigenous or local ruling elites, and ordinary political subjects. Although political alignments between aggressive princes—with often urgent fiscal and military needs—and local rulers—the jealous guardians of historic privileges that were the basis of their position locally—were nearly always uneasy and contentious, they nevertheless consolidated the power of local elites vis-à-vis their local populations... This pattern of elite consolidation was clearly ruptured in Catalonia as a result of popular political action that forced the local elites to choose between royal political favours and local solidarities. When an important faction of the Catalan elite openly chose the side of popular resistance, it opened up a revolutionary situation that entailed the possibility of a local consolidation of power under an independent Catalan republic... But the urgent need for military protection against the king's armies quickly resulted instead in what might well be called a coup d'etat in the sense that one very powerful prince replaced another and quickly consolidated his power in conjunction with a faction of the local elites with whom he had struck an alternative dynastic bargain. (Te Brake 1998: 127)

Such political turmoil could shake the positions of both individual courtiers and kings. The neat ordering from the king through the courtiers to the local communities never worked to create a uniform and universal European political landscape. Rather, situations and the compositions of interests, conflicts, and opportunities for forming coalitions gave each nation, if not each locality, its own foundations for constituting itself in a distinct way, furnishing Europe at its roots with the political variety from which it has suffered or prospered since then—depending on the perspectives of beholders. Instead of transforming from late-medieval composite states into autocratic monarchies and court societies (along the lines of France under Louis XIV), Europe became a landscape of very differently constituted states depending on how local elites and ordinary peoples succeeded in influencing politics (Te Brake 1998: 183 ff.). In autocratic states such as France and Spain, the court gained a distinct role as it was the space in which 'elite competitors for power were co-opted by guarantees of elite privilege' (ibid. 185). In other places 'the composite state maker was eliminated altogether' giving rise either to city states like Venice or Geneva or confederated provinces such as the Swiss Confederation of Cantons or the Dutch Republic (ibid.: 184). In yet other places 'dynastic princes were neither eliminated nor triumphant', as in Catalonia, the southern Netherlands and the constituent parts of Germany. Here 'locally segmented jurisdictions remained the primary arena for political interaction between subjects and rulers'. For obvious reasons, in the two latter cases any attempt to institutionalize the social figuration of the court only had limited effects. In instances where central powers are neither eliminated nor triumphant, the figuration remains extremely unsettled, and it is perhaps here—due to the intensity of volatility and conflicts—that some of the most promising lessons could be learnt (Te Brake 1998: 186).

If this is the case in Europe during the period of state formation, the situation may be similar in our epoch of globalization. It is quite obvious that local (or national) elites have too much to suffer if they plainly ignore the game played in the institutional equity nexus. If they ignore it altogether they may simply cut themselves off from cheap capital or waves of modernization of plants, as with the spread of Japanese production systems. But of course, it is possible to think that they can play this game to be able to play local games better. For instance a local bank may engage in modern financial transactions to create access for its local customers to novel forms of financing without thereby pushing these customers directly into the game of the institutional equity nexus. It is well known that banks often do the opposite as they channel local liquid capital into their centralized portfolio funds, from where they furnish the institutional equity nexus with the means that enable the game. In banks, it may be difficult to institutionalize a new ongoing system of negotiation between the local elite and 'subjects' that can determine the balance between local and global orientation, though exactly this seems to be what Wallenberg has done for Sweden (Lindgren 1994). But such bargaining might be possible to institutionalize where strong unions have created pension funds and other mutual funds, where local elites have created collective investment funds by which they participate in the global game to keep themselves collectively stronger in local or national games, etc. When searching, it is in fact possible to find numerous examples of new forms of financial institutions that exactly try to play the gobal game to the benefit of the local (Kristensen and Zeitlin, 2005, Chapter 12).

Perhaps the most remarkable step in this direction has been the development of Labour Sponsored Investment Funds (LSIFs) in Canada. Beginning with the creation of the Quebec Solidarity Fund in 1983, these funds have expanded rapidly with the support of tax credits from federal and provincial governments to account by 2000 for 50 per cent of the Canadian venture capital market.... Some LSIFs, based mainly in Ontario, Canada's largest province and financial center, were formed by existing investment firms purely to take advantage of tax concessions, with only a nominal connection to the sponsoring union. But others, notably the members of the LSIF alliance whose boards are directly controlled by union bodies, are committed to meeting broader economic and social objectives, including regional development, employee participation, and labor-management cooperation in investee firms.... These labor-sponsored funds also work with investee firms to enhance management capabilities, adopt new forms of work organization, improve communication with the workforce, build trust with the local union, and foster employee stock ownership. Taken together, the participatory investment and decision-making processes promoted by these funds may lead to an effective control of assets, thereby redefining the practical meaning of industrial property rights, while at the same time providing a powerful tool for local communities to tap into broader financial markets. (ibid.)

In a similar way, it is obviously possible for subsidiaries of MNCs to play the institutionalized game in such a way that they enable enlargement of local mandates (Birkinshaw and Hood 1998; Birkinshaw 2001), create tighter relations to localities (Sölvell and Zander 1998) and even make it attractive for headquarters to learn from them (as they become bench-markers). Thereby they might use the opportunity to institutionalize within the MNC novel systems of negotiation or innovate and create new practices through the use of such bodies as European Work Councils (Kristensen 2003; Kristensen and Zeitlin, 2005, Chapter 11).

Ironically by trying to deal with and through the institutional equity nexus, such new players enter into its game of mutual positioning with slightly changed codes of behaviour by which they may discover new ways of behaving. These new role-takers could easily have great impact on its functioning, being determined to civilize parts of it. By doing so they could reinforce the volatile potentiality of a system we have first described as being a set of complementary and self-reinforcing roles. As we see it, the institutional equity nexus is a game about mutual positioning on a global scale, and as long as the participants play the game by the given rules they will tend to reproduce a given mutual positioning. Thus, people positioned low in its hierarchy can not alter their position by playing by its rules. To move upwards demands that they find innovative ways to perform better than existing benchmarks, making the figuration of the institutional equity nexus possibly as unstable as was any court society, where a *coup d'etat* always risked shaking the cultivated hierarchy among courtiers.

Up to now this new financial court society combined with MNCs has exercised its power in a peculiar way. As we all know, Enron and other companies have benefited from such relations to a degree beyond imagination. Other corporations have, rather to the contrary, been punished and forced to reduce their work force every year. The main way for multinational corporations to grow is by merger and acquisitions, but rather than leading to more cost-effective ways for the expansion of employment this leads to the destruction of firms and reduction in employment. It could be said that in the financial court society, capitalism has become a mechanism for shrinking rather than enlarging social space. This can also be observed in the way this regime restricts states from public spending, either by increasing interests rates or by moving capital out of the country, a process very similar to how capitalism was used to 'civilize' princes who had an uneconomic passion for wars (Hirschmann 1977).

Most observers see, for good reasons, financial court society combined with globalization as leading to growing isomorphism among states and national economies. They must adapt to and adopt Anglo-Saxon inspired governance models in firms and society in exchange for 'privileges' that are allocated from the financial court society. Even former advocates of the diversity and vitality of national business systems see former highly variant forms becoming attuned to the new order. Witness in this book, two examples of this form of reasoning. Lane's account of Germany is one in which Germany must give up its former identity, but finds it difficult though necessary because so many German institutional complementarities have to be dismantled. Lilja and Moen give an account of Finland using its coordinated market economy to make a concerted change towards a financially coordinated economy. Whereas Lane sees the outcome of change in terms of rising inequalities and social conflict, Lilja and Moen identify the change in Finnish capitalism with an upgrading process that has led to increasing prosperity. In view of this there are of course good reasons to ask whether some other forms of capitalism still hold comparative advantages that may enable them to take up the challenge of the Anglo-Saxon 'model' and contest it by using these advantages in new ways on global markets.

This approach, however, tends to compare models statically rather than dynamically, and tends to reduce—as we have argued—our understanding of their capabilities to a focus on their ability to sustain capital accumulation. This neglects their ability to sustain a civilized society that cultivates its ability to mutually coordinate action among its complexes of institutions, social groupings, organizations in general and firms in particular.

If we take departure from Adam Smith's demonstration of how actors of humble station internalize the views of external spectators when planning their own actions and rewrite this through the language of symbolic interactionism and Mead's social psychology, we find that civilization improves to the degree that human actors or agencies learn to cultivate the ability in various social situations to take on the role of others. This does not mean an end to social strife and the conflict over social space, but it civilizes agent, and it encourages actors, mutually, to strategize in such a way that they make social use of, pay respect to, and give place to the role and strategic struggle of others. How societies enable and allow for mutual recognition could be the 'decisive' mechanism that gives it its character, variability, and difference from others. In this context, Crouch's comparative study of different forms of 'interest intermediation' becomes of central interest. It will become of great importance to study where and how different societies have institutionalized ongoing systems of negotiation and whether they are able to innovate, so that individual groups can satisfy these aspirations without destroying prospects for others.

Anglo-Saxon societies have, on the whole, handed the context for and power over, processes of mutual recognition to the financial court, with the effect that large institutional complexes of society have been deemed uneconomic. If that device for mutual recognition could be said to be hyper-rational with supreme forms of information-gathering and calculative methods, it would be necessary to take its effects on behaviour very seriously. However, even internal observers of the institutional equity nexus have shown how the behaviour of its web of actors is shaped by limited information processing capacity (Golding 2001; Plender 2003). At the very least, the system works in a boundedly rational way, leading to a systematic non-allocation of capital to the most promising sectors (SMEs) of economies and the most promising countries (developing countries or NICs). On the contrary, the financial system seems to fall into a trap of speculative bubbles that destroy huge amounts of capital.

The great promise, therefore, is that if other societies can develop more advanced forms or mechanisms for mutual assessment and recognition than those developed in contexts dominated by the financial court, then they will have a great chance to be able to outperform the allocative efficiency of the financial court society. If the financial system becomes recognized more from its failures than from its benefits, it may force investors to investigate more directly the potential of risky investments rather than relying on the game of misinformation that seems increasingly to rule the game of the financial equity nexus. That might start a whole new way of building an alternative 'financial system' as when royal courts were being overtaken by parliamentary bodies that could better align the local and central levels, and mediate different interests among social groupings.

13.6. The Creative Role of NBS Research in the Future

The possibility of genuine mutual recognition among social groupings becoming lost with the transformation from agrarian communities to footloose industrial cities, or with the invasion of mass media into the process by which communitarian new publics became established (Dewey 1927) has been frequently discussed in social science. Politics has turned into something very far from the business of creating and sustaining mutual recognition, and understanding the roles and contributions of others. Concepts such as 'good and evil' and division between 'us and them' if not 'me against all' seem to spread increasingly and undermine the possibilities for mutual recognition.

And yet it is often the case, when field researchers listen carefully to how narration takes place within a field, that even behind tough and seemingly cynical façades, people mutually recognize each other and try to move the division line between 'them and us' so that it is less narrowing. The dynamics of mutual recognition across agents and agencies may play a crucial role in mobilizing and changing mutual commitment, creating social space to allow agencies to experiment and to create rationalizations for them to be carried out (Weick 2001). At the core of this lies the process of creating a narrative of identity, cohesion and cooperation. These may tend to inclusion or to exclusion: good against evil, us against them. Depending on these narrative constructions, agents both create a predictable social environment and also a defining frame, in which experiments, novel behaviour and role-formations, new identities, and new projects may be detected and recognized.

Despite an overwhelming tendency for spreading the narration of exclusion by the mass media, supported by the financial nexus and Anglo-Saxon ways of constructing world politics, inclusive narrations on the micro-level can also be observed in a lot of instances. Such narrations take place when former conflict-ridden regions report on the creation of mutual trust, or where formally independent enterprises engage in and construct stories and measurement techniques in support of collaborative manufacturing; or where, for instance, workers and employers engage in partnership in which they sincerely try to mutually respect the interests of their former opponent by which they might learn how both parties can develop entirely new interests and mutual aspirations as they discover their joint worlds.

If these mechanisms are at work in some societies, it is my prediction that we will be able to discover novel ways of attempting to civilize MNCs and the institutional equity nexus in a multitude of different regions throughout Europe and other places. Alternatively it may be possible to create economic dynamism independently of the influence of MNCs and the institutional equity nexus. For me what seems to be one of the most urgent tasks for social scientists is to be able to capture such tendencies in their emergence, as neither the mass media nor politics are any longer able to do so. As field researchers we should try to see how independent actions and experiments do, or could, cohere so that a multitude of actors and voices are helped to discover both the contributions of others and the agglomerated outcome that may become possible.

Dorf and Sabel (1998) give in *A Constitution for Democratic Experimentalism* the most elaborated example for studying such processes. Here standard-techniques such as 'benchmarking' are used to extend situational narration in the service of building mutual understanding—if not trust—even when the actors, agencies, groupings, and institutions involved are engaged in a race of transformations fighting among each other over social space. Benchmarks simply become heuristic devices for searching for aims and means, and for communicating to others what this search is all about. This makes possible the mutual recognition of aspirations and transformation in roles and identities. Sabel has later applied this framework to search for the way in which for instance a school reform has led to the mutual recognition of the interest of politicians, school leaders, teachers, and pupils allowing for much more open-ended search and experimentalism in school reform.

Now the good side of the kind of 'partnership formations' that it enables is that it prepares the engaged actors directly for providing each other with the resources that would otherwise need to be bought and sold and therefore provided with the involvement and disciplining technology of the 'financial court' either directly or through public spending.

It seems, however, as if the press, the general political discourse and also the social sciences as a whole are often highly critical of such

experimentalist forms of new partnerships. Collaborative manufacturing could be either hiding dominance and power from the stronger
party or simply becoming a cartel-like conspiracy against the general interest. Unions can see employer and employee partnerships as
anti-union attempts to create and increase employee loyalty to the
employer. They may cast doubt on the political orientation of the
members that do engage in such experiments. Partnerships across
institutional divides could be seen as being partisan coalitions either
turned against other priorities within the state budget or ways to hold
up the normal market processes and competition.

It is obvious that neither normal economic theory nor political science and sociology in their usual forms provide appropriate measures
for evaluating whether such experimental partnerships are of any
good. In my view the national business system framework could
provide the tools for assessing in a more systematic way, whether
experimental partnerships in societies are promising for reconstructing
the larger 'system' or not.

However, for the study of comparative capitalism to become of such
relevance, these streams of research orientations should be more attentive to institutional developments that have not already made their
mark on the capitalist process, but are fighting to capture an emergent social space. This may only make its mark on the larger social
and economic process gradually. However, this effect in turn may be
an outcome of the active involvement of National Business Systems
scholars in narrating field studies in such a way that macro-actors
pay attention. Such actors may be forced to engage in inclusive politics rather than processes of exclusion, very much in the same way
as scholars and social reformers participated with social movements
and political parties in the construction of the international discourse
and practice of social reform that Rodgers identifies as the 'Atlantic
Crossing' (1870–1950) (Rodgers 1998).

Our advantage as comparative analysts is that we may narrate such
cases of experimentation with a much clearer view of the systemic
potentialities than is usually the case. But this again is dependent on
our ability to gradually move our modelling towards a more complex
and synthetic understanding of each society being studied, rather than
theorizing and aggregating them into ideal types or more negatively
already dead stereotypes.

The big scientific question is, of course, which forms of modelling of various capitalisms or National Business Systems allow for
the detection of such experimental processes when they are emergent

and ongoing, rather than when they have become already generally institutionalized. If we cannot provide such modelling, we will not be able to study the processes of formation from a system perspective, but only be able to summarize past history into models and types.

REFERENCES

Amable, Bruno (2003). *The Diversity of Modern Capitalism*. Oxford: Oxford University Press.

Baran, Paul A. and Sweezy, Paul M. (1966). *Monopoly Capital*. New York: Monthly Review Press.

Berle, A. A. and Means, Gardiner C. (1932). *The Modern Corporation and Private Property*. New York: Macmillan.

Bourdieu, Pierre (1994). *Raison practique. Sur la théorie de l'action*. Paris: Éditions du Seuil.

Casper, Steven (2000). 'Institutional Adaptiveness, Technology Policy, and the Diffusion of New Business Models. The Case of German Biotechnology'. *Organization Studies* 21(5): 887–914.

Crouch, Collin (1993). *Industrial Relations and European State Traditions*. Oxford: Clarenton Press.

Dewey, John (1927). *The Public and its Problems*. Dever: Allan Swanlow.

Dore, Ronald P. (1973). *British Factory—Japanese Factory. The Origins of National Diversity in Industrial Relations*. Berkeley: University of California Press.

—— (2000). *Stock Market Capitalism. Welfare Capitalism. Japan and Germany versus the Anglo-Saxons*. Oxford: Oxford University Press.

Dorf, Michael C. and Sabel, Charles F. (1998). 'A Constitution of Democratic Experimentalism'. *Columbia Law Review*, 98(2): 267–473.

Elias, Norbert (2000). *The Civilizing Process. Sociogenetic and Psychogenetic Investigations*. Oxford: Blackwell Publishers.

—— (1996). *The Germans. Power Struggles and the Development of Habitus in the Nineteenth and Twentieth Centuries*. Cambridge: Polity Press.

Esping-Andersen, Gösta (1990). *The Three Worlds of Welfare Capitalism*. Cambridge: Polity Press.

Fligstein, Neil (1990). *The Transformation of Corporate Control*. Cambridge, MA: Harvard University Press.

Galbraith, John Kenneth (1967). *The New Industrial State*. London: Hamish Hamilton.

Golding, Tony (2001). *The City. Inside the Great Expectation Machine. Myth and Reality in Institutional Investment and Stock Market*. London: Prentice Hall.

Guillén, Mauro F. (2000). 'Organized Labor's Images of Multinational Enterprise. Divergent Foreign investment Ideologies in Argentina, South Korea, and Spain'. *Industrial Labor Relations Review*, 53: 419–42.

Hall, Peter A. and Soskice, David (eds.) (2001). *Varieties of Capitalism. The Institutional Foundations of Comparative Advantage*. Oxford: Oxford University Press.

Hirschmann, Albert O. (1977). *The Passions and the Interests. Political Arguments for Capitalism Before its Triumph*. Princeton, NJ: Princeton University Press.

Hobbes, Thomas (1968). *Leviathan*. Harmondsworth: Pelican Books.

Julian, Birkinshaw (2001). 'Strategy and Management in MNE Subsidiaries'. In: Rugman and Brewer (eds.), pp. 380–401.

—— and Neil Hood (eds.) (1998). *Multinational Corporate Evolution and Subsidiary Development*. London: Macmillan.

Kristensen, Peer Hull (2003). *Et grænseløst arbejde. En fantastisk fortælling om danske tillidsvalgtes arbejde med at sikre arbejde, indflydelse og fremtid i multinationale selskaber*. Copenhagen: Nyt fra samfundsvidenskaberne.

—— and Zeitlin, Jonathan (2001). 'The Making of a Global Firm. Local Pathways to Multinational Enterprise'. In: Glenn Morgan et al. (eds.).

—— and—— (2005), *Local Players in Global Games. The Strategic Constitution of a Multinational Corporation*. Oxford: Oxford University Press.

Lewis, Bernard (2002). *What Went Wrong? Western Impact and Middle East Response*. London: Oxford University Press.

Lindgren, Håkan (1994). *Aktivt Ägande. Investor under växlanda konjunkturer*. Institut för ekonomisk-historisk forskning (EHF).

Maurice, M., Sellier, F., and Silvestre, J.-J. (1986). *The Social Foundations of Industrial Power. A Comparison of France and Germany*. Cambridge, MA: MIT Press.

Mjøset, Lars (2002). *An Essay on the Foundations of Comparative Historical Social Science*. Working paper, No. 22, August. ARENA and the Department of Sociology and Human Geography, University of Oslo.

—— (2003). 'National Systems and Global Trends—the Need for a Diversity-Oriented Foundation'. Paper for Workshop on National Business Systems in the New Global Context, Leangkollen, Oslo, Norway, 8–11 May.

Morgan, Glenn, Kristensen, Peer Hull, and Whitley, Richard (eds.) (2001). *The Multinational Firm. Organizing Across Institutional and National Divides*. Oxford: Oxford University Press.

Müller, Frank (1996). 'National Stakeholders in the Global Contest for Corporate Investment'. *European Journal of Industrial Relations* 2(3): 345–68.

—— and John Purcell (1992). 'The Europeanization of Manufacturing and the Decentralization of Bargaining. Multinational Management Strategies in the European Automobile Industry'. *International Journal of Human Ressource Management* 3(1): 15–31.

Ohmae, Kenichi (1990). *The Borderless World. Power and Strategy in the Interlinked Economy*. Harper Business.

Plender, John (2003). *Going off the Rails. Global Capital and the Crisis of Legitimacy.* Chichester: John Wiley and Sons.

Popper, Karl (1957). *The Poverty of Historicism.* London: Routledge and Keagan Paul.

Quack, Sigrid, Morgan, Glenn, and Whitley, Richard (eds.) (2000). *National Capitalisms, Global Competition and Economic Performance.* Amsterdam: John Benjamins Publishing Company.

Regini, M. (1991). *Uncertain Boundaries. The Social and Political Construction of European Economies.* Cambridge: Cambridge University Press.

Rodgers, Daniel T. (1998). *Atlantic Crossings. Social Politics in a Progressive Age.* Cambridge, MA: Harvard University Press.

Rugman, Alan M. and Brewer, Thomas L. (eds.) (2001). *The Oxford Handbook of International Business.* Oxford: Oxford University Press.

Sabel, Charles F. (1982). *Work and Politics. The Division of Labor in Industry.* Cambridge: Cambridge University Press.

Shonfield, Andrew (1965). *Modern Capitalism. The Changing Balance of Public and Private Power.* London: Oxford University Press.

Smith, Adam (1969). *The Theory of Moral Sentiments.* Indianapolis: Liberty Classics.

—— (1970). *The Wealth of Nations. Book I–III.* Hammondsworth: Penguin Press.

Sölvell, Örjan and Zander, Ivo (1998). 'International Diffusion of Knowledge. Isolating Mechanisms and the Role of MNE'. In: Chandler et al. (eds.), *The Dynamic Firm. The Role of Technology, Strategy, Organizations and Regions.* Oxford: Oxford University Press.

Streeck, W. (1992). *Social Institutions and Economic Performance Studies of Industrial Relations in Advanced Capitalist Economies.* London: Sage Publications.

Te Brake, Wayne (1998). *Shaping History. Ordinary People in European Politics 1500–1700.* Berkeley: University of California Press.

Veblen, Thorstein (1997). *Absentee Ownership. Business Enterprise in Recent Times. The Case of America.* New Brunswick: Transaction Publishers.

Weber, Max (1978). *Economy and Society. An outline of Interpretive Sociology. Vol. I.* Berkeley: University of California Press.

Weick, Karl E. (2001). *Making Sense of the Organization.* Oxford: Blackwell.

Whitley, Richard (1992a). *Business Systems in East Asia. Firms, Markets and Societies.* London: Sage.

Whitley, Richard (eds.) (1992b). *European Business Systems. Firms and Markets in their National Context.* London: Sage.

—— (1999). *Divergent Capitalisms. The Social Structuring and Change of Business Systems.* Oxford: Oxford University Press.

—— (2000). 'The Institutional Structuring of Innovation Strategies. Business Systems, Firm Types and Patterns of Technical Change in Different Market Economies'. *Organization Studies* 21(5): 855–86.

Whitley, Richard and Kristensen, Peer Hull (eds.) (1996). *The Changing European Firm. Limits to Convergence.* London: Routledge.
——and Kristensen, Peer Hull (eds.) (1997). *Governance at Work. The Social Regulation of Economic Relations.* Oxford: Oxford University Press.
Wood, Ellen M. (1991). *The Pristine Culture of Capitalism. A Historical Essay on Old Regimes and Modern States.* London: Verso.

14

Institutional Complementarities, Path Dependency, and the Dynamics of Firms

GLENN MORGAN

The contributions to this book have analysed the relationship between firms and institutions and how this influences change processes within national and international contexts. Building on different institutionalist approaches, all the contributions have emphasized that the degree of complementarity between institutions varies across societies and firms are able to use this variability, both within societies and across them, to develop new patterns of action that in turn contribute to the reshaping of institutions at the national and the international level. In this final chapter, I wish to draw out and make explicit some of the key points emerging from these contributions.

The broad orientation of this argument is twofold. First, I argue that firms are active participants in their own fate; they do not simply reproduce a dominant recipe but on the contrary search for their own position in markets. This process of search and experimentalism in a tight selection environment driven by the market is not always successful but when it is, the reasons may relate not just to an effective use of existing institutional resources, but also to the development of new combinations of resources. The institutionalist argument therefore needs to develop a stronger 'theory of the firm' that pays greater attention to firm-level dynamics and particularly the power of firms to innovate in new and unexpected ways. In this process, firms face institutions and the actors involved in them with new challenges.

Thus, second, we need to investigate more deeply how institutions evolve, complement one another, and change. Crucially, institutions do not simply reproduce old patterns, but rather a range of actors, from firms through to social movements and political groupings, are involved in adapting and reconstructing institutions over time. This necessitates that 'institutionalist' approaches should incorporate a stronger sense of, first, time and history (i.e. how the specific temporal ordering of 'events' and processes shapes the relationship between institutions and firms), second, the layered nature of social space (i.e. the simultaneity of the context and consequences of action and institutions at the local, regional, national, and international), and third, the idea that institutions do not simply incorporate an economic logic but are the outcomes of complex social processes of negotiation and conflict between a range of actors of which firms are only one component. In what follows, these arguments are developed in more detail.

In the first part of the chapter, I argue that a theory of the firm, built along what may be broadly labelled 'Penrosian' lines (for classic statements see Penrose 1959 and Richardson 1972), has three key insights for our understanding of changing capitalisms. First, it sees firms as actively developing and growing in the context of their environment, both using existing institutional resources but also searching for new combinations of resources that can strengthen firm uniqueness. Second, it identifies the engine of growth with the development of core capabilities through new combinations of resources inside the firm and through interactions outside the firm; this in turn relates to the centrality of innovation processes to firm growth. Third, it emphasizes the limitations to growth emerging from problems of managerial coordination.

In the second part of the chapter, I consider how institutions relate to this active model of firms. The primary danger, I argue, is to assume that institutions are functionally related to firms, that is, that they emerge in order to solve economic coordination problems for firms. On the contrary, I argue that institutions emerge from multiple sources that need to be much more broadly conceived than simply through a single economic logic. Similarly, the idea that institutions over time become complementary to each other and to firms as ways of ensuring a coherent and cohesive environment for firms is also flawed. I propose a view of institutions in which the emphasis is placed on the multi-layered nature and historical construction of institutional contexts. Three key areas that I emphasize are the political nature of institutions, the complexity and variety of complementarities between institutions and between institutions and firms and, finally, the importance of a historical approach towards processes of institutional emergence and selection.

14.1. Theorizing the Firm

Recent developments in the theory of the firm have moved from an interest in the aggregate level of firm dynamics in terms of supply and demand curves to opening up the 'firm as a black box'. The broad thrust of Penrosian theories of the firm is to argue that firms consist of a core of capabilities that are distinctive, unique, and developing. Such capabilities mean that firms respond to selection environments in two ways. First, they seek to establish the distinctiveness of their own capabilities and make markets that are effectively unique to them by ensuring that whatever they are providing cannot be imitated by others. However, since imitability at the level of products and services is limited and usually only temporary, the firm must, secondly, anticipate competition by establishing itself in new markets. What is distinctive to the firm, is therefore, not the products or services themselves but the capability to innovate and change, to learn through its actions and become dynamic in response to the challenges of the selection environment. How does the firm establish such capabilities in this model? In the first instance, these capabilities are constructed on the basis of the resources (financial, human, technological, etc.) made available by the institutional context. However, then, firms have to combine and coordinate them in distinct and historically unique ways. Thus, firms develop a distinctive set of capacities, ways of doing things, which emerge out of this process and make them different from other firms, both those within the same context and those in different contexts.

This argument distinguishes two levels of the firm. First, there are the products and services that the firm sells on the market. There must be a market for these products at a price that enables the firm to continue to survive and grow. However, success at this level can never be taken for granted. Other firms may copy, imitate, and take market share. Therefore successful firms are those that have in place within the organization capacities for innovation and change. This is the second level of the firm on which long-term survival is built—the ability to monitor changing environments and to learn in ways which continually upgrade or shift products and services in new directions. This ability is unique to individual firms and cannot be imitated by others as its distinctive character is embedded within a range of practices and procedures inside the firm that may even be invisible to members of the firm itself. Teece and Pisano, for example, claim that 'competences and capabilities are intriguing assets as they typically must be built because they

cannot be bought' (Teece and Pisano 1998: 197). They are a product
of organizational and managerial processes that enable learning to
occur in both the internal and the external environment. The firm
bridges the gap between the internal and the external process of
learning by alliances, mergers and acquisitions, participation in joint
product development, involvement in professional, industry, university, and governmental networks, etc. According to Teece and
Pisano, 'competitive success arises from the continuous development,
exploitation and protection of firm-specific assets' (ibid.: 209). Thus,
the Penrosian theory of the firm contrasts with some institutionalist models which assume a pattern of imitation and isomorphism as
firms seek to legitimate their structures by copying those which have
been deemed to be successful. In the Penrosian analysis, imitation
can only be a form of 'skin-deep' copying of 'observable characteristics', as 'capabilities' are not observable and are therefore resistant to
imitation.

Central to this argument is the importance of knowledge and knowledge development to the capabilities of the firm (see, for example,
Amin and Cohendet 2004; Nooteboom 2000). The capacity to recognize new knowledge, both from internal and external sources, to
identify its key elements and to transfer and integrate it more widely
in the firm requires that the firm have the absorptive capacity to facilitate these processes. Ideas of tacit knowledge point to the difficulties
of this in contexts where firms are trying to maintain their distinctiveness, avoid imitability, and ensure the appropriability of revenues from
their markets. Nevertheless, this process of learning and continually
upgrading the capabilities of the firm is essential in market selection
environments where in terms of products and services most firms are
able, given sufficient time and resources, to reach the same standards. Increasingly, firms are using internationalization as a means to
enhance this dynamic and increase internal variety and diversity with
a view to new learning and new developments. As firms internationalize, they have access to new resources. Capital becomes available on
different terms. New types of labour with different profiles in terms
of skills, discipline, and commitment become available. New forms
of knowledge embedded in different institutional systems of education, research, technology transfer, etc. are opened up. Firms use these
resources in new ways to improve their survival prospects.

The picture of firms that emerges from the Penrosian account is one
of continuous change and innovation as they seek to develop their
underlying capabilities and to produce goods and services that are

unique in the marketplace by accessing or producing new resources and combining them in innovative ways with existing complementary assets. This is a process of learning and experimentation in uncertain environments in which market selection mechanisms (mediated by institutional factors such as government involvement, bankruptcy laws, stakeholder involvement, etc.) weed out firms that 'fail'.

There are many reasons why firms may 'fail'. They may not have the capacity to learn quickly; they may be unable to integrate new knowledge; they may not have ways of changing products and services to meet new circumstances; they may overpay for new assets such as acquisitions or new technologies. A key element in this process concerns the capacity for coherent and effective managerial coordination of these processes. How do firms evolve the managerial capacity to develop these integrative processes of learning and coordination under conditions of uncertainty and ambiguity? How do these in turn relate to broader issues of coordination first within the firm (particularly in relation to sharing authority and control with skilled employees) and second between the firm and its owners, its suppliers, and its customers? Solving this problem concerns the interaction between the firm and the institutional context in which it exists. It therefore links back to the issue of how we conceive of this institutional context, the theme of the following part of this chapter.

In conclusion, the Penrosian theory of the firm offers an important way into understanding the dynamic processes within firms and how this relates to selection processes. Its emphasis on innovation and the continuous search for extensions to core capabilities is complemented by its concern with the difficulties and uncertainties of this. Furthermore the limitations on growth that arise from the problems of coordinating and developing managerial capabilities provide an important insight. Firms are not omniscient but they are dynamic and active. They can be expected to treat the institutional context not as a constraint, nor even as a fixed set of complementary processes that dictate a particular way of doing business. Rather the institutional context is a resource that the firm interacts with in order to pursue its own agenda of growth and survival. In the process, the firm may operate in ways that do not necessarily reflect the dominant institutional logic. They may find hidden legacies and new potential within the existing environment. They may bring new practices and processes in from the outside (from their international linkages and experience) which test the limits of variability in the existing institutions. They may, most obviously, become active participants in debates about institutional change. In all these respects, theorizing the firm from this Penrosian perspective emphasizes the need to focus on dynamics and change in institutional contexts.

14.2. Institutions and Institutionalism: the Basic Framework

Turning to the analysis of institutions, it is clear that most analyses within the institutionalist framework have seen institutions from the point of view of economic functionalism. The implicit assumption has been that institutions perform the function of providing a coherent set of rules of the game for firms which reduce the transaction costs which would otherwise emerge if every time that firms interacted they had to establish the rules for that interaction (North 1990). Aoki, for example, provides an account of institutions and 'the rules of the game' as enabling structured interaction to occur between actors with different interests. The rules are an 'equilibrium' solution to a coordination problem; the rules emerge from the interaction between actors and are expressive of their different interests and the necessity of balancing these interests in a way which satisfices for both sides in a context of bounded rationality where it is impossible to determine in detail every possible outcome. The rules offer a means of dealing with uncertainty and ambiguity and thus reducing the costs of attaining information, taking decisions, and negotiating with other actors. They are the outcome of rational processes of cost minimization under conditions of bounded rationality. Institutions 'represent the self-sustaining expectations of the agents who have actually played the game repeatedly. As such, an institution is "the product of long-term experiences of a society of boundedly rational and retrospective individuals" (Kreps)' (Aoki 2001: 11). According to Aoki, 'external' changes trigger an 'institutional crisis' in the cognitive sense:

the shared beliefs regarding the ways in which a game is played may begin to be questioned and the agents may be driven to re-examine the choice rules based on new information not embodied in existing institutions. A new institution will emerge only when agents' action-choice rules become mutually consistent in a new way and their summary representation induces convergent beliefs among them. (Aoki 2001: 18–19)

This period of uncertainty is characterized by patterns of search and experimentation as actors look for ways of re-establishing equilibrium. Particularly important here is the issue of how any particular equilibrium is linked to others (across time or at the same time). Equilibrium solutions that reinforce solutions in other areas are likely to emerge out of this period of uncertainty, thus creating complementarity. Milgrom and Roberts describe complementary activities as existing where 'doing more of one thing increases the returns to doing more of another' (Milgrom and Roberts 1995: 181; see also Milgrom and Roberts 1990). If activities are complementary, they generate higher returns than if they are not. As a result, when complementarities between institutions emerge, they 'crowd out' institutional solutions that are not complementary since their economic pay-offs are higher. As this happens, institutions become more tightly coherent as non-complementary patterns fade into insignificance. The result is a path dependent logic where the 'efficient pattern' is reproduced until conditions change the balance of advantages to actors. Milgrom et al. state that:

The momentum of the system of changes we analyze results entirely from the positive feedback effects that each of a group of core activities and practices has on the other activities and practices in the group . . . once the system begins along a path of growth of the core variables, it will continue forever along that path or more realistically, until unmodelled forces disturb the system. (Milgrom et al. 1991)

Hall and Soskice follow a similar logic; in their analysis of 'varieties of capitalism' they state that:

we construe the key relationships in the political economy in game-theoretic terms and focus on the kinds of institutions that alter the outcomes of strategic interaction. . . . Firms located within any political economy face a set of coordinating institutions whose character is not fully under their control. These institutions offer firms a particular set of opportunities; and companies are expected to gravitate toward strategies that take advantage of these opportunities. (Hall and Soskice 2001: 5, 15)

As with Aoki, the rules of the game that become established are those which provide the highest benefits to actors and these are in turn related to the higher levels of returns achieved through institutional complementarities. Firms respond to the incentives in the system to act in particular ways that fit the institutional context and thereby reproduce a path dependent trajectory of economic development.

The path dependency metaphor has increasingly come to the fore in analyses of institutions and institutional change. These ideas were originally developed through analyses in the area of technological development (David 1985) and have since evolved further to explain the growth of firms (Arthur 1994; David 1994). In essence, the argument is that when rules break down, actors look for new ways to coordinate their activity. Over time, a particular set of new rules tends to emerge which effectively locks actors into a distinctive path of behaviour. This path emerges as actors invest in assets specific to a particular way of doing things. This has the positive effect that as the rules spread and bind more actors into the network, they become more efficient as complementarities build and economies of scale and scope can be achieved. Put more negatively, actors are locked into a particular path because of the economic costs of switching even though new forms of coordination may, in abstract terms at least, offer lower costs, all other things being equal. Over time, commitments to this path of action are raised as others invest in it and reinforce it. Actors are not only bound in by the fact that they are invested in the particular technology or pattern of activities but also because they are rewarded for that investment in ways which they would not be if they acted differently. There is a positive pay-off to following the path arising from the gains achieved through complementarities.

In contrast to most economic accounts which assume that there is a point where continued investment will bring decreasing returns and that the goal for the firm is therefore to find the equilibrium moment at which returns are at the highest before the inevitable decline, the path dependency argument posits no such limits to returns. There is no endogenous economic factor that can lead to a change of direction or restructuring on the part of economic actors. Following the particular path that has emerged leads to increasing returns for the actors who conform. In this sense, paths lock-in actors because they bring gains and make a change of direction economically unviable. There is therefore a self-reinforcing quality to sequences of action over time and paths reproduce themselves because they perform a function for the system as a whole. The only way change can enter the system is through exogenous shocks or 'unmodelled forces' when some unexpected combination, and concatenation, of causes comes together to make it impossible to continue with the existing pattern. The result is that actors initiate new moves in a different direction and out of this process emerges a new pattern and a new process of lock-in. Thus the cycle starts again but with a new path.

Bringing these arguments together leads to a two-stage model of institutional contexts: a model of origins and a model of reproduction. One moment is the period of uncertainty when, for exogenous reasons, the previous institutional system is breaking down, that is, it does not provide returns to actors because the coordination mechanisms are no longer constraining actors and enabling predictability in interaction. This period of uncertainty can stretch over some time as actors look for new equilibrium solutions. Mahoney (2000) argues that which solution emerges, is determined by two factors. First, where there are high set up costs, positive network externalities, and immediate benefits from adoption of the practices, once actors have begun to invest they will find it difficult to turn back. They will in effect become locked in and will seek to make sure that others with whom they transact will also be locked in to the same set of practices. Second, where institutions clearly and quickly benefit a particular group of actors without immediately disadvantaging others, they are likely to be reinforced. The equilibrium solution itself is not the most efficient solution to the coordination problem in any universal sense; rather it is the most efficient solution in terms of the particular circumstances of the time. In retrospect, the chosen solution may appear in strict economic terms less 'efficient' than other solutions but once actors have made the initial investment this becomes irrelevant because the costs of changing are high. For Mahoney, therefore, there is a clear distinction between the moment of origin of an institution and the process of its reproduction (see Table 14.1). The former is explained as a contingent outcome of unexpected patterns of events and causal chains while the latter is explained by processes of lock-in and the returns that arise from path dependency.

The use of this model complements the broader framework developed by Aoki and others in its focus on the two distinct stages of institutional formation. Uncertainty enters the reproduction of the institutions from outside or from 'chance' interactions which make it

Table 14.1 *The two-stage model of path dependency.*

	Model of origins	**Model of reproduction**
Key concept	Contingency; unexpected interactions	Path dependency and institutional complementarities
Time scale	Short-term	Long-term
Selection mechanisms	First mover advantages that lock in participants	Actors locked into existing institutions and therefore alternatives, no matter how 'efficient' are unviable and 'selected out'
Implications for the firm	High uncertainty and low constraint	Low uncertainty and high constraint

difficult to simply continue the same rules of the game. In this phase of uncertainty, actors are looking for new rules. There are no 'objective' standards by which to set the new rules. They emerge out of a competition of rules where first mover advantages are important, particularly when they are combined with first, the interests of powerful actors and second, with solutions that offer sufficient rewards to a broad range of actors to make them invest in specific assets. The result is a rapid move towards a functionally efficient outcome and a new regime of stable reproduction that suits the new environment. In this model, there is strong complementarity between institutions that tend to reinforce each other and create a strong set of 'rules of the game' that constrain actions. Thus the model is one of 'strong institutions' and 'weak firms' where firms only make a difference at moments of institutional breakdown. The rest of the time they follow the patterns set by the institutions.

In contrast to these kinds of arguments, I propose an approach built on the idea of 'strong firms' and 'weak institutions'. Firms are 'strong' not in the sense that they are immortal but in the sense that even within institutional constraints, they are centralized decision-making actors which have to make choices if they are going to grow and develop. Institutions are 'weak' in the sense that they do not have a centre of decision-making. They grow out of historical circumstance and this means that in any particular context, there are a diverse range of institutions, where complementarities are many and varied, where not all institutions contribute to this complementarity and where the selection pressures on institutions to 'make' them contribute are weak. There are multiple institutional legacies, memories, and possibilities that vary in their significance across institutional contexts. Clearly the extent and variety of institutions varies between national contexts as described by Whitley in Chapter 8, this volume. On national business systems. Thus firms and other actors have diverse options open to them and 'paths' are much less determined and much more varied. In the following sections, I elaborate this argument in detail.

14.3. The Political Nature of Institutions

The starting point for such an analysis is to consider the origins of institutions not purely from the point of view of solving economic coordination problems but also from the point of view of their political nature. Contrary to views that institutions emerge out of economic selection processes, I argue that they are products of political agenda and actions. Amable, for example, states that:

Rather than optimal solutions to a given problem, institutions represent a compromise resulting from the social conflict originating in the heterogeneity of interests among agents. What we consider to be different 'economic' models are therefore based on specific social compromises over institutions. The question of institutional change is basically a question of political economy. (Amable 2003: 10)

Varied institutional structures emerge from this process of conflict and change. They represent institutional compromises between actors that have consequences for the distribution of power and rewards in a society by positioning actors in particular spaces and making them play the game over time from that position. The idea of institutional compromise is different from that of institutional reproduction as it implies the possibility of not just submitting to the rules of the game (and trying to succeed within them) but also testing the opportunities for rule change or game change as new circumstances arise for challenging the institutional compromise. Thus institutionalist analysis has more than just the two moments—origins and reproduction. It also involves an idea of the institutional order continually evolving and changing as actors and structures develop.

The role of time, events, and history is essential in this view of institutional change. With regard to time, Pierson (2003), for example, points out that beneath the surface of any seemingly stable institutional structure, there may be slow-moving changes that will eventually reshape institutions. He distinguishes between 'cumulative causes' and 'threshold effects'. Cumulative causes move slowly but continuously such that after a long period of time it becomes obvious that something fundamental has changed, for example, the 'industrial revolution'. Threshold effects occur where small incremental changes suddenly lead to a qualitative change in social relations because the point at which tensions can be held in place has been passed, for example, in the analysis of revolutions.

Pierson's argument links to Thelen's point that it is important to identify the types of change that may be occurring underneath a surface institutional stability. She points out:

Politics is characterized by disagreement over goals and disparities in power and in fact, institutions often reinforce power disparities .... However the losers do not necessarily disappear, and their adaptation can mean something very different from embracing and reproducing the institution . . . . For those who are disadvantaged by prevailing institutions, adapting may mean biding their time until conditions shift, or it may mean working within the existing framework, in pursuit of goals different from, even subversive to, those of the institution's designers. (Thelen 1999: 386; also Thelen 2003)

Thelen suggests that in these circumstances new institutions may be built alongside or within existing contexts, processes which she refers to as 'institutional layering' and 'institutional conversion' as actors with different powers test the limits of existing institutions and begin to play other games. In the case of what Pierson refers to as 'cumulative causes', what may happen is that new institutions emerge initially on the sidelines but gradually gain stronger adherence and become more central to the institutional order more generally. These authors suggest, therefore, that beneath any particular institutional setting, there are processes occurring that are leading to change. This requires that institutionalist analysis pays special attention not just to the surface level of continuity but underlying patterns of tension and conflict in institutional settings.

The concept of 'event', on the other hand, focuses on the particularities of distinctive moments in time. 'Events' have about them the qualities of first, unpredictability and second, consequentiality. With regard to the former, events often imply the coming together of a variety of causal chains into a particular and unpredictable combination. With regard to the latter, many 'events' happen that are of significance only to a few people. Events that have consequences tend to be triggers for the threshold effects which Pierson identifies. The assassination of Archduke Franz Ferdinand, in Sarajevo in August 1914 is typical in this respect; as a particular event it could not have been predicted but once it happened it set off a tightly linked causal chain and had huge consequences. Elections are another example of a category of events that, in certain situations, are high on both unpredictability and consequentiality. The election of George W. Bush in 2000 was determined by the outcome in Florida where, among other factors, the number of 'hanging chads' on ballot papers had a central influence on the result with major consequences for the whole world.

In terms of institutional analysis, bringing history back in requires that we discard the dualistic model of origins and reproduction. Instead, we consider institutional contexts as temporary outcomes of political conflict and change. Under the surface, it may be possible to identify forces that are changing the power distribution that brought about a particular institutional compromise, for example, shifts in demography, technology, social attitudes, patterns of living, etc. These may emerge in new institutions, initially on the margins, or they may emerge in new struggles within particular institutions. On the surface itself, so to speak, unpredicted events may serve to shift actors' perceptions and views and to destabilize existing institutional compromises.

Take, for example, Schmidt's (2002) recent analysis of the United Kingdom, France, and Germany which takes seriously all these different levels. She begins with the institutionalist argument that these three countries are characterized by different 'economic models' but what she shows is that each of them has over the last thirty years undergone institutional change. Britain has moved more closely towards market capitalism from the 1970s (when there were still elements of corporatism in the system) through to the late 1990s with some minor moves back under the Blair government (e.g. in terms of minimum wage legislation and trade union recognition). France has moved away from state capitalism towards market capitalism (though still much further away from it than Britain). It moved quite rapidly from 1983 through to the late 1990s but more recently has stalled particularly over reforms to the welfare state. Germany changed very little from the 1970s to the 1990s but from the mid-1990s there have been increased changes with challenges to key elements of the institutional settlement. Her argument is that institutions do change over time; that this is partly as a result of external pressures but also as a result of how actors internal to the system perceive the opportunities available to them and how they act in the light of particular events. Radical change, in the form of Thatcherism, came earliest to the United Kingdom because of increasing levels of economic and political conflict in the 1970s as different groups struggled to maintain their position in the face of UK economic decline. Events in the United Kingdom since then build on these institutional changes in the light of new circumstances. Schmidt emphasizes, in particular, the ability (and often inability) of politicians to create discourses that can create a broad constituency for change. This was what Thatcher was able to do for some time. In contrast, Schroeder and Jospin both failed to find a discourse that could sufficiently unite their own internal forces with a broader political constituency and thus have both produced in different and distinctive ways halfway houses to institutional change. Schmidt reinforces the point that timing matters, actors matter and institutional reform can make a difference.

14.4. **Institutional Complementarities**

The previous argument, of course, is antithetical to a strong 'institutional complementarities' position. In the dominant institutional model, as institutions become complementary they provide increasing returns to actors which lock-in participants and constrain possibilities for institutional change or for firm-level innovations which break the common mould. At least part of the reason for this is that, in much discussion, institutional complementarities and increasing returns are treated unproblematically in two respects. First, they are defined primarily in economic terms and second, the beneficiaries are assumed to be a single category of actor. Both of these assumptions are questionable.

With regard to the first point, actors are often as concerned with the power and status outcomes of institutions as with their economic consequences. They do not necessarily give up one set of institutions and seek to replace them with another just because the economic returns from them seem to be declining. With regard to the second point, changes in the level of returns may lead different groups to evaluate the benefits of institutions and the broad institutional settlement differently. What in the past was seen as an acceptable institutional settlement which brought an adequate level of returns for key groups in society may, as a result of either exogenous or endogenous change, come to be perceived differently by some groups, for example, as a barrier to them getting their 'fair share' of social wealth or welfare. Such groups can then start to change their allegiance to the dominant set of complementarities and search out others. Since actors have more interests than simply maximizing short-term economic returns, their willingness to engage in behaviour that may upset the existing system cannot be judged purely from an economic perspective.

For instance, the massive conflicts of the twentieth century and the institutional formation processes that accompanied them were central to economic outcomes. However, the forces which drove them went beyond issues of technical economic rationality to ideological constructions reflected in the totalitarianism of Nazism and Stalinism or in the more moderated discourse of late twentieth-century liberal democracy. Institutional settlements in states are political outcomes and in those processes, the impact of increasing returns from economic performance per se is mediated by social and political mechanisms of legitimation and representation.

Similarly the assumption that either states build their institutions to serve this economic function or that if they have not done so, they will come under pressure to reshape their institutions in that way, needs to be moderated. In a broader sociological institutionalist account, the values and compromises achieved at the political level and embedded in the institutions have economic consequences, but they are reinforced by wider mechanisms of legitimacy and consent. Thus economic outcomes that may send one society into crisis because its institutions are so tightly constructed around economic performance, may have little impact on another society where institutions have a broader platform of support and legitimacy making them resistant to change purely on economic efficiency considerations.

In this sense, the analysis of institutional complementarity is not simply about increased economic returns and functionalist processes of reproduction, but also about the broader social context within which those returns are perceived and distributed by different socio-economic groups. Thus the translation of the model of complementarities from the analysis of firms and markets to the analysis of institutions is not justified without moderating the definition of 'complementarities' to include political and normative considerations.

The complexity of this idea of institutional complementarities is exacerbated further by consideration of the issue of the social space within which institutions exist. The focus on the 'national' social space as the appropriate level of analysis for understanding complementarities has a number of problems. First, and most obviously, it ignores other forms of social space such as the regional and the international. It can be cogently argued that the focus on the national is justified by the fact that in the modern context this is the level at which power, authority, legitimacy, and representation tend to come together and thus exercise a strong shaping power over processes of institutional formation (see, for example, Whitley in this book). Equally, dimensions of social space, such as the international or the regional, lack the specific institutional form that comes from the existence of the nation-state. While there are many types of nation-states, there is some recognizable commonality between them, for example in terms of the Weberian idea of the nation-state's claim to sovereignty within particular geographical borders and the monopoly of the legitimate use of force within those borders. There is no simple analogue for the 'nation-state' at international or regional levels.

On the contrary, there are multiple forms of 'international' and 'regional' institutions. For example, the 'international' can refer to institutions built through agreement by nation-states or to agreements built by social actors from different states. Similarly the type of institutions built by these actors and how they interrelate to national institutional settings can vary hugely (see, for example, the discussions in Hewson and Sinclair 1999; Rosenau 1997; Young 1999). Institutional formation at the EU level, for example, is far more significant for the sovereignty and institutions of member states than is membership of the United Nations. Thus, there is no 'institutional' standardization across the sphere of the 'international' as there is in terms of the nature and function of the nation-state. Similarly, the 'regional' can admit of many meanings from a category applying to geographically proximate nation-states through to administrative or historical subunits of nation-states on to the identification of local cross-border connections (Breslin et al. 2002).

The fact that it is difficult to pin down a common institutional form to these multiple dimensions of social space, however, does not mean that they should be ignored. Most pertinently, national institutional formation and change is affected by the broader international economic and political context. Since the sixteenth century the ability of European states to build institutions that gave a social space that was coherent internally and defensible externally has to a significant degree been dependent on the nature of the international system.

This has been partly a function of trade and reliance on other countries for goods, capital, and labour. Clearly some countries have been generally more dependent on this trade than others and 'integration' into the world economy has tended to be a matter of degree. Some large economies, such as the United States in the twentieth century and Japan in the post-war period, have tended to be less dependent on this trade than other developed economies. The type of integration of 'weak' economies, for example, in Africa, Latin America, and Asia, has also varied in circumstances where particular forms of integration, for example, through the export of raw material commodities, can actually have destructive effects on the local system. Nevertheless, the general point is that the national and the international levels of analysis do not sit one inside the other like Russian dolls but are mutually constitutive. The capacity to develop a particular institutional compromise within a national context is, I suggest, dependent on how that affects the insertion of the society into the broader international political and economic environment. The interdependence that arises from this, sets particular constraints on and opportunities for national institutions, while at the same time offering actors in particular institutional contexts the opportunity to extend their reach outside this context through a process of internationalization. Thus, national systems are not hermetically sealed from each other but are variously permeable, offering opportunities for their own actors to extend their reach and for actors from other contexts to penetrate their own boundaries.

This implies that the idea of institutional complementarity cannot be confined to the national level. On the contrary in order for institutions to be effective in the national context, there must be international 'institutions' that both facilitate cross-border trade exchanges and constrain cross-border military action. So the Westphalian system of international law and order is complementary to the sovereignty of the modern nation-state. More specifically, the fixed exchange rates of the Bretton Woods era were complementary to economic policies of National Keynesianism (see, for example, Ruggie's account of 'embedded liberalism' 1998; also Morgan 1997).

An interesting question which has emerged over the last twenty years concerns the new forms of complementarity which exist between these two levels as fixed exchange rates are replaced by floating currencies, the volatility of international currency markets increases and national Keynesianism is abandoned. Clearly changing complementarities between national and international institutions create new frameworks within which actors can conceive the issue of increasing returns. Actors within national institutional contexts may see greater returns for themselves if they orient themselves to international markets than if they stick to their own home base. When they make such moves (if they do so in sufficient numbers), they may alter the returns received by other actors in the national context. This is particularly powerful for firms that are acting in competitive markets. An example of this would be the changing orientation of German private banks to international markets and their disengagement from the more traditional elements of the German context (see, for example, the discussions in Deeg and Lane, Chapters 2 and 4, this volume).

As has been suggested, complementarity of this sort does not have just an economic dimension. There is also a political dimension in the sense of states and their institutional orders fitting into the broader interstate system in a particular way. This struggle for hegemony between powerful states (and their satellites, colonies, and allies) both shapes the internal structures of the states themselves (e.g. the processes of military and ideological conflicts over empire which occurred in the nineteenth and twentieth centuries and served to shape economic and industrial orders as part of these battles) and the environment in which states can themselves develop, for example, by positioning them as dominant or subordinate within such global political and economic orders. In such contexts, states, like firms, develop alliance relationships to shore up or increase their power by allying themselves in the broader struggle for hegemony with other states as a way of gaining a favourable political and economic status.

The growth of Japan and Korea from the 1950s to the 1980s, for example, was very much helped by the US willingness to support them in terms of keeping its markets open and its currency high, thereby building up a large trade deficit for the political purpose of sustaining US-supporting political regimes as a bulwark against the spread of communism in the cold war era (LaFeber 1997; Woo-Cummings 1999). Similar linkages between the United States and European countries such as France, Italy, and West Germany were also crucial to the establishment of the post-war institutional settlement in those countries during the 1950s and 1960s (see, for example, Chapters 5 and 6 by Sorge and, Djelic and Quack, respectively, this volume; also Djelic 1998; Zeitlin and Herrigel 2000). Thus the national does not exist separately from the international; there is a process of mutual constitution and complementarity under conditions of uncertainty (Djelic and Quack 2003; Morgan 1997). The dynamics of international politics can have major impacts on processes within nation-states, as exemplified by the unification of Germany that has had profound consequences for the maintenance of the post-war social settlement that characterized West Germany, coinciding as it did with broader changes in the global economy and in the institutions of the European Union.

The suggestion that there are multiple complementarities to be constructed does not, however, mean that there is not a dominant set within any particular context. Amable, for example, has suggested the idea of an 'institutional hierarchy'. In an institutional hierarchy 'one institution somehow imposes the conditions according to which complementary institutions are going to supplement it in a specific institutional structure' (Amable 2003: 67). The dominant institutions are those that 'are most crucial for the socio-political groups that constitute the dominant bloc, that is, those where change is likely to modify substantially the distribution of income for individuals behind the socio-political groups' (ibid.: 69). Amable's point is that it is important to distinguish where institutional change occurs. If it involves change in terms of the interests of the dominant bloc and its key institutional means of reproduction, it will have wider ramifications than if it occurs at a 'lower' level of institutional generality or centrality.

Identifying the key institutional nexus and its complementarities in a society, however, is complex and may well vary over time as actors change their position inside and outside national systems. For example, Deeg (Chapter 2, this volume) suggests that the German institutional nexus has been changing from one in which the banking system was crucial to its structuring to one where at least central parts of the banking system are becoming detached (significantly through their internationalization). From this point of view, the dominant social bloc is characterized by a combination of owners, managers, and employees around a distinctive system of skill and training formation that shapes the strategy and structure of German manufacturing firms and thus the pay-offs to the groups and individuals concerned. The German banks are no longer as central to this as funds for investment are increasingly generated internally or through wider international capital markets. Foreign investors invest in German firms knowing that the firms are characterized by this particular system of skill and training. While they may pressure for more shareholder friendly policies they recognize that this is only going to involve marginal change. For international institutional investors, German shares (as with Japanese shares) are not a no-go territory; rather they are purchased with a specific view in mind and with a specific fit to the existing portfolio. Only in particular cases, such as hedge funds, are shares bought to leverage out-of-the-ordinary returns (in terms of what might be expected from German shares). So long as the German system delivers the high value/high technology engineering products that are encouraged by the existing institutional nexus, changes in terms of foreign ownership, increased transparency, share option incentive schemes, sell-off of shares by banks, and more shareholder friendly policies generally can be absorbed into the system at the same time as the central role of the German private sector banks reduces.

Interestingly therefore, the key pressure for change is less from the collapse of tight complementarity between the financial system and the strategies of particular firms and more from the linkages between the national and the international environment. So long as firms from other countries could not imitate sufficiently the distinctiveness of the German products, German firms could command a premium on world markets and return the rewards to the members of the dominant bloc; once firms from other countries began to be able to take some of these markets, then pressures on German firms to reduce costs became more acute. It was, then, the loss of complementarity between what German firms can make and sell and what international markets are willing to buy that has placed pressure on the system, not the collapse of the complementarity between the financial system and the firm per se.

This can be taken further in relation to Thelen's ideas of institutional conversion and layering. For example, it can be argued that actors within particular contexts will not reproduce institutions mechanically but will be aware of new opportunities that may emerge. Thus they may seek out new complementarities that provide a different level of pay-off. So, for example, major private banks in Germany may see, as deregulation occurs in both home and foreign markets, that it may be advantageous to them to work towards a new model of banking. They are shifting away from the traditional German 'universal banking model' built on long-term investments, loans and relationships with manufacturing companies and more towards the US model of 'investment banking' where profits are generated through financial market activities (Deeg 1999; Jackson 2003; Vitols 2003). As these banks begin to make such moves, they transform aspects of the financial system, building new complementarities, and dismantling others. In response, other financial institutions may move to fill potential gaps arising from this.

At the same time, manufacturing firms of different sizes and capacities will also move in different ways. Some might welcome the investment banking model as it gives them the chance to develop new complementarities, for example, by helping ease their entry into new international financial markets (and with this is a greater capability for mergers and takeovers in international contexts). Other companies may be concerned about it and therefore encourage other forms of financial institutions to fill the potential gaps. Thus a variety of accommodations and adjustments take place around these moves, transforming, as Thelen suggests, the institutional context (see also Chapter 12 by Lilja and Moen which describes the interrelationship between the institutional context of Finland and the international strategizing of Nokia).

New forms of complementarities therefore consist of the development of patterns of action that bring greater rewards to the actors involved in them. This may happen gradually and without anybody noticing anything much. 'Institutional entrepreneurs' may push this along further by either articulating the complementarities more clearly and communicating them to a wider audience or by simply working harder and more skilfully at making the new complementarities work. For example, it would be hard to analyse the emergence of the Silicon Valley institutional complex without recognizing the role of particular individuals in establishing links, for example, between universities and companies, or the role of academics and others in constructing a narrative of what this institutional complex consists of and how it works. On the other hand, many of the processes, for example, the interconnections between scientific research, company formation, innovation processes, and venture capitalists, were not designed by these institutional entrepreneurs but were outcomes of other processes which gradually became linked together because they were promoting high returns to those involved (see, for example, the analyses in Kogut 2003; Lee et al. 2000; Schoonhoven and Romanelli 2001).

Finally, it is necessary to recognize not all institutions in a society fit neatly into either this institutional hierarchy or a logic of complementarities. In any social setting, there are a variety of institutions and, while at a broad level it may be possible to think of them all interacting together in some way, only an extreme form of structural-functionalism would assume there has to be strong complementarity at all levels and across all institutions. Indeed, as Deeg (Chapter 7, this volume) and Crouch have pointed out, the idea of complementarity needs to be defined more carefully. Frequently, complementarity is taken to mean that two institutions share a basic orientation (e.g. they may be long-termist or short-termist in orientation). However, Crouch points out that complementarity in more exact terminology means that a failure or a gap in one area is made up for (complemented) somewhere else in the system. Thus complementarity implies not isomorphism of principles but rather its opposite, the coexistence of different principles. Carruthers et al. provide a neat illustration in their discussion of central bank monetary policy and bankruptcy laws. They suggest that as central bank monetary policy has become tighter, it has the consequence of potentially driving more firms into bankruptcy. However, simultaneously, bankruptcy laws have become 'looser', allowing firms time and space to restructure themselves rather than force the closure of potentially productive units (Carruthers et al. 2001). Crouch argues that this diversity is in fact crucial to enabling institutional contexts to become arenas for experimentation and change rather than 'institutional reproduction' and a central issue is how this diversity is 'governed' in any particular context so that it does not pull the society apart but rather provides it with greater vitality and robustness to respond to external and internal shocks (Crouch, Chapter 7, this volume).

Equally, it is clear that not all institutions are complementary to each other at any particular time. They may have been so in the past and they may be so again in the future. However at any particular time, it is an empirical question as to whether and how they are linked and whether this linkage can be conceived as 'complementary', that is, enhancing gains, or not. For example, the Weber thesis depends on the idea that at a particular time there was a complementarity between the Protestant Ethic and the 'spirit of capitalism'; how this actually worked out in practice and changed over time is an empirical question (Marshall 1982).

Indeed, it is possible to conceive of national contexts where institutions lack complementarity; each has its own logic that is often in conflict with others and the result is a society that cannot achieve stability, never mind a situation of increasing returns. Fragile societies where the state has little legitimacy and therefore property rights and the infrastructure of law and order are weak are contexts where either perverse complementarities may arise, for example, in Mafia-style activity across different institutional spheres, or no complementarities at all appear and actors pursue immediate goals in an uncertain environment (see, for example, debates on transformations in Eastern Europe and the ex-Soviet Union; Humphrey 2002).

What is more likely to be the case in developed societies is that there exists a core of institutional contexts that have over time become complementary because recognisably similar rules of the game have developed and reinforced each other. However, this is not a statement of ontological reality, that is, that institutions by definition reinforce each other, but rather an argument that in any particular society at a specific point of time, institutions vary in their degree of complementarity and thus in their ability to generate increasing returns. Some are core and essential; others are peripheral. Which institutions fall into which camp is an empirical and usually historical question.

From this perspective, the coherence of a particular institutional order is as much an artefact of a particular way of seeing social reality, that is, by taking a snapshot of society at a particular time, as an adequate representation of what is occurring within the society over time. From a historical perspective, the dynamics within particular institutional contexts and the way in which these connect with other contexts and create complementarities and increasing returns are much messier. There is not necessarily a single institutional logic tying all institutions together. Nor is there a single moment of 'origins' followed by a longer period of path dependent reproduction. There may be some 'historical hangovers', institutions which still exist, have their adherents, their own rules of action but, for most of the time, are relatively insignificant for the dominant rules of the game because their power has been sidelined and shifted to newer institutions. There may be other institutions that are becoming more closely entwined over time but where there are difficulties and tensions. Similarly there may be other institutions in a particular society that are becoming disentangled, pursuing their own logics and losing complementarities.

14.5. Selection, Complementarities, and Institutions

What are the underlying mechanisms of this process? What is causing this reinforcement or disentangling? How do complementarities emerge and become embedded? The theme of selection is central to this. One view is to take a straightforward Darwinian position in which institutions that fail to deliver complementarities and increasing returns to their participants are deselected and those that do deliver such benefits are reproduced. When we look at any particular array of institutions, in this view, we are seeing a snapshot of longer processes of growth in particular institutional patterns and decline in others, primarily determined by changes in the environment. Institutions that 'fit' the new context, that is, are complementary to other institutions and deliver benefits to participants in the system, grow and prosper whereas those that do not will wither.

Selection processes at the institutional level are, however, quite complex. The functionalist explanation that particular institutions emerge because they work best (in terms of generating efficiency gains) and are perceived to do so by key actors lacks historical credibility. It is fairly clear when one examines particular historical examples that institutions do not reflect the intentions of their originators and that the key complementarities emerge over time as institutions actually begin to change their function and manner of working as a result of adapting to contingent events and the impact of other institutions. In this sense, institutional complementarity can be considered as something that emerges from 'behind the backs of actors', not as a result of their intentional design.

Streeck has provided a graphic illustration of this in his discussion of the German context. He notes that throughout the post-war period, trade unions and their representatives tended to be extremely hostile to banks, arguing that banks had too much power and needed tighter control. Thus, at the same time as academics were arguing that one of the reasons for the relative stability of employment and the level of rewards received by German workers was the existence of 'patient capital' in the form of banks, trade union representatives were arguing for reducing the power of these institutions. The complementarity that emerged was not because powerful actors saw its usefulness and supported the process. As Streeck and Yamamura argue:

Although institutions embody constraints and opportunities or rights and obligations, their exact meaning can never be completely clear because no social norm is ever unequivocal and capable of speaking for itself. Interpretations of what an institution demands or allows are not only typically contested but may change over time as new facets of the institution are discovered. In fact what exactly an institution demands, makes possible or penalizes is continuously redefined by activities of what may be called 'interpretive entrepreneurs'. (Streeck and Yamamura 2003: 44)

The diversity of institutions, the ambiguity and uncertainty in how they constrain or facilitate behaviour reinforces Pierson's argument that in many situations, the problem of bounded rationality makes it impossible to arrive at a confident analysis of what the appropriate institutional solution is and how it might 'emerge' and be 'selected'. He states:

Economic theory is built in large part around the useful and plausible assumption that actors seek to optimize and are relatively good at it. Firms operate to maximize profits. The metric for good performance is relatively simple and transparent. Prices send strong signals that facilitate the analysis of how various features of the economic environment affect firm performance. Observable, unambiguous and often quantifiable indicators exist for many of these features.... Politics is a far murkier environment. It lacks anything like the measuring rod of price. Political actors pursue a range of goals. Furthermore it is often very hard to observe or measure important aspects of political performance.... There may be long lags and complex causal chains connecting political actions to political outcomes. The result is that mistaken understandings often do not get corrected. (Pierson 2000*b*: 260)

The basic point is that 'designing in' complementary institutions is an extremely precarious activity, subject to the uncertainties of broader social, political, and economic contexts. As Amable says:

There is no 'social engineer' in charge of the efficiency of institutional design and there is no pre-established fit of institutions either. Economic 'models', i.e. specific sets of institutional forms and the associated complementarities, are not designed from scratch with all the different pieces intended to nicely complement each other. The coherence of a model is usually defined *ex post* and the complementarities may sometimes come as a surprise even to the agents most closely concerned. (Amable 2003: 12)

In fact, political institutions in democratic contexts may most of the time militate against institution building and associated social engineering projects because actors faced with issues of winning elections are likely respond in ways which maximize short-term advantage rather than look to the long term. It is not clear what incentives politicians have to think about the long-term implications of what they are doing. Moreover, the characteristic of institutions, that is, that they constrain actors over the long term, may positively militate against institution building in politics where lock-in may be seen as something that ties the hands of politicians and therefore needs to be avoided (Pierson 2000*a,b*). Paradoxically, building stable institutions requires actors to give up power and lock themselves and their successors into a long-term deal (see North and Weingast 1989 for the classic statement of this process). This takes a particular institution out of the realm of party political debate, for example, as the Labour government's granting of independence to the Bank of England did in 1997. Building institutions relies on the establishment of credible commitments and evoking the 'shadow of the future' (Pierson 2000*b*). If politicians are serious about institutions they have to recognize that this will also lock them in and reduce their room for manoeuvre. All of this means that establishing the conditions for long-term reform of institutions is likely to be highly complex and deliberative institution building overall a rather small part of how institutions actually emerge.

Are there other pressures which select and deselect institutions behind the backs of actors? Pierson (2000*b*) argues that selection processes at the political level are very different from firm-level processes of selection. There is no single market that can determine the fate or survival of institutions. Agents find it difficult to discipline principals. For example, in electoral contexts, many factors come into play and signals from elections can be interpreted in many different ways. Thus the 'failure' of a particular institutional arrangement is unlikely to be clearly signalled in the electoral cycle. On the other hand, in an electoral context, 'Many of the goals pursued by political actors have a "lumpy" or "winner-takes-all" quality . . . . Unlike economic markets, in which there usually is room for many firms, in politics finishing second may not count for much.' (Pierson 2000b: 258).

Thus, on the one hand, it is difficult to read clear signals for institutional performance in the political realm while on the other hand, some types of institutions can be deselected in a radical way when power changes hands in elections. Change in institutions can therefore occur in many different ways. Some may be dismantled as a result of political action but this is often irrespective of their performance effects and cannot be explained in Darwinian fashion. Other institutions may gradually collapse and disappear over time as older generations die out and younger generations migrate to different institutions that are seen as more relevant. Sometimes, institutions may be sidelined, becoming less central to the core economic complementarities in a society, as in the case of religion in most Western societies. Alternatively, institutions may be converted and changed from the inside as actors give them new meaning, as has happened with education in general and universities in particular in the post-war period (Brown et al. 2001; Crouch et al. 1999). There is not a single institutional logic that ties all institutions together in a complementary fashion. As Milgrom and Roberts themselves state: 'Just how strongly are various elements of the systems linked? Also which subcollections of activities can be broken off successfully and grafted onto another system?' (Milgrom and Roberts 1995: 205).

How is it possible to understand this diversity of processes? In research terms, it is clear that there must be a historical perspective on how institutional coherence emerged and what such coherence consists of at any particular time. What social bloc supports any particular institutional formation (and how does this relate to those excluded)? What diversity of different institutional legacies may remain within an overall dominant mode of complementarity? How is this coherence and complementarity reinforced at other levels such as the international? Institutional fit may emerge at particular historical moments from processes of selection and change but such moments are both temporally limited and temporally structured, that is, the product of a particular concatenation of forces at various levels. This is not to suggest that there is no 'fit' between institutions most of the time. It seems a reasonable assumption that social institutions generally do fit together and do not contradict, in their principles or modes of operation, each other without leading to widespread disorder and breakdown. Rather the argument is that the fit/non-fit dichotomy is too crude to capture different evolving forms of fit (e.g. loose or tight fits, segmented patterns of fit—between some institutions but not others—emergent or transitional patterns of fit, historical survivals of other periods of 'social settlements', new patterns of fit between national and international levels of action and institution building, etc.).

14.6. Conclusions

In this respect, therefore, the next stage of institutionalist analysis is likely to be much more concerned with processes of historical formation, with interactions between the national and the international level of analysis and with a greater sense of the ambiguity, diversity, and variety of institutional contexts. Until recently, institutionalist analysis has been concerned predominantly with static models of divergent capitalisms and has tended to assume a strong path dependency approach in which institutional lock-in constrains actors and makes it highly costly to move in a new direction. Any such move would be seen as disrupting the gains from complementarity that arise from path dependency and therefore would only be likely to come from outside. There are, however, a number of problems with this approach in relation to institutions.

First, it does not take account of the capacity of actors to search for new complementarities. Thus while acceptance of the rules may be a dominant pattern, there are circumstances where actors look elsewhere. This may be because the rules actually disadvantage them in some way, for example, the existing financial institutions are predominantly serving large firms with stable markets and offer very little to small firms in more dynamic and uncertain markets. As they move elsewhere, the 'old' institutions become less used and may eventually be replaced. Given the dynamic view of the firm proposed earlier, it is necessary to place this search process more centrally in institutionalist analysis (as, for example, in the contributions by Herrigel and Wittke, Chapter 11; Moen and Lilja Chapter 12, this volume).

Second, there is a one-dimensional view of complementarities rather than a recognition that new combinations of institutions and contexts can occur. Thus the earlier discussion referred to institutions that become disconnected from the dominant groupings; these institutions or historical institutional legacies may be drawn upon to reactivate new types of complementarities. Even institutions that constitute part of the core social settlement in a particular society differ in their degree of malleability and significance for the dominant social bloc. Thus new complementarities can be picked out. The long-term consequences of such new practices cannot be determined in advance. In any particular situation they are clearly in competition with the existing rules of the game. Why should actors switch from one set of rules which are fairly clear and where the outcomes of following those rules are well known to a situation where the rules and the outcomes are unclear? Where the context is such that it provides a simple choice between acting in accordance with existing rules or acting in a different way the risks of picking the wrong horse may be very high. However, many social situations are not like that. There are, in effect, multiple causal chains linking different institutional contexts that may interact at specific moments of time and therefore open up new possibilities.

For example, the development of the Internet economy coincided with forms of financial deregulation that made it easier for prospective entrepreneurs to fund their activities. These were two independent causal chains that met at a particular juncture in time and created a sense of uncertainty about whether there were new opportunities. Firms and socio-economic groups wove these opportunities together and created new powerful movements that impacted on many institutional settings (e.g. speeding up the development of second and third tier stock markets in Germany and Japan). In particular institutional settings, this encouraged some actors to take a risk that there might be a new source of pay-offs for them if they began to play a different game. This in turn brought a wider debate about institutional changes that were required to facilitate this new game (Kogut 2003).

All societies have space for, first, path dependent complementary processes; second, institutions that are the legacy of previous periods; and, third, experiments that reflect current uncertainties and ambiguities. Where and how much of this space exists is the factor that distinguishes different societies not in the sense of a hidden essence of any society but rather as a specific time-related capacity reflecting the dynamics of both internal processes and the structuring of international economic and political regimes. For example, institutional legacies, in the sense of different institutional practices, that survive either in memory or in practice, are more likely to exist in societies where the key complementarities have become limited in scope, for example, to a small number of institutional settings. Actors have more diversity of opportunity to draw on different institutional legacies.

Similarly, experiments are more likely to occur outside the tightly defined core of institutional complementarities on the periphery in new industries (see, for example, Whitley, Chapter 8, this volume).

The institutionalist approach does not rely on the claim that every-body in a society does the same thing because of institutional pressure. This is clearly nonsensical. What is more significant is first, that the range of experimentation and differentiation in any society is institu-tionally determined and second, that while individuals can do things differently, whether that has a wider impact depends on whether it brings advantages to other actors to follow that practice rather than the existing rules of the game, in other words whether there is comple-mentarity and consequent increased returns. Thus any society is likely to have inside it variety and diversity but whether this has an impact on the core institutional formation is the important question. From this point of view, it is irrelevant to measure 'change' per se. There is always change and variety in a society; but is it change and variety in core institutions, and is it leading to changing complementarities and changing pay-offs?

In conclusion, this volume has advanced a new agenda for the study of 'changing capitalisms'. The issue is not simply one of chan-ging our focus from stability to change but rather of forging new concepts and ideas that place a more dynamic view of firms and insti-tutions at the centre of the analysis. This will happen as our studies become more intensively historical, more sensitive to diversity within institutional settings, more cognizant of the interrelationship between national and international contexts and finally more willing to recog-nize uncertainty, ambiguity, and experimentation at the level of firms and institutions. None of this requires jettisoning the key insights of previous analysis of 'national business systems', 'varieties of capit-alism', etc. Variety remains but not just variety at the national level but variety within and across national contexts. In this respect, this form of analysis is going to be central to the understanding of firms, as firms are prime movers (without being determinant) in stimulating and shaping institutional change. The integration of a dynamic model of analysis at the firm level with an understanding of the diversity and dynamics of institutional contexts is the key contribution of this book and it promises to be the start of a fruitful interaction between these intellectual traditions.

REFERENCES

Amable, B. (2003). *The Diversity of Modern Capitalism*. Oxford: Oxford University Press.

Amin, A. and Cohendet, P. (2004). *Architectures of Knowledge: Firms, Capabilities and Communities*. Oxford: Oxford University Press.

Aoki, M. (2001). *Toward a Comparative Institutional Analysis*. Cambridge, MA: MIT Press.

Arthur, W. B. (1994). *Increasing Returns and Path Dependence in the Economy*. Ann Arbor: University of Michigan Press.

Breslin, S., Hughes, C. W., Phillips, N., and Rosamond, B. (2002). *New Regionalisms in the Global Political Economy*. London: Routledge.

Brown, P., Green, A., and Lauder, H. (2001). *High Skills: Globalization, Competitiveness and Skill Formation*. Oxford: Oxford University Press.

Carruthers, B. G., Babb, S., and Halliday, T. C. (2001). 'Institutionalizing Markets or the Market for Institutions? Central Banks, Bankruptcy Law and the Globalizaiton of Financial Markets'. In: Campbell, J. L. and Pedersen, O. (eds.), *The Rise of Neoliberalism and Institutional Analysis*. Princeton: Princeton University Press, pp. 94–126.

Crouch, C., Finegold, D., and Sako, M. (1999). *Are Skills the Answer?* Oxford: Oxford University Press.

David, P. A. (1985). 'Clio and the Economics of QWERTY'. *American Economic Review* 75: 332–7.

—— (1994). 'Why are Institutions the "Carriers of History"?: Path Dependence and the Evolution of Conventions, Organizations and Institutions'. *Structural Change and Economic Dynamics* 5: 205–20.

Deeg, R. (1999). *Finance Capitalism Unveiled*. Ann Arbor: University of Michigan Press.

Djelic, M.-L. (1998). *Exporting the American Model*. Oxford: Oxford University Press.

—— and Quack, S. (2003). *Globalization and Institutions: Redefining the Rules of the Economic Game*. Cheltenham, UK: Edward Elgar.

Hall, P. and Soskice, D. (2001). *Varieties of Capitalism*. Oxford: Oxford University Press.

Hewson, M. and Sinclair, T. J. (1999). *Approaches to Global Governance Theory*. Albany, NY: State University of New York Press.

Humphrey, C. (2002). *The Unmaking of Soviet Life: Everyday Economies After Socialism*. Ithaca, NY: Cornell University Press.

Jackson, G. (2003). 'Corporate Governance in Germany and Japan: Liberalization Pressures and Responses During the 1990s'. In: K. Yamamura and W. Streeck (eds.), *The End of Diversity? Prospects for German and Japanese Capitalism*. pp. 261–305. Ithaca, NY: Cornell University Press.

Kogut, B. (2003). *The Global Internet Economy*. Cambridge, MA: MIT Press.

LaFeber, W. (1997). *The Clash: US–Japanese Relations Throughout History*. New York: W.W. Norton and Company.

Lee, C.-M., Miller, W. F., Hancock, M. G., and Rowne, H. S. (2000). *The Silicon Valley Edge*. Stanford: Stanford University Press.

Mahoney, J. (2000). 'Path Dependence in Historical Sociology'. *Theory and Society* 29: 507–48.
—— and Rueschmeyer, D. (2003). *Comparative Historical Analysis in the Social Sciences*. Cambridge: Cambridge University Press.
Marshall, G. (1982). *In Search of the Spirit of Capitalism: An Essay on Max Weber's Protestant Ethic Thesis*. London: Hutchinson University Library.
Milgrom, P. and Roberts, J. (1990). 'The Economics of Modern Manufacturing: Technology, Strategy and Organisation'. *American Economic Review* 80: 511–28.
—— and Roberts, J. (1995). 'Complementarities and Fit: Strategy, Structure and Organisational Change in Manufacturing'. *Journal of Accounting and Economics* 19: 179–208.
——, Qian, Y., and Roberts, J. (1991). 'Complementarities, Momentum and the Evolution of Modern Manufacturing'. *American Economic Review* 81: 84–8.
Morgan, G. (1997). 'The Global Context of Financial Services: National Systems and the International Political Economy'. In: G. Morgan and D. Knights (eds.), *Regulation and Deregulation in European Financial Services*. London: Macmillan.
——, Whitley, R., and Kristensen, P. H. (2001). *The Multinational Firm: Organizing Across Institutional and National Divides*. Oxford: Oxford University Press.
Nooteboom, B. (2000). *Learning and Innovation in Organizations and Economies*. Oxford: Oxford University Press.
North, D. C. (1990). *Institutions, Institutional Change and Economic Performance*. Cambridge: Cambridge University Press.
—— and Weingast, B. R. (1989). 'Constitutions and Commitment: The Evolution of Institutions Governing Public Choice in Seventeenth-Century England'. *The Journal of Economic History* 49(4): 803–32.
Penrose, E. (1959). *The Theory of the Growth of the Firm*. Oxford: Oxford University Press.
Pierson, P. (2000a). 'The Limits of Design: Explaining Institutional Origins and Change'. *Governance: An International Journal of Policy and Administration* 13: 475–99.
—— (2000b). 'Increasing Returns, Path Dependence and the Study of Politics'. *American Political Science Review* 94(2): 251–67.
—— (2003). 'Big, Slow-Moving and . . . Invisible: Macrosocial Processes in the study of Comparative Politics'. In: J. Mahoney and D. Rueschmeyer (eds.), *Comparative Historical Analysis in the Social Sciences*. Cambridge: Cambridge University Press, pp. 177–207.
Richardson, G. (1972). 'The Organisation of Industry'. *Economic Journal*, 82, 883–96.
Rosenau, J. N. (1997). *Along the Domestic–Foreign Frontier; Exploring Governance in a Turbulent World*. Cambridge: Cambridge University Press.

Ruggie, J. G. (1998). *Constructing the World Polity*. London: Routledge.

Schmidt, V. A. (2002). *The Futures of European Capitalism*. Oxford: Oxford University Press.

Schoonhoven, C. B. and Romanelli, E. (eds.) (2001). *The Entrepreneurship Dynamic: Origins of Entrepreneurship and the Evolution of Industries*. Stanford, CA: Stanford University Press.

Streeck, W. and Yamamura, K. (2003). 'Introduction: Convergence or Diversity? Stability and Change in German and Japanese Capitalism'. In: K. Yamamura and W. Streeck (eds.), *The End of Diversity? Prospects for German and Japanese Capitalism*. Ithaca, NY: Cornell University Press, pp. 1–50.

Teece, D. J. and Pisano, G. (1998). 'The Dynamic Capabilities of Firms'. In: G. Dosi, D. J. Teece, and J. Chytry (eds.), *Technology, Organization and Competitiveness*. Oxford: Oxford University Press, pp. 193–212.

Thelen, K. (1999). 'Historical Institutionalism in Comparative Politics'. *Annual Review of Political Science* 2: 369–404.

—— (2003). 'How Institutions Evolve: Insights from Comparative Historical Analysis'. In: J. Mahoney and D. Rueschmeyer (eds.), *Comparative Historical Analysis in the Social Sciences*. Cambridge: Cambridge University Press, pp. 208–40.

Vitols, S. (2003). 'From Banks to Markets: The Political Economy of Liberalization of German and Japanese Financial Systems'. In: K. Yamamura and W. Streeck (eds.), *The End of Diversity? Prospects for German and Japanese Capitalism*. Ithaca, NY: Cornell University Press, pp. 240–60.

Whitley, R. (1999). *Divergent Capitalisms*. Oxford: Oxford University Press.

Woo-Cummings, M. (ed.) (1999). *The Developmental State*. Ithaca, NY: Cornell University Press.

Yamamura, K. and Streeck, W. (eds.) (2003). *The End of Diversity? Prospects for German and Japanese Capitalism*. Ithaca, NY: Cornell University Press.

Young, O. (1999). *Governance in World Affairs*. Ithaca, NY: Cornell University Press.

Zeitlin, J. and Herrigel, G. (2000). *Americanization and Its Limits*. Oxford: Oxford University Press.

Index